ArtScroll® Series

Rabbi Nosson Scherman / Rabbi Gedaliah Zlotowitz
General Editors
Rabbi Meir Zlotowitz ז״ל, *Founder*

SAITSKIY EDITION

The Mystery

Published by

ARTSCROLL®

Mesorah Publications, ltd

ספר מגיד הרקיע

And the Majesty

ELUL • YAMIM NORAIM • SUCCOS

The grandeur and nobility
of the Days of Awe and Joy

RABBI DANIEL GLATSTEIN

FIRST EDITION
First Impression … August 2019

Published and Distributed by
MESORAH PUBLICATIONS, LTD.
4401 Second Avenue / Brooklyn, N.Y 11232

Distributed in Europe by
LEHMANNS
Unit E, Viking Business Park
Rolling Mill Road
Jarow, Tyne & Wear, NE32 3DP
England

Distributed in Australia and New Zealand
by **GOLDS WORLDS OF JUDAICA**
3-13 William Street
Balaclava, Melbourne 3183
Victoria, Australia

Distributed in Israel by
SIFRIATI / A. GITLER — BOOKS
POB 2351
Bnei Brak 51122

Distributed in South Africa by
KOLLEL BOOKSHOP
Northfield Centre, 17 Northfield Avenue
Glenhazel 2192, Johannesburg, South Africa

ARTSCROLL® SERIES
THE MYSTERY AND THE MAJESTY
© *Copyright 2019, by* MESORAH PUBLICATIONS, Ltd.
4401 Second Avenue / Brooklyn, N.Y. 11232 / (718) 921-9000 / www.artscroll.com

---

ISBN 10: 1-4226-2372-6 / ISBN 13: 978-1-4226-2372-5

Typography by CompuScribe at ArtScroll Studios, Ltd.

Printed in the United States of America
Bound by Sefercraft, Quality Bookbinders, Ltd., Brooklyn N.Y. 11232

Dedicated By:
Maksim and Oleg Saitskiy and Families

The word HONOR evokes a profound visceral response along my spine long after the simple meaning settles in my consciousness. I straighten my back, close my eyes, and conjure an image of my father, Shlomo Zalman ben Yechezkel, Solomon Saitskiy. The way I knew him, the way I remember him, and the way I want him to be remembered by my own children.

I have always respected my father for the man that he was, the truths he knew and believed in, the principles he stood for, and the military status which he ultimately achieved in the Soviet Army. Now, the time has come to honor him.

Born at the brink on World War II on the border of Romania and Russia, my father's earliest, most vivid memories were of chaos, air raid sirens, and explosions. Families ravaged and torn apart. Wails and screams became his lullabies, replayed in his memory for the rest of his life. He lost his mother and together with his sister spent years in an orphanage. He bore scars from beatings there as proudly as he bore his military medals. After the war, he tutored his peers in math and physics in exchange for food. When he turned 18, he enlisted in the army, because, as he recalled, soldiers were always fed and, because he was Jewish, there was no other way for him to get higher education. Despite all of the negative reactions he suffered, he proudly carried his Jewish name and his Jewish identity.

He met my mother during a visit to Tashkent and whisked her away from warmth and comfort to a part of Russia covered in permafrost most of the year. There he developed and tested the Russian Nuclear Arsenal. The Cold War was at its peak. There Maksim was born in 1969. They were the only Jewish family on base and yet they managed to have matzah on Pesach — my grandmother smuggled a box every year from Tashkent.

I was born ten years later. My father considered retiring from military service with the rank of Colonel, an accomplishment not many could have achieved. One of the few Jewish cadets to graduate from the highest Military Academy, he was sent to a small town near Moscow. Then, back to Tashkent, waiting to be arrested for requesting to immigrate and possibly betraying top military secrets, or for permission to leave. Years in waiting.

We came to America in 1992 — nothing short of a miracle. I learned to see the hand of Hashem in everything, and I recognize that with His strong and mighty hand He took us out of our own Mitzrayim. We achieved our own American dream in Boro Park. We received a great education, established families, and found our way back to Judaism.

My father spent the rest of his life watching us strive for higher goals and ideals, ensuring that the sacrifices he had endured were not made in vain. He taught us kindness and honesty, morals and integrity. He taught us the price of one word and the value of silence. I close my eyes and think of all the things he could have taught my sons....

And now, the time has come to honor him.

Oleg Saitskiy

לעילוי נשמת

אבי מורי

שמואל משה בן מאיר ז"ל

Sam Fuchs

נפטר י"ג טבת, תשס"ה

ואמי מורתי

חנה בת מאיר יצחק ז"ל

Helen Fuchs

נפטרה א' דראש חודש אדר ב' תשמ"ה

זקנתי מורתי

אסתר מלכה בת יוסף חיים ז"ל

נפטרה ח' תמוז תשנ"ב

Holocaust survivors who rebuilt their lives through tremendous *emunah* and *bitachon* in Hashem, accepting all of their experiences as Divine Providence.

It is our great *zechus* to dedicate this *sefer* by Rabbi Glatstein to their memory. May they be *meilitzei yosher* for their family and for Klal Yisrael.

Meir and Shandee Fuchs and Family

מוגש ומוקטר כמנחת זכרון

לעלוי נשמת

Moshe ben Adzizoi, Malka bat Sara (Cheeni),
Ogul bat Sara (Cheeni), Bachor ben Michal,
Lea bat Shoshana (Roza), Lazar ben Malka, Rachel bat Malta,
Shoshana (Roza) bat Ogul, Avrech ben Ogul, Rafoel ben Ester,
Miriam bat Lea, Lea (Luyba) bat Bitiya, Roshel ben Ester,
Abo ben Malka, Ester bat Sara, Abo ben Sara, Lea bat Sara,
Yechiel ben Devorah, Bitia bat Lea, Yashayo ben Mazal,
Avneu ben Malka, Sara bat Ketzia

שקרובם נדיב לב אוהב תורה הנדיב הנכבד שליט"א

הרים תרומה נכבדה להוצאת הספר לעלוי נשמתם.

זכות התורה תעמוד להם לעולמי עד

ושתהיה נשמתם צרורה בצרור החיים

ויעמדו לתחיית המתים בקרוב בימינו או"א.

וברכת ה' תלווהו להנדיב הנכבד שליט"א

שיזכה לראות ברכה בעמלו

ואך טוב וחסד ירדפוהו כל הימים

ובכל אשר יפנה יצליח.

המחבר

TEL. (718) 520-0115
FAX (718) 268-0186

קהל נחלת יצחק ד'הומנא

CONGREGATION NACHLAS YITZCHOK

141-43 73RD AVENUE
KEW GARDENS, HILLS, N. Y. 11367

NOACH ISAAC OELBAUM
RABBI
AUTHOR OF SEFORIM
MINCHAS CHEN

נח אייזיק אהלבוים
בעהמח"ס מנחת חן
רב ואב"ד דק"ק נחלת יצחק
בקיו גארדענס הילס, נ. י.

בס"ד

[illegible] תשס"ב

[illegible]

[illegible] "THE MYSTERY AND THE MAJESTY" [illegible]

[illegible]

[illegible]

נח אייזיק אהלבוים
בעהמח"ס
מנחת חן
רב דקהל נחלת יצחק בקיו גארדענס הילס

בס"ד

שמחתי לראות את ספרו של ידידי הנעלה והדגול מחשובי הרבנים בניו
יארק הגאון ר' **דניאל יעקב גלאטשטיין** שליט"א אשר משפיע הרבה
בתורתו ויראתו ומנהיג קהילות נפלאות ברוממות התורה וביר"ש טהורה
ומוציא לאור **ספר מגיד הרקיע** על עניני הפורים, וערדתי על כמה מאמרים
ומאד נהנתי מעומק הדברים ומהיקף הרב של הידיעות בכל נושא ונושא,
והוא מלא וגדול בדברי תורה ערבים ומתוקים המביאים את אורם של ימי
הפורים לכל המעיין בספר, ויש בו פתח גדול להיכנס בשערי פנימיות
הארת הימים ולהשכיל במשמעות ימים גדולים אלו. ובעז"ה יהיה הספר
לתועלת מרובה ולברכה.

ויזכה הרב המחבר שליט"א להמשיך ולהשמיע מתורתו הרחבה בכתב
ובע"פ ויפוצו מעיונותיו לזכות הרבים.

הכו"ח לכבודו של עמלי תורה

(ה) ? ו ?

דוד כהן

Michtav Berachah to the author's Hebrew sefer

יא טבת תשע"ט

הסכמה מראשי ישיבת חפץ חיים

הנה ראינו גליונות מהספר 'מגיד הרקיע' על ענייני פורים, שתלמידינו היקר והחביב
הרב דניאל יעקב גלטאשטיין שליט"א מתכונן להוציא לאור, והן מלאות דברי
תורה נעימים ונחמדים בהלכה ובאגדה האמורים בשכל ישר ובקיאות רבה והבנה
עמוקה כיד ה' הטובה עליו. המחבר שליט"א למד בישבתינו הקדושה שנים רבות,
והצליח ועשה פרי בלימודו וזכה לעלות גם בתורה גם ביראה. כעת הוא מכהן
כמרא דאתרא בית הכנסת אהבת ישראל, ומנהל קהילתו הקדושה על דרך התורה
היראה והמוסר כרוח ישיבתינו. גם זכה ללמד תורה ברבים, ונתקבלו שיעוריו אצל
הצבור ושותים בצמא את דבריו. וכעת רחש לבו דבר טוב, להעלות דברים עלי
ספר ורבים יאותו לאור תורתו ויהנו מדבריו.

המחבר שליט"א מחזיק בדרך רבותיו, ויהיב חיליה לאורייתא להרביץ תורה
לרבים. וכל שיעוריו מיוסדים על דברי חז"ל ורבותינו הראשונים והאחרונים, וכמו
שאמרו חז"ל (ירושלמי פי"ט ה"א) 'כל תורה שאין לה בית אב אינה תורה'. ולכן
באנו בזה לברכו באהבה שיצליח מאד בכל דבריו וישרה שכינה במעשי ידיו.

החותמים לכבוד התורה ולומדיה,

הרב דוד הריס   הרב עקיבא גרונבלאט

Michtav Berachah to the author's Hebrew sefer

פנחס פרידמאן
ראש הכוללים דחסידי בעלזא
בעל מחבר פרי הדר על הפמ"ג
ושבילי פנחס על התורה
ירושלים תובב"א

ב"ה

יום ד' פרשת וישב כ' כסליו תשע"ט לפ"ק
פה ירושלים עיה"ק ת"ו

הן בא לפני ידיד נפשי הנעלה והנכבד הרה"ג **מוה"ר דניאל יעקב גלאטשטיין
שליט"א** רב ומרא דאתרא של הקהילה קדושה **"אהבת ישראל"**, ובידו ספר יקר
"מגיד הרקיע" דרושים נפלאים על חודש אדר ופורים, המבוססים על הקדמות
יקרות מספרים הקדושים, ועוד הוסיף לן מדיליה כהנה וכהנה מאשר חנן אותו
הקב"ה ברוב רחמיו וחסדיו, וחפץ ה' בידו הצליח להעלות הדברים על הכתב
כדי לזכות בהם את הרבים.

והנה הרב הנזכר כבר נודע בשערי בת רבים בדרשותיו המתוקים על פרשיות
השבוע המשמחים לב אלקים ואנשים, בהיותו פה מפיק מרגליות. אולם מעל
כל הוא ידוע וביודעי ומכירי קאמינא, שמלבד היותו תלמיד חכם גדול הוא
ירא שמים אמיתי, מדקדק במצוות ובכל מנהגי ישראל בקלות כבחמורות בלי
לנטות ימין ושמאל, ומנהל את בית מדרשו בדברי חיזוק לעורר את המתפללים
להתקרב לה' ולתורתו. וכבר שוחחנו עמו רבות בעניני תורה ברוב תענוג
ונחת.

על כן ידי תיכון עמו להיות נטפל לעושי מצוה, לחזקו ולברכו בברכת הדיוט,
יהי רצון שספר חשוב זה יתקבל באהבה רבה בבית מדרשא, וחפץ ה' בידו
יצליח שיתפשטו דבריו בבי מדרשא וימצאו חן ושכל טוב בעיני אלקים ואדם,
ויזכה לחבר עוד ספרים ככל אות נפשו להגדיל תורה ולהאדירה.

הכותב וחותם לכבוד התורה ולומדיה

פנחס פרידמאן

Michtav Berachah to the author's Hebrew sefer

Table of Contents

Shemini Atzeres/Simchas Torah

Acknowledgments

חֲבָלִים נָפְלוּ לִי בַּנְּעִמִים אַף נַחֲלָת שָׁפְרָה עָלָי (תהלים טז:ו).

The Ribbono shel Olam has bestowed upon me the greatest happiness, joy, good fortune, and privilege: the opportunity to study and share the beauty, grandeur, mystery, and majesty of the *Torah HaKedoshah* with other *Yidden*.

אוֹדֶה ה׳ מְאֹד בְּפִי וּבְתוֹךְ רַבִּים אֲהַלְלֶנּוּ (תהלים קטט:ל).

May the Ribbono shel Olam continue to grace me with this sacred privilege מִתּוֹךְ שִׂמְחָה וָנַחַת, בַּרְיוּת גּוּפָא, וּנְהוֹרָא מַעַלְיָא, מְנוּחַת הַנֶּפֶשׁ וְהַרְחָבַת הַדַּעַת עַד כִּי יָבוֹא שִׁילֹה.

Seventy-five years ago, my dear grandfather, HaRav Mordechai Leib Glatstein, may he live and be well, experienced the horrors of the Holocaust. He witnessed the extent of human suffering, and emerged with a soaring spirit of *emunah* in HaKadosh Baruch Hu, compassion for his fellow Jew, and an indefatigable drive to resuscitate and resurrect the lives of *acheinu beis Yisrael*, our Jewish brethren. Having come within inches of the crematoria, and moments from the Next World, he dedicated his life to breathe life into others לְהַחֲיוֹת רוּחַ שְׁפָלִים וּלְהַחֲיוֹת לֵב נִדְכָּאִים. My grandmother of blessed memory, Rebbetzin Cyna Glatstein, was the daughter of the last Rav of Sochaczew, Rav Yehuda Leib Wolman H"yd, who died *al kiddush Hashem* in the Warsaw Ghetto, not forsaking his *kehillah* in their time of need. Together, my grandparents devoted their lives to educate, elevate, resurrect, and revitalize the lives of countless *Yidden* of the *She'eiris HaPleitah* in the Displaced Persons camps in Europe and the lives of countless *Yidden* in Pittsburgh, Pennsylvania where my grandfather served as a Rav for more than seventy years. May their merit continue to stand for me to follow in their ways, לְקַדֵּשׁ שֵׁם שָׁמַיִם וּלְהַגְדִּיל תּוֹרָה וּלְהַאֲדִירָה.

My dear grandparents, Rabbi and Mrs. Shimon and Miriam Devorah Hershfang, have been living examples of *Ahavas HaTorah, Ahavas Yisrael, Kavod HaTefillah*, and true modesty for me and for all who know them. I fondly remember that, as a young boy, I was privileged to learn Gemara and a number of *sefarim* with my grandfather, and although I learned in Beis Midrash and Kollel for a number of years, there is a special *yiras Shamayim* that I was able to observe in the house of my grandparents. Their guidance has influenced me deeply.

The memory of my great-grandfather, Rav Shlomo Zalman Glick, is still etched in my heart. He was a trailblazer in introducing the concept of *Kavod HaTefillah* in the early days of Flatbush, and his profound impact has reached many shuls, including, *b'ezras Hashem*, the new *Beis HaKnesses* that our *kehillah* will be moving into coinciding with the publication of this *sefer*.

May this *sefer* be a tribute to my dear grandparents, for their impact on me can be felt on every page.

Special thanks to my dear uncle and aunt, Rabbi and Mrs. Tzvi and Yehudis Hershfang, for their love and support, and for being true exemplars of our family's ideals.

My dear parents have transmitted these teachings to me and my siblings, Rabbi Aharon Glatstein and Racheli and their family; my brother is a noted Rebbe and *maggid shiur* in Yerushalayim, who made valuable additions to this work; Ilana and Ari Lebovics and her family; and my brother Elie. My father, Rabbi Yossi Glatstein *shlita*, an attorney by profession, traveled the Jewish world for many decades to shuls, yeshivos, and college campuses, bringing the message of the eternity, majesty, and grandeur of the Torah to audiences of all stripes and affiliations. These presentations affected the lives of thousands of Yidden, perhaps none more so than this author. The moving and stirring lectures imparting the glory of the Torah that I heard as a young boy still reverberate in my soul until this very day. My father's advice has been my guiding light and has added immeasurably to the quality of this *sefer*.

To my dear mother, Mrs. Ettie Glatstein שתחיה, endless gratitude for the love and warmth that she invests in me *ad hayom hazeh*, to this very day. I have never met anyone more diligent and hardworking than my mother. Simultaneously caring for and supporting four generations of our family, her devotion knows no bounds.

As my humble *sefer* on Purim, *Maggid HaRakia*, was dedicated to the honor of my parents (see the Introduction there), so, too, should this *sefer* be a tribute to honor my parents שיחיו.

I was *zocheh* to marry into the Pinter family. I am deeply indebted to my in-laws, Dr. and Mrs. Avraham and Naomi Pinter, for their unwavering support, assistance, and dedication throughout the years to me, my wife, and our children. The values and ideals that they have been able to impart to us are what guide us and help us to continue to give over these ideals to our children. May they continue to see much *nachas* from us and from the entire family.

I have been privileged to learn in the Chofetz Chaim yeshivah system from the time I was a young *bachur*, first in Yeshiva Tiferes Yisroel in Brooklyn under the leadership of HaRav Yehuda Jacobson and HaRav Tzvi Turk, and then in the Rabbinical Seminary of America under the *nesius* of the legendary Rosh HaYeshivah Maran HaGaon Rav Alter Chanoch Henoch Hakohen Leibowitz *zt"l*, now led by the Roshei Yeshivah HaRav Dovid Harris *shlita* and HaRav Akiva Grunblatt *shlita*. This yeshivah, which has made such an important contribution to Klal Yisrael across America and around the world, has imparted to me and so many of its *talmidim* the legendary *mesorah* of the yeshivah, the methodology of in-depth *iyun* and *lomdus*, as well as the emphasis on the rigorous study of *mussar* in the approach of Slabodka. Above all, the yeshivah has inspired the great joy to be able to share the beauty of the Torah with other *Yidden*. For all of this, and more, I am deeply grateful.

A special thanks to one of my very esteemed Rebbeim, HaRav Eliyahu Maza *shlita*, who taught me in the summer months, in *shiur* and privately, the *sefarim* of Rav Itzele Peterburger: *Kochavei Ohr* and *Shaarei Ohr*. These *limudim* made a deep impression on me, and two chapters in this *sefer* are based on the essays of Rav Itzele (see "The Secret of Successful *Teshuvah*— First Come, First Served" and "The Urgency of *Teshuvah*").

As I reached my final years of kollel, and my interest in Rabbanus was burgeoning, I had the *zechus* to learn from and closely observe one of the great Rabbanim of our time, HaRav Noach Isaac Oelbaum *shlita*. Rav Oelbaum's ability to relate to so many varied and complex areas of Torah and convey it to the masses in such an engaging and exhilarating fashion really captured my heart. The Rav's ability to share a warm relationship with his *baalebatim*, and at the same time elevate them without lowering himself, is an ideal to which I aspire. The Rav has always made himself available to me personally and he continues to be a source of great *chizuk* and advice. יְהִי רָצוֹן שֶׁיִּזְכֶּה לְהַרְבֵּה שָׁנִים עַל מַמְלַכְתּוֹ מִתּוֹךְ שִׂמְחָה וָנַחַת לְהַגְדִיל תּוֹרָה וּלְהַאֲדִירָהּ.

I have been privileged to benefit from the masterful Torah and advice of one of the foremost *darshanim* of our time, the Rosh Kollel of Chassidei Belz, HaRav Pinchas Friedman *shlita*. The Rav has gone out of his way to teach, guide, advise, and inspire me. May Rav Friedman continue to illuminate עֵינֵי יִשְׂרָאֵל בְּתוֹרָתוֹ וּבְחָכְמָתוֹ, the eyes of Bnei Yisrael with his Torah and his wisdom.

When I assumed my first position in Rabbanus nine years ago, I was straight out of kollel with limited experience. The *shiurim* I gave in my first *kehillah*, Khal Toras Emes in Queens, were modestly attended. Someone suggested that I start video-recording the *shiurim*. A start-up organization called TorahAnytime.com was videoing *shiurim* and offering them online. I did not own a computer, nor had I ever been online, and I wasn't quite sure what the benefit would be. After enough pressure, I began to have the *shiurim* recorded.

I would like to acknowledge my dear friends at TorahAnytime.com, the founders, Shimon and Reuvain Kolyakov, together with the Executive Director, my dear friend Yosef Davis. These *tzaddikim* have changed the world. Slowly, *b'chasdei Hashem*, more people were introduced to the *shiurim* and live attendance grew, as did the online viewership. Special thanks to my friend Meir Sommers, who would drive by in his ambulance to pick up the SD card and upload the *shiur*. I remember being amazed when I was told seven hundred people had watched the *shiur* — in that week alone. Now, *baruch Hashem*, the numbers have exceeded my wildest expectations. I was also giving *shiur* at the time in the Young Israel of Kew Gardens Hills under the leadership of Rav Fabian Schoenfeld. Rav Fabian, and now his son Rav Yoel, have continued to graciously host a number of my weekly *shiurim* for ten years now. I began giving a *shiur* in Rav Noach Isaac Oelbaum's shul as well, under the auspices of the *Agra D'pirka Kollel* network, led by the Rosh Kollel, R' Ezra Klein. Those *shiurim* were videoed as well, and from these modest beginnings the *shiurim* were disseminated worldwide. *Yidden* all over the world are thirsty for Torah, and TorahAnytime is bringing it to them. It is my honor to partner with this worthy team of idealistic and dedicated group of people to share our heritage with those who yearn for it. A special thank-you goes to Rachamim Segev, Yossi Farbowitz, Yossi Sommers, Mr. Yaakov Gandjian, and Mr. Alvin Roslyn for their technical support.

One facet of the *shiurim* that many attendees enjoyed was the source sheet booklet that accompanied the *shiurim*. I feel that it is critical for people not only to hear and learn new ideas and profound concepts, but also to be able to see and study from the original text.

About eight years ago I received a call from R' Aharon Subar of Monsey, New York. R' Aharon had been listening to and enjoying the *shiurim* and wanted to know how he could obtain the *maareh mekomos*. So, I started faxing — yes, faxing — the sheets to R' Aharon, and the rest is history. R' Aharon has amassed an email list of many hundreds of people to whom he faithfully sends out the source material a number of times each week. This has really expanded the *shiur* viewership and the number of people who benefit from the *shiurim*. R' Aharon also uploads the *shiurim* to Kol HaLashon. If anyone would like to receive the source sheets for any of the recorded *shiurim*, email Rabbiglatsteinsourcesheets@gmail.com and R' Aharon will be happy to send them to you. May the Ribbono shel Olam shower R' Aharon and his whole family with great *berachah* for all of his incredible efforts on behalf of *harbatzas haTorah*.

I've always been on the lookout for new ideas and novel concepts in Torah, which has led to an unending search for rare and hard-to-find *sefarim*. At first my weekly jaunts to the used *sefarim* stores were enjoyable adventures, but eventually, due to time constraints, they were no longer possible. When my friend Gedaliah Schwartz of Norfolk, Virginia would hear me mention in a *shiur* that I was looking for a hard-to-find sefer, he would take it upon himself to track it down. R' Gedaliah's *sefarim* finds have contributed significantly to the source material to which I have access.

Another of R' Gedaliah's initiatives was the WhatsApp groups. R' Gedaliah created groups for the *Parashah shiurim*, *Mishnah Berurah shiurim*, and *Daf HaShavua*; these groups comprise people from all over the world, ranging from Jews in South Africa and Australia to members of the Bnei Menashe in Northeast India. In fact, when I had the opportunity to speak in Gibraltar, I was literally stopped on the street by members of Gedaliah's WhatsApp group. May HaKadosh Baruch Hu bless you and your entire family for your tremendous efforts in spreading Torah to the farthest corners of the world.

Three and a half years ago, our family was privileged to

accept the opportunity to lead a young, burgeoning, wonderful *kehillah* in Cedarhurst, New York — Kehillas Ahavas Yisrael. It is a *kehillah* of energetic, lively, genuine *mevakshim* who strive to grow ever higher in their *ahavas haTorah* and *ahavas Yisrael*. May I continue to be worthy of their trust and devotion. I am especially grateful to those who attend the *shiurim* in the shul. We are at the verge of moving into our brand-new building and may we be *zocheh* to cultivate a מְקוֹם תּוֹרָה וּתְפִילָה לְשֵׁם וּלְתִפְאֶרֶת לְקַדֵּשׁ שֵׁם שָׁמַיִם.

This project is yet another page in the ArtScroll Revolution, whose efforts in *harbatzas haTorah* know no bounds. Rabbi Gedaliah Zlotowitz's encouragement from the beginning was the driving force in bringing this project to fruition. May HaKadosh Baruch Hu grant him continued success in spreading the published word throughout the Jewish world. When I was a young boy, Rav Nosson Scherman's pen and scholarship were the legendary standard. It is the honor of a lifetime to have this association with the gold standard of Jewish publishing.

I offer my deepest heartfelt thanks to my dear friend Dr. Chaim Moeller for producing the manuscript for this *sefer*. I marvel how Dr. Moeller, a renowned cardiologist, found the time to listen to the numerous recordings, study the source material, and consult with me to format the manuscript with great love and attention to detail. It is only Reb Chaim's aspiration *l'kadeish Shem Shamayim* and be a *marbitz Torah* that energized him to carve out time from when it's neither day nor night to produce this great contribution. Special thanks to Mrs. Sara Moeller and their children, Azriel, Adina, Raphael, and Aryeh, for lending me their husband and father so the project could see the light of day.

Mrs. Felice Eisner worked tirelessly around the clock to enhance the literary excellence of this book. Her talents, advice, creativity, and skill have elevated this work to a different stratosphere. May HaKadosh Baruch Hu bless her with good health and much *nachas*, to continue to upgrade so many Torah publications.

Mrs. Judi Dick reviewed the entire manuscript with a keen eye and a wealth of knowledge that has improved every page. May HaKadosh Baruch Hu bless her with good health and much *nachas*, to continue to elevate the work of each author fortunate enough to work with her.

Thank you to the ArtScroll team of experts who brought this *sefer* safely through the intricacies of publication: Mendy Herzberg, Eli Kroen, Mrs. Estie Dicker, and Mrs. Faygie Weinbaum.

I am deeply grateful to my dear friends whose dedications have made this *sefer* possible.

I am truly humbled that this *sefer* is dedicated by Mr. Oleg Saitskiy in memory of his father, Mr. Solomon Saitskiy, שלמה זלמן בן יחזקאל, a Jew who emerged from the Iron Curtain, and who, at great personal sacrifice and in the most trying of times, would use only his Jewish name. With great self-denial, he brought his family to America, and insisted on giving his children *brissim* and providing them an authentic Torah education. His memory is an inspiration to his family and to all of Klal Yisrael. May this *sefer* bring an *aliyah* to his *neshamah*.

I am honored to yet again be the beneficiary of the kindness and generosity of my dear friends Dr. Meir and Mrs. Shandee Fuchs, who have been the first to graciously assist with all of my projects and have been there from the beginning of my publication ventures. Reb Meir enjoys telling me that he knows a good spiritual investment when he sees one; may I be worthy of their friendship and trust. The Fuchs' extraordinary love for Torah and Eretz Yisrael is matched only by their *ahavas Yisrael*, love for their fellow Jews. May they be blessed with continued *hatzlachah* and *nachas* from their beautiful family.

My dear friends Yossi and Malka Melohn were the driving force behind getting this project off the ground, recommending this *sefer* to Mesorah Publications and generously ensuring that the project would take off. The Melohn family has become synonymous with Torah philanthropy, and Yossi has entered into new vistas of *hachzakas haTorah* in his own right through his creativity and Torah Initiatives. May Yossi and Malka continue the family legacy of being among the worthy Torah supporters of our time.

To my beloved friends, Dr. Reuvain and Adina Fatakhov, who have been ardent supporters since my early days of Rabbanus in the good old days of Khal Toras Emes of Queens. The *middos* and refinement of the Fatakhov family have made them one of the great treasures of the Kew Gardens Hills Torah community. Thank you for your many years of friendship and kindness.

Special thanks to the many kind individuals whose contributions have made this *sefer* possible: Mrs. and Mrs. Eli Cizma, Mr. and Mrs. Hillel Meltz, Mr. and Mrs. Yitzi Friedman, Mr. and Mrs. Gedaliah Schwartz, Mr. and Mrs. Daniel Rosenthal, Mr. and Mrs. Bentzi Barenbaum *l'ilui nishmas* Tziporah Rochel bas R' Elazar, Mr. and Mrs. David Kallus, Mr. and Mrs. Mendy Reich, Mr. and Mrs. Uriel Rodriguez, Mr. and Mrs. Mechel Rosenberg, Mr. and Mrs. Yitzi Gedalowitz, Mr. and Mrs. Lev Lerner, Mr. and Mrs. Michoel Shugal *l'ilui nishmas* Inna bas R' Eliyahu, Mrs. and Mrs. Mordechai Jacobs, Mr. and Mrs. Avi Schreier *l'ilui nishmas* Maxine and Bernard Selevan and Uncle Lester Freedman, Mr. and Mrs. Zev Schreier *l'ilui nishmas* Toiba bas R' Shabsi HaLevi Schreier, Mr. and Mrs. Dan Moeller *l'ilui nishmas* Yaakov ben Yitzchak, Miriam bas Yitzchak, Moshe Aryeh ben Yaakov HaKohain, Finkel bas Menachem Mendel, Zaida Raphael Yonah ben Yaakov, Mr. and Mrs. Alan and Anna Rothenberger, and Mr. and Mrs. Teddy and Renee Pollak *l'ilui nishmas* Mordechai ben Moshe, Rivka bas Yaakov HaKohen, Moshe ben Yehudah, Sarah bas Chaim, Baruch ben Moshe.

I want to thank my *chaver tov* Rav Aharon Jacoby, who was the chief editor of my *sefer* on the *moadim* — *Maggid HaRakia* on Purim and *b'ezras Hashem* the upcoming edition on Pesach. Thank you for your valuable suggestions, advice, and guidance.

Thank you to my *yedid ne'eman*, Rabbi Moshe Bamberger, Mashgiach Ruchani of Beis Midrash L'Talmud, and author of the acclaimed ArtScroll series, *Great Jewish ...*, for your many years of encouragement to get the ball rolling with this project, and for your sound advice.

To my partner in life, my dear wife Suri, who graciously and wonderfully shoulders the myriad burdens of the household and children, with supernatural patience, to allow me to fulfill the joyous and sacred opportunity to try to follow in the pathways of Hashem, Who teaches Torah to His nation, Yisrael, with love. Your unwavering kindness has enabled this book to come to light. May HaKadosh Baruch Hu grant us the *zechus* to continue to share with Klal Yisrael the Mystery and the Majesty of the Torah — גַּל עֵינַי וְאַבִּיטָה נִפְלָאוֹת מִתּוֹרָתֶךָ, *Reveal to my eyes and I will see wonders from Your Torah*. In your merit, may we be *zocheh* to see abundant *nachas d'kedoshah* from our wonderful children: Ahuva, Yehuda, Meir, Naftali, Leah, Shlomo, and Dovid.

וּבְצֵאתִי מִן הַקוֹדֶשׁ אֶפְרוֹשׂ כַּפַּי אֶל אָבִינוּ שֶׁבַּשָּׁמַיִם בְּהוֹדָאָה עַל הָעָבַר וּבַקָּשָׁה עַל הֶעָתִיד, דְּכְּשֵׁם שֶׁעֲזַרְתַּנִי לְהוֹצִיא סֵפֶר זֶה, כֵּן תַּעֲזְרֵנִי לְהַתְחִיל סְפָרִים אֲחֵרִים וּלְסַיְּימָם. עַד הֵנָּה עֲזָרוּנוּ רַחֲמֶיךָ, וְלֹא עֲזָבוּנוּ חֲסָדֶיךָ, וְאַל תִּטְּשֵׁנוּ, ה' אֱלֹקֵינוּ לָנֶצַח, שֶׁנִּזְכֶּה לַעֲשׂוֹת נַחַת רוּחַ לְפָנָיו, לְזַכּוֹת אֶת הָרַבִּים וּלְהַגְדִּיל תּוֹרָה וּלְהַאֲדִירָה, אָמֵן כֵּן יְהִי רָצוֹן.

דניאל יעקב גלאטשטיין
מנחם אב תשע"ט

For the full text of any of the sources in this *sefer*, kindly send a request to themysteryandthemajesty@gmail.com.

Introduction

Our *tefillos* on the Yamim Noraim are replete with heart-wrenching requests to merit to behold the great era of *Acharis HaYamim* and the ultimate redemption. In *Shemoneh Esrei*, we pray, מְלוֹךְ עַל כָּל הָעוֹלָם כֻּלּוֹ בִּכְבוֹדֶךָ, וְהִנָּשֵׂא עַל כָּל הָאָרֶץ בִּיקָרֶךָ, וְהוֹפַע בַּהֲדַר גְּאוֹן עֻזֶּךָ עַל כָּל יוֹשְׁבֵי תֵבֵל אַרְצֶךָ, *Reign over the entire universe in Your glory; be exalted over all the world in Your splendor, reveal Yourself in the majestic grandeur of Your strength over all the dwellers of Your inhabited world.* שִׂמְחָה לְאַרְצֶךָ, וְשָׂשׂוֹן לְעִירֶךָ, *Gladness to Your land and joy to Your city;* we ask Hashem to bring happiness and joy to our Holy Land and to the city of Yerushalayim, which is בֵּית חַיֵּינוּ, the very lifeblood of the Jewish people.

וּצְמִיחַת קֶרֶן לְדָוִד עַבְדֶּךָ, וַעֲרִיכַת נֵר לְבֶן יִשַׁי מְשִׁיחֶךָ, בִּמְהֵרָה בְיָמֵינוּ, *[and bring] flourishing pride to David, Your servant, and preparation of a lamp for the son of Yishai, Your anointed, speedily in our days;* we fervently beseech that the influence of the *Malchus Beis David* be realized and that the flourishing of the *Melech HaMashiach* come to fruition.

We declare that the *tzaddikim* will exult when they witness the ultimate sanctification of the Name of Hashem, when all evil will be vanquished and Hashem's *Malchus*, Sovereignty, will be recognized and acknowledged the world over.

This is the focus of our *tefillos* on the most solemn and

awe-inspiring days of the year, and yet we must wonder why we focus on these ideas when teshuvah should be the order of the day. While we consistently await the redemption and yearning for the *Geulah* is a central principle of Judaism,* what is teshuvah's specific relevance to the Yamim Noraim?**

I was then struck by the words of the Rambam, who writes,[1] כָּל הַנְּבִיאִים כּוּלָן צִוּוּ עַל הַתְּשׁוּבָה, *all the prophets have commanded us regarding teshuvah*, וְאֵין יִשְׂרָאֵל נִגְאָלִין אֶלָּא בִּתְשׁוּבָה, *and Klal Yisrael will only be redeemed through teshuvah*, וּכְבָר הִבְטִיחָה הַתּוֹרָה שֶׁסּוֹף יִשְׂרָאֵל לַעֲשׂוֹת תְּשׁוּבָה, *and the prophets have assured that the Jewish people will indeed do teshuvah in the End of Days*, וּמִיָּד הֵן נִגְאָלִין, *and they will immediately be redeemed.*

The Rambam teaches us that the national teshuvah of Klal Yisrael is a prerequisite to the *Geulah*. In fact, the Gemara[2] declares that גְּדוֹלָה תְּשׁוּבָה שֶׁמְּקָרֶבֶת אֶת הַגְּאוּלָה, *Teshuvah is great since it brings the Geulah closer*, as the verse states, וּבָא לְצִיּוֹן גּוֹאֵל וּלְשָׁבֵי פֶשַׁע בְּיַעֲקֹב נְאֻם ה׳, *A redeemer will come to Tzion, and to those of Yaakov who repent from willful sin — the word of Hashem (Yeshayahu 59:20)*; the Gemara asks, What is the reason that "a redeemer will come to Tzion"? It is because of "those of Yaakov" who repent.

Thus, our *tefillos* focus on **the ultimate objective of teshuvah**: גְּדוֹלָה תְּשׁוּבָה שֶׁמְּקָרֶבֶת אֶת הַגְּאוּלָה. The prayers are centered around the national objective of the process of repentance — the Final Redemption.

Perhaps, even, the *succah*, which is a microcosm of the Beis HaMikdash,*** is in some small measure Hashem's response to all of our prayers of the Yamim Noraim. We may say that

---

* See סמ"ג מצוה א who considers צפיה לישועה, *yearning for salvation*, one aspect of the very first mitzvah of the Torah: אָנֹכִי ה׳ אֱלֹהֶיךָ אֲשֶׁר הוֹצֵאתִיךָ מֵאֶרֶץ מִצְרַיִם מִבֵּית עֲבָדִים. [According to the listing of the Smag, the first of the *Aseres HaDibros* is the first mitzvah.]

** See "Are We Ignoring Our Own Needs on Rosh Hashanah?," page 75.

*** See "The Sanctity of the Beis HaMikdash in the *Succah*," page 273, and "The Borders of Eretz Yisrael Encompassed in Your *Succah*," page 287.

Hashem answers that if we sincerely want to return to Eretz Yisrael, and bask in the Glory of the Beis HaMikdash, He will give us a small semblance of that experience as we take shelter under His Divine Presence, under the shade of the *succah*. We are not satisfied with a mere microcosm of the Beis HaMikdash, and so we continue to pray for the ultimate *succah*: הָרַחֲמָן, הוּא יָקִים לָנוּ אֶת סֻכַּת דָּוִד הַנּוֹפָלֶת.

Bearing in mind this teaching, that the objective of teshuvah is the ultimate redemption of the Jewish people, we can appreciate a very difficult Rambam.

The very first halachah in *Hilchos Teshuvah*[3] teaches us, כָּל הַמִּצְוֹת שֶׁבַּתּוֹרָה ... אִם עָבַר אָדָם עַל אַחַת מֵהֶן ... כְּשֶׁיַּעֲשֶׂה תְּשׁוּבָה וְיָשׁוּב מֵחֶטְאוֹ, חַיָּב לְהִתְוַדּוֹת לִפְנֵי הַקֵל בָּרוּךְ הוּא. If a person transgresses any mitzvah in the Torah, when he does teshuvah he is obligated to confess before Hashem. *"When"* a person does teshuvah? Isn't a person *required* to do teshuvah? "When" implies that it is not absolutely obligatory; rather, if one does choose to do teshuvah, he is obligated to follow a specific protocol that entails *Vidui*, confession.

Surprisingly, the Rambam implies — and this is the *Minchas Chinuch's*[4] understanding of the Rambam — that there is no mitzvah in the Torah to do teshuvah. Can it really be that teshuvah is not a mitzvah?

The Ramban in *Parashas Nitzavim* advances that when the Torah writes, כִּי הַמִּצְוָה הַזֹּאת אֲשֶׁר אָנֹכִי מְצַוְּךָ הַיּוֹם לֹא נִפְלֵאת הִוא מִמְּךָ וְלֹא רְחֹקָה הִוא, *For this commandment that I command you today — it is not hidden from you and it is not distant* (Devarim 30:11), it is referring to the mitzvah of teshuvah that the Torah had mentioned earlier in the passage: וְשַׁבְתָּ עַד ה' אֱלֹקֶיךָ, *and you will return to Hashem* (ibid., 30:2).

Unlike the Rambam, the Ramban clearly maintains that teshuvah **is** a mitzvah. The Rambam implies it is optional — but how can teshuvah be discretionary?

Rav Betzalel Zolty[5] offers a brilliant interpretation. Certainly, if a person sinned, he would be obligated to repent. Although the Rambam does not reckon teshuvah as one of the mitzvos of the Torah, he maintains that teshuvah is a prerequisite for *Geulah*.[6] As such, we are vouchsafed that just as the redemption will come, so will Klal Yisrael ultimately do teshuvah. וְכְבָר הִבְטִיחָה הַתּוֹרָה שֶׁסּוֹף יִשְׂרָאֵל לַעֲשׂוֹת תְּשׁוּבָה, the Torah already promises that, in the end, Bnei Yisrael will do teshuvah.

Says Rav Zolty, if perforce the time will come that we will do teshuvah, that means that we will not always have absolute free choice in regard to teshuvah. There will be a time when HaKadosh Baruch Hu will compel Klal Yisrael to return. It is the fundamental definition of a mitzvah that it is always in the arena of Man's free will to perform or desist. As this is not the case with teshuvah, teshuvah cannot be reckoned a mitzvah. The Rambam understands וְשַׁבְתָּ עַד ה' אֱלֹקֶיךָ not as a command, but rather as a prediction.

HaGaon HaRav Noach Isaac Oelbaum comments in his *sefer*, *Minchas Chein* on *hilchos teshuvah*, that this interpretation works well with another passage in the Rambam.[7] There, the Rambam writes, יִשְׁתַּדֵּל הָאָדָם לַעֲשׂוֹת תְּשׁוּבָה, A person should *try* to do teshuvah. The Rambam merely recommends trying to do teshuvah. Isn't it a *mitzvas asei*? No! Technically, it is not. We do need to do it, but fundamentally it is an assurance, not a command, that ultimately the Jewish people will do teshuvah.

And this is a הַבְטָחָה, *promise*, that we have been privileged to see fulfilled to some degree, in our time.

There is a chilling *remez* that was revealed by the Vilna Gaon.[8] The *Gra* states that *Sefer Devarim* corresponds to the sixth millennium of world history. Each of the ten *parshiyos* in *Devarim* corresponds to a discrete century. Although there are eleven *parshiyos* in *Devarim*, the *parshiyos* of *Netzavim* and *Vayeilech* can be reckoned as one. So, for instance, *Parashas Devarim* corresponds to the years 1240 – 1340 (5000 – 5100) and *Va'eschanan* to 1340 – 1440 (5100 – 5200). The years 1840 – 1940 are predicted in *Ki Savo*, as the devastating upheaval of World War I and the onset of the Holocaust could not be described more vividly by the *tochachah* in *Parashas Ki Savo*. But the Holocaust continued for five more years and is clearly alluded to in the *pesukim* of

Netzavim-Vayeilech as well, which is our century of 1940 – 2040 (5700 – 5800).

וַיִּחַר אַף ה' בָּאָרֶץ הַהוּא לְהָבִיא עָלֶיהָ אֶת כָּל הַקְּלָלָה הַכְּתוּבָה בַּסֵּפֶר הַזֶּה. וַיִּתְּשֵׁם ה' מֵעַל אַדְמָתָם בְּאַף וּבְחֵמָה וּבְקֶצֶף גָּדוֹל וַיַּשְׁלִכֵם אֶל אֶרֶץ אַחֶרֶת כַּיּוֹם הַזֶּה, *So God's anger flared against that Land, to bring upon it the entire curse that is written in this Book, and Hashem removed them from upon their soil, with anger, with wrath, and with great fury, and He cast them to another land, as this very day* (Devarim 29:26-27). Can it be more explicit? Incredibly, the *sefer De'ah Es Hashem*[9] points out that the words בְּאַף וּבְחֵמָה וּבְקֶצֶף גָּדוֹל are the precise numerical value of הפתרון הסופי, *the final solution.*

But the *Torah HaKedoshah* continues: Yes, you will be scattered to new lands between the years 1940 and 2040. But וְשַׁבְתָּ עַד ה' אֱלֹקֶיךָ, there will be a teshuvah movement in Klal Yisrael to an extent that our people have never experienced. As the *pasuk* states, וּמָל ה' אֱלֹקֶיךָ אֶת לְבָבְךָ וְאֶת לְבַב זַרְעֶךָ, *Hashem, your God, will circumcise your heart and the heart of your offspring* (ibid., 30:6). I will inspire your hearts to seek out My word.

In *Parashas Vayeilech*, which continues to refer to our century, we have the greatest of all promises: כִּי לֹא תִשָּׁכַח מִפִּי זַרְעוֹ, *for [the Torah] shall never be forgotten from the mouth of its offspring* (ibid., 31:21). This is the promise of the eternity of the Torah, that the Torah will never be forgotten. The yeshivos will be rebuilt, and there will be a renaissance of Torah learning the likes of which we have never seen. The Chassidic Courts decimated in the Holocaust will be restored in all their majesty and grandeur.

At first glance, the unending publication and dissemination of *sefarim* was seemingly disparaged by Shlomo HaMelech, as he writes, וְיֹתֵר מֵהֵמָּה בְּנִי הִזָּהֵר עֲשׂוֹת סְפָרִים הַרְבֵּה אֵין קֵץ וְלַהַג הַרְבֵּה יְגִעַת בָּשָׂר, *Beyond these words, my son, beware: The making of many books is without limit, and much study is weariness of the flesh* (Koheles 12:12). However, this verse can be understood to mean that it is precisely this publishing revolution in the aftermath of the near destruction of our people seventy years ago that will herald the ultimate redemption of our people.

Rav Shlomo Kluger[10] interprets this *pasuk* as follows: עֲשׂוֹת

סְפָרִים הַרְבֵּה, produce many, many *sefarim!* אֵין קֵץ, for the *Geulah* has not yet come. Additional *sefarim* are needed to usher in the *Geulah*. Likewise, the Abarbanel interprets that Shlomo HaMelech is encouraging the continuous dissemination of the written word of Hashem.

As we have seen the *Tochachah* come to fruition, so, too, we have seen the *nechamah* of the teshuvah movement and the rebuilding and dissemination of Torah in our times.

May this modest contribution of the printed word about doing teshuvah — שֶׁמְּקָרֶבֶת אֶת הַגְּאוּלָה — and the Yamim Noraim, culminating with the זְמַן שִׂמְחָתֵינוּ be counted among the עֲשׂוֹת סְפָרִים הַרְבֵּה, so that we no longer have to be in a state of אֵין קֵץ, but rather may our *tefillos* of וּצְמִיחַת קֶרֶן לְדָוִד עַבְדֶּךָ, וַעֲרִיכַת נֵר לְבֶן יִשַׁי מְשִׁיחֶךָ be fulfilled in the fruition of הָרַחֲמָן, הוּא יָקִים לָנוּ אֶת סֻכַּת דָּוִד הַנּוֹפָלֶת.

ENDNOTES

1. הלכות תשובה פרק ז הלכה ה.
2. יומא פו, ב.
3. הלכות תשובה פרק א הלכה א.
4. מצוה שס"ד, מצות וידוי על החטא.
5. משנת יעב"ץ או"ח סימן נד.
6. הלכות תשובה פרק ז הלכה ה.
7. הלכות תשובה פרק ז הלכה א.
8. פנינים משולחן הגר"א, פרשת כי תצא, פרק כ"ה פסוק ט"ו, ובהגהה שם.
9. ספר דעה את ה' מרב אברהם ישעיהו טרוף דפים 289, 342.
10. הקדמה לטוב טעם ודעת חלק ב'.

eLuL

The Secret of Successful Teshuvah: First Come, First Served

❧ *Four Days of Judgment*

בְּאַרְבָּעָה פְרָקִים הָעוֹלָם נִדּוֹן, בַּפֶּסַח עַל הַתְּבוּאָה, בָּעֲצֶרֶת עַל
פֵּרוֹת הָאִילָן, בְּרֹאשׁ הַשָּׁנָה כָּל בָּאֵי הָעוֹלָם עוֹבְרִין לְפָנָיו כִּבְנֵי
מָרוֹן, שֶׁנֶּאֱמַר "הַיּוֹצֵר יַחַד לִבָּם, הַמֵּבִין אֶל כָּל מַעֲשֵׂיהֶם"[1]וּבַחַג
נִדּוֹנִין עַל הַמַּיִם (משנה ראש השנה א:ב).

*The world is judged on four separate occasions. On
Pesach, Hashem judges the grain; on Shavuos, Hashem
judges the fruits. On the Yom Tov of Rosh Hashanah, all
the inhabitants of the world pass before Hashem like a
flock before a shepherd. And on Succos, Hashem passes
judgment on water (Mishnah Rosh Hashanah 1:2).*

❧ *What Are the* בְּנֵי מָרוֹן?

The Mishnah uses the phrase בְּנֵי מָרוֹן to describe mankind as
it passes before Hashem in judgment. The Gemara[2] offers three
possible explanations for this unusual term. The first explanation translates *bnei maron* as *young sheep*. Rashi[3] explains that
this analogy refers to an owner who counts his flock to mark

every tenth sheep that will be given to the Levi as *maaser*. The sheep exit the corral through a narrow opening that allows them to pass through only one at a time. He then counts them as they pass, marking every tenth sheep for *maaser*. Likewise, on Rosh Hashanah, we pass before Hashem one at a time.

Reish Lakish offers a second explanation, stating that the Mishnah refers to a path used to ascend to the house of Maron. The path was very steep and narrow; it led to the top of the mountain. As they made their way to the top, climbers were forced to walk in single file to prevent them from falling from the cliffs at the edge of the path.

A third explanation is presented by R' Yehudah, who said in the name of Shmuel that בְּנֵי מָרוֹן, which can be translated, *soldiers of the master,* refers to the soldiers in David HaMelech's army. The general would decide the order in which the soldiers marched, and they would maintain that strict order as they proceeded to march in single file.

The Gemara provides three definitions for the term בְּנֵי מָרוֹן, but each one seemingly refers to the same thing: On Rosh Hashanah, all the inhabitants of the world come before Hashem in single file — one at a time, stating that we are each judged individually. Let us uncover the deeper messages of these three analogies.

ဆ *Why So Cryptic?*

Why does the Mishnah not simply state that on Rosh Hashanah all the inhabitants of the world come before Hashem individually — "*zeh achar zeh,* one after the other"— to be judged? Typically, *Chazal* use parables only to elucidate complex topics, while the simple concept of passing before God individually is easily understood. Furthermore, when the Gemara is seeking an explanation, why does it provide three explanations that all reach the same conclusion? These questions are raised by Rav Yitzchak Blazer, known as Rav Itzele Peterburger (1837 – 1907), in his great work, *Kochvei Ohr.*[4]

✑ Meet Rav Itzele Peterburger

Rav Itzele Peterburger was one of the three primary students of the founder of the *mussar* movement, Rav Yisroel Salanter, along with the Alter of Kelm and Rav Naftali Amsterdam. Rav Yisroel would praise these *talmidim*; the accolade with which he praised Rav Itzele was that he was a *lamdan*. This is certainly evident from his classic work of halachic responsa, *Sheilos U'Teshuvos Pri Yitzchak*. We can get a glimpse of Rav Itzele's saintliness through a comment of the Chofetz Chaim,[5] who wrote that in order not to sin with one's words during the Yamim Noraim, one must be very careful to curtail one's speech, emulating ways of the Gaon and the *tzaddik* Rav Yitzchak Blazer, the *Av Beis Din* of St. Petersburg, who did not speak from Rosh Chodesh Elul until after Yom Kippur. Each year, he was completely silent for these forty days.

✑ What the Mishnah Is Really Teaching Us

Rav Itzele answers by offering a revolutionary understanding of the first Mishnah in *Rosh Hashanah*: In fact, the Mishnah is not teaching us that we pass before Hashem one at a time; that goes without saying. Rather, the Mishnah is teaching us that as we pass before Hashem in single file, it is our position on this procession that is crucial to the outcome of our *Yom HaDin* and is a key component as to the type of year we will have.

The closer one is to the front of the line, the better off he is!

✑ Why "One by One"?

Rav Itzele asks an even more basic question: Why does Hashem require us to pass before Him to be judged one at a time? Can't Hashem judge the whole world simultaneously?

The Gemara[6] describes the judgment on Rosh Hashanah. Hashem begins by judging the Jewish People, and He then proceeds to judge the other nations of the world. And, as Rav Chisda says, when Hashem judges the Jews, He begins with the king and then moves onto the *tzibbur*. The Gemara offers two explanations as to why the king must be judged before the masses. The first is that it is not *derech eretz* to keep the king waiting as his subjects are judged.

The Gemara's second answer is the key to understanding the secret of the judgment on Rosh Hashanah: The king is privileged to be judged מִקַּמֵּי דְּלֵיפּוּשׁ חֲרוֹן אַף, *before the anger of God flares*. Rashi[7] explains that as the *Yom HaDin* progresses, Hashem is increasingly faced with a multitude of people who have committed all sorts of *aveiros*. Hashem has great patience, *kavayachol*, at the beginning of the day, but as time wears on and more and more sins are presented before Him for judgment, Hashem conducts Himself as if His patience were being tried. Subsequent judgments are not as lenient or forgiving. Were the king to be judged after the people, he would face a much harsher and more stringent judgment than if he were to be judged before them. Therefore, Hashem judges the king first.

❧ *Can Hashem's Din Be Influenced?*

Rav Itzele[8] is troubled by this Gemara as well. Can we say that Hashem's *din* for one person is swayed by the sins of others? Hashem's judgment is absolutely objective; He is the ultimate *Dayan Emes* — He is completely and perfectly just and can certainly judge each person on the basis of his own merits. How can we possibly say that Hashem will be negatively influenced and that His patience will be tried as the day of judgment progresses?

Therefore, Rav Itzele derives from this Gemara that Hashem established the procedures of the Heavenly Court analogously with mortal courts. Just as in a human court, earlier cases impact and affect the way a judge decides and sentences later cases, so too, the *Beis Din shel Maalah* allows those who are judged earlier on the *Yom HaDin* to impact the judgment of those who come before Hashem later in the day. Each member of Klal Yisrael, while judged individually, is actually very much affected by earlier judgments of other Jews. Rav Itzele explains that the reason the Heavenly Court is conducted this way is in order to help us relate better to the judgment process; we are thus able to think of it as if it were a judgment of flesh and blood.

∾ *Why We're Not All Judged at the Same Time*

According to Rav Itzele, this is why Hashem does not judge us all simultaneously. If Hashem were to look at everyone at once, with our many collective sins, His patience would, so to speak, soon be exhausted and we would each be in danger of receiving a harsh judgment. By judging us individually, Hashem gives us a fighting chance to have an easier and more lenient sentence. To those who come before Hashem earlier in the day — those at the front of the line — the Judge is patient; His patience has not been tried and worn thin. The all-important question, then, is how does one merit placement at the head of the line rather than at the tail end?

∾ *How Do We Get to the Front of the Line?*

The Gemara tells us that Hashem places the king at the very front of the line so that he will be in a better position to receive a positive judgment, so how do *we* move up and get as close as possible to the front? Every place on the line is of critical importance. As the *pasuk* states, וְחוֹטֶא אֶחָד יְאַבֵּד טוֹבָה הַרְבֵּה, *a single rogue can ruin a great deal of good* (*Koheles* 9:18). Every additional person, with his *aveiros*, who precedes us on the line can greatly affect the outcome as we are judged. It would be worthwhile to get ahead of even one person on line; that may make all the difference in what the ultimate *din* is.

While awaiting judgment, our fate is very much dependent on the position we occupy, so how do we secure a better position on the line of judgment?

✑ Rav Itzele's Incredible Explication of the Mishnah

Says Rav Itzele, this is precisely what the Mishnah tells us with the statement that on Rosh Hashanah we come before Hashem like *bnei maron*: The Mishnah teaches us how to get to the front of the line, and the Gemara offers us three ways to accomplish this. To understand this, we must first explore how the *din* on Rosh Hashanah actually takes place.

✑ The Basis of the Din on Rosh Hashanah

How does Hashem, in fact, judge a person? On what is the *din* based? The Gemara states[9] that there are three books open before Hashem on Rosh Hashanah. One is the book of *tzaddikim gemurim*, the totally righteous; the second book is that of *reshaim gemurim*, the totally wicked; the third is the book of *beinonim*, those who fall between the above categories. *Tzaddikim gemurim* are registered in the Book of Life, and their verdict is immediately sealed for life, while *reshaim gemurim* are immediately registered and sealed for death. However, the *din* of the *beinonim* is in limbo; it is suspended until Yom Kippur. At that time, if they merit, they then are registered for life, and if not, they are sentenced to death.

✑ The Ran Defines Tzaddik, Rasha, and Beinoni

In this context, who is considered a *tzaddik*? What defines a *rasha*? A *beinoni*? Is a *tzaddik* only a *gadol hador* and a *rasha* always a completely wicked person?

The Ran comments[10] that upon first analysis, the Gemara seems to use the term *beinoni* to describe someone who has precisely the same number of *zechusim* as *aveiros*. This implies that to be a *tzaddik*, one might have even only one more mitzvah than he does *aveiros*. Using this rationale, a *rasha* would be someone whose sins outnumber his mitzvos — again, even by just one.

Yet, says the Ran, this cannot be the correct understanding. Looking around, we have seen that many people who clearly had many more mitzvos than *aveiros* did not all survive the year. The opposite is also true: People who are known to be evil survive and even thrive. The Gemara therefore cannot be defining a *tzaddik* simply as someone who has more mitzvos than *aveiros* and a *rasha* as someone who has more *aveiros* than mitzvos.

According to the Ran, the word *tzaddik* does not refer to a righteous person, and the word *rasha* does not refer to a wicked person. Rather, the Ran states, a *tzaddik* is one who is found to be צָדִיק בַּדִּין, one who has been acquitted; a *rasha* is defined as a רָשָׁע בַּדִּין, one who was found guilty. Thus, a *tzaddik* is a person to whom Hashem decides to give life on Rosh Hashanah; a *rasha* is one on whom Hashem has passed the verdict that he will not survive the year. Hashem can decide that a special act of kindness warrants another year of life for the one who performed it — even if that person is truly wicked. When this person comes to the *Beis Din shel Maalah* after 120 years, he will definitely be held accountable for all the sins he committed during his lifetime, and he will be punished accordingly. But in terms of the *din* on a particular Rosh Hashanah, he can merit a victorious judgment based on the merit of a mitzvah or action that found favor with Hashem. In this instance, the person who is a true *rasha* is labeled a צָדִיק בַּדִּין — he has emerged righteous in his judgment on that Rosh Hashanah.

The *din* on Rosh Hashanah is administered differently from the judgment one faces after his demise. That later *din* weighs and considers **all** a person's actions, and it balances the good against the bad. On Rosh Hashanah, however, Hashem does not necessarily look at the balance in the spiritual ledger of mitzvos and *aveiros*. Instead, He may examine individual deeds that a person may have done that will lead him either to a *din* of life or, *chas v'shalom*, the opposite. Hashem may see a *tzaddik* who performed one act that He feels is unacceptable for one of his stature. This *tzaddik* may then emerge as a רָשָׁע בַּדִּין — not receiving another year of life.

The Ran states that the proof that the *din* of Rosh Hashanah is administered in this way is apparent in the world around us. We see many righteous people who pass away and many evil people who survive.

➣ *The Rambam's Approach to the Din of Rosh Hashanah*

However, the Rambam[11] differs with the Ran's conclusion. The Rambam writes that the *din* on Rosh Hashanah actually is a calculation and a tallying of all of a person's mitzvos and *aveiros*, and the judgment is based on the balance between them. More mitzvos result in life; more *aveiros* result in death. The Rambam says the judgment on Rosh Hashanah is the same *din* that one will face after he passes away; i.e., it depends solely on a person's merits and demerits.

How does the Rambam then explain the phenomenon of a *tzaddik* passing away and a *rasha* surviving? Rav Itzele[12] explains that the Rambam is referring to most cases, wherein a *tzaddik* will have a long and fulfilling life, while a *rasha* will not. In the vast majority of instances, Hashem weighs the mitzvos and *aveiros*, and the *din* is based on which side of the scale is heavier.

The Rambam agrees that there are exceptions to this paradigm. There are times when a true *tzaddik* receives an unfortunate *din* because of a specific *aveirah* he may have done. There are cases when a *rasha* is judged for life because of a specific mitzvah he may have done that found favor with Hashem. But these occasions are the exception, not the rule. Rav Itzele states a Jew must believe that the basis for judgment on Rosh Hashanah is primarily based on the number of one's mitzvos weighed against the number of one's *aveiros*, regardless of the exceptions.

➣ *The Secret Aspect of Din*

However, there is yet a third aspect of *din*. Moshe Rabbeinu[13] asked the Ribbono shel Olam, הוֹדִעֵנִי נָא אֶת דְּרָכֶךָ, *Make Your way known to me* (*Shemos* 33:13). Moshe Rabbeinu wanted to understand the phenomena of *tzaddik v'ra lo* and *rasha v'tov lo*: How can a *tzaddik* experience hardship, while a *rasha's* life is pleasant and smooth? Why do we sometimes see a perfect *tzaddik*, who never sinned, pass away in his prime, while a *rasha*, who continually sins, lives and prospers? Hashem responded that He would not reveal the secret to Moshe: וְחַנֹּתִי אֶת אֲשֶׁר אָחֹן וְרִחַמְתִּי אֶת אֲשֶׁר אֲרַחֵם, *I shall show favor when I choose to show favor, and I shall show mercy when I choose to show mercy* (ibid. v. 19). That is, Hashem is gracious to the person He chooses, and He will be compassionate to the person He chooses. This decision is not made because of a specific mitzvah or a specific *aveirah*; rather it is based on hidden reasons that we mortals cannot be privy to nor understand.

◈ Summary of the Three Main Methods of Judgment:

1) In the vast majority of cases, Hashem uses a scale to weigh one's mitzvos against the *aveiros*, and He bases His judgment on which side of the scale is heavier (Rambam).

2) Out of the ordinary cases, in which Hashem identifies a specific action and bases the *din* on that action. There may be a mitzvah that found favor with Hashem, and a *rasha* may be spared, or there may be a single *aveirah* that causes Hashem to judge a *tzaddik* unfavorably (Ran).

3) A seemingly completely undeserving person may receive Hashem's compassion, or vice versa, for reasons we cannot understand: וְחַנֹּתִי אֶת אֲשֶׁר אָחֹן וְרִחַמְתִּי אֶת אֲשֶׁר אֲרַחֵם (*Berachos* 17a).

These are the methods of judgment.

◈ Three Ways to Be Placed at the Head of the Line

Correspondingly, there are three ways to be placed at the all-important head of the judgment line. The first is to deserve it. If a person has numerous mitzvos and *zechusim,* and his *zechusim* far outweigh his *aveiros,* then Hashem may move him up the line. Thus, the first way to move up in the line is to accumulate more mitzvos than *aveiros.* However, this suggestion is not very helpful at the eleventh hour, as we may not have enough time to achieve this goal right before the *Yom HaDin.*

A second way to move up in the line can apply even to someone whose *aveiros* far outweigh his mitzvos. If the person has a unique mitzvah, a special *zechus,* that finds favor with Hashem, the Ribbono shel Olam may move that person up in the line. Even though according to his balance sheet the person does not deserve to be advanced, Hashem decides to move him there based on a specific mitzvah he did.

There is a third way to be placed at the head of the line. Hashem is merciful and, based on His hidden reason, may decide that a certain individual warrants being moved up in the line. However, from a practical standpoint, we have no way of influencing this decision and taking advantage of this method.

The most useful method of moving toward the head of the line is the second way described above. If we were able to identify a mitzvah that would fit into the category of a special *zechus* that really finds favor with Hashem, then perhaps we could influence our positioning. Thus, even if we are not really deserving, we may be able to improve our outcome by having our place moved up in the line.

✒ *What Is That Special Zechus?*

Can we, in fact, identify a special *zechus* that might find favor with Hashem so that He will move us forward and thereby increase our chance for a favorable *din*?

Rav Itzele Peterburger states that by uncovering the hidden meanings of the three definitions of *"bnei maron,"* as noted above, we discover three ways one can move to the head of the line during the *Yom HaDin.*

The first *pshat of bnei maron* was that we file before Hashem like the sheep who exit the corral one at a time. The order in which the sheep walk through the gate is not decided by the owner; it is determined by the sheep. The stronger and more powerful sheep push the weaker animals out of their way and exit first. This parable teaches us that the strongest and the biggest — in a spiritual sense — are at the front of the line. Those with the most *zechusim* are the strongest spiritually, and they can muscle their way to the head of the line to be judged first. *Tzaddikim* are therefore afforded a better spot on line than those who are not as righteous.

The Gemara[14] tells us that there are some people whom Hashem feeds and provides for out of His good grace, while others are provided for because they are strong. Rashi[15] says that the strength of these "strong" people lies in their mitzvos. Thus, this latter group, for whom Hashem provides because of their strength, is comprised of the *tzaddikim*. If we want to know who goes first, who is judged at the head of the line on Rosh Hashanah, this *mashal* teaches us that it is the strong ones, namely, the mighty *tzaddikim* with their many *zechusim*.

Who are the weak people? The Torah states, אֲשֶׁר קָרְךָ בַּדֶּרֶךְ וַיְזַנֵּב בְּךָ כָּל הַנֶּחֱשָׁלִים אַחֲרֶיךָ, *that he [Amalek] happened upon you on the way, and he struck those of you who were hindmost, all the weaklings at your rear…* (*Devarim* 25:18). Rashi[16] explains הַנֶּחֱשָׁלִים, *the weaklings*, as a reference to those who are spiritually weak because of their sins. As we see, sinners are termed weak and *tzaddikim* are called strong. Thus, the first group of people who are granted positions at the front of the line are the strong, the *tzaddikim*, symbolized by the more powerful sheep who push their way through the gate at the head of the flock.

The second *mashal* the Gemara gives for *bnei maron* is the steep and narrow ascent up the mountain. Uncovering the message of this *mashal* will prove to be the secret of achieving a more successful *din* on Rosh Hashanah. This steep pathway must be climbed in single file. Who goes up the mountain first? Whoever gets to the path first! There is no specific order; access to the path is granted on a first-come-first-served basis. Rav

Itzele Peterburger says that this *mashal* is telling us a very practical way to move up in the line and therefore be assured a better judgment on Rosh Hashanah. If we get to the line first — if we start doing teshuvah early — then we will be ahead of those who begin to prepare after us.

Just as one who is truly worried about an important court case prepares extensively and starts his preparation as soon as he can, one who takes the *Yom HaDin* seriously prepares for it in advance, rather than waiting until the last minute. This will help for the judgment on Rosh Hashanah, and the earlier one starts preparing the farther up the line and the better off he will be. Even if a person is not a *tzaddik*, and even if he does not have many *zechusim*, starting to prepare earlier grants him an earlier place on the line.

There is a third way to be moved to the front of the line, which parallels the third understanding of the *bnei maron*. Similar to the general whose choice of who should go to battle and when seems arbitrary, Hashem can choose to (seemingly) randomly assign a person an earlier and more coveted spot on line.

✑ The Three Methods Summarized

To get to the front of the line, one has the option to act like a strong sheep and power his way forward, as it were, by performing mitzvos and gathering *zechusim* throughout the year. This will increase his spiritual muscle, enabling him to move to the front of the line. However, this option is not easy to achieve for everyone. Likewise, the third way to get to the front of the line is not something that we can influence, as Hashem acts in mysterious ways and decides on His own to advance someone's position on the line. Therefore, it is imperative to employ the second method, which will prove to be the most practical for most people. As Elul begins, and the *Yemei HaDin* approach, this second method is critical for one to be aware of and to take advantage of. Like those who are attempting to climb the path up the mountain, getting there first ensures an earlier spot on line. By commencing preparations early, by being among the first to begin the teshuvah process, a person can move himself up the line. This favorable position provides the opportunity to receive a more favorable judgment. As soon as the *shofar* sounds on the very first day of Elul, it behooves one to think about the impending judgment and to begin to do teshuvah.

The Gemara in *Rosh Hashanah* is not simply telling us three ways to understand how we pass before Hashem single file. There is a much deeper message. The Gemara is teaching us about the order of the line of judgment on Rosh Hashanah as a means of instructing us as to how we can move our place on line closer to the front.

◈ *Eimas Hadin Engenders Rachmanus*

Rosh Chodesh Elul marks the beginning of the days of mercy, *yemei rachamim*, because it is the day that Moshe Rabbeinu went up to *Shamayim* for the third time to obtain the second set of *Luchos*.[17] Rav Itzele adds[18] that the more fearful one is regarding the judgment, the more *rachmanus* Hashem will have on that person. By preparing early, one demonstrates that he has a genuine *eimas hadin*, fear of judgment, which is a *zechus* to arouse the mercy of Hashem. The *yesod* of preparing for the *din* is to awaken this fear in oneself. This fear, acquired with introspection and reflection, can facilitate a person receiving a more advantageous decision on the *Yom HaDin*.

◈ *The Chiddush of the Tzaddik M'Raanana*

The *sefer Ben L'Ashri* — *Berachah M'shuleshes* was written by the Gaon and *Mekubal* Rav Yitzchak HaKohen Huberman. He learned in Yeshivas Chachmei Lublin, where he was the *chavrusa* of my great-grandfather, the last Rav of Sochaczew, Reb Yehuda Leib Wolman *Hy"d*. After his family was murdered in the Holocaust, Rav Huberman moved to Eretz Yisrael, where he became known as the *Tzaddik M'Raanana*.* The Gerrer Rebbe used to study the righteous practices of this *tzaddik*.

The Tzaddik M'Raanana was so poor that he could not even afford a new *tallis katan*; he could not even afford to purchase paper. My grandfather, HaRav Mordechai Leib Glatstein, has many letters of correspondence with the Tzaddik M'Raanana in which this *tzaddik* wrote on the inside of the envelope, since he did not have other stationery. He was a venerated *mekubal* to whom the Beis Yisrael of Gur traveled weekly to study kabbalah. This great *tzaddik* was not blessed with children, and the *sefer, Ben L'Ashri,* is his legacy. In his *sefer,*[19] the Tzaddik M'Raanana sets down an incredible promise. He writes that he will pray daily for anyone who learns his *sefer* and relates *the divrei Torah in his name.* The Tzaddik vowed to *daven* that these people will be saved from any *tzarah* in both This World and in the World to Come.

The *Ben L'Ashri*[20] expounds on the *pasuk*: כִּי אִם אֶל הַמָּקוֹם אֲשֶׁר יִבְחַר ה' אֱלֹקֵיכֶם מִכָּל שִׁבְטֵיכֶם לָשׂוּם אֶת שְׁמוֹ שָׁם לְשִׁכְנוֹ תִדְרְשׁוּ וּבָאתָ שָׁמָּה, *Rather, only at the place that Hashem, your God, will choose from among all your tribes to place His Name there shall you seek out His Presence and come there (Devarim* 12:5). The word לְשִׁכְנוֹ has its root in the word *shachein,* neighbor. We know that the halachah is that we are obligated to begin learning about and expounding upon the halachos of a Yom Tov thirty days before it arrives. Therefore, in preparation for Rosh Hashanah, which is a day of teshuvah, preparations must begin on Rosh Chodesh Elul, thirty days earlier.

Says the *Tzaddik M'Raanana*: Don't wait for Elul! לְשִׁכְנוֹ תִדְרְשׁוּ — seek out Hashem, start preparing during the neighbor of Elul — during the month of Av. Start doing teshuvah during the month of Av. If you do, then וּבָאתָ שָׁמָּה, you will come to the desired place. If you do, then you will have a blessed and successful year.

---

* This appellation was given to Rav Huberman by the Gerrer Rebbe, the Beis Yisrael.

True, if you start doing teshuvah on Rosh Chodesh Elul, you have a good chance to be placed on an advantageous spot on the line. Even better would be to start earlier, during the month of Av. In fact, it is brought down[21] that the two letters of the word Av are the *roshei teivos* for אֱלוּל בָּא — Elul is coming. During the month of Av one should be cognizant that Elul is coming, and Rosh Hashanah is not far behind. When it comes to the judgment of Rosh Hashanah, it is location, location, location — being at the front of the line can help us merit a favorable judgment on the *Yom HaDin*.

ENDNOTES

1. תהלים לג, טו.
2. ראש השנה יח, א.
3. רש"י, שם.
4. כוכבי אור, סימן ד.
5. חובת השמירה, פרק י.
6. ראש השנה ח, א.
7. רש"י, שם.
8. כוכבי אור, שם.
9. ראש השנה טז, ב.
10. ר"ן, ראש השנה טז, ב.
11. הלכות תשובה, פרק ג הלכה ג.
12. כוכבי אור, שם.
13. ברכות ז, א.
14. ברכות יז, ב.

15. רש"י, שם.
16. רש"י, שם.
17. טור או"ח סימן תקפא.
18. כוכבי אור, שם.
19. בן לאשרי, ברכה משולשת (מהגאון הצדיק ר' יצחק הכהן הוברמן זצ"ל), בשער הספר: והנני מוסר עוד מודעה שהחלטתי להתפלל בלי נדר בכל יום על כל אלה שיעיינו בספר ויגידו בשמי דברי תורה לאחרים שיוושעו מכל צרה שצריכים ישועה בעולם הזה ובעולם הבא.
20. ראה עמוד שמ"ה.
21. טיב המועדים, אלול-תשרי עמוד כט.

CPremium CTeshuvah

～ *Parashas Re'eh and Chodesh Elul: A Connection to Explore*

A *parashah* that is read at a specific time of the year contains the lessons and teachings relevant to that time period. The Gemara[1] mentions this concept specifically in reference to the reading of the *Tochachah* of *Parashas Bechukosai* before Shavuos and the *Tochachah* of *Parashas Ki Savo* before Rosh Hashanah. The Shelah HaKadosh applies this to the Torah portions that are read throughout the year.[2] Interestingly, *Parashas Re'eh* is always read at the beginning of Chodesh Elul. In light of the above teaching of the Shelah, let us explore what we can glean from *Parashas Re'eh* at the start of Elul as we embark on our voyage of teshuvah.

～ אֲנִי לְדוֹדִי וְדוֹדִי לִי :*Why* דּוֹדִי, *My Beloved?*

There are many allusions to the month of Elul, none more well-known than the *remez* in the verse in *Shir HaShirim*: אֲנִי לְדוֹדִי וְדוֹדִי לִי, *I am my Beloved's, and my Beloved is mine* (*Shir HaShirim* 6:3). The *Mishnah Berurah*[3] writes that the *roshei teivos*, initial letters, of these four words form the word אלול.

The *Mishnah Berurah* further notes that each of the *sofei teivos*, final letters, of these four words is a *yud*; numerically, combining the four *yuds* gives us 40, representative of the 40 days from Rosh Chodesh Elul until Yom Kippur. It was during these 40 days that Moshe Rabbeinu went up to *Shamayim* to obtain the second set of *Luchos*, a period culminating in Yom Kippur, when Hashem stated, סָלַחְתִּי כִּדְבָרֶךָ, *I have forgiven because of your words* (*Bamidbar* 14:20). In light of Hashem's magnanimity, during this time of the year, our hearts should be close to that of our Beloved by engaging in teshuvah. Hashem reciprocates this closeness and accepts our teshuvah wholeheartedly. As well-known as this *remez* may be, there is an important detail that is often overlooked.

The Ribbono shel Olam is referred to by many different names; for example, *Elokim*, the *Shem Adnus, Tzavakos, Shakkai*, and, most notably, *Yud Kei Vav Kei*. Why, then, doesn't Shlomo HaMelech refer to Hashem using one of these more familiar names rather than דּוֹדִי, *Beloved*? Why not *Ani l'Elokim v'Elokim li*? That would be a more typical way to refer to Hashem. As noted, this verse alludes to Elul, and it is only here we refer to Hashem using this unusual appellation. Why is it that when the month of Elul is suggested, we opt to use this rare designation for Hashem? What is the connection between the month of Elul and Hashem being our Beloved?

⚬ *An Analysis of the Pasuk*

The opening *pasuk* of *Parashas Re'eh* already outlines for us a number of insights into the teshuvah process. The *parashah* begins with the verse: רְאֵה אָנֹכִי נֹתֵן לִפְנֵיכֶם הַיּוֹם בְּרָכָה וּקְלָלָה, *See, I present before you today a blessing and a curse* (*Devarim* 11:26). The Vilna Gaon[4] teaches us that these words delineate for us a number of important concepts about the process of teshuvah.

The verse states, נֹתֵן, using the present tense. Why not say "*nasati*, I have given," using the past tense? The Vilna Gaon explains as follows: If someone chooses to act wrongly, such as speaking during *chazaras hashatz,* and he continues to do so for many years, does he still have *bechirah,* a choice? Each time he speaks in shul, it is no longer a conscious decision — it is merely a habit. It would seem that he no longer has *bechirah chofshis,* free will, to choose to do the right thing and listen silently to the *chazzan.* The Gra says that this suggestion is incorrect. As the saying goes, "past performance has no bearing on future results." Despite previous choices and actions, a person always has the ability to choose. That is why the *pasuk* is written in the present tense: Each and every day, Hashem נֹתֵן, actively *gives* us the ability to make a new choice all over again, regardless of what we have done until that point.

The Gra further explains that the word הַיּוֹם, today, is telling us that on any day — today — a person can choose to repent and start over with a clean slate. One should never feel that since he has sinned in the past, he is unable to come close to Hashem. Any day — even הַיּוֹם — a person can change and repent and start over as if he was born הַיּוֹם, today. In addition, Hashem uses the word אָנֹכִי to indicate that He Himself provides encouragement and support to anyone who wants to repent. Even if the teshuvah process seems daunting, and one feels that he can never accomplish it on his own, he should be reassured, because Hashem will provide him the assistance he needs. Now, although this assistance is provided to us, initiating teshuvah still lies before us — לִפְנֵיכֶם — it is up to us to take the step in the right direction and then Hashem will help. We cannot throw up our hands and expect Hashem to independently guide us in the right direction; teshuvah still requires us to take the initiative, and then Hashem will provide the assistance we need.

The opening word of the *parashah,* רְאֵה, in the singular, rather than רְאוּ, in the plural, also conveys a powerful message. Hashem instructs each of us to be introspective, to look inside ourselves to choose what we will do, rather than be influenced by those around us and by what other people are doing.

✑ The Gift of Teshuvah

In the opinion of most *Rishonim*, it is a mitzvah to do teshuvah. The Rambam, however, does not assert that teshuvah is a mitzvah. He writes, "כְּשֶׁיָּשׁוּב הָאָדָם"; i.e., when a person does teshuvah, he should say *Vidui*. Teshuvah is not obligatory, but it is available to us should we desire it.

We have to recognize that teshuvah is a special gift given to us by Hashem. Imagine that someone is arrested for committing a crime. When he comes before the judge, he admits to robbing the bank, but tells the court that he should be released because he has admitted doing the deed, feels sorry that he committed the robbery, and accepts upon himself to never rob a bank again. The judge will not be impressed by the criminal's remorse and admission, and he will sentence the culprit to prison. Repentance does not work in the physical, material world; it does not erase the act. In contrast, Hashem has created a unique concept for Klal Yisrael: Teshuvah **can** erase our *aveiros*. Perhaps surprisingly, this gift is not given to all mankind. The gift of teshuvah has only been given to the Jewish people, not to the nations of the world.

✑ Why Does Teshuvah Work Only for the Jewish People?

The *Midrash Tanchuma*[5] discusses an apparent contradiction between two verses. One *pasuk* states, יָאֵר ה' פָּנָיו אֵלֶיךָ, *Hashem will illuminate His countenance to you* (Bamidbar 6:26). Another *pasuk* says, אֲשֶׁר לֹא יִשָּׂא פָנִים וְלֹא יִקַּח שֹׁחַד, *[Hashem] does not show His countenance and does not show favoritism* (Devarim 10:17). The Midrash explains that Hashem will not show His countenance to someone who did not do teshuvah. However, if a person does do teshuvah, then Hashem will favor him. By adding the word אֵלֶיךָ, *to you*, to the Jews, to the *pasuk* stating that Hashem will show favor to one who does teshuvah, the Torah is teaching us that only *Yidden* can do teshuvah. The word אֵלֶיךָ excludes non-Jews from this capability.

Even the inhabitants of Nineveh, who we typically under-stand did do teshuvah after hearing the admonishments of Yonah and it was accepted, in reality were not able to do proper teshuvah. They were merely able to suspend punishment for a period of time,[6] but they were not able to be forgiven. Only a Jew can erase his record with complete teshuvah.

The *Mabit*,[7] Rav Moshe MiTrani, in his *sefer Beis Elokim*, writes similarly that teshuvah is only effective for Bnei Yisrael. Likewise, the *Bnei Yissaschar*[8] quotes the aforementioned *Midrash Tanchuma* and concludes that teshuvah applies only to Jews, mentioning that this follows the *psak* of the *Rama MiFano*.

◌ *An Astounding Explanation*

The *Bnei Yissaschar* quotes the *sefer Limudei Hashem*, which offers a remarkable reason that teshuvah was gifted only to the Jewish people. This reason is also cited in the name of the *Chida* and has its source in our *parashah*, *Parashas Re'eh*. The *pasuk* states, "בָּנִים אַתֶּם לַה׳ אֱלֹקֵיכֶם, *you are children to Hashem your God*" (*Devarim* 14:1). Only the Bnei Yisrael are Hashem's chil-dren. The non-Jews of the world are indeed made in the image of Hashem; however, they are the subjects of Hashem their King, but they are not His children. That privilege is reserved for Klal Yisrael alone. This special relationship has halachic ramifications as well.

The Gemara[9] states, מֶלֶךְ שֶׁמָּחַל עַל כְּבוֹדוֹ אֵין כְּבוֹדוֹ מָחוּל; i.e., a king is not permitted to turn a blind eye to someone who infringed on his honor. If someone insults the king, he is guilty of rebellion, and he must be punished severely, without any tolerance.

However, הָאָב שֶׁמָּחַל עַל כְּבוֹדוֹ כְּבוֹדוֹ מָחוּל; that is, a father can forgive a child who insulted him or caused him pain. Thus, says the *Chida*, the reason teshuvah is effective is because WE are Hashem's children. As our Father, Hashem can overlook our wrongdoings. When it comes to the sins of the other nations, however, since their relationship with Hashem is strictly that of king and subject, and a king is not permitted to be *mochel*, to pardon a rebel, teshuvah is therefore not possible for any nation other than the Bnei Yisrael.[10]

This insight into the mechanism of teshuvah gives us a novel perspective as to why the first *parashah* we read when Elul starts is *Parashas Re'eh*. It is because this *parashah* includes the fundamental principle, the verse that explains why teshuvah works for us: בָּנִים אַתֶּם לַה׳ אֱלֹקֵיכֶם. This is the first lesson that we must learn in Elul. We are Hashem's children, and this relationship avails us of the world of teshuvah.

◁ *Teshuvah: Mei'ahavah or Mi'yirah — Out of Love or From Fear?*

There are many levels of teshuvah and some are more effective than others. In a discussion about teshuvah, the Gemara[11] presents what appears to be a contradiction in the words of Reish Lakish. Initially, Reish Lakish teaches us that teshuvah is great since it can change intentional *aveiros* into inadvertent sins. As the *pasuk* states: שׁוּבָה יִשְׂרָאֵל עַד ה׳ אֱלֹקֶיךָ כִּי כָשַׁלְתָּ בַּעֲוֹנֶךָ, *Return, Yisrael, unto Hashem your God, for you have stumbled in your iniquity* (Hoshea 14:2). We know that an עָוֹן is defined as *meizid*, a sin committed with intent. "בַּעֲוֹנֶךָ" refers to sins committed deliberately, yet the verse subsequently refers to these sins as a mere מִכְשׁוֹל, *stumble*. We see from here, says the Gemara, that with teshuvah an עָוֹן, which is *meizid*, intentional, is transformed into a מִכְשׁוֹל — from מֵזִיד, *intentional*, to שׁוֹגֵג, *unintentional*.

The Gemara then offers another citation of Reish Lakish, in which he taught that teshuvah is great because intentional sins actually are converted into זְכוּיוֹת, merits. Teshuvah is so remarkable that it does not merely lessen the severity of the sin; it actually converts the sin into a mitzvah! As the verse states, וּבְשׁוּב רָשָׁע מֵרִשְׁעָתוֹ וְעָשָׂה מִשְׁפָּט וּצְדָקָה עֲלֵיהֶם הוּא יִחְיֶה, *... and if a wicked person turn back from his wickedness and acts with justice and righteousness, he shall live for [his acts]* (Yechezkel 33:19). That is, the sinner who does teshuvah will actually live through his sins — because they will be converted into mitzvos.

Although the two statements of Reish Lakish seem to be at odds, the Gemara answers that, in fact, both citations are correct: The first refers to someone who performs teshuvah out of fear, while the second refers to a person who does teshuvah out of *ahavah*, his love for Hashem. If someone repents because of his fear of Hashem, his *aveiros* are transformed from *meizid* to *shogeg*. But if someone repents out of *ahavah*, love for Hashem, this higher level of teshuvah transforms the sins into mitzvos.

Rav Itzele Peterburger elucidates that teshuvah from *yirah*, fear, means that the repentant's remorse is to the degree that he would never have committed the *aveirah* had he known the punishment he would receive. This reassigns the *aveirah* to the *shogeg* category, since he did not realize the severity of the punishment. However, if someone accomplishes the higher level of teshuvah out of love for Hashem, not only is the sin totally erased, but it actually is transformed into a mitzvah.

✎ How Can We Ask Hashem to Increase Our Merits for Us?

On Rosh Hashanah, we eat many *simanim*, symbolic foods, and utilize them in order to request a year of blessing and success. There is a particular *minhag* to eat carrots, *meren* in Yiddish, on Rosh Hashanah, accompanied by a *tefillah*, "*yehi ratzon… sheyirbeh zechuyoseinu*," asking Hashem to increase our merits. However, *zechusim* are earned, not granted by Hashem. If we want more *zechusim*, we must do more mitzvos. If so, what do we mean by this *tefillah*? The *sefer Toras Chaim*[12] explains that when one does *teshuvah mei'ahavah*, out of love, all his *aveiros* are transformed into *zechusim*. This *tefillah* is thus a prayer asking Hashem to assist us in doing *teshuvah mei'ahavah*, which will then transform our *aveiros* into *zechusim*. This is how Hashem assists us in increasing our merits.

∾ The Four Levels of Kapparah:

The Gemara[13] teaches us that there are four levels of *aveiros* and how to do teshuvah for each. The requirements for being granted forgiveness vary, based on the type of sin committed. The first and lowest level of sin is failure to perform a *mitzvah asei*, a positive commandment. Teshuvah for this type of sin wipes away the sin immediately. Yom Kippur is not even required to achieve this atonement. The second level of *aveirah* is violation of a *lav*, such as wearing *shaatnez* or eating *tereifah*; if the sinner subsequently does teshuvah with all that it entails, he is still not forgiven. Teshuvah suspends the punishment until he reaches Yom Kippur, which cleanses him of the sin.

Interestingly, the Meiri[14] innovatively states that the necessity for Yom Kippur in this case is not absolute. Yom Kippur is an aid that can help someone's teshuvah be completely sincere and definitive. However, if one would muster that level of teshuvah on his own, he would in fact be able to attain forgiveness without the need for the assistance of Yom Kippur.

Violating a *chiyuv kareis* is a third level of sin. Teshuvah and Yom Kippur together are not enough to achieve atonement. For this type of *aveirah*, teshuvah with Yom Kippur suspend the punishment; however, the sinner must also experience *yissurim*, suffering, in order to be totally forgiven.

The fourth level of sin is causing a *chillul Hashem*. Teshuvah, Yom Kippur, and *yissurim* together do not suffice to atone for this severest of *aveiros*. For *chillul Hashem*, מִיתָה, death, is required in order to receive forgiveness.

This is quite an alarming Gemara for one who studies it seriously. The Gemara is teaching us that there are severe sins that teshuvah and Yom Kippur cannot wipe away on their own. However, there is a great *pesach tikvah*, a great opening of hope, that can give us a more positive perspective on our approach to teshuvah. The *Chida* writes[15] that this Gemara is referring to someone who does *teshuvah m'yirah*. He explains that when one commits a sin and does *teshuvah mi'yirah*, the sin is transformed to a *shogeg*, as noted above. Thus, he still needs Yom Kippur to eliminate the remnant of sin. *Teshuvah mi'yirah* only has the ability to transform the *aveirah* to a *shogeg* — but the sin, the *chiyuv kareis*, and the *chillul Hashem* all remain — albeit as a *shogeg*. Additional requirements must be met to eradicate all these and obtain forgiveness. Doing *teshuvah mei'ahavah*, on the other hand, ***does*** have the power to eradicate every type of sin — even *chillul Hashem*. The reason is that if one does *teshuvah mei'ahavah*, the sins become mitzvos, and nothing more than teshuvah itself is needed to achieve this. Once these sins are converted into mitzvos, Yom Kippur and *yissurim* are superfluous, since there is no longer a sin for which to atone. Amazingly, the Chasam Sofer[16] writes that an *aveirah* such as eating *neveilah* is transformed by *teshuvah mei'ahavah* into a mitzvah such as eating the *korban pesach*!

The *Minchas Chinuch*[17] similarly states that although there are *aveiros* for which teshuvah alone does not suffice, this is only when the person is engaging in *teshuvah mi'yirah*, which he refers to as incomplete teshuvah. *Teshuvah mei'ahavah*, on the other hand, is a higher level of teshuvah that independently serves to atone for even the most serious violations. With *teshuvah mei'ahavah*, *aveiros* are retroactively converted into mitzvos. Rav Yitzchak Elchanan Spector writes the same in his introduction to *Nachal Yitzchak* 2:12.

❧ *Vidui on Yom Kippur — Yes, a Song!*

This helps us understand the seemingly unbelievable practice we have to chant the *Vidui* on Yom Kippur in a *niggun* that is somewhat less than somber; perhaps it may even be referred to as joyous. *The Tiferes Yisrael* explains[18] that the goal of doing teshuvah is to attain the level of *teshuvah mei'ahavah*. Accomplishing that goal on Yom Kippur changes the *aveiros* into mitzvos, and therefore we sing in celebration of all the new mitzvos we are acquiring and adding to our repertoire through our *teshuvah mei'ahavah*.

❧ Why Does Blowing the Shofar Twice Silence the Satan?

The Gemara[19] discusses the reason we blow both *tekios d'myushav* and *tekios d'm'umad*, that is, we blow two sets of *tekios*, one before and one during Mussaf. We blow two times so as to confuse the *Satan*. *Tosafos* explains that the *Satan* thinks that the first set of *tekios* is for the mitzvah of *shofar*, and he thinks that the second set is blown to herald Mashiach's arrival. Rashi[20] offers a different explanation, writing that we blow twice so as to prevent the *Satan* from instigating against Klal Yisrael. When he sees that we love mitzvos so much that we even blow the *shofar* twice, he is silenced and his efforts against us are thwarted.

Rav Akiva Eiger[21] asks why this would deter the *Satan* from enumerating our sins and prosecuting the Jews for the *aveiros* they committed. Why would he be silenced just because we are performing the mitzvah of *shofar* twice? On the contrary, it seems logical that seeing us do more mitzvos would motivate him to prosecute us even harder.

Rav Akiva Eiger explains that when the *Satan* hears us blowing the *shofar* the first time, he knows that we are doing teshuvah. He starts to list the *aveiros* we have committed during the year, and he works hard to prosecute us before the Ribbono shel Olam. Then, he hears us blow the *shofar* a second time. This second time is a testament to the fact that we love doing mitzvos. Since by doing so we show that we truly love Hashem and his mitzvos, then the teshuvah we are doing must be *teshuvah mei'ahavah*. All of our *aveiros* would then be converted into mitzvos. Each sin in our ledger that the *Satan*, as prosecutor, enumerates to Hashem, will be transformed into a mitzvah! Realizing this, he is silenced, since every *aveirah* he mentions would only work against him, increasing the *zechusim* on the other side of the scale. This, affirms Rav Akiva Eiger, is why the second set of *tekios* silences the *Satan*.

Why Is the Baal Teshuvah on a Higher Level Than a Tzaddik Gamur?

Chazal teach us,[22] "*B'makom shebaalei teshuvah omdim, ein tzaddikim gemurim yecholim la'amod*, in a place where *baalei teshuvah* are standing, even complete *tzaddikim* cannot stand. It is difficult to understand why this would be true. Shouldn't someone who has lived his entire life in purity and in the service of Hashem be on a higher level than someone who began to follow Hashem and His mitzvos much later in life? The *baal teshuvah* seemingly has much lost time to compensate for, many years during which the *tzaddik* was doing mitzvos and he was not. Why is the *baal teshuvah* on a higher *madreigah*?

The *Chida*[23] explains that one who has performed mitzvos his entire life certainly can reach lofty levels. But he has never had the opportunity to convert his *aveiros* into mitzvos. By performing *teshuvah mei'ahavah*, the *baal teshuvah*, whose catalogue of sin may have contained the most severe of *aveiros*, now undergoes a transformation whereby all his sins become *zechusim*. A *tzaddik* can perform only the 248 positive commandments in the Torah. A *baal teshuvah*, on the other hand, who may have violated numerous *aveiros*, including those for which he is liable to *misah* and *kareis*, has among his *zechusim* these severe *aveiros* that have been transformed into mitzvos — something the *tzaddik gamur* certainly does not have.

Premium Teshuvah: Ani L'Dodi

The *Chida*[24] teaches that this helps us understand why the *remez* for Chodesh Elul, the month dedicated to teshuvah, is *Ani L'Dodi V'Dodi Li*. Shlomo HaMelech is bringing to our attention that when we engage in the process of teshuvah, we should not settle for average, mediocre, pedestrian teshuvah. What we seek is "premium teshuvah" — the teshuvah of *L'Dodi* — the teshuvah of love! *Teshuvah mei'ahavah* is the goal; therefore, in this context Hashem is referred by us as our Beloved. We strive to perform the kind of teshuvah that does not merely allow us to evade punishment, but the type of teshuvah that transforms our sins into *zechusim*. This *remez* encourages us to pursue the type of teshuvah that will leave us on a higher level than when we started, with many more merits than before.

This is why the first *parashah* we read in Elul contains the all-important phrase בָּנִים אַתֶּם לַה׳ אֱלֹקֵיכֶם. This is the entire basis for the concept of teshuvah, which can only be effective because we are the beloved children of Hashem.

⚲ Zechusim Acquired With Teshuvah Are Uniquely Perfect Mitzvos

The Dubno Maggid[25] relates the following parable:

A couple were engaged to be married. The *chassan* came from a simple family that did not have much by way of material possessions. The *kallah's* family, who resided in another city, was very affluent. When the parents met to plan the wedding, the bride's father told the parents of the groom that it would be his pleasure to cover the entire cost of the wedding. He understood that the *chassan's* family could not afford it, and he offered to pay for the entire evening. The only thing he asked was that the *chassan's* father purchase a suit for his son to wear to the wedding. With difficulty, the father scraped together enough money to purchase an inexpensive suit that the groom then wore as he traveled to the wedding. On the way, he tripped and fell, ripping the suit in several places. He arrived at his bride's home the day before the wedding in a torn and muddied suit that clearly was not appropriate garb in which to be married. His father-in-law took one look at the suit and whisked the *chassan* off to his tailor to purchase a custom-made suit of the finest fabric. The *kallah's* father tells his son-in-law, "Now that I am the one buying you a suit, I am not going to buy you the type of suit you would buy for yourself. I am going to buy you the kind of suit that I would wear: the best fabric, beautifully tailored, and a perfect fit."

The Dubno Maggid explains: Even the mitzvos performed

by a *tzaddik* likely have imperfections. Mitzvos are inevitably impacted by human limitation. Perhaps he did not have complete *kavannah* while performing the mitzvos, or they may have been tainted by a small measure of ulterior motive. Perhaps his mitzvah lacked the appropriate *zerizus*, *simchah*, or *yiras Shamayim*. Although he has many *zechusim*, they are not perfect; they are limited by human shortcomings. A *baal teshuvah*, on the other hand, has the advantage that Hashem transforms his *aveiros* into mitzvos. And into what type of mitzvos does Hashem transform these *aveiros*? They are the very best possible mitzvos, performed the way He would like each and every mitzvah to be done. Thus, the newly generated mitzvos of the *baal teshuvah* are perfect and beautiful, without any deficiencies. His mitzvos are generated by Hashem, and they are therefore the essence of perfection. Hashem says, "Now that I am giving you the mitzvah, I am not going to give you the type of mitzvah you might do yourself. I am going to give you the kind of mitzvah that I would want: performed perfectly with all the right *kavannos*."

This, says the Dubno Maggid, is why *b'makom shebaalei teshuvah omdim, ein tzaddikim gemurim yecholim la'amod*. A *tzaddik* has plenty of mitzvos and *zechusim*, but they are all mortal mitzvos performed on a human level. But when the *baal teshuvah* does *teshuvah mei'ahavah*, he acquires mitzvos of a much loftier, Divine nature.

❧ How Does One Reach the Level of Teshuvah M'ahavah?

Ahavas Hashem is a very high *madreigah*, and the *Chovos HaLevavos* discusses it as the final *madreigah* and the ultimate achievement of the *oveid Hashem*. Nevertheless, the basic feeling of *ahavas Hashem* is already inherent and programmed into the heart of the Jew; and we just have to work on tapping into it and bringing it to the forefront. The Ramchal[26] writes that our love for Hashem must be a love that is not dependent upon any external factor. We don't love Hashem because of the benefits that He gives us. It is not our money, success, or fame that is the basis for why we love Hashem. Our love toward Hashem is that of a child toward his father. A child has a natural love for his father, not only due to what his father does for him or buys for him. Human nature compels a child to love his parent. Similarly, our very nature as Jews causes this innate love toward the Ribbono shel Olam. This is expressed in *Parashas Haazinu*: הֲלוֹא הוּא אָבִיךָ קָּנֶךָ, *Is He [Hashem] not your Father, your Master?* (*Devarim* 32:6).

⌈ *How Can We Be Commanded to Love?*

Rav Akiva Eiger[27] presents a beautiful idea: Hashem commands us to love Him, but how can we be instructed to love someone or something? If one has a dislike for another person, for example, he cannot learn to love that person by merely being commanded to do so. So how can Hashem expect us to love Him simply because we are told we must? The answer is that there is a rule in relationships: כַּמַּיִם הַפָּנִים לַפָּנִים כֵּן לֵב הָאָדָם לָאָדָם , *As water reflects a face back to a face, so one's heart is reflected back to him by another* (*Mishlei* 27:19); i.e., if someone loves you, then you will love him back. Love is reciprocated. The *Shema* that we recite daily states, וְאָהַבְתָּ אֵת ה', *you shall love Hashem.*[28] However, immediately preceding the *Shema* is the phrase, הַבּוֹחֵר בְּעַמּוֹ יִשְׂרָאֵל בְּאַהֲבָה! Hashem has selected us with love! Once we recognize that Hashem loves us, then we can readily be instructed to love Hashem, since love is reciprocal.

⌈ *Ahavas Hashem: A Daily Fulfillment*

The Chofetz Chaim writes[29] that although *ahavas Hashem* is one of the few *mitzvos asei d'Oraisa* that we can perform daily, it is a mitzvah whose actual fulfillment is, for some reason, often neglected. Indeed, the Chofetz Chaim recommends that we should be careful not to eat in the morning until we are certain we have fulfilled this mitzvah. We should bear this thought in mind when we say the *pasuk V'ahavta es Hashem Elokecha*, as noted above, or at least contemplate our love for Hashem before leaving the shul in the morning to return home.

In *Sefer Ahavas Chessed*,[30] the Chofetz Chaim notes that *ahavas Hashem* is not a very lofty *madreigah*. He points out that there is a difference between *ahavah* and *deveikus*. The Torah tells us, וּבוֹ תִדְבָּק, *and to Him shall you cleave* (*Devarim* 10:20); *deveikus*, cleaving to Hashem, means that the feeling of *ahavah* is constantly in one's heart. It is always present. *Ahavas Hashem*, on the other hand, may be present only on occasion, when a person is motivated and stirred to love Hashem. The *madreigah* of *ahavas Hashem* is reached even if it is not on one's mind at all times.

Rav Avigdor Miller[31] would say that a person should not let a single day pass by without articulating, at least once, "I love You, Hashem." Although the Rambam describes *ahavas Hashem* as a very exalted *madreigah*, nevertheless, the Gra felt that *ahavas Hashem* can be taught even to young children. Perhaps the highest levels of *ahavas Hashem* can be achieved only by noteworthy *tzaddikim*, but there are more basic levels of *ahavas Hashem* that are within the reach of each and every one of us. Therefore, we can utilize even a basic level of *ahavas Hashem* as an impetus for *teshuvah mei'ahavah* that can then catapult us to garner *zechusim* that surpass the *zechusim* of *tzaddikim gemurim*.

◈ *Love for a Parent —*
and Thus for Hashem — Is Innate

My grandfather, Rav Mordechai Glatstein, *zol ehr gezunt zein*, was a Rav in Pittsburgh for many years. As Rav, he was often asked to officiate at the unveiling of a *matzeivah* for one of his congregants. On one particular occasion, he was not feeling well, and my father, Rav Yosef Glatstein, who was not a practicing rabbi but was familiar with the procedure, stepped in to officiate in his place. He received a phone call from a Western Pennsylvanian man who would drive up in his pickup truck to take him to the cemetery. When he arrived at my grandparents' house, my father met a gruff, six-foot-five man who was clearly rough around the edges. At the cemetery, as they walked to the grave, this man stopped to show my father the graves of numerous members of his family. They visited the graves of his aunt, uncle, sister, brother, and various other family members. Without emotion, he took my father around the cemetery, without sentiment, pointing to the different graves as one would point to a bottlecap collection. This emotionless tour continued even at the final resting places of his own son and daughter. Then they arrived at the graves of his parents, who had passed away about fifty years earlier. At this point, this giant of a man broke down, crying like a baby. For his father and mother, gone for over half a century, his tears flowed.

What is the strongest love in this world? The love for a spouse? The love for a child? One can make the case that it is the love for a parent, the very first love implanted in the human heart. The love for a child, in certain respects, may be more compelling. Nevertheless, this feeling only develops much later in life and in some ways is not as strong as the love one has for his parents. We are born with love for our parents. The *Mesillas Yesharim*[32] writes that the love we have for HaKadosh Baruch Hu, our Father, is an *ahavah tiviis,* a natural love. It is innate, and we must merely access it. And when we do, this will allow us to access a level of teshuvah that will transform our actions into the most magnificent *zechusim* and allow us to truly hope for a blessed and successful year and a *kesivah vachasimah tovah.*

ENDNOTES

17. מצוה שסד אות לה.
18. תפארת ישראל, תענית ד, ח.
19. ראש השנה דף טז, א-ב.
20. רש"י שם.
21. חידושי רבי עקיבא איגר, הובא בחוט המשולש דף קעח-קעט.
22. ברכות כו, ב.
23. ספר פני דוד, פרשת שופטים דף קסו.
24. חומת אנך, שיר השירים ו, כו.
25. המגיד מדובנא, הובא באוצרות התורה אלול-ראש השנה-יוה"כ דף של.
26. מסילת ישרים פרק יט, בבאור חלקי החסידות.
27. דרושי וחידושי רבי עקיבא איגר דף קסז.
28. דברים ו, ה.
29. ספר שמירת הלשון, חתימת הספר פרק ב.
30. פתיחה לאהבת חסד, בהג"ה.
31. אור עולם חלק א' דף ב-ג.
32. מסילת ישרים, שם.

1. מגילה לא, ב.
2. ספר שני לוחות הברית (של"ה), פרשת דברים, תורה אור אות יד.
3. משנה ברורה סימן תקפא ס"ק א.
4. פנינים משלחן הגר"א, פרשת ראה דף טו-טז.
5. האזינו (ה) [ד].
6. מלבים יונה ג, ד.
7. בית אלקים, שער התשובה פרק יד.
8. בני יששכר, מאמרי חדש סיון מאמר ב אות ה.
9. קידושין לב, ב.
10. אהבת דוד, דרוש ד לשבת שובה דף לד; ספר אורות ימי הרחמים דף קנ.
11. יומא פו:
12. אוצרות התורה, אלול-ראש השנה-יוה"כ דף קעג.
13. יומא פו, א.
14. יומא פה, א.
15. מדבר קדמות, מערכת ת אות יח.
16. דרשות חתם סופר, חלק א דף יט.

The Journey of Teshuvah — One Small Step

∽ *The Challenge of Teshuvah*

The *Aseres Yemei Teshuvah* offer us the opportunity of a life-time. Rav Yonason Eibeshutz teaches[1] that through the seven days between Rosh Hashanah and Yom Kippur, one can repair all of one's sins committed on all the corresponding days of the week of the prior year. For instance, if one does teshuvah and performs *maasim tovim* on the Sunday of the *Aseres Yemei Teshuvah*, he can rectify the sins he did on all of the Sundays of the previous year. The same applies to each of these seven days.

While, on the one hand, this is a unique opportunity, on the other hand, the teshuvah process can appear to be a very daunt-ing task because it is very difficult for a person to truly change his ways. Although it is a real challenge to improve and to change our habitual behavior, studying the following concepts can be a great source of encouragement.

∽ *The Mikveh Analogy*

The days of teshuvah are analogous to a *mikveh*. Rabbi Akiva declares at the end of *Meseches Yoma*,[2] מַה מִקְוֶה מְטַהֵר אֶת הַטְּמֵאִים,

אַף הַקָּדוֹשׁ בָּרוּךְ הוּא מְטַהֵר אֶת יִשְׂרָאֵל, *Just as a mikveh purifies the impure, so too will Hashem purify the Bnei Yisrael.* When one immerses in a *mikveh*, whether he is spiritually ready or not, he becomes *tahor*, pure. The same is true for the Yamim Noraim. Even if a person puts in minimal effort and is not truly prepared to make a drastic change in his conduct, he still emerges a different person.

The *Bnei Yisasschar* extends this analogy.[3] Just as a *mikveh* contains forty se'ah of water, there are forty days during which to do teshuvah from Rosh Chodesh Elul through Yom Kippur. Calculating further, we can compute forty se'ah equal 960 *lugin.**** Thus, there are 960 *lugin* in a *mikveh*. Correspondingly, the forty days between Rosh Chodesh Elul through Yom Kippur contain a total of 960 hours during which we can do teshuvah (24 hours x 40 days = 960 hours).

These analogies between *mikveh* and the *Yemei Teshuvah* teach us that just as someone who immerses in a *mikveh* emerges purified, as a new person, regardless of his preparation and readiness, so, too, does one emerge from the *Yamim Noraim* purified, as a new person.

The *Bnei Yissaschar* adds an interesting detail. He calculates the numerical value of the word תִּשְׁרֵי with its *nekudos*. Tishrei itself has a *gematria* of 910: 10 = י, 200= ר, 300 = שׁ, 400 = ת. *Al pi kabbalah*, the *nekudos* also have *gematria***: The *chirik*, which is formed by one dot, has the numerical value of 10. The *shva* and the *tzeirei* each have two dots, and thus each has the numerical value of 20, for a total of 50.*** Thus, Tishrei with its *nekudos* has the *gematria* of 960: the same value as the *lugin* in a *mikveh* and as the hours in the *Yemei Teshuvah*. This is an additional *remez*

---

* The halachic measurements of liquid are: 6 eggs = 1 log; 4 log = 1 kav; 6 *kav* = 1 se'ah; 3 se'ah = 1 *eifah*.

** For example, see של״ה הקדוש cited by באר היטב או״ח סימן קפז ס״ק א.

*** The *gematria* of the remaining *nekudos* is as follows: A *cholam*, which is formed by one dot, has the numerical value of 10. A *segol*, with three dots, is valued at 30. A *patach*, which is a horizontal *vav*, has the *gematria* of 6. A *kamatz* is made up of a horizontal *vav* and a *yud*, rendering 16.

hinting that the month of Tishrei functions as does a *mikveh*. Even if insufficient teshuvah is done, Tishrei can purify a person to some extent; it will elevate us spiritually.

∾ *Bitul of a Beriyah: 1/960*

If a very small amount of *tereifah* falls into kosher soup, the soup remains kosher; utilizing the principle of *batel b'shishim*, the *tereifah* element is nullified in content that is sixty times larger in volume. However, if a single ant falls into a huge vat of kosher food, the food becomes prohibited. This is because the rule of *batel b'shishim* does not apply to a complete *beriyah*, a complete creature. The Talmud Bavli rules that it is not *batel* even in a ratio of 1:1000. However, the Talmud Yerushalmi[4] disagrees, stating that an entire *beriyah* is *batel* in a ratio of 1:960.

Although we, too, are complete *beriyos*, we still have the opportunity to be *mevatel* our spiritual impurities through the mechanism of immersion into the 960 *lugin* of a *mikveh*. Likewise, the *Bnei Yisasschar* teaches us that we can be *mevatel* our sins and purify ourselves through experiencing the 960 hours of the 40 days of teshuvah.

∾ *Sprinkle or Immerse*

The Mishnah at the end of *Yoma* cited above states: אָמַר רַבִּי עֲקִיבָא, אַשְׁרֵיכֶם יִשְׂרָאֵל, לִפְנֵי מִי אַתֶּם מְטַהֲרִין, וּמִי מְטַהֵר אֶתְכֶם, אֲבִיכֶם שֶׁבַּשָּׁמַיִם, שֶׁנֶּאֱמַר, (יחזקאל לו:כה) וְזָרַקְתִּי עֲלֵיכֶם מַיִם טְהוֹרִים וּטְהַרְתֶּם. וְאוֹמֵר (ירמיה יז:יג) מִקְוֵה יִשְׂרָאֵל ה', מַה מִּקְוֶה מְטַהֵר אֶת הַטְּמֵאִים, אַף הַקָּדוֹשׁ בָּרוּךְ הוּא מְטַהֵר אֶת יִשְׂרָאֵל. Rabbi Akiva declares that Klal Yisrael is fortunate, for it is Hashem, our Father in heaven, Who purifies us. As the verses state: *Then I will sprinkle pure water upon you, that you may become cleansed* (Yechezkel 36:25) and *Hashem [is] our Mikveh*" (Yirmiyah 17:13). Just as a *mikveh* purifies the impure, so too will Hashem purify the Bnei Yisrael.

Rav Avraham Pam[5] was fond of quoting the son of Rav Yitzchak Elchanan Spector, who asks why Rabbi Akiva quoted the two aforementioned *pesukim* when it seems that one would have sufficed. He explains that these two *pesukim* are cited because there are two types of *taharah* and thus two corresponding types of teshuvah.

We are most familiar with the purification of the *mikveh*, in which complete immersion renders a person or object pure. There can be no *chatzitzah*, interposition, between the object or person being purified and the waters of the *mikveh*, and the immersion must be total. If even one tiny part, one hair, is not immersed, the purification is not effected. Although 99 percent of the object may have been immersed, the object or person is not 99 percent purified. Without complete and total immersion, purification in the *mikveh* is not effective at all.

The second type of purification is through the waters of purification that are sprinkled on the impure. If a *tamei* person is sprinkled with the water in which the ashes of the *parah adumah* are mixed, even if the water touches only a part of the body, even merely one hair, the person has achieved a significant level of purification.

✑ *Two Types of Teshuvah*

There are also two types of teshuvah that directly parallel these two methods of purification. One type of teshuvah occurs when a person says that he regrets all his *aveiros*, and avers that he is never going to repeat his mistakes. In this type of teshuvah, the penitent is transformed into an entirely new person. It is as if his entirety is immersed in the teshuvah process, and he emerges from this purification as a new being. This is the perfect teshuvah, which at times may seem very daunting to attempt.

The second type of teshuvah, however, is analogous to the water used to purify someone who is *tamei*. With this method, a person realistically knows he is not going to become a perfect *tzaddik* in the coming year. But he chooses one action, such as reciting one *berachah* in *Shemoneh Esrei* with *kavannah*. He knows he cannot commit himself to never speaking *lashon hara* again, but he can at least ensure that his Shabbos table is free from *lashon hara*. A commitment to one small thing — something that is truly a change for the better — can also be considered teshuvah. While it is not complete teshuvah, it is meaningful teshuvah nonetheless.

The ultimate goal that we strive for is complete and total teshuvah — *teshuvah sheleimah*. But even if this seems to be beyond our reach, we can take heart knowing there is another valid option as to how to do teshuvah.

❧ *Teshuvah Is Great* — *It Reaches the* כסא הכבוד!

This approach to teshuvah is illustrated by introducing an expanded and novel system of *gematria*. *Parashas Ki Savo* states, וְכָתַבְתָּ עַל הָאֲבָנִים אֶת כָּל דִּבְרֵי הַתּוֹרָה הַזֹּאת בַּאֵר הֵיטֵב, *You shall inscribe on the stones all the words of this Torah, well clarified* (*Devarim* 27:8). On the words בַּאֵר הֵיטֵב, *well clarified*, Rashi comments that the Torah was to be written in all seventy languages. The Mizrachi explains the source for Rashi's comment. When the word הֵיטֵב is written out as follows: ה׳, ה״י, הי״ט, היט״ב, starting with the first letter alone and then adding each subsequent letter one at a time, the *gematria* is 70.

Rav Shamshon M'Ashtropoli[6] introduced a *chiddush* that he said was revealed to him from Heaven, which applies this expanded system of *gematria* to the words כִּסֵא הַכָּבוֹד: כ׳, כ״ס, כס״א, כס״א ה׳, כס״א ה״כ, כס״א הכ״ב, כס״א הכב״ו, כס״א הכבו״ד. Tallying the *gematria* of these letter combinations gives the same numeric value as the word תשובה: 713. This alludes to what we have been taught; i.e., teshuvah is great because it reaches to the *Kisei HaKavod* of the Ribbono shel Olam.

The Ladder of Teshuvah — One Rung at a Time

Sefer Mishnas Yosef writes[7] that this *chiddush* teaches us an incredible lesson in teshuvah. One does not reach the *Kisei HaKavod* in one leap. One cannot suddenly become a completely new person. Rather, one must climb the ladder of teshuvah one rung at a time — one letter at a time.

Sometimes, what it takes is changing one's ways in one small area every year. Eventually the sum of these small steps will add up to complete teshuvah. For example, as noted, one may want to work on his *davening* by adding one *berachah* every year that he *davens* with extra devotion. After nineteen years, he will have improved his entire *Shemoneh Esrei*! It is important for us to be *mekabel* upon ourselves one small thing that we know we can uphold throughout the year.

To perform the type of teshuvah that will reach the *Kisei HaKavod*, one must approach it one letter at a time. Hashem simplifies the teshuvah process for us, accepting even small steps and small changes from us, rather than demanding complete reform all at once.

The King Will Come to You

The *Pesikta Rabbasi*[8] teaches us a parable that illustrates this concept of teshuvah. A prince is very far from the palace where the king, his father, resides. He is at a distance of a hundred days' travel from the palace when he receives word that his father wants him to come home. The distance, however, seems too far for him to traverse, and he does not think he can make the long and arduous journey. The king sends word that if the prince starts heading out — if he takes even just a few steps in the right direction — then the king will travel the remaining miles to meet his son and bring him home. "You take a few steps, and I will travel the rest of the way to get you; I will take you the rest of the way."

This is what the *pasuk* means when it says, שׁוּבוּ אֵלַי וְאָשׁוּבָה אֲלֵיכֶם, *Return to Me and I will return to you!* (*Malachi* 3:7). We have to do the best we are capable of, and then Hashem will come to us — He is willing and ready to cover the vast majority of the distance that separates us from Him, so long as we make an honest effort. When we try to do teshuvah, Hashem will elevate us to levels we never thought we could achieve.

✍ *Taking the Elevator of Teshuvah*

The Chofetz Chaim was very interested when the invention of the elevator came to his attention, saying that it was the perfect metaphor for teshuvah. One simply presses the button to summon the elevator and enters the compartment; then the elevator carries him the rest of the way. So too, if one merely makes a meaningful effort to return to Him, Hashem will provide the *siyata d'Shmaya* to elevate him to even higher levels of teshuvah.

✍ *A Tiny Opening Is Enough*

Rav Meir Shapiro was invited to give a *derashah* in a city he was visiting. His *derashah* focused on the *pasuk* in *Parashas Balak*, said at the beginning of Shacharis, מַה טֹּבוּ אֹהָלֶיךָ יַעֲקֹב, *How goodly are your tents, O Yaakov* (*Bamidbar* 24:5). The simple *pshat*, as explained by Rashi,[9] is עַל שֶׁרָאָה פִּתְחֵיהֶם שֶׁאֵינָן מְכוּוָנִין זֶה מוּל זֶה, *he saw that the doors were not aligned*. Bilaam was very impressed by the modesty he noted in the arrangement of the tents of Bnei Yisrael, as the doorways of their tents were not situated opposite their neighbors', preventing them from seeing into one another's homes.

Rav Meir Shapiro[10] explained the verse homiletically. The Midrash[11] says that Hashem tells Bnei Yisrael, "You open a small opening [of teshuvah], as small as the point of a needle, and I will open for you an entrance to allow wagons to enter." Hashem is telling us that we must make one small improvement, and then He will take us the rest of the way. This is what pained Bilaam: He saw that the "doorways were not aligned"

— a Jew's "doorway" of teshuvah is required to be only a tiny opening and then Hashem will open a vast entrance for him. Bilaam was very jealous that even the smallest effort on our part is matched many times over by Hashem. Bilaam was commenting on what he felt was an expression of Hashem's unparalleled love for Klal Yisrael.

≈ The Shofar

Perhaps we can suggest that this concept is alluded to by the shape of the *shofar* that we sound on Rosh Hashanah, which has a very small opening on the bottom, while the top has a much wider opening. This indicates that even if we sincerely open our hearts only a small amount to do teshuvah, then Hashem will widen that small opening and elevate us.

Let us take advantage of this extraordinary opportunity of the *Aseres Yemei Teshuvah* and utilize this gift from Hashem by making even the smallest — albeit sincere — effort at coming back to Hashem with teshuvah. When we accept upon ourselves a modest attempt to improve, the Ribbono shel Olam will provide *siyata d'Shmaya* and enable us to return to Him completely, *b'teshuvah sheleimah*.

ENDNOTES

1. יערות דבש דרוש א, הובא במשנה ברורה סימן תרב ס"ק ב.

2. יומא פה, ב.

3. בני יששכר, תשרי מאמר א אות ג.

4. תרומות י, ה.

5. עטרה למלך עמוד קעג.

6. ניצוצי שמשון, פרשת נצבים.

7. הובא בספר אוצרות התורה, ימים נוראים עמוד שער-שעה.

8. פסיקתא רבתי פרק מד.

9. רש"י במדבר כד, ה.

10. אמרי דעת, פרשת בלק עמוד רצב-רצג.

11. מדרש שיר השירים ה, ב.

ROSh hashanah

Praying for the Shechinah — the Greatest Source of Berachah on the Yom HaDin

◆ Are We Ignoring Our Own Needs on Rosh Hashanah?

Rav Yitzchak Meltzen, in his *Siddur HaGra*,[1] poses a question that is extremely fundamental to understanding the objective of our *tefillos* on Rosh Hashanah. Why did our early authorities arrange the *Shemoneh Esrei* of Rosh Hashanah in the form that we use today? On the Day of Judgment, why is our entire *tefillah* focused only on being *mispallel* for the *Kavod HaShechinah*? Shouldn't we be imploring Hashem for *banei, chayei, u'mezonei,* children, life, and sustenance? Shouldn't we be begging for *selichah* and *mechilah*? Furthermore, asks Rav Meltzen, shouldn't we specifically mention our sins instead of ignoring them; as we know, *modah b'knas patur,* one who admits to guilt warrants exemption. Would it not improve the Heavenly judgment if we confessed, admitted our sins, and asked for forgiveness? When our lives and our entire future hang in the balance, shouldn't we be begging for what is certainly foremost in our minds? Why do we seem to be ignoring our own needs on the *Yom HaDin*?

❧ *Pray for Hashem … and He Will Provide*

Rav Meltzen answers that on Rosh Hashanah we definitely would want to *daven* for our needs, for our *parnassah*, and for our children. However, there is something that transcends our own personal needs: the *Shechinah*. The *Shechinah* is in pain. The *Shechinah* is in exile. Hashem is, so to speak, without a home, disrespected and disgraced throughout the world. How can we bring ourselves to ask for our physical and worldly needs when Hashem Himself is not afforded the proper *kavod* and *yirah* to which He is entitled!? Therefore, *Chazal* instructed us to focus first and foremost on restoring *Kavod Shamayim*, making sure that Hashem's needs, so to speak, are addressed. We ask for only the bare minimum of our own needs on Rosh Hashanah; we ask only for life — *Zachreinu L'Chaim* — and even then, our *tefillah* is framed by our intention to bring more *kavod* to Hashem with the life He would grant us. We say, *"L'maancha Elokim chaim"*; we ask for life only so that we can serve You better.

We focus our *tefillos* on Rosh Hashanah on asking Hashem to make His Name and honor revealed and manifest throughout the entire world. When we put our own needs on the back burner, and focus on asking for the *kavod Shamayim* to be magnified, the prosecuting angels are silenced, since they see that our concerns are first and foremost those of the Ribbono shel Olam. And then, the *pasuk* "אֲנִי לְדוֹדִי וְדוֹדִי לִי" is applicable in its truest sense: We are for our Beloved: We are using our *tefillos* and requests on the *Yom HaDin* for the sake of the honor of our Beloved — and then our Beloved will be for us and will provide for our needs.

Furthermore, says Rav Meltzen, we can apply *Chazal's* principle that *"kol hamispallel b'ad chaveiro v'hu tzoreich l'oso davar, hu yaaneh techilah*, one who *davens* for a friend, while simultaneously having similar unmet needs of his own, will be answered first." By *davening* for the "needs" of Hashem, while we ourselves have significant needs, we ensure that our needs will be answered first.

❧ All Blessing and Goodness Result From the Manifestation of God's Malchus

Perhaps we can answer this all-important question raised in the *Siddur HaGra* in a different vein, based on a principle set forth in the *Derech Hashem*.[2]

Rav Moshe Chaim Luzzatto writes that the mechanism and the dynamic of how Creation is set up are such that when Hashem's Authority is known and recognized by mankind, all good and prosperity exists in the world. Blessing is increased, and the world abides in peace. When Hashem's subjects, however, do not subjugate themselves to Hashem and recognize His sovereignty, then goodness is lacking, darkness prevails, and evil dominates. Whenever any reason exists for the Creator to manifest Himself in His Kingdom and demonstrate His rulership over His world, it results in great blessing and prosperity among mankind. There is an increase in the holy illumination of Hashem's beneficence while the forces of evil are humbled and subjugated, so that they are not able to undermine the good of the world.

Based on this principle of the Ramchal, we can understand the focus of our *tefillos* on the *Yom HaDin*, as we ask Hashem:

וּבְכֵן תֵּן פַּחְדְּךָ ה׳ אֱלֹקֵינוּ עַל כָּל מַעֲשֶׂיךָ וְאֵימָתְךָ עַל כָּל מַה שֶּׁבָּרֵאתָ וְיִירָאוּךָ כָּל הַמַּעֲשִׂים וְיִשְׁתַּחֲווּ לְפָנֶיךָ כָּל הַבְּרוּאִים. *And so, grant that Your awe, Hashem, our God, be upon all Your works, and Your dread upon all You have created; and then all Your works will fear You and prostrate before You.*

וְתִמְלוֹךְ אַתָּה ה׳ לְבַדֶּךָ עַל כָּל מַעֲשֶׂיךָ, *And You, Hashem, will reign Alone over all Your works.*

מְלוֹךְ עַל כָּל הָעוֹלָם כֻּלּוֹ בִּכְבוֹדֶךָ וְהִנָּשֵׂא עַל כָּל הָאָרֶץ בִּיקָרֶךָ וְהוֹפַע בַּהֲדַר גְּאוֹן עֻזֶּךָ עַל כָּל יוֹשְׁבֵי תֵבֵל אַרְצֶךָ וְיֵדַע כָּל פָּעוּל כִּי אַתָּה פְעַלְתּוֹ וְיָבִין כָּל יְצוּר כִּי אַתָּה יְצַרְתּוֹ וְיֹאמַר כֹּל אֲשֶׁר נְשָׁמָה בְאַפּוֹ ה׳ אֱלֹקֵי יִשְׂרָאֵל מֶלֶךְ וּמַלְכוּתוֹ בַּכֹּל מָשָׁלָה. *Reign over the entire world with Your glory, and be uplifted over all the earth with Your honor, and appear in the splendor of Your majestic might over all who dwell in the inhabited world of Your earth; so everything that has been made will know that You have made it, and it will be understood by everything that was formed that You formed it. And they will say, everyone who has breath in his nostrils, "Hashem, God of Israel, is King, and His Kingship rules over all."*

When Hashem's *Malchus* is recognized and His Glory is revealed, what will naturally follow for all are goodness, peace, blessing, tranquility, light, and holiness. Everything we need, everything that we would want to ask for on the *Yom HaDin*, will naturally flow forth if only Hashem's *Malchus* were to be recognized and accepted throughout the world. By asking for the world to recognize and honor Hashem in the proper fashion, we are, in essence, asking that we receive all the *berachos* we want, since that is the natural outcome of Hashem's *Malchus* being recognized properly throughout the world.

ENDNOTES

1. סידור הגר״א, פתיחה לתפילת ראש   2. חלק ד פרק רביעי אות ג.
השנה בד״ה והביטה,עמוד 396.

CRosh CHashanah:
CThe CTime CIs CNow

❧ וְעַתָּה, *and Now*

At the depiction of the sin of the *Eitz Hadaas*, the Torah tells us, וַיֹּאמֶר ה' אֱלֹקִים הֵן הָאָדָם הָיָה כְּאַחַד מִמֶּנּוּ לָדַעַת טוֹב וָרָע וְעַתָּה פֶּן יִשְׁלַח יָדוֹ וְלָקַח גַּם מֵעֵץ הַחַיִּים וְאָכַל וָחַי לְעֹלָם, *And Hashem God said, "Behold, Man has become like the Unique One among us, knowing good and bad; and now, lest he put forth his hand and take also of the Tree of Life, and eat and live forever!"* (Bereishis 3:22). The *Midrash*[1] comments that this *pasuk* indicates that Hashem gave Adam HaRishon the opportunity to do teshuvah. The word וְעַתָּה, *and now*, is the source for this explication, since we find that the word וְעַתָּה is used in reference to teshuvah in the *pasuk,* וְעַתָּה יִשְׂרָאֵל מָה ה' אֱלֹקֶיךָ שֹׁאֵל מֵעִמָּךְ כִּי אִם לְיִרְאָה אֶת ה' אֱלֹקֶיךָ, לָלֶכֶת בְּכָל דְּרָכָיו וּלְאַהֲבָה אֹתוֹ וְלַעֲבֹד אֶת ה' אֱלֹקֶיךָ בְּכָל לְבָבְךָ וּבְכָל נַפְשֶׁךָ, *Now, O Israel, what does Hashem, your God, ask of you? Only to fear Hashem, your God, to go in all His ways and to love Him, and to serve Hashem, your God, with all your heart and with all your soul* (Devarim 10:12). However, since this *pasuk* seems to have nothing to do with teshuvah, this explanation is difficult to understand. In fact, in the *sefer Ahavas Chessed*,[2] the Chofetz Chaim pointedly asks how teshuvah is hinted at in the word

וְעַתָּה. He states that although the subsequent words of the *pasuk* — כִּי אִם לְיִרְאָה, *only to fear [Hashem]* —may hint at the concept of teshuvah, that does not answer how the word "וְעַתָּה, *and now*" specifically refers to repentance.

❧ *HaYom, Today*

The *pasuk* in *Parashas Netzavim* states, אַתֶּם נִצָּבִים הַיּוֹם כֻּלְּכֶם לִפְנֵי ה' אֱלֹקֵיכֶם רָאשֵׁיכֶם שִׁבְטֵיכֶם זִקְנֵיכֶם וְשֹׁטְרֵיכֶם כֹּל אִישׁ יִשְׂרָאֵל, *You are standing today, all of you, before Hashem, your God: the heads of your tribes, your elders, and your officers — all the men of Israel* (*Devarim* 29:9). The Yom Tov of Rosh Hashanah is known by several different names in the Torah, including *Yom Teruah* and *Yom HaZikaron*, and we call it Rosh Hashanah. Yet, as we will soon see, throughout Tanach, rather than these appellations, the term *HaYom*, today, is often used to refer to Rosh Hashanah. This would provide us with a powerful and compelling reason why *Parashas Netzavim* is consistently read on the Shabbos before Rosh Hashanah as it portrays dramatically the *Yom HaDin* that we are about to face: אַתֶּם נִצָּבִים הַיּוֹם כֻּלְּכֶם לִפְנֵי ה' אֱלֹקֵיכֶם, that very soon, we will all be standing before Hashem הַיּוֹם, on the fateful day of Rosh Hashanah. There are numerous *pesukim* in Tanach where הַיּוֹם is employed to describe the day of Rosh Hashanah.

❧ *Examples in Tanach Where* הַיּוֹם *Refers to Rosh Hashanah:*

1) In *Iyov* 1:6 we read, וַיְהִי הַיּוֹם וַיָּבֹאוּ בְּנֵי הָאֱלֹקִים לְהִתְיַצֵּב עַל ה' וַיָּבוֹא גַם הַשָּׂטָן בְּתוֹכָם, *And it happened on the day: The angels came to stand before Hashem, and the Satan, too, came among them.* Rashi[3] says that this הַיּוֹם, *the day*, was Rosh Hashanah, the *Yom Teruah*, the day of the shofar-blowing, when Hashem commands the *Satan* to bring the merits and demerits of the Bnei Yisrael before Him.

2) In *II Malachim* 4:8, the *pasuk* reads, וַיְהִי הַיּוֹם וַיַּעֲבֹר אֱלִישָׁע אֶל שׁוּנֵם וְשָׁם אִשָּׁה גְדוֹלָה וַתַּחֲזֶק בּוֹ לֶאֱכָל לָחֶם. *And it happened on*

the day that Elisha traveled to Shunem. There was a prominent woman and she importuned him to eat a meal. The *Zohar HaKadosh* writes[4] that "the day" Elisha went to the *Ishah HaShunamis* was Rosh Hashanah.

3) At *Akeidas Yitzchak*, the Torah states, וַיִּקְרָא אַבְרָהָם שֵׁם הַמָּקוֹם הַהוּא ה' יִרְאֶה אֲשֶׁר יֵאָמֵר **הַיּוֹם** בְּהַר ה' יֵרָאֶה, *And Avraham called the name of that place Hashem Yireh, as it is said, This day, on the mountain Hashem will be seen* (*Bereishis* 22:14). What does Avraham mean by saying, "As it is said, *this day*"? On that day, no one knew about the *Akeidah* so no one was able to talk about it. The *sefer Meor V'Shemesh*[5] explains as follows: Avraham's statement that "as it is said this day" is a *remez* that through the *Akeidah* that took place there, Hashem decreed that the strict judgment of Rosh Hashanah would be sweetened: אֲשֶׁר יֵאָמֵר הַיּוֹם, as it [will be] said on this day of Rosh Hashanah, בְּהַר ה' יֵרָאֶה. The word הַר forms the *roshei teivos*, initial letters, of Rosh Hashanah. Avraham is stating that הַיּוֹם, on *this day* of the *Akeidah*, בְּהַ"ר, on Rosh Hashanah, Hashem appeared on the mountain in order to have *rachmanus* on Klal Yisrael during the days of judgment.

4) *Tehillim* 119:91 states: לְמִשְׁפָּטֶיךָ עָמְדוּ **הַיּוֹם** כִּי הַכֹּל עֲבָדֶיךָ, *For Your judgment they stand today, because all are Your servants.* Rav Yosef Chaim Sonnenfeld[6] points out that, remarkably, the *gematria* of this entire *pasuk* is the numerical equivalent to that of the words רֹאשׁ הַשָּׁנָה. Once again, הַיּוֹם is used in reference to Rosh Hashanah.

5) In Mussaf of Rosh Hashanah we say, **הַיּוֹם** הֲרַת עוֹלָם **הַיּוֹם** יַעֲמִיד בַּמִּשְׁפָּט כָּל יְצוּרֵי עוֹלָמִים, *Today is the birthday of the world; today they will stand in judgment, all of creation.* Again, clearly the redactors of this *tefillah* are referring to Rosh Hashanah with the word הַיּוֹם.

∾ *Why "HaYom"?*

Of all the potential terms that could be used to refer to Rosh Hashanah, why is the word *HaYom* chosen? The word *HaYom* means *today*. Why would we call Rosh Hashanah "today"? "Today" can be used to refer to any day of the year. Would it not be more logical to refer to Rosh Hashanah as *"that* day"?

✆ *Procrastination*

The *Mesillas Yesharim*[7] writes that there are many people in this world who are delinquent and ineffective in fulfilling their obligation to observe Torah and mitzvos. It is not out of a lack of a clear understanding about man's mission in life. They are fully aware that Hashem created Man to serve Him, to learn Torah, and to do mitzvos for the purpose of meriting *Olam Haba*. When pressed to explain why his daily activities and practices apparently contradict this stated objective, his response is that while he recognizes the critical necessity to do mitzvos, he merely has not yet started on his quest to fulfill them. He consistently plans to begin to perform mitzvos tomorrow. Thus, the *Mesillas Yesharim* continues, people do genuinely recognize the obligation they have to serve Hashem and to make this the primary objective of their lives, but often they are overcome by laziness and they perpetually postpone initiating their life of service to Hashem.

In *Ahavas Chessed*,[8] the Chofetz Chaim says similarly: Some people are not involved in the performance of mitzvos or *chessed*, not because they are stingy, but rather as a result of laziness. Laziness is the reason that people do not perform the mitzvos or *chessed* they should. A person's nature is to continually procrastinate, postponing performing the mitzvos until another day, meanwhile remaining deficient in Torah and *maasim tovim*.

✆ *Understanding Why V'atah Refers to Teshuvah*

The Chofetz Chaim[9] offers a piercing explanation for why *v'atah* is the word that refers to teshuvah. Doing teshuvah is not a matter of learning *what* to do — we know what to do. Teshuvah is about *when* to do it—we must do it *now!* Capitalize on the moment *now*; there is no time like the present. The main technique of the *yetzer hara* is to trick a person into believing that he has no time today to learn Torah or do mitzvos. The *yetzer hara* knows that he cannot convince a Jew that learning Torah, giving *tzedakah*, and doing *chessed* are all unimportant. Rather, he takes a different approach: He agrees that these are critical elements in our lives. But the *yetzer hara* convinces a person that *today* he has too many pressing matters that need his attention, and therefore the mitzvos must wait until another day. This recurs daily, with the *yetzer hara* continually coaching a person that the opportunity to do mitzvos will always be better *tomorrow*, as on every *today* there is simply too much to do.

This is the catchphrase of the *yetzer hara*: Tomorrow, tomorrow, tomorrow.

When the *pasuk* states, אַל תֹּאמַר לְרֵעֲךָ לֵךְ וָשׁוּב וּמָחָר אֶתֵּן וְיֵשׁ אִתָּךְ, *Do not tell your neighbor, "Leave and come back; tomorrow I will give it," when it is [already] by you (Mishlei 3:28)*, the word רֵעֲךָ, *friend*, alludes to the *yetzer tov*, who is a person's true friend. We are being taught not to tell our true friend to wait until tomorrow.

The Torah tells us, הַיּוֹם הַזֶּה ה' אֱלֹקֶיךָ מְצַוְּךָ לַעֲשׂוֹת אֶת הַחֻקִּים הָאֵלֶּה וְאֶת הַמִּשְׁפָּטִים וְשָׁמַרְתָּ וְעָשִׂיתָ אוֹתָם בְּכָל לְבָבְךָ וּבְכָל נַפְשֶׁךָ, *This day, Hashem, your God, commands you to perform these decrees and the statutes, and you shall observe them and perform them with all your heart and with all your soul (Devarim 26:16)*. This *pasuk* teaches us that we need to perform the mitzvos הַיּוֹם, today. Additionally, *Chazal*[10] teach us, Repent הַיּוֹם, *this day*, for tomorrow one may pass away.

Chazal are consistently coming to teach us that we should not allow ourselves to fall victim to the blandishments of the *yetzer hara*, who is constantly trying to convince us to procrastinate. Instead, we should be regularly asking ourselves, "What does Hashem want me to do with my time הַיּוֹם, today —i.e., *now*?"

Thus, whenever one is faced with a choice and must decide what activity to perform next, he should ask himself, "What does Hashem want me to do *now*?" When you wake up, when you finish *davening* Shacharis, when you finish work, etc., always ask yourself, "What would Hashem want me to do at this moment?"

✑ If Boaz Had Procrastinated … The Eternal Ramification of Delaying a Mitzvah

In *Megillas Rus*, we learn that Rus is concerned, wondering whether her *yavam*, Boaz, will take her as his wife. Naomi tells her, שְׁבִי בִתִּי עַד אֲשֶׁר תֵּדְעִין אֵיךְ יִפֹּל דָּבָר כִּי לֹא יִשְׁקֹט הָאִישׁ כִּי אִם כִּלָּה הַדָּבָר הַיּוֹם, *Sit [patiently], my daughter, until you know how the matter will turn out, for the man will not rest unless he settles the matter today* (*Rus* 3:18). The Chofetz Chaim[11] vividly portrays what would have happened had Boaz equivocated about whether he should marry Rus or if he had delayed even a single day: The opportunity would have been lost forever — for Boaz passed away that very night. We are taught that the very night Boaz married Rus, Oved was conceived; he, in turn, fathered Yishai, who fathered David HaMelech. Had Boaz waited, the possibility of Mashiach would have been lost forever. What enabled Boaz to capitalize on this opportunity and become the progenitor of Mashiach was his *middah* of *Now*. *Malchus Beis David* came about because of Boaz's *zerizus*. Naomi knew that Rus could rely on this *middah* of Boaz when she told Rus not to be concerned, because she knew that Boaz was a *zariz*. One should never postpone an opportunity for a mitzvah, since he can never know if he will be here tomorrow to complete the task.

✑ Amalek Is Always Machar, Tomorrow

The antithesis of this *middah* of *zerizus* exemplified by Boaz is embodied by Amalek. When Amalek is mentioned in the Tanach, his name is juxtaposed to the word *machar*, tomorrow. We see this in numerous places:

1) וַיֹּאמֶר מֹשֶׁה אֶל יְהוֹשֻׁעַ בְּחַר לָנוּ אֲנָשִׁים וְצֵא הִלָּחֵם בַּעֲמָלֵק מָחָר אָנֹכִי נִצָּב עַל רֹאשׁ הַגִּבְעָה, *Moshe said to Yehoshua, "Choose people*

*for us and go do battle with Amalek; **tomorrow** I will stand on top of the hill …"* (Shemos 17:9).

2) וַיַּכֵּם דָּוִד מֵהַנֶּשֶׁף וְעַד הָעֶרֶב לְמָחֳרָתָם, *And David smote them [Amalek] from twilight until the evening of the **next day**…* (II Shmuel 30:17).

3) יָבוֹא הַמֶּלֶךְ וְהָמָן אֶל הַמִּשְׁתֶּה אֲשֶׁר אֶעֱשֶׂה לָהֶם **וּמָחָר** אֶעֱשֶׂה כִּדְבַר הַמֶּלֶךְ, *"…Let the king and Haman [Amalek] come to the banquet that I shall prepare for them, and **tomorrow** I shall fulfill the king's word"* (Esther 5:8)

4) וַתֹּאמֶר אֶסְתֵּר אִם עַל הַמֶּלֶךְ טוֹב יִנָּתֵן גַּם **מָחָר** לַיְּהוּדִים אֲשֶׁר בְּשׁוּשָׁן לַעֲשׂוֹת כְּדַת הַיּוֹם וְאֵת עֲשֶׂרֶת בְּנֵי הָמָן יִתְלוּ עַל הָעֵץ, *Esther replied, "If it pleases the king, let **tomorrow** also be given to the Jews who are in Shushan to act as they did today, and let Haman's ten sons [Amalek] be hanged on the gallows"* (ibid. 9:13).

When we deal with Amalek, it is always "tomorrow." Rav Yosef Chaim Sonnenfeld explains[12] that this is because the *middah* of Amalek is the *middah* of tomorrow. They are the embodiment of the *yetzer hara*, whose main tactic is to always postpone everything until tomorrow. This *middah* of Amalek, this trait of "tomorrow" must be completely uprooted from within us, because "tomorrow" is one of the chief methods utilized by the *yetzer hara* to encourage us to constantly come up short in fulfilling the *ratzon* of Hashem.

∾ *Bribe the Satan*

Interestingly, there are times that we can employ the concept of *tomorrow* against the *yetzer hara*. Just as the *yetzer hara* always tries to push us to postpone doing a mitzvah or *chessed* until tomorrow, so too can we convince him to push off the *aveirah* until "tomorrow." For example, if someone has an urge to view something inappropriate, the more he says he won't look, the more the *yetzer hara* will try to convince him to look. But by telling the *yetzer hara*, "Sure, it is great to look at; I will look at it first thing tomorrow," the *yetzer hara* will back off. This method can be used creatively in various circumstances to postpone and thwart the efforts of the *yetzer hara*. The *Michtav Me'Eliyahu*[13] refers to this as *shochad l'Satan*, bribing the *Satan*. If one seems to be giving in to the *Satan* on some small level, the *Satan* retreats, and then overcoming the *yetzer hara* becomes easier.

◎ Inspired? Change Today!

There are times when a person may be inspired by something that he learns from a *sefer* or by a *shmuess* he hears or by an experience in life. He tells himself that he is going to make changes in how he conducts himself. In comes the *yetzer hara* and implants a negative message in his mind: "Yes, this was a great *shmuess*; you should make these changes — just wait until tomorrow." But when the next day dawns, the inspiration has receded and the desire to change is no longer the same. This is one way the *Satan* stunts our spiritual growth.

Rav Gamliel Rabinovitch teaches[14] that in the *pasuk* אַתֶּם נִצָּבִים הַיּוֹם, quoted above, the word אַתֶּם is the *roshei teivos* for: אל תאמרו מחר, *Do not say tomorrow!* By not saying "tomorrow," — נִצָּבִים , *you will stand tall* and you will be successful— on הַיּוֹם — Rosh Hashanah.

A person who acquires this *middah* of אַתֶּם, of not pushing off mitzvos and opportunities until tomorrow, but who instead is in the habit of grabbing every moment and opportunity that he is presented with, and makes the most of them, will be in position to have a successful judgment on *Yom HaDin*.

◎ Why Rosh Hashanah Is Called HaYom and V'atah Refers to Teshuvah:

We now understand why Rosh Hashanah is given the appellation *HaYom* and why teshuvah is implied by the word "*v'atah*," now. In order to be *zocheh* to a positive *din* on Rosh Hashanah, we must master the *middah* of not postponing until tomorrow the mitzvos we can do today. Our attitude must be one of הַיּוֹם, *today*. *Zerizus*, seizing the moment, is the ultimate formula to receiving a good judgment. Furthermore, teshuvah requires that we acquire the *middah* of וְעַתָּה, meaning that we learn to discard the attitude of procrastination and make the changes we need to, in order to live our lives seeking to do Hashem's will *now*, in every moment. This is a seminal part of the teshuvah process. Living our lives in this manner, capitalizing immediately on every moment and on each opportunity, will ensure that we emerge from *Yom HaDin* with a *kesivah va'chasimah tovah*.

ENDNOTES

1. בראשית רבה פרשה כא, ו.
2. אהבת חסד חלק ב׳ פרק י״א בהג׳ה.
3. רש״י איוב א, ו.
4. הובא פרדס יוסף נצבים א־כז.
5. מאור ושמש רמזי ר״ה כב.
6. חכמת חיים עמוד רכה.
7. מסילת ישרים פרק ו ובביאור מידת הזריזות.
8. אהבת חסד שם.
9. אהבת חסד בהגה שם.
10. אבות דרבי נתן טו, ד.
11. חפץ חיים, הובא באוצרות התורה אלול־ראש השנה עמוד קב.
12. חכמת חיים, הובא באוצרות התורה דף קכא־קכב.
13. מכתב מאליהו: כרך א׳ עמוד רסב־סג, יום הכפורים ב.
14. טיב המועדים שם עמוד שסה.

The Shofar of Rosh Hashanah —
The Piercing Cry of the Neshamah

∾ Why Does Tefillah Set Klal Yisrael Apart?

In *Parashas Va'eschanan*, Moshe Rabbeinu declares the praise of Klal Yisrael. כִּי מִי גוֹי גָּדוֹל אֲשֶׁר לוֹ אֱלֹקִים קְרֹבִים אֵלָיו כַּה' אֱלֹקֵינוּ בְּכָל קָרְאֵנוּ אֵלָיו, *For which is a great nation that has a God Who is close to it, as is Hashem, our God, whenever we call out to Him?* (*Devarim* 4:7). Moshe Rabbeinu is saying that Klal Yisrael is a great nation because we have the gift of *tefillah* — the ability to call out to Hashem and know that He will answer us.

The Brisker Rav[1] wonders why this is considered a unique and special quality of the Bnei Yisrael, since even non-Jews can pray to Hashem. Moshe Rabbeinu mentions the special quality that is unique to the Bnei Yisrael: כִּי מִי גוֹי גָּדוֹל, *For which is a great nation.* Moshe Rabbeinu could have mentioned a mitzvah such as *tzitzis, tefillin, talmud Torah, mezuzah,* or Shabbos, which is truly unique to Klal Yisrael; the *umos haolam* don't have these. Why choose *tefillah,* which belongs not only to the Jewish people but also to the *umos haolam*? On the rare occasion in the Torah that Moshe Rabbeinu declares the uniqueness of Klal Yisrael, he chooses the one mitzvah that is applicable to non-Jews as well!

In *Selichos* we say, כִּי בֵיתִי בֵּית תְּפִלָּה יִקָּרֵא לְכָל הָעַמִּים, *For My House will be called a house of prayer for all the peoples* (*Yeshayah* 56:7). When Shlomo HaMelech inaugurated the first Beis HaMikdash, he asked Hashem to accept the prayers of non-Jews who would come there to pray. On Yom Kippur we read *Maftir Yonah*, and we learn that the people of Nineveh were *mispallel* to the Ribbono shel Olam and Hashem accepted their *tefillos*. Clearly, then, *tefillah* is not a feature unique to the Bnei Yisrael. Moshe Rabbeinu is discussing the distinctive quality of Klal Yisrael, and he picks one of the few mitzvos enjoyed by all mankind.

‿ *Hashem Is Our* תרועה

Let us endeavor to discover the meaning behind Moshe's praise of the Bnei Yisrael. One of the *pesukim* we recite in Mussaf on Rosh Hashanah, as part of *Shofaros*, is a verse in *Parashas Balak*. When Bilaam speaks about the admirable qualities of Klal Yisrael, he says: לֹא הִבִּיט אָוֶן בְּיַעֲקֹב וְלֹא רָאָה עָמָל בְּיִשְׂרָאֵל ה' אֱלֹקָיו עמּוֹ וּתְרוּעַת מֶלֶךְ בּוֹ, *He [Hashem] perceived no iniquity in Yaakov, and saw no perversity in Yisrael. Hashem, his God, is with him, and teruas melech bo — the friendship of the King is in him* (*Bamidbar* 23:21). Klal Yisrael's special status is that *teruas melech bo.*

What is meant by *teruas melech*? To which special trait in Klal Yisrael does this term refer? Rashi[2] explains the term to mean "*chibah* and *rei'us*, love and friendship." Bilaam was jealous of the fact that the Jewish people are blessed with the friendship of the Ribbono shel Olam. Hashem is the *Borei*, Creator, *Manhig*, Leader, and *Mefarneis*, Provider, for the *umos haolam* as well, but the concept that Hashem is תְּרוּעָה, a close and dear friend, is applicable only to the Bnei Yisrael. Bilaam is pointing out that this level of closeness, this endearing friendship exists solely between Hashem and Klal Yisrael.

The *Ibn Ezra*,[3] however, interprets this phrase differently, stating that Bilaam is highlighting something else entirely. He says that Bilaam is bothered by the fact that the Bnei Yisrael have the mitzvah of *tekias shofar*. That is what he envied: the mitzvah of shofar.

Of all the mitzvos of the Torah, of all the mitzvos that Klal Yisrael does that demonstrate the greatness of the Jewish people, why, asks the Brisker Rav,[4] is the one mitzvah Bilaam selects the mitzvah of shofar? Why is this the one mitzvah that Bilaam is jealous of? What is unique about the mitzvah of shofar that Bilaam singled it out as the catalyst for his ire? Let us try to uncover the inner dimension of the mitzvah of shofar.

∾ Choosing the Right Horn for the Best Defense

The Gemara[5] discusses the type of horn that can be used for the mitzvah of shofar on Rosh Hashanah.

When the Kohen Gadol enters the *Kodesh HaKodashim* on Yom Kippur he does not wear his *bigdei zahav*, golden vestments, to do the *avodah*. The reason for this is based on the principle of *ein kateigor naaseh saneigor*, the prosecutor cannot be the advocate. The gold vestments are a reminder of the sin of the *Eigel HaZahav*, the Golden Calf. Gold, which would serve as a prosecuting agent before Hashem and which would remind Hashem of the *Cheit HaEigel*, cannot now be employed by the defense. Wearing gold into the *Kodesh HaKodashim* on Yom Kippur would be a reminder of Klal Yisrael's *aveirah* and could sway the judgment of Yom Kippur against us. To forestall this possibility, the Kohen Gadol does not wear gold.

The Gemara then asks, why then does the Kohen Gadol wear the gold vestments on Yom Kippur when he is not in the *Kodesh HaKodashim*? Why does the Kohen Gadol wear the golden vestments when performing other parts of the avodah? Why present the opportunity to remind Hashem about the *Cheit HaEigel*? The Gemara answers that our only concern of *ein kateigor naaseh saneigor* is in the innermost Sanctum, the *Kodesh HaKodashim*, *lifnei v'lifnim*. Outside of the *Kodesh HaKodashim*, however, we are not concerned that the Kohen Gadol's defense will unintentionally serve to prosecute.

For this very reason, the horn of a cow or bull cannot be used on Rosh Hashanah to fulfill the mitzvah of shofar. Here too the Gemara employs the principle of *ein kateigor naaseh saneigor*. Using the *keren*, horn, of a cow would remind Hashem of the sin of the Golden Calf at a time when we want Hashem to be considering only our merits. We avoid using a horn that could remind Hashem of the *Cheit HaEigel* and would serve as a prosecuting agent rather than as a tool for the defense.

However, this seem to be at odds with the principle the Gemara stated with regard to the *bigdei zahav* that were worn outside of the *Kodesh HaKodashim*, that we are concerned with *ein kateigor naaseh saneigor* only in the *Kodesh HaKodashim*. The shofar is not blown in the *Kodesh HaKodashim*, it is blown in the shul, so why do we employ the principle of *ein kateigor naaseh saneigor* when it comes to choosing the appropriate horn to use as a shofar?

The Gemara answers that since the mitzvah of shofar is employed as a favorable remembrance of the Bnei Yisrael before Hashem, it is as if it is being used in the *Kodesh HaKodashim*. What does this mean? The shofar is not permitted to be blown in the *Kodesh HaKodashim* — and in fact no one, not even the Kohen Gadol, even entered the *Kodesh HaKodashim* at all on Rosh Hashanah. How does the fact that the shofar's purpose is as a remembrance cause it to be considered as if it were being blown in the *Kodesh HaKodashim*?

∾ *Does Hashem Listen to the Shofar?*

There is an important principle employed in *tefillah*. When the *Anshei Knesses HaGedolah* arranged the text of our prayers, they did not randomly choose nice words to be incorporated into the *tefillos*. Each word of the *Shemoneh Esrei* is based on a *pasuk* in Tanach. This is especially true of the *chasimos*, conclusions, of the *berachos*. However, there seems to be an exception to this rule. The *berachah* of *Shofaros*, recited as part of Mussaf on Rosh Hashanah, contains wording that does not seem to appear anywhere in Tanach.

We conclude the *berachah* of *Shofaros* by saying, כִּי אַתָּה שׁוֹמֵעַ קוֹל שׁוֹפָר וּמַאֲזִין תְּרוּעָה וְאֵין דְּוֹמֶה לָךְ, *For You hear the sound of shofar, and listen to the teruah, and there is none like You.* בָּרוּךְ אַתָּה ה׳ שׁוֹמֵעַ קוֹל תְּרוּעַת עַמּוֹ יִשְׂרָאֵל בְּרַחֲמִים, *Blessed are You, Hashem, Who hears the sound of the teruah of His people, Yisrael, with compassion.*

However, there is no source in Tanach for the concept that Hashem listens to our *shofar*-blowing.[6] Furthermore, what is the meaning of this *berachah*? Hashem is not the One Who listens to the *teruah* — it is *we* who are required to listen to the *teruah*! That is our mitzvah of *shofar* on Rosh Hashanah: to listen and hear the sounds of the *shofar*. The Rambam writes in at least eight places* that there is a mitzvah for us to hear the sound of the *shofar* on Rosh Hashanah. What do we mean when we say that *Hashem* listens mercifully to our *teruos*?

❧ Does the Shofar of Elul Take the Place of the Sephardim's Selichos?

The *Shulchan Aruch*[7] writes that the *minhag* is to get up early in the morning to recite *Selichos* and *Tachanunim* from Rosh Chodesh Elul until Yom Kippur. The *Rema* comments that the *minhag Ashkenaz* is rather that, instead of reciting *Selichos*, we blow the *shofar* after *davening* Shacharis.

What does the *Rema* mean? Why doesn't he just write that *minhag Ashkenaz* is to not say *Selichos* from Rosh Chodesh Elul? What does he mean by saying that in place of the *Selichos*, *minhag Ashkenaz* is to blow *shofar*? How is *tekias shofar* a substitute for *davening* to Hashem and reciting *Selichos*?

---

* See שו״ת אבני נזר חלק או״ח סימן תל״א, who writes that this view of the mitzvah of *shofar* is the basis for the custom of covering the *shofar* at the time of the *berachah*. Considering that the mitzvah is to hear the sound of the *shofar* and not the act of blowing, the *shofar* would not even be considered a *cheftzah shel mitzvah*, but rather relegated as a tool used to create a sound that is the entity with which we perform the mitzvah. Thus, we cover the *shofar*, similar to the custom of covering the challah during *Kiddush*, to avoid humiliating the *shofar*, as it has been reduced to an item of secondary importance.

∽ Bent or Straight

There is a *machlokes*[8] as to whether the *shofar* should be bent or straight. The Gemara explains the two viewpoints. One opinion is that on Rosh Hashanah, the more bent and humble one's mindset, the better it is. Therefore, the *shofar* should be bent. The other opinion is that on Rosh Hashanah a person's outlook and mindset should be straight, and therefore the *shofar* should be straight as well.

The shape of the *shofar* is intended to resemble the kind of *da'as* a person should have on Rosh Hashanah. Should one feel humbled and bent over, or should one focus on being straight and upright, rather than bent?

Interestingly, this same *machlokes* is found in the Gemara[9] with regard to how a person should stand while *davening Shemoneh Esrei*. Should a person *daven* with a bent-over posture, with his eyes cast downward as a sign of a humble mindset, or should one *daven* standing upright, with one's eyes toward the heavens as he *davens*, because as one stands before Hashem he should be standing straight, not bent.

Furthermore, Rashi[10] in *Rosh Hashanah,* in explaining the two views as to the halachically correct shape of the *shofar,* cites *pesukim* in support of each respective position — the very same *pesukim* quoted in *Yevamos.* Rashi applies the *pesukim* that the Gemara used to explain how a person should stand as he prays to the shape the *shofar* should have on Rosh Hashanah. Rashi writes that the position that holds that the *shofar* should be bent maintains that the more a person bends his face toward the ground while he is *davening,* the better, which is sourced in the *pasuk,* וְהָיוּ עֵינַי וְלִבִּי שָׁם, *My eyes and My heart shall be there* ... (I Melachim 9:3); that is, when a person *davens,* his eyes and his heart should be bent downward. This opinion would likewise hold on Rosh Hashanah that the *shofar* should be bent. The dissenting opinion holds that the *shofar* should be straight, as the *pasuk* states, נִשָּׂא לְבָבֵנוּ אֶל כַּפָּיִם, *Let us lift our hearts with our hands* (Eichah 3:41). This is the very *pasuk* from which the view emanates that one should be in a completely erect position when *davening*. Therefore, on Rosh Hashanah one should utilize a straight *shofar*.

◈ The Deeper Meaning of Tekias Shofar

The *sefer Hararei Kedem* of Rav Michel Shurkin[11] advances that from this *sugya* in *Rosh Hashanah*, we glean a significant *yesod*. If the shape of the *shofar* is akin to our posture during *tefillah*, clearly there is another, deeper, component to the *shofar*! It shows us that the *shofar* is, in fact, a *cheftzah shel tefillah* and *tekias shofar* is an aspect of prayer! More than just producing stirring sounds to listen to, it is actually a form of *tefillah*. This is enunciated explicitly in the words of Rashi. In explaining the position that the *shofar* should be bent, Rashi says,[12] הלכך בר"ה בא בענין כפופין. . .דלתפלה, that since on Rosh Hashanah the *shofar* is for prayer, it needs to be bent. Likewise, when in explaining the other position, of utilizing the straight *shofar*, Rashi says, דלתפלה הוא הלכך בר"ה בפשוטין. Rashi is clearly stating the principle that the *shofar* is an item of *tefillah*.

◈ Doing a Mitzvah During Shemoneh Esrei: Shofar Is the Exception

This concept is further reinforced by the fact that we sound the *shofar* during *Shemoneh Esrei*. One does not shake his *lulav* and *esrog* during *Shemoneh Esrei*; it would be highly inappropriate. One cannot even give *tzedakah* while *davening Shemoneh Esrei*. Yet, *minhag Sefard* does blow *shofar* during *Shemoneh Esrei*. *Minhag Ashkenaz* does not blow *shofar* during the silent *Shemoneh Esrei*, but the *shofar* is sounded during *chazaras hashatz*. This too is a deviation from the norm. During the *chazzan's* repetition of *Shemoneh Esrei* one is not permitted to perform other mitzvos; even learning Torah is not allowed.* During

---

* See ארחות יושר פרק ל' ס"ק כח' of Rav Chaim Kanievsky, where he advances the possibility that one who is *ma'avir sedra* during *chazaras*

the *chazzan's* repetition, one must pay full attention to the words the *chazzan* is saying, as if he himself were *davening Shemoneh Esrei*. How then can we blow the *shofar* during *Shemoneh Esrei* and during *chazaras hashatz*?

It is apparent, then, that blowing the *shofar* is in itself *tefillah*.[13] Blowing the *shofar* is not an interruption of *tefillah* — it *is tefillah*! The sound of the *shofar* is *tza'akah*, it is crying out to Hashem.

◈ Why Ein Kateigor Naaseh Saneigor Applies to the Shofar

The *sefer Hararei Kedeim*[14] uses this to explain why *ein kateigor naaseh saneigor* applies to the *shofar* even though the *shofar* is not used in the *Kodesh HaKodashim*. The *Rambam*[15] writes that when one stands to *daven Shemoneh Esrei*, he should envision himself as if he were standing directly in front of the *Shechinah*. Further, the Rambam[16] adds that when one *davens,* his heart should be meditating about Hashem, as if standing before Him in Heaven.

During *Shemoneh Esrei* one should be thinking that he is standing in *Shamayim,* and he should consider himself as if he is standing directly in front of Hashem. When the *shofar* is sounded, it is also *tefillah,* and, just like *Shemoneh Esrei*, it is to be viewed as if it were being sounded directly before Hashem, as if it were being blown in *Shamayim*. This, posits the *Hararei Kedem*, is equivalent to standing *lifnei v'lifnim* in the *Kodesh HaKodashim*! It is as if the *shofar* is being blown in the actual *Kodesh HaKodashim*! No wonder we can apply the principle of *ein kateigor naaseh saneigor* to the *shofar*! It is considered *tefillah,* and *tefillah* is regarded as taking place in the *Kodesh HaKodashim*.

I would add an even more explicit support to this idea.

---

hashatz would not even be *yotzei* post facto, as it is a *mitzvah haba'ah ba'aveirah*; i.e., a mitzvah performed through sin.

The *Shulchan Aruch*[17] tells us that when one *davens Shemoneh Esrei* he should have intention toward Yerushalayim, toward the Beis HaMikdash, and toward the *Kodesh HaKodashim*. The *Mishnah Berurah*[18] explains that this means that one's frame of mind should be as if he were physically standing in the Beis HaMikdash, in the *Kodesh HaKodashim*. He must envision himself as standing in the *Kodesh HaKodashim* as he *davens*. By the same token, blowing the *shofar*, too, should be imagined as if it is taking place in the *Kodesh HaKodashim*. Using a *shofar* that recalls the sin of the *Eigel* would then be inappropriate, because *ein kateigor naaseh saneigor* would apply.

∾ *The Tandem of the Shofar and Tefillah*

Rabbi Shlomo Wahrman[19] points out that this explains the *tefillah,* אֲרֶשֶׁת שְׂפָתֵינוּ יֶעֱרַב לְפָנֶיךָ קֵל רָם וְנִשָּׂא. מֵבִין וּמַאֲזִין מַבִּיט וּמַקְשִׁיב לְקוֹל תְּקִיעָתֵנוּ , *May the utterances of our lips be pleasing unto You, Almighty, Most High and Uplifted, Who understands, and gives ear, Who perceives and listens to the sound of our shofar blast.* This *tefillah* starts with a reference to *tefillah*: אֲרֶשֶׁת שְׂפָתֵינוּ, *May our tefillah be sweet to You.* We then ask Hashem to *listen to the sounds of our shofar blasts,* לְקוֹל תְּקִיעָתֵנוּ. Which are we asking Hashem for? The answer is that since sounding the *shofar* is a form of *tefillah*, it is really only one request: We are asking Hashem to listen to our *tefillos* in all their forms — in the form of the *shofar* blasts and in the form of the words that we pray with our mouths.

∾ *Tekiah Is the Praise*

An original thought was presented by Rabbi Isaac Bernstein, a renowned rav and master orator. The Gemara[20] says that *teruah* can be translated as either גַּנּוּחֵי גָּנַח or יַלּוּלֵי יַלֵּיל, either a moan or a wailing. Either way, it is a form of crying: a *tefillah*. The *tekiah* serves a different purpose. In *Tehillim*[21] we say, "*halleluhu be-seika shofar*, praise Hashem with the *tekiah* of the *shofar*." *Tekiah* is *shevach*, praise of Hashem.

We know that a person is always supposed to first praise Hashem, and only then begin to *daven*. Therefore, we first blow a *tekiah*, as praise of Hashem. This is then followed with the *teruah*, which is the actual *tefillah* of the *shofar*: גַּנּוּחֵי גָנַח or יַלּוּלֵי יַלִּיל. Then, since *tefillah* also concludes with *shevach* to Hashem, we conclude with a second *tekiah*. Each *tefillah* of the *shofar*, each *teruah*, is sandwiched between two *tekios*, two praises of Hashem. Thus, the blowing of the *shofar* follows the halachic format of *tefillah*.

∾ *The Cry of the Shofar*

The Brisker Rav[22] extrapolates the *yesod* that the *shofar* is a form of *tefillah* from the words of the Rambam. The Torah says that when going out to war: וְכִי תָבֹאוּ מִלְחָמָה בְּאַרְצְכֶם עַל הַצַּר הַצֹּרֵר אֶתְכֶם וַהֲרֵעֹתֶם בַּחֲצֹצְרֹת וְנִזְכַּרְתֶּם לִפְנֵי ה' אֱלֹקֵיכֶם וְנוֹשַׁעְתֶּם מֵאֹיְבֵיכֶם, *When you go to wage war in your Land against an enemy who oppresses you, you shall sound short blasts of the trumpets, and you shall be recalled before Hashem, your God, and you shall be saved from your foes (Bamidbar 10:9).*

The Rambam[23] codifies this mitzvah as follows: It is a *mitzvas asei* to "cry out — to *daven* — and to sound the חֲצֹצְרֹת, *trumpets*." However, the *pasuk* does not mention *davening*; it states only that the Bnei Yisrael are to וַהֲרֵעֹתֶם, *sound … the trumpets*. How does the Rambam derive that there is a mitzvah to also *daven*? It is very clear that the Rambam understands that the function of blowing the חֲצֹצְרֹת or the *shofar* is a form of *tefillah*, and that is why he describes the mitzvah of the חֲצֹצְרֹת also as *tefillah*.

∾ *Ashkenaz's Shofar = Sefard's Selichos!*

Now we can understand why the *Rema* implies that the *shofar* that is blown during Elul according to *minhag Ashkenaz* is in lieu of the *Selichos* that are recited by Sefardim. *Shofar* is a powerful form of *tefillah* itself. While the Sefardim increase their prayers in Elul by adding *Selichos*, the Ashkenazim increase their prayers by the daily blowing of the *shofar*.

✑ Why Do We Need the Shofar's Tefillah?

Rosh Hashanah is a day in which we spend many hours *davening* to Hashem. What does the *tefillah* of the *shofar* add to the numerous *tefillos* we already recite?

The *Beis HaLevi*[24] offers a very profound approach. On Rosh Hashanah, as we stand before Hashem being judged, we *daven* extensively, hoping for a good year. We do not want to use any items that may remind Hashem of our *aveiros*, and that is why, as we mentioned above, we don't use a *shofar* made from a cow's horn. We apply the principle of *ein kateigor naaseh saneigor*, which also explains why the Kohen Gadol would not serve in the *Kodesh HaKodashim* while garbed in his gold vestments. Both the *shofar* of the cow and the gold garments would remind Hashem of the sin of the *Eigel*. We do whatever we can to avoid recalling and highlighting *aveiros* we may have committed in the past, so that they cannot be held against us.

We possess a faculty that is used consistently throughout the year, and not always in the right way. At times we use our mouths to speak *lashon hara, rechilus, motzi shem ra, sheker*, etc. The last thing we want to do on Rosh Hashanah is remind Hashem of the improper ways in which we have used our mouths over the past year. There is probably a much greater concern of *ein kateigor naaseh saneigor* with regard to our own mouths than there is for the *Eigel* with which our ancestors had sinned. When our *tefillos* come up to Hashem on Rosh Hashanah, beseeching Hashem, "*Zachreinu l'chaim*," the *malachim* will highlight the other words our mouths have said, words we are likely less than proud of, and which may steer our judgment in an unfavorable direction.

We therefore are gifted with a form of *tefillah* that bypasses the mouth. The *Beis HaLevi* writes that the *shofar* is *tefillah* that arises from the depths of the heart, and it does not use the mouth in the same manner that it had been used to commit the *aveiros* that involve speech. Its *tefillah* goes straight from the heart to Hashem. It can be termed a quadruple bypass — bypassing the larynx, tongue, teeth, and lips — and it allows our *tefillos* to come before Hashem without the downside of being offered through the same vehicle that had been used for sin. It is *tefillah* without utilizing the faculty of speech. The *shofar* is the cry from the heart of a Jew. And the heart of a Jew is holy and pure.

❧ Why Tefillah Sets Us Apart and Bilaam's Jealousy Explained

As we noted above, *tekias shofar* is the mitzvah of which Bilaam was envious. Why specifically the *shofar*? We have many mitzvos. We also asked why Moshe Rabbeinu praised the Bnei Yisrael by focusing on a unique ability of Klal Yisrael: the *koach ha'tefillah*. But non-Jews can also pray, so why is this a praise of Klal Yisrael?

The *shofar* is a unique, special type of *tefillah*. It is a cry to Hashem *m'umka d'liba*, from the deepest recesses of the heart. The content of this cry to Hashem depends on what is in the heart of the person who is sounding the *shofar*. Innately, the heart of a Jew contains the deepest desire to serve Hashem. When a person does not agree to divorce his wife and *beis din* rules that he should, "*kofin oso ad sheyomar rotzah ani*, we force him until he says that he wants to give the *get*." The *Rambam* explains[25] that even though he is being forced, this person's *get* is still considered as having been given of his own will, because, deep down, every Jew has the same desire: *Ritzoneinu la'asos ritzonecha*, Our will is to do the will of Hashem.

When the *shofar* is in the mouth of a Jew, sounding *teruos* to Hashem, what emanates from his heart is pure desire to serve Hashem and do His will. The *tefillah* of the *shofar* is therefore the purest of *tefillos*.

But the heart of a non-Jew does not have this deep-rooted innate desire to serve Hashem and do His will. When the heart of a non-Jew is tapped and its desires are revealed, it would not prove to be as worthy and meritorious.

The *tefillah* of the *shofar*, which comes *m'umka d'liba*, is the deepest, most intense desire of a Jew: namely, to come closer to *Avinu she'baShamayim*, to do the will of Hashem. This is what Bilaam envied. He was jealous of the purity of the yearning that lies in the deepest recesses of the heart of a Jew, the desire that emanates from the power of the *tefillah* of the *shofar*. This uniqueness of our spiritual character and DNA is what made Bilaam envious.

This, perhaps, is also the special power of *tefillah* that Moshe Rabbeinu referred to when he said כִּי מִי גוֹי גָּדוֹל אֲשֶׁר לוֹ אֱלֹקִים קְרֹבִים אֵלָיו כַּה׳ אֱלֹקֵינוּ בְּכָל קָרְאֵנוּ אֵלָיו, *For which is a great nation that has a God Who is close to it, as is Hashem, our God, whenever we call to Him? (Devarim 4:7)*. The *tefillah* of the *shofar* that emanates directly from the *neshamah* of the Jew is the form of *tefillah* that exemplifies the praise of Klal Yisrael.

When we recite the *berachah* of *Shofaros*, we conclude by stating, כִּי אַתָּה שׁוֹמֵעַ קוֹל שׁוֹפָר וּמַאֲזִין תְּרוּעָה. Where in Tanach does it say that Hashem listens to the sound of the *shofar*? It is the *pasuk* that states, שֹׁמֵעַ תְּפִלָּה עָדֶיךָ כָּל בָּשָׂר יָבֹאוּ, *O Heeder of prayer, unto You does all flesh come (Tehillim 65:3)*.

May HaKadosh Baruch Hu be attentive to the piercing cry of our *shofar*, accompanied by all of our *tefillos* and accept them with mercy and good will, and may we all merit a *gut gebentched yahr*.

ENDNOTES

1. חידושי הגרי״ז על התורה פרשת ואתחנן.

2. במדבר כג, כא.

3. אבן עזרא שם.

4. ספר שי לתורה-ראש השנה עמוד קסב, בשם הגרי״ז.

5. ראש השנה כו, א.

6. הררי קדם סימן ז אות ד.

7. או״ח, מחבר ורמ״א סימן תקפא סעיף א.

8. ראש השנה כו, א.

9. יבמות דף קה, ב.

10. רש״י ראש השנה כו, א.

11. הררי קדם סימן ז אות א.

12. רש״י ראש השנה כו, ב.

13. אורות ימי הרחמים סימן י עמוד מט.

14. הררי קדם ז אות ד.

15. הלכות תפילה פרק ד הלכה א.

16. הלכות תפילה פרק ה הלכה ד.

17. או״ח סימן צד סעיף א.

18. שם ס״ק ג.

19. אורות ימי הרחמים סימן י עמוד מח.

20. ראש השנה לג עמוד ב.

21. תהילים קנ.

22. ספר שי לתורה, ראש השנה, דף קסב-קסג.

23. ריש הלכות תענית.

24. דרוש ט״ו (הובא בסוף הספר שו״ת בית הלוי).

25. יד החזקה הלכות גירושין פרק ב הלכה כ.

Personal Revivification and the Revivification of the Dead

❧ Why Do We Say No One Is Comparable to Hashem During Shofaros?

In the Mussaf of Rosh Hashanah, at the end of the *berachah* of *Shofaros*, we state, כִּי אַתָּה שׁוֹמֵעַ קוֹל שׁוֹפָר וּמַאֲזִין תְּרוּעָה וְאֵין דּוֹמֶה לָךְ. בָּרוּךְ אַתָּה ה' שׁוֹמֵעַ קוֹל תְּרוּעַת עַמּוֹ יִשְׂרָאֵל בְּרַחֲמִים. The words וְאֵין דּוֹמֶה לָךְ, *and there is no one comparable to You*, seem superfluous; they seemingly do not lend anything to the *berachah*. They are a truism that can be inscribed in any *berachah*, to any *tefillah*, yet, it is added only to the *berachah* of *Shofaros*. Why?

In addition, there is a concept in halachah that we require "*me'ein hachasimah samuch lachasimah*, the words near the conclusion of a *berachah* must be similar to and reflect the subject of the *berachah's* closing words." The words that immediately precede the *Baruch Atah* at the end of a *berachah* must address the same subject as the closing words of the *berachah*. The addition of the words וְאֵין דּוֹמֶה לָךְ, however, seem to be in contradiction to this halachic rule, as they are completely unrelated to the conclusion of the *berachah*. It would seem more logical to omit the words וְאֵין דּוֹמֶה לָךְ so that the praise of Hashem — that He is attentive to our *shofar* blasts — will flow seamlessly into the conclusion of the *berachah*. These words, וְאֵין דּוֹמֶה לָךְ, therefore, must be articulating a central theme fundamental to Rosh Hashanah and the mitzvah of *shofar*.

⧉ *The Tefillah of the Shofar*

We have learned that* in addition to the fact that *tekias shofar* is one of the 248 *mitzvos asei*, positive commandments, there is another dimension of *tekias shofar*: It is a form of *tefillah*, of prayer to Hashem.

What type of *tefillah* is *shofar*; what is it requesting? *Merubim tzarchei amcha*, the needs of Hashem's nation are numerous. We all have many wants and needs to request of Hashem: health, *parnassah*, children. Everyone has *nisyonos*, challenges for which they need assistance.

The Ribbono shel Olam recognizes this, and therefore He gives us a gift: the *shofar*. The sound of the *shofar* is the unarticulated cry of the Jew. "Ribbono shel Olam, I throw my burden on You! I cannot articulate the many needs I have, but from the sound of the *shofar* You are able to understand what we need! כִּי אַתָּה שׁוֹמֵעַ קוֹל שׁוֹפָר; You are able to understand the *tefillah* of the *shofar*, which includes even needs of which we are unaware. וְאֵין דּוֹמֶה לָּךְ, *and there is no one like You*, Who could hear in the sound of the *shofar* the myriad requests and needs that we have, both those we wish to articulate and those that we cannot articulate. You, Hashem, are able to uncover and discover the true requirements of every Jew. It is the sound of the *shofar* that encapsulates and encompasses the unarticulated cry for all of man's needs. There is no one like You, Hashem — for only You can hear all of this in the cry of the *shofar*." [1]

There is, however, a deeper explanation for the words וְאֵין דּוֹמֶה לָּךְ, *There is no one like You*, as these words have a very specific connotation. These words refer to the ability, specific to Hashem, of divining these unarticulated prayers.

---

* For a complete treatment and explanation of this concept, see preceding essay, "The Shofar of Rosh Hashanah — The Piercing Cry of the *Neshamah*," page 88.

✑ Expectations of a Miracle — What Miracle?

The *Tur*[2] cites the following, based on a Midrash: We groom ourselves before Rosh Hashanah. We take haircuts and bathe, despite the *Yom HaDin* that is approaching.

There is no nation like Klal Yisrael, who know the methodology of their God, His customs and laws. When one is about to be judged, especially for a capital offense, he wears black clothing as if in mourning, he lets his hair grow wild and unkempt, he does not cut his nails, and he does not bathe. He is so frightened of the upcoming trial, he is so consumed with fear, that he cannot even focus his mind on personal hygiene.

The Bnei Yisrael, however, are different. As the *Yom HaDin* approaches, we dress in white clothing, we cut our hair, we trim our beards, we cut our nails. We do groom ourselves irrespective of the upcoming judgment. We even go so far as to have festive meals, replete with delicacies. The Tur concludes: We are confident that Hashem will perform a miracle.

What does the Tur mean, we are confident in the performance of a miracle? What miracle occurs on Rosh Hashanah? The Tur should simply write that we are confident that we will be *zocheh* in the judgment, that we will have a favorable *din*, and that we conduct ourselves in this fashion because we feel assured that we will be acquitted. What is the miracle to which he is referring?

✑ The Key: וְאֵין דּוֹמֶה לָךְ

Rav Moshe Shapiro, cited in the *sefer Az Yashir*[3] by Rav Moshe Schwerd, teaches that the key to understanding what transpires on Rosh Hashanah is contained in the three words: וְאֵין דּוֹמֶה לָךְ. We use this expression in two places in *davening*. Every day, in every *Shemoneh Esrei*, in the *berachah* of *Atah gibor*, we say, מִי כָמוֹךְ בַּעַל גְּבוּרוֹת וּמִי דּוֹמֶה לָךְ מֶלֶךְ מֵמִית וּמְחַיֶּה, *Who is like You, Master of mighty deeds, and who can be compared to You, King Who causes death and restores life.* The words וּמִי דּוֹמֶה לָךְ in this context refer specifically to *Techiyas HaMeisim*. Hashem has infinite abilities, and He can perform endless wonders.

Here is one example worth mentioning: A fetus *in utero* does not breathe through its lungs. It receives oxygen from the mother, via the umbilical cord. The lungs are not used for respiration. As the baby's blood returns to its heart, to the right atrium, there is no need for that blood to proceed to the right ventricle and subsequently to the pulmonary artery — to the lungs — since the baby's blood does not receive oxygen from its lungs. Rather, the blood from the right atrium proceeds directly to the left atrium via an opening in the heart, the foramen ovale, bypassing the lungs and pulmonary circulation. But a baby couldn't survive after birth, even briefly, with a hole in its heart. Miraculously, when a baby is born and cries for the first time and starts to breathe, the lungs inflate and the foramen ovale closes. This forces the blood in the right atrium to now go to the right ventricle and then to the lungs in order to receive oxygen.

This incredible miracle enables a child to survive after birth, and yet it is not classified as וּמִי דּוֹמֶה לָךְ. There is only one single miracle, one *neis*, that we reference by saying, "Hashem, there is no one like You. No one can do this except You, Hashem." This is the miracle of *Techiyas HaMeisim*.

The Gemara[4] states that the day will come when Hashem will knock on a person's grave and rouse him. Hashem will reconstitute each person. The Gemara[5] tells us, "*Hashem mibashan ashiv*, Hashem will restore even from the Bashan." If, *chas v'shalom*, someone drowned and his body decomposed and his atoms were deposited in all corners of the world, when it comes time for *Techiyas HaMeisim*, Hashem will reconstitute and re-create the person; He will gather all the tiny particles from all over the world and rebuild the person. This is the greatest miracle in This World. In reference to this miracle of *Techiyas HaMeisim* we declare, וּמִי דּוֹמֶה לָךְ.

The second place in *davening* that we use this phrase is in the *birchas Krias Shema* that we recite on Shabbos morning: אֵין כְּעֶרְכֶּךָ. וְאֵין זוּלָתֶךָ. אֶפֶס בִּלְתֶּךָ וּמִי דּוֹמֶה לָךְ. Once again, this phrase about the incomparable nature of Hashem refers to *Techiyas HaMeisim*, as the *piyut* concludes, וְאֵין דּוֹמֶה לָךְ מוֹשִׁיעֵנוּ לִתְחִיַּת הַמֵּתִים!

∾ Why Reference Techiyas HaMeisim in the Berachah of Shofaros?

Why, then, in the *berachah* of *Shofaros* do we utilize the phrase וְאֵין דּוֹמֶה לָּךְ? What does *Shofaros* have to do with *Techiyas HaMeisim*?

A halachah brought in *Shulchan Aruch*[6] states that when one sees a friend whom he has not seen during the past thirty days, he recites the *berachah Shehecheyanu*. We do not observe this custom in our times; as there are many forms of communication nowadays, we are safe to assume that our friend is still alive even though we have not seen him; otherwise, we would have expected to have heard of his demise.

The halachah further states that when one sees a friend whom he has not seen in over twelve months, he recites the *berachah Mechayeh HaMeisim*. The *Mishnah Berurah*[7] discusses the basis and rationale for this *berachah*. He quotes the *Maharsha*, who explains that since on every Rosh Hashanah a person is judged either for life or for the alternative, on every Rosh Hashanah each person's life is on the line. Therefore, if one has not seen his friend in twelve months, that means that his friend has experienced and survived the *din* of Rosh Hashanah. Surviving the *din* is comparable to *Techiyas HaMeisim*. Therefore, since his friend has experienced a form of *Techiyas HaMeisim*, it is appropriate for him to recite the *berachah* of *Mechayei HaMeisim*.

∾ Rosh Hashanah Is Revivification!

We are learning that we have a fundamental misinterpretation in our understanding of Rosh Hashanah. We tend to think that what is occurring on Rosh Hashanah is that we, who are alive and in good health, come before Hashem and ask Him to maintain the status quo. Hashem, please continue to keep matters just as they are; after all, each of us is a *muchzak*, is in possession of his resources and success and *hamotzi mechaveiro alav hara'ayah*, the burden of proof is on You, Hashem, to repossess them. I have health, I have life, and I have money – the onus is on You, Ribbono shel Olam, to come up with a valid reason to change the existing circumstances. Meanwhile, let everything remain the way it's always been.

But this is not what is happening. We learn from the *Maharsha* and from the *Anshei Knesses HaGedolah's* use of וְאֵין דּוֹמֶה לָךְ in our *davening* on Rosh Hashanah that when Rosh Hashanah comes and a new year begins, all bets are off. The lease has ended. The eviction notice has arrived in the mail. The status quo enjoyed until now is no longer viable — it has been terminated.

There is no *chazakah*, established right, there is no status quo, and there are no assumptions. We stand before Hashem, not with life in hand and a request to continue it, but rather with nothing at all, and we ask Hashem to please revivify us.

We come before Hashem on Rosh Hashanah like *meisim*, the dead, but, as the Tur says, we are confident that Hashem will perform a miracle for us. And what is the miracle that we anticipate? It is the miracle of וּמִי דּוֹמֶה לָךְ, the miracle of *Techiyas HaMeisim*.[8]

❧ *K'dalim U'krashim Dafaknu Delasecha*

Rav Shlomo Heiman, the illustrious Rosh Yeshivah of Yeshivah Torah Vodaas, related with great emotion the moving *derashah* he heard on *Leil Selichos,* the first night of *Selichos,* from the *Granat,*[9] the Gaon Rav Naftali Tropp, before he led the *davening* in the yeshivah in Radin as the *chazzan* for *Selichos.* In *Selichos* we say, *"K'dalim u'krashim dafaknu delasecha,* like paupers and poor men do we bang on Your door." What does this *tefillah* mean?

It does not matter how much money a person has in his bank account, or how healthy he may be. On Rosh Hashanah we stand before Hashem like paupers. We stand before Hashem with no *chazakah*, no status quo, no money, no family, and we hope that Hashem will revivify us, for the lease has ended. "Like paupers and poor men, we bang on Your door."

The *sefer Az Yashir*[10] cites, in the name of Rav Moshe Shapiro, that the *Arizal* taught that on Rosh Hashanah, Hashem does not grant a person years for the duration of his life. He does not give one person a *din* for a longevity of a hundred years, and another person for eighty-two. Hashem is judging us solely for the upcoming year. Hashem takes it one year at a time. Our lease on life is only extended for a year; it must be renewed annually. Nothing decreed on Rosh Hashanah affects more than just the one year that is starting.

At the end of each year, every person's lease on life is up. He has to come before Hashem in judgment and be adjudicated. The lease on life may or may not be renewed. When one merits the gift of another additional year, when he is victorious in *din*, it is truly as if he is experiencing *Techiyas HaMeisim*.

When we stand before the Ribbono shel Olam on Rosh Hashanah, we are asking Hashem to please perform this miracle for us. Please perform the greatest miracle in Your repertoire, the miracle whose key was never given over even to the *malachei hashareis*.[11] That is why it is a miracle that is referred to with the phrase וְאֵין דּוֹמֶה לָּךְ.

מִי כָמוֹךָ בַּעַל גְּבוּרוֹת וּמִי דוֹמֶה לָּךְ refers to the power Hashem has to give life and to restore life.

During the *Aseres Yemei Teshuvah*, we insert a sentence into the *berachah* of *Gevuros*: מִי כָמוֹךָ אָב הָרַחֲמָן זוֹכֵר יְצוּרָיו לְחַיִּים בְּרַחֲמִים. It is appropriately added to the *berachah* of *Atah Gibor* because that is the *berachah* whose subject is *Techiyas HaMeisim*! What better place to mention the fact that Hashem is incomparable because He remembers His creations, and mercifully grants them life. This granting of life is precisely the topic of the *berachah*: *Techiyas HaMeisim*.

~ *The Judgment: Daily vs. Annually*

The Gemara[12] states, "*Adam nidon b'chol yom*, man is judged daily." Rav Eisele Charif[13] poses an incisive question: If we are judged every single day of the year, why is it that only on Rosh Hashanah do we take the *din* so much more seriously? What is different about the *din* of Rosh Hashanah than that of all the other days of the year?

He answers that the daily judgment is subject to the laws of *chazakah,* to the status quo. Every day when we are judged by the Ribbono shel Olam the judgment takes the *chazakah,* the person's current state, into account. The person existed yesterday, and Hashem allows that to continue because he is a *muchzak* in his life. *Hamotzi mechaveiro alav hara'ayah* is invoked, and the burden of proof is incumbent upon the one who wants to change the status quo.

But on Rosh Hashanah, there is no longer a status quo to invoke, there is no longer *chazakah.* Past existence has no bearing on future outcome. This is the difference between the daily judgment and the annual judgment of Rosh Hashanah. Once again, we encounter this principle of the miracle of *Techiyas HaMeisim* on Rosh Hashanah.

꧁ *Why Mention the Akeidah on Rosh Hashanah?*

One of the main *zechusim* that we try to tap into on Rosh Hashanah is the extraordinary *zechus* of *Akeidas Yitzchak.*

Why do we mention *Akeidas Yitzchak* on Rosh Hashanah? Not all opinions agree that it even took place on Rosh Hashanah, so why mention it in the *davening* on Rosh Hashanah?* Why is the *Akeidah* such a central theme on Rosh Hashanah to the point that we mention it during *Shemoneh Esrei,* we blow the horn of a ram to remind Hashem of the *Akeidah,*[14] and we read about the *Akeidah* in the *krias HaTorah* of the second day of Rosh Hashanah?

---

* While פסיקתא רבתי פרשה מ' אות ח' writes that indeed the *Akeidah* took place on Rosh Hashanah, the דרשות אבן שועיב and ילקוט ראובני פרשת וירא דרש ליו"כ write that it took place on Yom Kippur. Interestingly, see שמות רבה טו:יא that it took place in Chodesh Nissan!

❧ Tashlich at the Water Recalls the Akeidah

The *Rama*[15] codifies the custom of performing *Tashlich* at a river on Rosh Hashanah. It is sourced in the *Maharil*,[16] who says that we go to the river to say *Tashlich* to remind Hashem of the *Akeidah* and to invoke the *zechus* of that event, because the *Satan* created a river to prevent Avraham from going to the *Akeidah*. Avraham walked into the water until it reached his nostrils. He cried out, "הוֹשִׁיעֵנִי אֱלֹקִים כִּי בָאוּ מַיִם עַד נָפֶשׁ, *Save me, for the water has risen to my soul.*" Thus, the purpose of *Tashlich* is to invoke the *zechus* of *Akeidas Yitzchak*. The *Mishnah Berurah*,[17] in fact, cites this *Maharil*, that the purpose of *Tashlich* is to recall the momentous event of *Akeidas Yitzchak*.

❧ The Head of a Ram

The Shulchan Aruch[18] brings the custom of using a head as one of the *simanim* on Rosh Hashanah. This is to symbolize that we would like to be the head, and not the tail — *n'hi'yeh l'rosh v'lo l'zanav*. Interestingly, the *Shulchan Aruch* specifically recommends using the head of a ram, in commemoration of the ram that was sacrificed in place of Yitzchak at the time of the *Akeidah*. Again, we see the centrality of the *Akeidah* in the customs of Rosh Hashanah, but why is it so significant, since it is not unanimously believed to have occurred on Rosh Hashanah?

❧ The Akeidah: The First Techiyas HaMeisim

On Rosh Hashanah we are not merely asking Hashem to keep matters the way they were. What we are asking Hashem for is *Techiyas HaMeisim*, for Him to revivify us in every dimension of our lives. And when was the first time in the history of the world that Hashem was *mechayeh meisim*? It was at *Akeidas Yitzchak*!

The *Shibbolei HaLeket*[19] brings the teaching that the *berachos* of the weekday *Shemoneh Esrei* are actually an historical account of the story of the world. When Avraham Avinu was saved from the fires of Ur Kasdim, the *malachei hashareis* cried out, "*Baruch Atah Hashem, magen Avraham.*"

When Yitzchak Avinu was bound on the *mizbei'ach* to be offered as a *korban* to Hashem at the *Akeidah*, he became ashes that were then scattered all about Har HaMoriah. Although the familiar and oft-quoted sequence of events dictate that Yitzchak emerged unscathed from the *Akeidah*, numerous *midrashim* state otherwise. According to the *Midrash* cited in *Shibbolei HaLeket*, Yitzchak Avinu in fact did die, as his *neshamah* left him — *parchah nishmaso.*

The Ribbono shel Olam then performed *Techiyas HaMeisim*; He placed dew on Yitzchak and brought him back to life. It is about this event that David HaMelech wrote, כְּטַל חֶרְמוֹן שֶׁיֹּרֵד עַל הַרְרֵי צִיּוֹן, *So the dew of Chermon descends upon the mountains of Tzion* (*Tehillim* 133: 3). Dew on Har Tzion is a reference to the dew that Hashem sprinkled on Yitzchak Avinu as He brought him back to life.

Immediately upon Yitzchak's revivification, the *malachim* said the *berachah*, "*Baruch Atah Hashem, mechayeh hameisim.*"

There is another version of the *midrash*[20]: Yitzchak's soul departed, and when his *neshamah* returned to his *guf*, when he experienced *Techiyas HaMeisim*, it was he who stated, "*Baruch Atah Hashem, mechayeh hameisim.*"

Likewise, *Pirkei D'Rabbi Eliezer* states,[21] in the name of R' Yehudah: Once the knife was placed upon Yitzchak's neck, at the time of the *Akeidah*, his *neshamah* departed from his body. When his *neshamah* heard the voice of Hashem coming from between the two *Keruvim*, stating, אַל תִּשְׁלַח יָדְךָ אֶל הַנַּעַר, "Do not stretch out your hand against the lad" (*Bereishis* 22:12), the *neshamah* immediately returned to Yitzchak's body. He was then untied and he stood up. Yitzchak realized that *Techiyas HaMeisim* is *min haTorah*, and he understood that those who pass away will be revivified in the future. He immediately composed and recited the *berachah*, *Baruch Atah Hashem, mechayeh hameisim.*

We have a tradition[22] that the first *berachah*, *Magen Avraham*, corresponds to Avraham Avinu, and the second *berachah*, *Atah Gibor*, which is the *berachah* of *Techiyas HaMeisim*, corresponds to Yitzchak. With these *midrashim*, we can appreciate how the *berachah* of *Gevuros* corresponds to Yitzchak, because he was the very first person to experience *Techiyas HaMeisim*.

✺ *Why the Central Theme Is the Akeidah*

Now we understand why the central theme of Rosh Hashanah is *Akeidas Yitzchak*. It is not merely because of timing, as not everyone is in agreement that it took place on Rosh Hashanah. The reason to invoke the *Akeidah* on Rosh Hashanah is to point out that this is the *maaseh avos siman labanim*, all events that occurred to the forefathers are portents for their descendants, a pre-enactment to what takes place annually on Rosh Hashanah: *Techiyas HaMeisim*.

This is a particularly strong connection according to the view that the original *Techiyas HaMeisim* did in fact take place on Rosh Hashanah, at the *Akeidah*. This action is then forever fused to the day of Rosh Hashanah, and Rosh Hashanah will always be a day of *Techiyas HaMeisim*. Hashem revivifies all of us every Rosh Hashanah.

We stand before Hashem *k'dalim u'krashim*, and like *meisim mamash*, actual corpses. We *daven* and ask Hashem to please sprinkle upon us the dew of *Techiyas HaMeisim*. We are confident, as the Tur says, that Hashem will perform this miracle for us. This is why we invoke the remarkable capability of Hashem, כִּי אַתָּה שׁוֹמֵעַ קוֹל שׁוֹפָר וּמַאֲזִין תְּרוּעָה וְאֵין דְּוֹמֶה לָּךְ. The powerful and poignant meaning of the final phrase, וְאֵין דְּוֹמֶה לָךְ, is now understood as a reference to the greatest of all miracles, *Techiyas HaMeisim*, and explains why on Rosh Hashanah we focus on *Akeidas Yitzchak* — the source of the power of *Techiyas HaMeisim* in This World.

✺ *Another Dimension of Techiyas HaMeisim*

Another dimension of *Techiyas HaMeisim* is worthy of note. There is a *Kaf HaChaim*[23] that Rav Shneur Kotler would often repeat during this time of the year in the name of his father, Rav Aharon.

There are forty days from Rosh Chodesh Elul until Yom Kippur. These forty days correspond to the forty days of *yetziras hav'lad*, the forty days of the formation of a baby. Even though the baby is in the mother's womb for nine months, the primary creation, including the determination of the gender, takes place in the first forty days. The *neshamah* then enters the baby on the fortieth day. In what way do the forty days of Chodesh Elul and the *Aseres Yemei Teshuvah* correspond to the forty days of *yetziras hav'lad*?

Rav Yerucham Olshin explains,[24] using the *Midrash* on the *pasuk,* תִּכָּתֶב זֹאת לְדוֹר אַחֲרוֹן וְעַם נִבְרָא יְהַלֶּל קָהּ, *Let this be recorded for the final generation, so that the newborn people will praise Hashem* (*Tehillim* 102:19). Who is this new nation that is being created? The *Yalkut Shimoni*[25] explains that this verse refers to us, who come before Hashem like *meisim b'maaseihem*, lifeless in our actions, *davening* to Hashem on Rosh Hashanah and Yom Kippur. Hashem responds to our *tefillos* by creating us anew, allowing us to proceed to Succos, when we will hold the *lulav* and *esrog* as we say *Hallel* — thereby fulfilling the verse, *the newborn people will praise Hashem.*

Rav Yerucham understands that the *Midrash* is adding an important point to our understanding of our status on Rosh Hashanah. When we stand before Hashem on Rosh Hashanah, not only do we have nothing to count on, not only is there no *chazakah*, and we cannot rely on the past. But it is more than that: We are actually considered *meisim b'maaseihem,* because *reshaim bechayehem k'ruim meisim,* the wicked are considered dead even as they live.[26]

We stand before Hashem, proclaiming that our actions, our *maasim,* do not render us worthy of being considered to be spiritually alive before Him. We implore Hashem not just to revive us physically, but to revive our *neshamos* as well. Allow us to start again, and help us achieve the level where we can be considered alive both physically and spiritually.

This is the concept of how the forty days before Yom Kippur correspond to the forty days of *yetziras hav'lad*. During Elul and during the *Aseres Yemei Teshuvah*, we are striving to re-create ourselves. We are trying to be reborn, to start over. Whatever was, was, and we are now going through a forty-day process that is reminiscent of the forty-day process we experienced *in utero*. We go through this process on a yearly basis as we ask Hashem for spiritual revival, spiritual re-creation.

With this understanding, the teshuvah process becomes akin to *Techiyas HaMeisim*. *Teshuvah* is a process by which we try to revive ourselves and come back to life.

✐ Teshuvah: A Form of Techiyas HaMeisim

In his commentary to *Shemoneh Esrei*,[27] Rav Yonasan Eibeshutz discusses the *kavannos*, intentions, we should have during *Shemoneh Esrei*. In his commentary to the second *berachah*, *Atah Gibor*, Rav Yonasan writes that Hashem's acceptance of our teshuvah is a form of *Techiyas HaMeisim*. A *rasha*, even while alive, is considered to be deceased: *reshaim bechayehem k'ruim meisim*. When he then does teshuvah, he is considered to have experienced *Techiyas HaMeisim*. Therefore, when we say the words אַתָּה גִבּוֹר לְעוֹלָם ה' מְחַיֵּה מֵתִים אַתָּה רַב לְהוֹשִׁיעַ, one of the *kavannos* to have in mind is that Hashem should revivify us by accepting our teshuvah.

Rav Tzadok HaKohen[28] brilliantly points out that the period of *Techiyas HaMeisim* will be ushered into the world by Eliyahu HaNavi who is also the one who ushers in the era of teshuvah. These are not two distinct roles of Eliyahu HaNavi, and these are not two different eras. These are one and the same, since, as we said, *reshaim bechayehem k'ruim meisim*. Eliyahu inspiring all to do teshuvah will be a form of *Techiyas HaMeisim*. Physical and spiritual revivification are both part of the same function that Eliyahu HaNavi will perform in the End of Days.

∾ Starting Selichos
From the First Day of Creation

The Tur[29] brings down three *minhagim* relating to *Selichos*. Some have the custom to start reciting *Selichos* from Rosh Chodesh Elul. There is another *minhag* to recite *Selichos* only during the *Aseres Yemei Teshuvah*. The Tur then mentions a third custom, which is to start reciting *Selichos* on the Sunday before Rosh Hashanah, and, if that is fewer than four days, then to start from the previous Sunday.

The *Gra*[30] disagrees with the Tur. He says we are to begin saying *Selichos* on the twenty-fifth day of Elul. This is the anniversary of *Berias HaOlam*, the Creation of the world. Hashem created Adam on Rosh Hashanah, as we say in *davening*, *zeh hayom techilas maasecha*. Since Adam was created on the sixth day of Creation, the first day of Creation must have been the twenty-fifth day of Elul. Therefore, the *minhag* is to start saying *Selichos* on כ"ה אלול.

The *Ran*[31] cites this *minhag* as well, stating that in Barcelona the custom was to start reciting *Selichos* on the twenty-fifth day of Elul, since that was the first day of *Berias HaOlam*.

How do we understand this custom cited by the *Ran* and endorsed by the *Gra*? Why is reciting *Selichos* connected to the first day of *Berias HaOlam*?

As noted, teshuvah is a forty-day process, *k'neged yetziras hav'lad*, as we try to re-create ourselves. We understand that our lease is over, and we ask Hashem to please re-create us, our families, and the entire Creation, in all dimensions, physical and spiritual. It is a time to re-create our *middos*, our character, our personality, our entire spiritual repertoire.

We begin the process on Rosh Chodesh Elul, *mem yom kodem yetziras hav'lad*. We start saying *Selichos* on the twenty-fifth day of Elul, which is the first day of *Berias HaOlam*, as we endeavor to re-create ourselves and our entire world.

≈ Every Moment Is Vital

The analogy of the forty days of teshuvah compared to the formation of a fetus, teaches Rav Yerucham Olshin, has critical significance. When a baby forms, the first forty days are very tenuous. Each and every moment of those first forty days is indispensable to the baby's development. Every second is another building block of life, and it may be when the key part of the brain, heart, kidney, or lung is forming. We cannot tamper with these forty days. They are vital, and not even a single second can be bypassed. This crucial time in a baby's gestation cannot be made up in another manner.

During Chodesh Elul and the *Aseres Yemei Teshuvah*, we are re-creating ourselves for the entire year to come, and we are preparing ourselves for the great miracle we are counting on Hashem to perform. We are readying ourselves for *Techiyas HaMeisim*, both physically and spiritually. Similar to the creation of a baby, here too, every single day is vital, every single second is critical to our re-birth. Each day is crucial and each moment is irreplaceable. There is not a single moment to waste.[32]

≈ The Navi of Teshuvah

Who in Tanach is the *navi* of teshuvah? It is the *navi* whom we read about as the holiest day of the year, Yom Kippur, is waning, the *navi* who teaches us that anyone can do teshuvah, that anyone can turn his life around. He is Yonah ben Amitai.

The *Malbim*[33] says that Yonah was the son of the *ishah almanah*, the widow who provided for and sustained Eliyahu HaNavi. Her child, Yonah, had died, and Eliyahu HaNavi performed *Techiyas HaMeisim*, bringing him back to life. Yonah was the first person recorded in Tanach who experienced *Techiyas HaMeisim*.*

In Rav Dovid Luria's commentary on *Pirkei D'Rabbi Eliezer*,[34]

---

* As noted above, the first instance of *Techiyas HaMeisim* is that of Yitzchak at the *Akeidah*, but that incident is not found in the Tanach. It is written in the *Midrash*.

he writes that when Yonah says the words וַתַּעַל מִשַּׁחַת חַיַּי... בְּהִתְעַטֵּף עָלַי נַפְשִׁי אֶת ה' זָכָרְתִּי, *Yet, You lifted my life from the pit ....* *When my soul was faint within me, I remembered Hashem* (Yonah 2:7-8), he alludes to the fact that when he was a child he died and Eliyahu HaNavi revivified him.

The *peirush* on *Sefer Yonah* called *Razei Yonah*[35] connects Yonah's experience of physical *Techiyas HaMeisim* to his being the *navi* of teshuvah. Yonah, who experienced physical *Techiyas HaMeisim*, is able to teach the world to do teshuvah, which is spiritual *Techiyas HaMeisim*. Having experienced the engine that powers teshuvah, namely *Techiyas HaMeisim*, he was able to teach the world what teshuvah was all about.

✑ *Personal Revivification*

A person might say, "Teshuvah — how is that possible for me? I'm in such a rut; I have so many bad habits." A person may think that he has a dark past and that he cannot overcome the darkness and the feelings of spiritual lifelessness. Yonah comes to teach us that teshuvah is possible. He testifies firsthand that just as *Techiyas HaMeisim* is possible, so is teshuvah. He experienced physical *Techiyas HaMeisim*, so he can teach the world about spiritual revivification.

Yonah tells the world, וּמִי דּוֹמֶה לָךְ, about Hashem's incomparable ability to revive the *baal teshuvah*.

At the end of *Shaarei Teshuvah* there is a brief *kuntres* called *Yesod HaTeshuvah*.[36] In it, Rabbeinu Yonah writes that when a person embarks on doing teshuvah, he should throw away all his sins. This is not a reference to actual teshuvah, as the halachic components of teshuvah are not being fulfilled. Rather, Rabbeinu Yonah is teaching us that a person has the ability to say, "I have a clean slate. The past is the past. It is as if I am born on this very day, with no *zechus* and no *chovah*, debt. Today is the start of my actions, a clean slate."

This is what is happening on Rosh Hashanah—a new beginning, a clean slate. We are experiencing *Techiyas HaMeisim*.

אַתָּה גִבּוֹר לְעוֹלָם ה׳ מְחַיֶּה מֵתִים אַתָּה רַב לְהוֹשִׁיעַ. We *daven* to Hashem, saying, we are like *meisim* before You, and we beseech You, please give us another year of life, both physical and spiritual. We are confident that Hashem is going to answer us in the affirmative, and that He is going to perform the greatest miracle of all for us, the miracle of *Techiyas HaMeisim*.

May we all be *zocheh* to a year of *chaim* and *shalom*, *shefa*, *berachah*, *v'hatzlachah b'chol inyaneinu*.

ENDNOTES

1. אז ישיר, רב משה שווערד דף א״ב.
2. או״ח סימן תקפ״א.
3. אז ישיר דף ד.
4. תענית ב, ב.
5. גיטין נז, ב.
6. אורח חיים סימן רכה סעיף א.
7. שם ס״ק ד.
8. שו״ת הלכות קטנות סימן ריד.
9. חידושי גרנ״ט, הנותן אמרי שפר, עמוד יח.
10. אז ישיר דף ד.
11. תענית ב, א.
12. ראש השנה טו, א.
13. עמק יהושע דרוש ד.
14. ראש השנה טז, ב.
15. או״ח סימן תקפ״ג סעיף א.
16. ראש השנה אות ט, רעז.
17. משנה ברורה סימן תקפ״ג ס״ק ח.
18. או״ח סימן תקפ״ג סעיף ב.
19. שבלי הלקט סימן יח.
20. אוצר המדרשים ויושע p. 149

21. פרקי דרבי אליעזר פרק לא.
22. בית יוסף או״ח סימן קיב.
23. כף החיים סימן תקפ״א ס״ק יד.
24. ירח למועדים ימים נוראים מאמר ג עמוד רכג.
25. תהילים רמ״ז תתנה.
26. ברכות יב, ב.
27. יערות דבש חלק א דרוש א עמוד י״יא.
28. פרי צדיק חנוכה עמוד תא.
29. או״ח סימן תקפ״א.
30. ביאור הגר״א שם.
31. ראש השנה דף ב בדפי הריי״ף.
32. ירח למועדים ימים נוראים מאמר ג עמוד רכד.
33. יונה א, א.
34. פירוש רד״ל פרקי דרבי אליעזר פרק לג, הובא במשבצות זהב על יונה עמוד לו.
35. הובא במשבצות זהב על יונה שם.
36. יסוד התשובה.

The Ascendancy of the Jewish People Over Yishmael Through the Akeidah

❧ Whose Test Was It Really?

וַיְהִי אַחַר הַדְּבָרִים הָאֵלֶּה וְהָאֱלֹקִים נִסָּה אֶת אַבְרָהָם.

And it happened after these things that Hashem tested Avraham… (Bereishis 22:1).

Tosafos asks in the name of R' Yehudah HaChassid[1]: Why does the Torah tell us that Hashem tested *Avraham*? Would it not be more accurate to state that Hashem tested *Yitzchak*? If all were to go as Avraham expected, he would return from the *Akeidah*, while Yitzchak's life would have ended as an offering to Hashem. It would seem that the Torah, then, at the very least, might have included both: *And Hashem tested Avraham and Yitzchak*. Yitzchak was 37 years old at this time, and he could have objected, so it seems that it was at least as much a test for him as it was for his father Avraham.

❧ Why Didn't Hashem Make His Wishes Clear Immediately?

The Torah states, וַיֹּאמֶר קַח נָא אֶת בִּנְךָ אֶת יְחִידְךָ אֲשֶׁר אָהַבְתָּ אֶת יִצְחָק, *Please take your son, your only one, whom you love*

— *Yitzchak* (ibid. v. 2). Rashi explains the verse as a conversation between Hashem and Avraham. Hashem tells Avraham to take his *son*, to which Avraham replies that he has two sons. Hashem becomes more specific and tells Avraham to take the son who is the *yachid*, only one, to which Avraham answers that each of his sons is *yichud l'imo*, his mother's only son. Hashem specifies further by adding, *the son whom you love*. Avraham's response is that he, in fact, loves both of his sons. To this Hashem adds the final qualification, stating that He is referring to Yitzchak. Why does Hashem not begin by specifying Yitzchak by name? Rashi explains that Hashem did not want Avraham to be startled or shocked, which might have been the case if Hashem had immediately said that Avraham was to bring Yitzchak as an offering. People might have said that since Avraham had to rush into the *Akeidah*, he had no time to think and to truly consider the consequence of his actions, and that his behavior was a rash decision that he would ultimately regret. They might say that had he had time to think and to consider what was really being asked of him, he never would have obeyed. Therefore, Hashem gave Avraham time to think and consider, and yet he willingly went along with whatever Hashem had instructed him to do.

Still, there are many ways to break news in a manner that would not be startling. We know that not even a single letter in the Torah is extraneous, so why does the Torah use all these descriptive phrases?

✑ *Why Would Hashem Be Referring to Yishmael?*

Furthermore, did Avraham really assume that Hashem would be referring to Yishmael? Avraham knew that Yishmael was an idol worshiper and an adulterer. The Torah tells us that Sarah had seen Yishmael "מְצַחֵק, *mocking*" (ibid. 21:9), indicating that he was completely corrupt, and that was why she had him sent away. Why would it even occur to Avraham that Hashem could possibly mean Yishmael?

Tosafos[2] says that it must be that Yishmael was visiting on the day of the *Akeidah*. Precisely on the day that Hashem gave Avraham the instructions about the *Akeidah*, Yishmael chose to return home to visit his father. On that specific day, Hashem tells Avraham, קַח נָא אֶת בִּנְךָ אֶת יְחִידְךָ אֲשֶׁר אָהַבְתָּ. Avraham's immediate reaction was that Hashem must mean Yishmael, for if Hashem had meant Yitzchak, He could have given the instruction at any time during the prior thirty-five years! The fact that Hashem gave the instruction of the *Akeidah* specifically on the day that Yishmael was there clearly seemed to imply that Yishmael was the son Avraham was instructed to sacrifice.

The *Maharal* says that דְּבָרִים גְּדוֹלִים אֵינָם בְּמִקְרֶה, important things don't happen coincidentally. Why did *hashgachah* have it that the *Akeidah* would take place on the one specific day that Yishmael chanced to be visiting? His happening to be there was not coincidental; it must have been planned by Hashem.

❧ *Why Was Yishmael at the Akeidah?*

וַיַּשְׁכֵּם אַבְרָהָם בַּבֹּקֶר וַיַּחֲבֹשׁ אֶת חֲמֹרוֹ וַיִּקַּח אֶת שְׁנֵי נְעָרָיו אִתּוֹ וְאֵת יִצְחָק בְּנוֹ.

So Avraham woke up early in the morning and he saddled his donkey; he took his two young men with him and Yitzchak, his son (ibid. v. 3).

Rashi[3] tells that the two young men who accompanied Avraham were Yishmael and Eliezer. An eminent personage does not travel unless he is accompanied by at least two people; therefore, Avraham took two men with him, in addition to Yitzchak.

Tosafos queries: We understand why Avraham would take Eliezer with him. After all, he was Avraham's chief steward. But why was Yishmael there after having been banished? How did Yishmael come to be at the *Akeidah*? We know that when Yishmael was sent away, Yitzchak was at least 2 years old. At the time of the *Akeidah*, Yitzchak was 37 years old, and Yishmael had been exiled for 35 years and had been living in Midbar

Paran (ibid. 21:21)! No *pasuk* in the Torah tells us explicitly that he had returned, yet we see that he had returned just in time to be a participant in the narrative of the *Akeidah*.

In fact, when Avraham then took Eliezer and Yishmael with him to the *Akeidah*, they quarreled. Yishmael said, "Now that my father is going to sacrifice Yitzchak, I will inherit Eretz Yisrael." Eliezer disagreed, saying that since Yishmael had already been banished, he, like a woman who received a *get*, no longer has any claim as an heir. "However," Eliezer states, "since I serve Avraham day and night, I am the rightful heir." Hashem then made it clear that neither of them would actually inherit Eretz Yisrael.

≈ Why Does Avraham Tell the Men to Remain "With the Chamor"?

The Torah tells us: וַיֹּאמֶר אַבְרָהָם אֶל נְעָרָיו שְׁבוּ לָכֶם פֹּה עִם הַחֲמוֹר, *And Avraham said to his young men, "Stay here by yourselves with the donkey."* Why add the seemingly superfluous words, *with the donkey*? The *Beis HaLevi* explains: The Gemara[4] states that we learn from here that a child who is born to a maidservant has the halachic status of a *chamor*, donkey: עַם הַדּוֹמֶה לַחֲמוֹר. Thus, בֶּן יִשְׂרָאֵל הַבָּא מִן הַשִּׁפְחָה אֵינוֹ מְיוּחָס אַחֲרָיו, a child born to a maidservant does not inherit his father's property.

The *Beis HaLevi* asks[5]: Since the Torah could have related this halachah at any time, why is it told here, at the time of the *Akeidah*? And why is this *derashah* being taught through the words of Avraham Avinu?

≈ אוֹיֵב *and* שׂוֹנֵא, *Enemy and Adversary: Same or Different?*

After the *Akeidah*, the Torah states, a *malach* told Avraham that because he passed the test, כִּי בָרֵךְ אֲבָרֶכְךָ וְהַרְבָּה אַרְבֶּה אֶת זַרְעֲךָ כְּכוֹכְבֵי הַשָּׁמַיִם וְכַחוֹל אֲשֶׁר עַל שְׂפַת הַיָּם. Hashem *will surely bless you and greatly increase your offspring like the stars of the heavens* and like the sand on the seashore, וְיִרַשׁ זַרְעֲךָ אֵת שַׁעַר אֹיְבָיו, and your offspring shall inherit the gate of its enemy (Bereishis 22:17). Over the course of time, the Yidden have had many enemies to whom this pasuk may be referring.

In this instance, however, the word enemy has a very specific connotation. This root of the word אֹיְבָיו, its enemy, is אוֹיֵב. In Lashon HaKodesh, there are two words that can be translated as enemy: אוֹיֵב and שׂוֹנֵא, and they have different connotations. A pasuk in Parashas Nitzavim uses both words: וְנָתַן ה׳ אֱלֹקֶיךָ אֵת כָּל הָאָלוֹת הָאֵלֶּה עַל אֹיְבֶיךָ וְעַל שֹׂנְאֶיךָ אֲשֶׁר רְדָפוּךָ, Hashem, your God, will place all these curses upon אֹיְבֶיךָ, your enemies, and upon שֹׂנְאֶיךָ, those who hate you, who pursue you (Devarim 30:7). Says Rabbeinu Bachya[6]: Throughout history, Klal Yisrael has had two primary enemies, Yishmael and Eisav. These two are routinely vying to see who could be more vicious toward the Bnei Yisrael. Michah prophesied about them as well; referring to the two nations that will subjugate us and among whom we will be dispersed, Michah says, תָּרֹם יָדְךָ עַל צָרֶיךָ וְכָל אֹיְבֶיךָ יִכָּרֵתוּ, Your hand will be raised above your enemies, and all your adversaries will be eliminated.

Whom would you categorize as the שׂוֹנֵא and whom as the אוֹיֵב? We know that Eisav is the שׂוֹנֵא, since when Yaakov Avinu encounters him (Bereishis Ch. 33), Rashi there brings the Chazal that הֲלָכָה בְּיָדוּעַ עֵשׂוֹ שׂוֹנֵא לְיַעֲקֹב, It is a well-known halachah: Eisav is Yaakov's enemy. Thus, Yishmael is the אוֹיֵב and Eisav is the שׂוֹנֵא.

Rabbeinu Bachya says that an אוֹיֵב is much worse than a שׂוֹנֵא. A שׂוֹנֵא, even when inflicting pain, may still conduct himself in a somewhat merciful manner, with רַחֲמָנוּת, mercy. He may be cruel and hurtful, but may at times show mercy. However, an אוֹיֵב has a burning, eternal hatred that never wanes. He creates unbearable stress and will never show mercy. The word אוֹיֵב is a derivative of אֲבוֹי, which has the same letters, and is reminiscent of the cry אוֹי וַאֲבוֹי, oy-va-voy. When one sees the אוֹיֵב, he cries out, "Oy-va-voy." Yishmael is much worse than Eisav: he is the אוֹיֵב.

The Akeidah Gives Klal Yisrael Power Over Yishmael

After the *Akeidah*, the Ribbono shel Olam tells Avraham Avinu through the *malach*, וְיִרַשׁ זַרְעֲךָ, *and your offspring shall inherit*. Whose children are considered Avraham's offspring? Yitzchak's! אֶת שַׁעַר אֹיְבָיו, *the gates of its enemy*: To which enemy is this phrase referring? Yishmael! From now on you will win over and prevail against your אויב: Yishmael. The *Akeidah* gave us the tools with which we can now overcome the challenge of Yishmael.

Hashem promises Avraham that through the merit of the *Akeidah*, his children will inherit Eretz Yisrael, and will overcome the enmity of Yishmael. The ascendency of Klal Yisrael over Yishmael is brought about by the *Akeidah*. Let's understand why Yishmael's presence to the *Akeidah* was necessary for it to serve as the way to overcome him.

After Which Words Did the Akeidah Take Place?

As noted, the narrative of the *Akeidah* begins with the phrase וַיְהִי אַחַר הַדְּבָרִים הָאֵלֶּה, *And it was after these words*. This implies a connection to an earlier conversation. To what is this referring? Rashi[7] tells us (in his second *pshat*) that this narrative begins following a conversation that Yitzchak had with Yishmael.

Who Was More Moser Nefesh, Self-Sacrificing?

Rashi tells us that Yishmael and Yitzchak were arguing over who would be the spiritual heir of Avraham Avinu. Yishmael told Yitzchak that it all would come down to who sacrificed more for the ideals of the *Avos*. The superior *moser nefesh*, the one who was more self-sacrificing, would be the rightful heir. Yishmael gloated over Yitzchak, stating that he is better than

Yitzchak, that he is the true *eved Hashem*, Hashem's servant, since his *bris milah* took place when he was 13 years old, and he willingly agreed to proceed, while Yitzchak was a mere infant of eight days and had no other option. Therefore, said Yishmael, "I am the obvious choice to be the heir of Avraham Avinu." Thereupon Yitzchak declares, "Do you think you are frightening me with one limb that you sacrificed? Were Hashem to instruct me to slaughter myself, to give my whole entire body to Hashem, I would do so willingly! I would not delay!"

Yitzchak states that he would gladly sacrifice his entire body, not simply a single limb, for Hashem. Thus, says Yitzchak, I am the heir of Avraham Avinu. I am the true *eved Hashem*, as I am the greater *moser nefesh*.

The purpose of the *Akeidah* was thus intended to demonstrate to Yishmael that he is not the *eved Hashem* par excellence, but that Yitzchak is greater than him in his service of Hashem and superior in his *mesirus nefesh*.

This explains why the *pasuk* must say וְהָאֱלֹקִים נִסָּה אֶת אַבְרָהָם, *and Hashem tested Avraham*, and not "and Hashem tested Yitzchak." For all intents and purposes, Yitzchak had vowed that he would gladly be slaughtered if Hashem requested it. When this is followed by an instruction from Hashem to do just that, it can hardly be called a *nisayon*! He already committed himself to this, without being asked. This is not a test; rather, it is an opportunity for him to make good on his promise. Avraham Avinu, on the other hand, never promised to sacrifice his son! Thus, for him it definitely was a test.

❧ Why the Interruption Before the Akeidah?

However, there is a difficulty with this way of understanding what the phrase אַחַר הַדְּבָרִים הָאֵלֶּה is referring to. This conversation between Yitzchak and Yishmael, where Yishmael uses his *milah* as the evidence that he should be Avraham Avinu's heir, took place after each of them had had his *bris milah*. If so, the *parashah* of the *Akeidah* should immediately follow the *pesukim* about the *milah*! Why is the incident of Avimelech coming to Avraham to make a treaty (*Bereishis* 21:22) inserted into the Torah before the *Akeidah*?

The Rashbam explains the connection between the story of Avimelech and the *Akeidah*. He translates that the words אַחַר הַדְּבָרִים הָאֵלֶּה as *It happened after these things*, referring to the treaty Avraham made with Avimelech. Rashbam writes that Hashem was very displeased with Avraham Avinu for making a treaty with Avimelech, thereby granting him land in Eretz Yisrael, which Hashem had gifted to Avraham and his descendants for the *Yidden* to live there! As a punishment, Hashem then told Avraham to bring his son as an offering. וְהָאֱלֹקִים נִסָּה אֶת אַבְרָהָם, *and Hashem tested Avraham*. The Rashbam tells us that the word נִסָּה, *test*, connotes torment. Hashem was tormenting Avraham because of the treaty he made. Hashem was telling Avraham that he had no right to give portions of Eretz Yisrael to non-Jews. According to the Rashbam, the flow from one incident to the next is understandable and clear.

But this is not what Rashi says. Rashi says that the *Akeidah* follows the conversation between Yishmael and Yitzchak, which took place after the *bris milah*. Why, then, does the Torah interject the story of Avraham and Avimelech making a treaty? This is the question of Rav Yaakov Kamenetsky in *Emes L'Yaakov*.[8]

ও *Who Sees What I See?*

When Avraham was on the way to the *Akeidah*, the Torah says, וַיַּרְא אֶת הַמָּקוֹם מֵרָחֹק, *[Avraham] perceived the place from afar* (*Bereishis* 22:4). Says the *Daas Zekeinim MiBaalei Tosafos*[9]: The *Midrash* tells us[10] that the word הַמָּקוֹם, *the place*, refers to the *Shechinah*. Avraham says to Yitzchak, "Do you see what I see?" Yitzchak responds that of course he sees the mountain and the cloud covering it. Avraham then turns to his lads with the same query, "Do you see what I see?" And their response is, "What should I see?" Avraham asks, "Do you not see the *Shechinah*?" "No, I don't see anything," was the answer. Avraham Avinu replies, "Yitzchak and I see the cloud representing the *Shechinah*, but you don't. This is something you have in common with the *chamor*, the donkey. The *chamor* does not see the *Shechinah*, and you don't see the *Shechinah*. שְׁבוּ לָכֶם פֹּה עִם הַחֲמוֹר, *Stay here by yourselves with the donkey.* You and the donkey are equally spiritually handicapped — you are on the same *madreigah*, spiritual level."

Yishmael's connection to the *Har HaBayis* is similar to the connection of a *chamor*. At times a donkey may find its way onto the *Har HaBayis*; so, too, Yishmael may occasionally be found there. That is the sum total of his connection.

Since Yishmael could not see the *Shechinah* and could not appreciate the *Kedushas Har HaBayis*, he obviously can have absolutely no claim to Eretz Yisrael. There can be no doubt that Yishmael, who is likened to a *chamor*, has no stake whatsoever in Eretz Yisrael.

❧ *Does Milah Give Yishmael a Claim?*

However, on further reflection, there is one *zechus*, merit, that the *bnei Yishmael* have, and one might think that this one merit gives them some right to Eretz Yisrael. This *zechus* is *bris milah*, the very subject debated between Yitzchak and Yishmael prior to the *Akeidah*. Yishmael himself thought that the *milah* gave him a right to Eretz Yisrael.

In *Emes L'Yaakov*, Rav Yaakov Kamenetsky[11] quotes the *Zohar*, who writes that for four hundred years the angel of Yishmael came and stood before Hashem, asking Hashem if someone who has a *bris milah* has a connection to Him. As a result, Hashem granted Yishmael a portion in Eretz Yisrael in the merit of his *milah*, and therefore Yishmael ruled over Eretz Yisrael, forestalling the return of Bnei Yisrael. The Zohar states that Yishmael eventually will be the cause of great wars in the world. Hashem will then ultimately demonstrate His superiority and His Sovereignty over Yishmael and Mashiach will come. Then — בַּיּוֹם הַהוּא יִהְיֶה ה' אֶחָד וּשְׁמוֹ אֶחָד, *on that day Hashem will be One* and *His Name will be One* (*Zechariah* 14:9). The Zohar is telling us that Yishmael's sole *zechus* to Eretz Yisrael is *bris milah*.

Yishmael says that Eretz Yisrael, Yerushalayim, and the *Har HaBayis* are his because of his sacrifice in performing the *bris milah* at the age of 13, which, he says, trumps Yitzchak's *bris milah* at a mere 8 days, without any knowledge of what a *bris* is.

◈ *Pilishtim = Areilim;*
It Is NOT About the Milah

However, Rav Yaakov Kamenetsky continues:[12] At this point, after Yishmael's claim of superiority, the Torah advises us to take a closer look at the peace treaty between Avraham and Avimelech.

Avimelech was the king of the Pilishtim. What is the distinguishing characteristic of a Pilishti? Whenever the Pilishtim are discussed in Tanach, the word used to describe them is עֲרֵלִים, *areilim*: uncircumcised.

We see this in multiple places in Tanach; e.g., in *Shoftim*, in *Shmuel*, and in *Divrei HaYamim*. All these contain discussions about the Pilishtim and refer to them as *areilim*. The quintessential symbol of עֲרֵלוֹת, *arelos*, the uncircumcised, is the Pilishti.

By inserting the incident of the treaty with the Pilishtim into this precise spot, the Torah is telling us that we should not be too troubled by the fact that Yishmael has a *bris milah*. Don't be concerned about this merit. The *milah* is not that important. Just look at the Pilishtim, who are *areilim*, and yet they have a portion in Eretz Yisrael. We see that the *zechus* of *milah* is not the most important factor in staking a claim to Eretz Yisrael. This incident is the foreword to the *Akeidah*: Don't worry about the *bris milah* — that is not at all the critical ingredient. The proof is that the Pilishtim, who *are* uncircumcised, *did* have a portion in Eretz Yisrael.

The *Akeidah* is the medium through which Hashem demonstrates who has control over Eretz Yisrael and the *Har HaBayis* for eternity. While Hashem tested Avraham, יִצְחָק נִיסָה אֶת יִצְחָק, Yitzchak himself tested Yitzchak.

✑ *Avraham Must Choose*

When Hashem informs Avraham about the *Akeidah*, Avraham wonders if the fact that he already sent away Yishmael is not already a clear message as to whom he has selected as his heir, and as the heir of Eretz Yisrael. Hashem informs Avraham that the action of sending away Yishmael did not project this message, because Avraham did not send out Yishmael because he felt with the utmost conviction that Yishmael was not his spiritual heir. Avraham sent away Hagar and Yishmael simply because Hashem told him to listen to Sarah. Avraham did not overtly select Yitzchak over Yishmael; he just followed the command to send away Hagar and Yishmael.

Through the *Akeidah*, Hashem gave Avraham a clear message. Hashem wanted Avraham to openly, clearly, and explicitly dictate that Yitzchak will be his only heir.

Hashem therefore had Yishmael return to Avraham's house for one night, right before the *Akeidah*. Hashem then tells Avraham, קַח נָא אֶת בִּנְךָ אֶת יְחִידְךָ אֲשֶׁר אָהַבְתָּ, and Avraham thinks that perhaps, because of the timing, Hashem is referring to Yishmael. Hashem says that He is absolutely not referring to anyone other than Yitzchak. Using all these adjectives clearly conveys Hashem's message to Avraham that He considers him to only have one son upon whom to shower his love

When Avraham was commanded to perform the *Akeidah*, it was not enough for him to take only Yitzchak but he had to take both Yitzchak and Yishmael, and then leave one of them behind, sending the message that his brother is superior. In addition, Avraham also was to convey to Yishmael that he is actually so unworthy as to be considered like a *chamor*! Yishmael had to be rejected, and not just because Avraham listened to Sarah. It must be clearly understood that Yishmael has no connection to Eretz Yisrael! He has no connection to the *Har HaBayis*! He cannot even *see* the *kedushah* of the *Har HaBayis* whereas Yitzchak and Avraham can. Regarding the *Har HaBayis*, Yishmael is comparable to the donkey.

The *Akeidah* proves that Yitzchak is connected to the *Har HaBayis*, to Yerushalayim, and to Eretz Yisrael. Yishmael is actively excluded.

Christians do not tamper with the Torah text, in what they refer to as the Old Testament. The Yishmaelites, on the other hand, change the narrative of the *Akeidah*, replacing Yitzchak's name with that of Yishmael. Why do they alter the narrative? It is because this incident as written in the Torah proves the superiority and ascendency of Klal Yisrael over the bnei Yishmael, thereby giving us rightful claim to the *Har HaBayis*. The bnei Yishmael apparently understand that this narrative is more than a simple story; it is the battle for the rights to the holiest place on earth! That is why they place Yishmael into the text.

Yes, the *Akeidah* was a test for Avraham. But it was also a self-imposed challenge to Yitzchak so that he can overcome Yishmael. Hashem is orchestrating everything. בִּנְךָ אֶת יְחִידְךָ אֲשֶׁר אָהַבְתָּ can refer only to Yitzchak. And as for Yishmael, גָּרֵשׁ הָאָמָה הַזֹּאת וְאֶת בְּנָהּ, *drive out this slave-women with her son* (Bereishis 21:10). And what will you eventually tell him? שְׁבוּ לָכֶם פֹּה עִם הַחֲמוֹר. Yishmael has no connection with the *Har HaBayis*. Even the Pilishtim, who are *areilim*, have a portion in Eretz Yisrael. Yishmael's *milah* will not benefit him.

Now we can understand what takes place at the end of the *Akeidah*. The *Akeidah* concludes with the words וְיִרַשׁ זַרְעֲךָ אֵת שַׁעַר אֹיְבָיו, *and your offspring shall inherit the gate of its enemy*, demonstrating that we will inherit our enemy, but it is not referring to Eisav here. Eisav is not relevant to the chronicle of the *Akeidah*. Through the *Akeidah* we gained the merit needed to overcome our אֹיֵב — who is none other than Yishmael.

As noted above, the *malach* returns to tell Avraham, כִּי בָרֵךְ אֲבָרֶכְךָ וְהַרְבָּה אַרְבֶּה אֶת זַרְעֲךָ כְּכוֹכְבֵי הַשָּׁמַיִם וְכַחוֹל אֲשֶׁר עַל שְׂפַת הַיָּם וְיִרַשׁ זַרְעֲךָ אֵת שַׁעַר אֹיְבָיו, Hashem *will surely bless you and greatly increase your offspring like the stars of the heavens and like the* sand on the seashore and your offspring shall inherit the gate of its enemy (ibid. 22:17). Thus, for all eternity, when Yishmael and his descendants say that they want Eretz Yisrael, that they want the *Har HaBayis*, we inform them that they have no claim. They have *milah*, but we have true *mesirus nefesh*. We serve Hashem בְּכָל לְבַבְכֶם וּבְכָל נַפְשְׁכֶם (*Devarim* 11:13), prepared to give up everything, even our lives, for Hashem.

Yishmael's being there that day was no coincidence; it was carefully orchestrated by the Ribbono shel Olam. Choosing Yitzchak becomes a decision and a choice only if there is a second option. Choosing the only option is not making a choice and is not showing preference. Therefore, Yishmael had to be there to allow Avraham to demonstrate that he was making a choice, and he was choosing Yitzchak. Yishmael had to be there for Hashem to say, בִּנְךָ אֶת יְחִידְךָ אֲשֶׁר אָהַבְתָּ is not *that* son! He is *this* one! He is Yitzchak. And that other son? He is compared to a *chamor*!

‌‌ *Hagar Disrespects Sarai —* *With Consequences — and We Pay the Price*

In *Parashas Lech Lecha*, we learn that Avram and Sarai were married for many years without having been blessed with children. Sarai then came to Avram with an idea: Why don't you marry Hagar? אוּלַי אִבָּנֶה מִמֶּנָּה, *perhaps I will be built up through her* (*Bereishis* 16:2). Hagar conceived immediately, and the Torah tells us, וַתֵּרֶא כִּי הָרָתָה וַתֵּקַל גְּבִרְתָּהּ בְּעֵינֶיהָ, *and when she saw that she had conceived, her mistress was lowered in her esteem* (ibid. v. 4). Rashi states[13] that Hagar made disparaging remarks to Sarai, calling her a hypocrite, pretending to be a *tzaddekes* and behaving as if she were truly righteous. Hagar said that if Sarai really were a *tzaddekes*, how is it that after so many years of marriage she did not have a child, while she, Hagar, had conceived immediately? It must be that Hagar was the true *tzaddekes* here.

Such comments hurt Sarai, and she said to Avram, "חֲמָסִי עָלֶיךָ, *The outrage against me is due to you!*" (ibid. v. 5). Why didn't you defend me? Avram responded, "הִנֵּה שִׁפְחָתֵךְ בְּיָדֵךְ עֲשִׂי לָהּ הַטּוֹב

בְּעֵינָיִךְ, *Behold!— your maidservant is in your hand; do to her as you see fit."* וַתְּעַנֶּהָ שָׂרַי, *And Sarai dealt harshly with her* (ibid. v. 6). Sarai afflicted Hagar, insulted her, and caused her pain. Immediately after this a *malach* came to Hagar and told her that she will give birth to a son, וְהוּא יִהְיֶה פֶּרֶא אָדָם, *and he shall be a wild-ass of a man.*

Says the Ramban,[14] it is not a coincidence that the announcement that Hagar would have a son, whom she should name Yishmael and who will be a פֶּרֶא אָדָם, comes immediately after וַתְּעַנֶּהָ שָׂרַי. The reason we suffer at the hands of Yishmael to this day is because Hashem is punishing us for how Sarai treated Hagar. The Ramban maintains that Sarai sinned by causing Hagar pain. Hagar then had a son Yishmael who would cause Klal Yisrael so much pain and anguish. The Ramban tells us that Avram, too, is at fault for allowing it to happen. Hashem heard her painful cries, and gave her a son who would be wild and who would cause excessive pain to the descendants of Avram with all types of suffering.

Sarai caused Hagar pain, and *middah k'neged middah*, measure for measure, Hashem allows Yishmael to cause us pain. According to the Ramban, all the pain and suffering that Klal Yisrael experiences at the hands of Yishmael is a result of וַתְּעַנֶּהָ שָׂרַי.

℘ *The Riva and Ramban Disagree: Sarai Was Right*

However, the Riva[15] disagrees with the Ramban. The Riva writes that Sarai was justified in paying Hagar back in kind. וַתֵּקַל גְּבִרְתָּהּ בְּעֵינֶיהָ; Hagar had hurt and insulted Sarai, and Sarai was allowed to insult and pain her in return. This is according to the position of the Smag, who writes that revenge for a monetary loss is prohibited, but one is allowed to take revenge if someone hurts his feelings. Someone who insults another Jew is not included in עֲמִיתֶךָ, *your friend,** and it is therefore permissible to take revenge.

------

* See *Vayikra* 19:17.

The Abarbanel[16] quotes the Ramban, but he agrees with the Riva. Sarai did do the right thing. The way to help someone fix a bad character trait is to take them to the other extreme. Hagar became very haughty and arrogant toward Sarai. Sarai had to then humiliate her to put her in her place. In doing so, Sarai did not sin.

❧ Hagar Repents Many Generations Later

There is an astounding incident recounted in the writings of the *Arizal* that is referred to by some of the *Rishonim* as well (see *Moadim U'Zemanim*,[17] where Rav Moshe Shternbuch also brings this story). The *Chida* often quotes *Rishonim* whose manuscripts were not discovered until this century. One such *Rishon*, whose writings we did not have but whom the *Chida* quotes in his *sefer, Maaras HaAyin*, was R' Yaakov Skili.

The *Chida*[18] tells us that R' Yaakov Skili, a *talmid* of the *Rashba*, documented the story of Yishai, who was a descendent of Moav. He relied on the same *pasuk* that Boaz had relied upon when he held that Rus was permitted to marry into Klal Yisrael (see *Devarim* 23:4). Therefore, Yishai maintained that his children were the continuation of *Malchus Yehudah*. However, toward the end of his life Yishai became concerned that perhaps Doeg was right, and Boaz was really not allowed to marry Rus. He decided to separate from his wife of many decades. He then propositioned his maidservant, with the understanding that any children they would have together would be slaves. They could subsequently be freed, which would then render them into true, kosher, and pure members of Klal Yisrael, without the stigma of being descendants of Moav.

However, this maidservant was very loyal to Yishai's wife, and she informed her of her husband's intentions. She then gave her clothing to Yishai's wife, who masqueraded as her and proceeded to rendezvous with her husband, while he thought he was with the maidservant. David HaMelech was conceived that night. A few months later, when it was clear to all that Yishai's wife had conceived, everyone — especially Yishai's sons, who knew he had separated from his wife — thought that she had committed adultery (as she had not been given a *get*). Yishai's sons wanted to impose the death penalty on their mother, because they were certain she had been adulterous, but Yishai discouraged them from doing so.

When David was born, his brothers *paskened* that he was a *mamzer*, illegitimate. As the *pasuk* states, מוּזָר הָיִיתִי לְאֶחָי, *I became a stranger to my brothers* (*Tehillim* 69:9). When he was born, they threw him to the dogs, as David writes, הַצִּילָה מֵחֶרֶב נַפְשִׁי מִיַּד כֶּלֶב יְחִידָתִי, *Rescue my soul from the sword, my essence from the grip of the dog* (ibid. 22:21). It is possible that they did not know he was of pure lineage until Shmuel HaNavi came and told them that not only is David legitimate, but he will also become the king of Klal Yisrael (see *I Shmuel* 16:12-13).

We have a debt of gratitude to the maidservant of Yishai who informed his wife of her husband's intentions. Had she not done so, we may never have had a David HaMelech or even perhaps Mashiach! Then the *Chida* tells us something incredible. He writes in the name of the *Rama MiFano* that Yishai's maidservant, who subjugated herself to her mistress, was a *gilgul* of Hagar, who came back to This World to rectify the attitude of superiority she had displayed toward Sarai. She came back to rectify the sin that she committed by lowering Sarai in her esteem. She returned to This World to rectify this by subjugating herself to Yishai's wife.

ꕥ *Two Mashiachs*

We learn from many sources (e.g., *Medrash Shocher Tov*,[19] Rashi in *Zechariah*,[20] and the *Arizal*[21]) that the final *galus* is a dual exile, of both Edom (Eisav) and Yishmael. We are currently witnessing the transition from *Galus Edom* to *Galus Yishmael*. We see the ascendency of Yishmael in the world today.

We are also taught that we are going to merit two Mashiachs, namely Mashiach ben Yosef and Mashiach ben David.

Why are two Mashiachs needed? The Vilna Gaon,[22] in his

commentary on *Safra D'Tzniusa*, discusses the need for both of them. Eisav, Edom is referred to as פָּרִים אַבִּירִים, *a mighty ox*. As we saw, Yishmael is called a *chamor*. So Eisav is called an ox and Yishmael is called a donkey.

The Vilna Gaon tells us that this is why we must be very careful not to plow with an ox and a donkey together! If Eisav and Yishmael ever work together, if they ever get along, together they will destroy the world. *Baruch Hashem*, they don't get along. The Torah tells us, in the laws of *kilayim*, prohibited or forbidden mixtures, לֹא תַחֲרֹשׁ בְּשׁוֹר וּבַחֲמֹר יַחְדָּו, *You shall not plow with an ox and a donkey together* (*Devarim* 22:10). The ox is Eisav and the donkey is Yishmael.

Therefore, says the Vilna Gaon, we will have two Mashiachs: Mashiach ben Yosef and Mashiach ben David. Yosef is called an ox, as the *pasuk* says, בְּכוֹר שׁוֹרוֹ הָדָר לוֹ, *A sovereignty is his oxlike one* (*Devarim* 33:17). David is called עָנִי וְרֹכֵב עַל חֲמוֹר, *a humble man riding upon a donkey* (*Zechariah* 9:9). Thus, Mashiach ben Yosef will take us out of *Galus Edom*, and Mashiach ben David will take us out of *Galus Yishmael*.

The *Rama MiFano* quoted above says that Hagar came back to this world in the guise of Yishai's maidservant to rectify her having humiliated Avram's wife. Therefore, she came back and subjugated herself to Yishai's wife.

Now we may ask an even more fundamental and perhaps more important question: Wasn't there something more vital for Hagar to correct? How could Hagar rectify the catastrophic issue of having brought the *chamor*, Yishmael, into this world to torment the *Yidden*?

Hagar rectified this sin by helping bring the antidote to the *chamor* into this world as well. By revealing Yishai's intentions to his wife, Hagar brought about the birth of the humble man riding upon a donkey: David HaMelech, who is the one who will save us from *Galus Yishmael*, from the *chamor*. She came back not only to rectify her sin of how she treated Sarai, but also to help eradicate Yishmael, the *chamor*, that she had previously brought into the world.

❧ Why Did Rabbi Akiva Laugh?

At the end of *Makkos*,[23] the Gemara relates an incident regarding Tannaim who went to the *Har HaBayis*, where they witnessed a painful, frightening scene. They saw foxes running about in the ruins, and they began to weep. They said, מָקוֹם שֶׁכָּתוּב בּוֹ "וְהַזָּר הַקָּרֵב יוּמָת", *A place about which it says that a stranger who enters will die*, now has foxes walking around!? And Rabbi Akiva laughed. What's the meaning of this Gemara? Why is Rabbi Akiva laughing?

A *talmid* of the *Rama MiFano*, R' Binyamin Vitale, writes in his *sefer Alon Bachos*: Do you know who these foxes are? The word שועלים, *foxes*, has the same *gematria*, and even the same letters, as the word *Yishmael* (without the *aleph*). When seeing Yishmael on the *Har HaBayis*, we are reminded that Yishmael's connection to the *Har HaBayis* consists of only שְׁבוּ לָכֶם פֹּה עִם הַחֲמוֹר. He has no spiritual connection whatsoever. Yishmael's perception of *kedushah* is on the same level as that of the *chamor*. Rabbi Akiva laughed because he knew that once the chamor Yishmael laid his stakes to the *Har HaBayis*, it is only a matter of time before the עָנִי וְרֹכֵב עַל חֲמוֹר comes and demonstrates our ascendancy. Rabbi Akiva knew that in the end it will be *chamor* (Yishmael) vs. the man riding the *chamor* (Mashiach) — first Yishmael's rule, followed soon after by Mashiach ben David.

The *Baal HaTurim* says[24] that *Parashas Chayei Sarah* concludes with the words, עַל פְּנֵי כָל אֶחָיו נָפָל, *over all his brothers [Yishmael] dwelt*, while *Parashas Toldos* begins, וְאֵלֶּה תּוֹלְדֹת יִצְחָק , *And these are the offspring of Yitzchak*. This tells us that after Yishmael will fall, at the End of Days, then Mashiach ben David, who is מִתּוֹלְדוֹת יִצְחָק, will sprout.

When will Klal Yisrael merit to see the flourishing of Mashiach ben David? When will we be *zocheh* to see the triumph of וְאֵלֶּה תּוֹלְדֹת יִצְחָק? Only when עַל פְּנֵי כָל אֶחָיו נָפָל! Only when Yishmael falls! Edom will fall first, through the salvation of Mashiach ben Yosef. Then Yishmael will fall through the coming of Mashiach ben David.

May we be *zocheh* to witness the עַל פְּנֵי כָל אֶחָיו נָפָל. We should see the fall of all the enemies of Klal Yisrael, Eisav, our שׂוֹנֵא, and especially Yishmael, our אוֹיֵב. And we should be *zocheh* to וְאֵלֶּה תּוֹלְדֹת יִצְחָק, to see the sprouting of Mashiach ben David, שֶׁיָּבֹא בִּמְהֵרָה בְּיָמֵינוּ, אָמֵן!

ENDNOTES

12. אמת ליעקב שם.
13. בראשית טז, ד.
14. בראשית טז, ו.
15. פירוש הריב"א על בראשית פרק טז, ו.
16. אברבנאל על בראשית פרק טז, א-טז.
17. מועדים וזמנים חלק ז סימן רמב.
18. מראית העין חיד"א פסחים דף קיט.
19. תהלים ו, ב.
20. זכריה ה, יא.
21. ספר ליקוטי תורה, פרשת כי תצא.
22. פירוש הגר"א על ספרא דצניעותא.
23. מכות כד, ב.
24. בעל הטורים בראשית פרק כה, יח.

1. בעלי התוספות, וירא, פרק כב פסוק א אות ט.
2. בעלי התוספות, וירא, פרק כב פסוק ג אות ט.
3. בראשית כב, ג.
4. קדושין סח, א.
5. שבו לכם פה עם החמור.
6. רבינו בחיי פרשת נצבים ל, ז: על אויביך ועל שונאיך.
7. בראשית כב, א.
8. בראשית שם.
9. בראשית כב, ה.
10. בראשית רבה נו, ב.
11. אמת ליעקב בראשית כב:א.

"The Great Shofar": The Ramchal Reveals the Universal Reverberations of the Shofar

⤴ *Malchiyos, Zichronos, Shofaros*

Two central parts of our *avodah* on Rosh Hashanah are the mitzvah of *tekias shofar* and the expanded *Tefillas Mussaf*. On Rosh Hashanah, three special *berachos* are inserted in the *Shemoneh Esrei* of Mussaf: *Malchiyos*, *Zichronos*, and *Shofaros*. During the *tefillah* of *Malchiyos*, we declare God's sovereignty over the world and we proclaim Him as our King. The *berachah* of *Zichronos* delineates Hashem's Divine Providence and His Omniscience, knowledge, and control of history. *Shofaros* encompasses the concept of the shofar.

The importance of the shofar on Rosh Hashanah is self-evident. The one and only mitzvah *d'Oraisa* on Rosh Hashanah is the mitzvah of shofar.

During the *tefillah* of *Shofaros*, we recite ten *pesukim* from Tanach that mention the shofar.

The introduction to the *berachah* of *Shofaros* reads:

אַתָּה נִגְלֵיתָ בַּעֲנַן כְּבוֹדֶךָ	You were revealed in Your Cloud of Glory
עַל עַם קָדְשֶׁךָ	to Your holy people
לְדַבֵּר עִמָּם	to speak to them.
מִן הַשָּׁמַיִם	From the heavens,
הִשְׁמַעְתָּם קוֹלֶךָ	You let them hear Your voice,
וְנִגְלֵיתָ עֲלֵיהֶם	and revealed Yourself to them
בְּעַרְפְּלֵי טֹהַר	in thick, pure clouds.
גַּם כָּל הָעוֹלָם כֻּלּוֹ חָל מִפָּנֶיךָ	So too, the entire world trembled before You,
וּבְרִיּוֹת בְּרֵאשִׁית	and the works of creation
חָרְדוּ מִמֶּךָ	trembled before You,
בְּהִגָּלוֹתְךָ מַלְכֵּנוּ	when You, our King, revealed Yourself
עַל־הַר סִינַי	upon Mount Sinai
לְלַמֵּד לְעַמְּךָ תּוֹרָה וּמִצְוֹת	to teach Your people Torah and mitzvos.

This introduction clearly refers to *Mattan Torah*, when Hashem gave us the Torah on Har Sinai.

✑ *Why Reference Kabbalas HaTorah on Rosh Hashanah?*

Why do we emphasize *kabbalas haTorah* as a central theme on Rosh Hashanah? Would this *tefillah* not be better suited for the *davening* on Shavuos? Why would *Shofaros*, in the central *tefillah* of Rosh Hashanah, begin with a description of *kabbalas haTorah*?

Let us examine the *pesukim* in the *berachah* of *Shofaros*:

כַּכָּתוּב בְּתוֹרָתֶךָ	as it is written in Your Torah:
וַיְהִי בַיּוֹם הַשְּׁלִישִׁי	"And it was on the third day,
בִּהְיֹת הַבֹּקֶר	as morning dawned
וַיְהִי קֹלֹת וּבְרָקִים	there was thunder and lightning,
וְעָנָן כָּבֵד עַל הָהָר	and a dense cloud over the mountain,
וְקֹל שֹׁפָר	and the sound of a shofar
חָזָק מְאֹד	was exceedingly loud;

וַיֶּחֱרַד כָּל הָעָם אֲשֶׁר בַּמַּחֲנֶה. and all the people in the camp trembled."

Once again, we reference *Mattan Torah,* and now we mention the shofar that was heard at Har Sinai.

The second *pasuk* brought in this *berachah* is also a reference to *kabbalas haTorah:*

וְנֶאֱמַר	And it is said:
וַיְהִי קוֹל הַשֹּׁפָר	"And the sound of the shofar
הוֹלֵךְ וְחָזֵק מְאֹד	became increasingly louder;
מֹשֶׁה יְדַבֵּר	Moshe spoke
וְהָאֱלֹקִים יַעֲנֶנּוּ בְקוֹל:	and God answered him by voice."

The third *pasuk* continues this theme:

וְנֶאֱמַר	And it is said:
וְכָל הָעָם רֹאִים אֶת הַקּוֹלֹת	"And all the people saw the sounds
וְאֶת הַלַּפִּידִם	and the flames,
וְאֶת קוֹל הַשֹּׁפָר	and the sound of the shofar,
וְאֶת הָהָר עָשֵׁן	and the mountain in smoke;
וַיַּרְא הָעָם וַיָּנֻעוּ	and the people saw and were shaken,
וַיַּעַמְדוּ מֵרָחֹק:	and stood from afar."

Thus, we see that the first three *pesukim* of *Shofaros* that contain the word shofar refer to the shofar that was heard at *Mattan Torah.* This is extremely curious, since this has nothing to do with Rosh Hashanah. On Rosh Hashanah we blow the shofar because the Ribbono shel Olam gave us the mitzvah of *tekias shofar.* Why would we invoke the shofar of *kabbalas haTorah*? The shofar of Har Sinai and the shofar of Rosh Hashanah reflect two completely different concepts that are seemingly unrelated.

What, then, is the connection between the shofar of Rosh Hashanah and the shofar of *kabbalas haTorah*?

❧ *The Shofar of L'asid Lavo*

The *pasuk* states: וְהָיָה בַּיּוֹם הַהוּא יִתָּקַע בְּשׁוֹפָר גָּדוֹל וּבָאוּ הָאֹבְדִים בְּאֶרֶץ אַשּׁוּר וְהַנִּדָּחִים בְּאֶרֶץ מִצְרָיִם וְהִשְׁתַּחֲווּ לַה' בְּהַר הַקֹּדֶשׁ בִּירוּשָׁלָם. *And it will be on that day, He will blow the great shofar, and all those lost in the land of Assyria will come, and all those cast away in* the land of Egypt, and they will bow down to Hashem at the holy mountain in Yerushalayim (*Yeshayah* 27:13). This is another of the ten *pesukim* that we recite in the *berachah* of *Shofaros*. In contrast to the *pesukim* mentioned above, the shofar in this *pasuk* refers to the shofar of Mashiach, in the time of *L'asid Lavo*, in the future.

Why do we mention the shofar that will be blown to herald the coming of Mashiach when we are reciting the *berachah* of *Shofaros* describing the shofar of Rosh Hashanah? Why do we include a reference to the shofar of *kibutz galiyos*, the gathering of the exiles, in our *tefillos* on Rosh Hashanah?

≈ Shofar Gadol: The Great Shofar

In our daily *Shemoneh Esrei*, we *daven*: תְּקַע בְּשׁוֹפָר גָּדוֹל לְחֵרוּתֵנוּ, וְשָׂא נֵס לְקַבֵּץ גָּלֻיוֹתֵינוּ, וְקַבְּצֵנוּ יַחַד מֵאַרְבַּע כַּנְפוֹת הָאָרֶץ. *Sound the great shofar for our freedom and raise the banner to gather our exiles, and gather us together from the four corners of the earth*. The shofar that will be sounded *L'asid Lavo* is called the *Shofar HaGadol*, the Great Shofar. Why is this shofar specifically given the title *great*?

≈ Two Sets of Shofar Blasts

The Gemara[1] discusses the two sets of *tekios* that we sound on Rosh Hashanah. The *tekios d'meyushav*, the *tekios* that are permitted to be listened to while sitting, are blown before *Shemoneh Esrei*. The *tekios d'meumad*, the *tekios* while standing, are blown during *chazaras hashatz*.

The Gemara explains that the reason we blow both sets is to confuse the *Satan*. And, in fact, the Gemara states[2] that any year that does not begin with the blowing of these two sets of *tekios* will not be a good year, as the *Satan* will not be confused. Tosafos[3] asks: What is so confusing to the *Satan*? Why does blowing two sets of *tekios* confuse him? Tosafos answers that, on Rosh Hashanah, when the shofar is sounded for the first time, the *Satan* begins to be befuddled. He does not know why the shofar is being sounded. When he then hears the second set of *tekios*, he concludes that this most certainly must be the *Shofar*

HaGadol, the Great Shofar of Mashiach. The time has come, he thinks, for his services to come to an end. He is no longer needed to induce people to sin and then to prosecute them for having sinned. This results in a degree of confusion that preoccupies the *Satan*, and he is no longer able to prosecute us before Hashem.

✑ Why Is the Satan Fooled Year After Year?

The *Satan* is smart, and he utilizes creative tactics in his efforts to instigate a person to sin. The *Satan* is able to convince people to forgo their *Olam Haba*, their eternal reward, for the transient pleasure they may receive from committing a specific *aveirah*. How can he be so fooled as to think our shofar is the *Shofar HaGadol* of Mashiach, especially on the second day of Rosh Hashanah? Once the shofar of the first day did not herald the coming of Mashiach, shouldn't he have figured out that it is not the sound of Mashiach's Shofar? And furthermore, from year to year, does the *Satan* not recall that we blew the same shofar last year and the years before that, and nevertheless we did not experience the *Geulah*?

Why is the *Satan* so confused? There must be a strong similarity between the shofar we blow in shul and the *Shofar HaGadol* of Mashiach, and that is why he continues to be fooled, year after year.

✑ Avoid a Shofar With a Hole

Halachah states[4] that if the body of a shofar develops a hole that is not repaired, even if the sound is changed as a result of the hole, the shofar is kosher. However, says the Rema, if one has another shofar without a hole in its body, it is preferable that he not use the shofar with the hole. The Rema reasons that there are some *poskim* who are of the opinion that one should never use a shofar with a hole in its body; therefore, even though the *Shulchan Aruch* rules its use is acceptable, one should not use it if he has another shofar available that does not have a hole.

❧ Why Does a Hole Make the Shofar Pasul?

What is the rationale behind the *poskim* who rule that a small hole in a shofar renders it *pasul*? The Torah never states that a shofar must be *shaleim*, whole.

The Vilna Gaon[5] quotes a *midrash* stating that if the hole is an impediment to the sound, even though the opening has been plugged, then the shofar is *pasul*. If, however, the sound is not altered, then the shofar is valid for use. The shofar with the hole is *pasul* based on the *pasuk*: וַה' עֲלֵיהֶם יֵרָאֶה וְיָצָא כַבָּרָק חִצּוֹ וַה' בַּשׁוֹפָר יִתְקָע וְהָלַךְ בְּסַעֲרוֹת תֵּימָן, *Hashem will appear to them, and His arrow will go forth like lightning; and the Lord will blow with a shofar and go forth in southern tempests* (Zechariah 9:14). The shofar in this *pasuk* is the shofar of *Techiyas HaMeisim*. The Vilna Gaon understands that the Shofar of Hashem is a complete shofar, without any cracks or holes. Therefore, since Hashem's Shofar does not have any cracks or holes, the shofar we use on Rosh Hashanah should also be free of cracks and holes. The shofar we use must resemble the Shofar of Hashem.

Why must the shofar we use on Rosh Hashanah resemble the Shofar of Hashem that will be sounded at *Techiyas HaMeisim*? Our shofar is not being used to awaken those who have passed away, so why do the same conditions apply to it? For no other mitzvah do we find a requirement to perform the mitzvah in a certain fashion because that is how Hashem would do it, so let us investigate why this is required specifically in regard to the shofar of Rosh Hashanah.

❧ The Ram of Avraham Avinu

Avraham Avinu was commanded by the Ribbono shel Olam to bring Yitzchak as an offering. When Hashem saw Avraham was prepared to slaughter his precious son on His command, He told Avraham that he had passed the test and he should not harm Yitzchak in any way. Avraham then wanted to bring a *korban* to Hashem, and he noticed a ram entangled in the bushes nearby, which he then offered as a *korban* in place of his son (see

Bereishis Ch. 22). *Pirkei D'Rabbi Eliezer*[6] informs us what was done with the two horns of the ram Avraham Avinu offered. They were both used as Hashem's Shofars. The Shofar made from the left horn was sounded by Hashem at Har Sinai when the Torah was given. The larger, right horn was made into the Shofar that will be used at the time of Mashiach to herald the ingathering of all the Jews from the four corners of the world. When we say, *Teka b'shofar gadol* in *Shemoneh Esrei*, the term *shofar gadol* refers to this Shofar — the Shofar that will be used in the time of Mashiach.

Why was it necessary that these two *Shofaros* originate from the same animal? Why couldn't one Shofar have been procured from one ram, and the second Shofar from a second ram? The fact that they originated from the same animal is indicative of a connection between the Shofar of Mashiach and the Shofar of *Mattan Torah*. In what way are they connected?

∾ *The Revolutionary Approach of the Ramchal*

Rav Moshe Chaim Luzzatto, the Ramchal, authored *Maamer HaChachmah*, a remarkable work on the *davening* of Rosh Hashanah and Yom Kippur. In this short volume, the Ramchal completely revolutionizes our understanding of the Yamim Noraim, the mitzvah of shofar, and the *tefillos* we offer on these hallowed days.

He writes[7] that blowing the shofar on Rosh Hashanah is so powerful, its effects reverberate throughout creation. The shofar's *koach* boosts the forces of good and subdues the forces of evil. These good and evil forces were created to exist in opposition to each other, as separate entities. However, when Adam and Chavah sinned, good and evil became intermingled. The forces of evil overtook and overpowered the forces of good. When Hashem gave us the Torah, the good extricated itself from the clutches of evil. Good then gained momentum and set out to conquer evil. When the Torah was given, it was the sounding of the shofar that prompted the good to attempt to break free. The shofar served as the signal for the good to cast off the shackles of evil and strive to rid the world of all wrongdoing.

However, the good only succeeded in escaping from the influence of evil, thus achieving independence. It was unable to destroy evil. There will eventually be a time when the good will be able to completely vanquish and eliminate the forces of evil from the world. *L'asid Lavo*, in the Time to Come, when Hashem gathers in the Jews from exile, the good will be victorious over evil, and evil will be eradicated from the world. Simultaneous with *Techiyas HaMeisim*, all evil will be destroyed.

Here, too, it will be the sound of the shofar blasts that will usher in this period, heralding the coming of Mashiach and the eradication of evil from the world.

Thus, the purpose of the sounding of the shofar is to provide strength to the good in the world, enabling it to triumph over evil. There were two times in history when the shofar was sounded and the forces of good were given the ability to overcome the forces of evil.

The first time the Shofar sounded, at *Mattan Torah*, it gave good the power and the ability to overthrow the evil that was holding it captive. Prior to the giving of the Torah, evil was rampant, manifesting control over the world. Whatever form evil took — *Dor HaMabul, Dor HaHaflagah, Shibud Mitzrayim* — evil dominated the world prior to the giving of the Torah. Once there was a Torah to guide mankind, however, evil no longer controlled the world. The Torah allowed the forces of good to be freed from submission to evil and good was then able to exhibit control over that which was bad in the world.

The second time there will be an era during which the forces of evil are pushed away — this time completely — will be when Mashiach comes. After *Techiyas HaMeisim* we will see the emergence of the forces of good as the only driving force in the universe, as the forces of evil will be completely destroyed. This time period will also be ushered in by the sounds of the shofar.

The first time the Shofar sounded, at the Giving of the Torah, it was successful only to an extent. True, good was released from captivity and was allowed to participate in the shaping of world events, but evil continued to exist. The second time the Shofar is sounded, it will be completely successful, and evil will be thoroughly annihilated. This, says the Ramchal, is why the second Shofar is called the *Shofar HaGadol*! It is the Shofar that will herald the complete eradication of evil from the world.

The Ramchal adds that the shofar we blow on Rosh Hashanah has the same *koach*: to enhance, magnify, and empower the forces of goodness in the world and to subdue and push away the powers of evil. It is a microcosm of the two Shofaros of *Mattan Torah* and *L'asid Lavo*. The annual shofar-blowing serves as a bridge that connects these two momentous soundings of the shofar. It strengthens and reaffirms what was already accomplished by the Shofar of *Mattan Torah*, and prepares us for what is to come when the Great Shofar will blow at the time of Mashiach.

This is why the Satan becomes very confused when he hears the sound of the shofar on Rosh Hashanah. He hears the shofar and is reminded of the effects of the shofar Hashem had sounded at Har Sinai. He feels the effects of the shofar of Rosh Hashanah, which is similar in nature (albeit on a lesser scale) to what he knows will be accomplished by the Great Shofar that will be sounded when Mashiach comes, and he becomes frightened. He may be aware that it is not the Shofar of Mashiach, but he feels that the shofar being blown on Rosh Hashanah has the same capability, and he knows that it can destroy him, it can eradicate evil.

❧ *What Are These Forces of Good and Evil?*

What are the forces of evil that will be overcome? What are the forces of goodness that will prevail?

The *Nefesh HaChaim*[8] explains as follows. We see in *Bereishis* (Chapters 1-2), Hashem created Adam HaRishon and placed him into Gan Eden. He was instructed not to eat from the fruits of the *Eitz HaDaas*. At this point, Adam HaRishon exemplifies human perfection. He had no *yetzer hara*; in fact, there was no evil prevalent in the world, except for one specific force of evil, in the form of the *nachash*, the serpent. This force was external to Adam and Chavah, who had no evil in their nature. They were *kadosh* and *tahor*, without any negative characteristics or bad traits in their makeup.

❧ The Tree of Life

Hashem had told Adam that if he were to violate the commandment not to eat from the Tree, he would die. Once the *nachash* induced Adam and Chavah to eat from the *Eitz HaDaas*, Hashem expresses a concern that Adam might subsequently eat from the *Eitz HaChaim*, which would allow him to live forever.

Why was Hashem concerned the Adam would eat from the Tree of Life only now, after he had sinned? Why didn't Hashem forbid Adam from eating the fruit of the *Eitz HaChaim* initially, just as He had commanded him not to eat from the *Eitz HaDaas*? It seems that only after Adam had eaten from the Eitz Hadaas did Hashem decide that Adam should not live forever! Before Adam sinned, it seems that Hashem would not have been concerned if Adam had eaten from the *Eitz HaChaim* and lived forever.

❧ What Happened to the Nachash?

After the *nachash* had convinced Adam and Chavah to partake of the forbidden fruit, we never hear about the serpent again. Why not? What happened to the him? Why is he no longer trying to induce people to sin?

The *Nefesh HaChaim* explains that when Hashem created Adam, he was perfect, and he had no internal attraction to anything evil. When the *nachash*, which personifies the external force of evil, convinced Adam to sin, this external force of evil entered Adam's body and became a part of his composition, poisoning and defiling him. This external force transformed into the internal force of evil that we know as the *yetzer hara*. It became part of a person's personality. Adam's eating from the *Eitz HaDaas* is what gave us the evil inclination.

This defiled us, and brought *tumah* into our bodies. This internal force of *Ra*, this *yetzer hara*, is very strong. Hashem informed Adam that the only way to rid himself of this evil force was to die; after his body was buried in the ground, it would become purified and the *Ra* would be purged from his body. Therefore, it was only after eating from the *Eitz HaDaas* that Adam living forever posed a problem, for if he was never buried, then he would never be cleansed of the evil that was now contained within him. Thus, by living forever he would be eternally doomed. Hashem did not want Adam to eat from the *Eitz HaChaim* so that he would be able to eventually die and subsequently, through burial, be purified from the evil within him.

When the shofar sounded at Har Sinai, thousands of years later, the *Satan* was expelled from our bodies. The *yetzer hara* left us and once again became an external force. That is how the *Satan* was able to create imagery in the sky, depicting Moshe as a corpse, thereby tricking the Bnei Yisrael and contributing to the eventual making of the *Eigel HaZahav*, the Golden Calf. The forces of evil were no longer part of each person, but reverted back to their original external state, attempting to convince people to sin from the outside rather than from within the individual.

However, this freedom from an intrinsic force of evil was short-lived. The sin of the *Eigel* caused the *yetzer hara* to return and once again become a part of our very bodies. The *yetzer hara* was once more internalized; however, it was not to the same extent. The Shofar of *Mattan Torah* did give the *yetzer tov* some degree of power, so that the forces of evil no longer have complete dominion over us.

The Shofar of *Mattan Torah* was therefore not successful in fully eradicating the *yetzer hara*. When the Great Shofar will be blown *L'asid Lavo*, then the *yetzer hara* will be destroyed forever. He will be slaughtered by the Ribbono shel Olam at the time of

Techiyas HaMeisim. This will usher in a utopian era in which things will return to as they were with Adam HaRishon before the *cheit*, when each person was filled only with *kedushah*, without any internal evil.

Until the coming of Mashiach, during the time period between the Shofar of *Mattan Torah* and that of *L'asid Lavo*, the *tekias shofar* of Rosh Hashanah strengthens the good, to some extent, and helps us rebuff the *yetzer hara*.

❧ The Power of the Shofar: Why on Rosh Hashanah?

Why do we blow the shofar on Rosh Hashanah? Of all the days of the year, why is it specifically on Rosh Hashanah that we work toward suppressing the evil and strengthening the *tov*? It is because Rosh Hashanah was the sixth day of creation. It was the very day on which Adam briefly existed in his state of perfection, and the day on which he internalized the forces of evil after partaking of the fruit of the *Eitz HaDaas*. Therefore, on the anniversary of this event, we utilize the shofar to revert to that utopian state. And while the shofar of Rosh Hashanah does not have the same power as the Shofar of *Mattan Torah* or of Mashiach, it does serve as a bridge between them and it does help us, on a much smaller scale, to enhance the power of good and suppress the forces of evil and attempt to return us to the original state of man.

The Shofar of *Mattan Torah* and the Shofar of *Techiyas HaMeisim* both serve the same purpose.[9] Their shared function, to strengthen the forces of good in the world and to subdue the *kochos hara* in the world, is also shared by the shofar of Rosh Hashanah.

❧ The Tefillos of Shofaros

The main focus of our *tefillah* is asking Hashem to restore the world to the way it was on the first Rosh Hashanah of history, prior to the *cheit* of Adam HaRishon: a time when there was no evil force, no *yetzer hara*. Adam was still perfect, just as he had been created.

This is not only the purpose of our *tefillah*, it is also the purpose of the shofar on Rosh Hashanah: to bring us back to the state things were in prior to Adam's sin. The shofar on Rosh Hashanah is similar to the Shofar of Har Sinai and the Shofar of *L'asid Lavo*, and this explains the *pesukim* we say in the *berachah* of Shofaros.

We begin Shofaros with *pesukim* about Hashem having revealed Himself on Har Sinai with the blast of the Shofar. Even though this event did not take place on Rosh Hashanah, we still mention it because the purpose and objective of that Shofar blast was the same as what we are striving to achieve on Rosh Hashanah when we blow the shofar. With our *tefillah* referencing Har Sinai, we are telling HaKadosh Baruch Hu, "Hashem, at Har Sinai You brought the world back to the way it was originally, at the very first Rosh Hashanah. You achieved this with the blowing of the Shofar, and that is also what we are hoping to accomplish today when *we* blow our shofar."

✒ Two Shofaros From the Same Ram — Explained

Rav Dovid Cohen, Rosh Yeshivah of Yeshivas Chevron, adds that this is why the *ayil*, the ram sacrificed in place of Yitzchak, provided both of its horns to be used at the most momentous occasions: One horn for Har Sinai, and the second horn to be used when Mashiach comes. Since the function of each Shofar is identical, it is only fitting that they should come from the same source, the same ram. Each horn is intended to overcome evil, to subdue the *kochos hara* and to give strength to the *kochos hatov*. They both work toward allowing the *yetzer tov* to be actualized and to eliminate the *yetzer hara*. This was accomplished on Har Sinai, it will be accomplished more completely *L'asid Lavo*, and it is accomplished to some extent every year on Rosh Hashanah. This is what makes the *yetzer hara* so confused when he hears the sound of the shofar: He knows that every shofar has some capacity to render him harmless — similar to the Shofar that was sounded at *Kabbalas HaTorah*.

✑ Why a Hole Makes a Shofar Pasul

We can now understand why a shofar with a hole in it is *pasul*. Since the shofar is being used on Rosh Hashanah to accomplish the same task as the Shofar that will sound at *Techiyas HaMeisim*, it stands to reason that just as Hashem's Shofar is intact, without any holes, so too the shofar we use should also not have holes.[10] Our shofar possesses the same power and mystical properties of enabling good to triumph over evil as does the Shofar of Hashem, and therefore it must parallel Hashem's Shofar in its physical characteristics as well.

✑ One of the World's Biggest Mysteries

As stated, *L'asid Lavo*, when Mashiach comes, Hashem will bring the world to its ultimate perfection when the forces of evil will be completely obliterated. This process was started at Har Sinai, continues in small increments every Rosh Hashanah, and will ultimately be fully realized in the future when Mashiach comes.

If Hashem is eradicating all evil and gradually bringing the world to a state of perfection — a utopia — where the forces of evil are rendered powerless, doesn't that indicate that Hashem is interfering with mankind's *bechirah*, free will, and ability to choose between good and evil?

The Ramchal[11] writes that this is one of the biggest mysteries of the world. Hashem operates the world using two simultaneous processes. On the one hand, every individual has free choice. Hashem does not interfere with a person's ability to choose freely. In this vein, He does not make it easier or harder for anyone to choose to do good. On the other hand, Hashem is slowly moving the whole world on a trajectory toward an objective of total eradication of all evil. These two modes operate simultaneously. Mode one is personal free choice, and mode two is Hashem bringing the entire world to ultimate perfection.

The Earth rotates on its axis, making one complete rotation every twenty-four hours. This explains the day and night cycle that we experience daily. The Earth is simultaneously revolving around the sun, a journey that takes an entire year to complete. There are two motions acting on the Earth at any given moment: It is rotating, and at the same time it is revolving. Each of these motions is independent of the other. Neither impacts the other.

This is analogous to how Hashem runs the world. Each person rotates on his own axis, making his own choices. These personal choices are based on each individual's free will. At the same time, Hashem is maneuvering the entire world, moving it toward a time when there will no longer be evil. These are independent modes in which the world operates, neither of which affects the other; they are independent of each other. Somehow, Hashem is eradicating evil without interfering with our free will. In our limited, human understanding we may not comprehend how this can be, but it is the reality. Somehow, the process of the eradication of evil still leaves our free will intact.

This is the prayer of Rosh Hashanah. We *daven* that the world should return to how it was prior to the sin of Adam HaRishon and to how it was at *Mattan Torah*. We pray that our shofar will also serve to accomplish this lofty goal.

ஐ *Why Shofaros From the Akeidah?*

What is the connection between these Shofaros and the *Akeidah*? Why did these two horns specifically have to originate from the ram of the *Akeidah*?

The *Midrash*[12] tells us that Avraham Avinu was called "*Adam hagadol b'anakim*, the greatest of all giants." He was called a giant because he was greater than Adam HaRishon. Adam HaRishon ruined the world, and Avraham Avinu repaired the world, rectifying Adam's wrongdoing. Avraham was the *tikkun*, rectification, of Adam HaRishon's sin. In actuality, Avraham was greater and should have been created before Adam. However, Hashem knew that Avraham's greatness would be required to repair any wrongdoing that Adam may have done, so Hashem brought Avraham to the world after Adam. This is analogous to having a cleaning crew scheduled to come after a party, to clean up the debris. Avraham, who had the power to rectify, had to come after Adam.

Adam HaRishon was the first person to inject *kochos hara* into the world, incorporating the *yetzer hara* into mankind, and Avraham was chosen to start the process of removing these evil powers.

The Ramchal[13] explains that after Adam HaRishon sinned, Hashem offered one more opportunity to Man, one more chance to get it right. He would give Man a chance to get the world back to the way it was before the sin. Hashem provided a single opportunity, and whoever would avail himself of this opportunity would ensure that his descendants would form the nation that would ultimately be able to enjoy a utopian world, a world that would revert to how it was before the sin: a world without evil. Everyone else would not be availed of this opportunity.

As the generations subsequently progressed, Hashem sought the one person who would try to restore the world to the way it was. That individual was Avraham Avinu, who worked to restore an evil-free existence. Therefore, it is only Avraham and his descendants who could ever enjoy that level of existence of complete good and a total absence of sin: namely, the world of the End of Days.

It was Avraham Avinu who rectified that which Adam HaRishon had damaged. At what point in his life did Avraham achieve this?[14] Presumably, it was when he passed his tenth and final test: the *Akeidah*. After *Akeidas Yitzchak*, Hashem told Avraham, "כִּי עַתָּה יָדַעְתִּי כִּי יְרֵא אֱלֹקִים אַתָּה, *For now I know that you are a God-fearing man ...*" (*Bereishis* 22:12). At this point Avraham had merited the right to restore the universe to how it had been prior to Adam and Chavah's sin, with only a *koach* of *tov*. Thus, it is quite understandable that the ram he used for a *korban* at that moment would serve to provide the Shofaros necessary for the task to be complete. This is the connection between the *Akeidah* and the two Great Shofars.

౿ What Is the Power of the Shofar?

We stated above that twice in history the forces of good receive a boost and the forces of evil are suppressed. The first occurred at *Kabbalas HaTorah*, when the *koach hatov* was given a boost, although it was incomplete. It did release goodness from the clutches of evil, but did not eradicate evil completely. The second occasion is yet to come: at the time of Mashiach, when evil will be completely wiped out. Each of these epic time periods are announced by the sounding of a Great Shofar.

What is it about the shofar that gives it this ability to elevate the *koach hatov* and suppress the *koach hara*? What is the source of this power? How does the shofar empower the good and eradicate the evil?

We will offer two explanations.

౿ The Secret of the Shofar?

The *Yesod V'Shoresh HaAvodah*[15] quotes the *Zohar* stating that merely blowing or hearing the shofar on Rosh Hashanah does not suffice. As we say in *davening*, "*Ashrei ha'am yod'ei teruah*, fortunate is the nation that understands the *teruah*." The *tefillah* does not say *fortunate are those who sound or hear the teruah*, as these would not be enough. What is required is understanding the secret of the shofar.

Hashem created numerous holy worlds in *Shamayim*. One of these worlds is called Shofar, *Olam HaShofar*, the World of the Shofar. This world is also known by another name: *Olam HaTeshuvah*, the World of Repentance. This special world is accessible only to Hashem.

Truth be told, it does not seem logical for teshuvah to be a possibility. Picture a thief who is convicted and brought before a judge for sentencing. All the remorse, commitment to change, and apologies in the world will not prevent the judge from sentencing him to what he deserves. The judge hands down the appropriate sentence, regardless of the prisoner's apologies and promises to change. The guilty must pay the price of his transgressions.

Only Hashem can grant a person the ability to do teshuvah, and therefore the *Olam HaTeshuvah* is available only to Him. However, He allows us to benefit from this world, thus, in *Olam Hazeh*, even if a person sinned numerous times, he can be forgiven with the proper teshuvah. When we sound the shofar, we are stirred to do teshuvah. We awaken the powers of the *Olam HaShofar*, the *Olam HaTeshuvah*, and we can then hope for a merciful and forgiving judgment.

Rav Yitzchak Isaac Chaver* adds[16] that this *Olam HaShofar*, the *Olam HaTeshuvah*, is forbidden to the *Satan*. This further explains why he becomes terrified when he hears the sound of the shofar. When he hears the shofar in *Olam Hazeh*, he knows it is activating the *Olam HaShofar* in *Shamayim* — a World of *Teshuvah* to which he has no right and in which he is powerless.

The *Nefesh HaChaim*[17] adds that the *Olam HaTeshuvah* is also referred to as the World of Freedom. To what does this freedom refer?

The *Sifsei Chaim*[18] explains the words of the *Nefesh HaChaim*. The *Olam HaTeshuvah* is referred to as the World of Freedom in that it is free of the filth and poison of Adam's *cheit*. It is the one corner of the universe where the effects of the sin of Adam are not felt.

This, then, is the secret power of the shofar: There is a world in *Shamayim* that is called the *Olam HaShofar, Olam HaTeshuvah*, and *Alma DeCheri* (the World of Freedom), which remains unaffected and unsullied by the sin of the *Eitz HaDaas*. In this world, evil does not exist and cannot enter. Only the *koach* of good exists there. The shofar's power is that it activates that world, which in turns enables us in This World to come closer to the

---

* Rav Yitzchak Issac Chaver was referred to as the "*peh shlishi*, the third mouth," of the Vilna Gaon; he was a *talmid* of a *talmid* of the Vilna Gaon.

state that the world was in prior to the sin of Adam HaRishon.

This is the explanation of Rav Dovid Cohen, Rosh Yeshivah of Chevron, based on kabbalistic sources.

◈ A Novel Approach

I would like to offer another understanding regarding the power of the shofar and how it is able to bring the state of the world back to how things were prior to the sin of the *Eitz HaDaas*.

The Ramchal we quoted above taught that there are two moments in history when the sounding of the shofar attempted to bring the world back to its original perfect state, without evil: the Shofar of *kabbalas HaTorah* and the Shofar of *L'asid Lavo*.

Wasn't there a third time in history when the world was in its idyllic state? When Hashem first created Adam HaRishon and placed him in Gan Eden, the world was most certainly in its original state, before the forces of evil took hold. The two Shofaros are intended to bring us back to that state, but that original state was perfection itself.

Why was no shofar sounded when Hashem created Adam HaRishon? If it is the shofar that gives strength to the good and subdues and diminishes the bad, then shouldn't the shofar have sounded when Adam was first created?

I would venture to suggest that there actually was a *tekias shofar* when Hashem first created Adam and placed him in Gan Eden. When Hashem created Adam, the Torah tells us, 'וַיִּיצֶר ה אֱלֹקִים אֶת הָאָדָם עָפָר מִן הָאֲדָמָה וַיִּפַּח בְּאַפָּיו נִשְׁמַת חַיִּים וַיְהִי הָאָדָם לְנֶפֶשׁ חַיָּה, *And Hashem God formed the man of dust from the ground, and He blew into his nostrils the soul of life; and man became a living being* (Bereishis 2:7). The *Sefer HaPeliah* says[19] that just as when a person blows into a balloon, the air comes from inside the person blowing, when Hashem blew the *neshamah* into Adam, the *neshamah* came from Hashem, as it were, from the One Who did the blowing. The *neshamah* is a *chelek Eloka mima'al*, literally, a piece of the Divine.

This *pasuk* teaches us one of the most important concepts of the Torah: Every Jew has a *neshamah* within that is a Divine entity, breathed into the nostrils by Hashem Himself.

Rav Yonasan Eibeshutz[20] writes that the appearance of the shofar is similar to that of a nose. Some shofars are shorter, some are longer, but the overall features remain consistent with that of the human nose. This is because the blowing of the shofar is reminiscent of the first blowing in history — when Hashem blew the *neshamah* into Adam via his nostrils. Thus, Rav Eibeshutz states, the blowing of the shofar on Rosh Hashanah directly parallels וַיִּפַּח בְּאַפָּיו נִשְׁמַת חַיִּים.

The *Shem MiShmuel*[21] adds in the name of his father, the *Avnei Nezer*, that this is the meaning of the *Sifri* stating that when Hashem blew our soul into us, He was the *Tokeiah*. Thus, even the original creation of Adam, placing him in the idyllic world of only *Tov* and no *Ra*, was also heralded with a blowing, with a *Tekiah*.

Thus, all three periods of history when the world was (or will be) in its perfect state were ushered in with *tekiyas shofar*! One was at *Mattan Torah*, and another will be *L'asid Lavo* when Mashiach comes. But the first was when Hashem Himself was the *Baal Tokeiah*, blowing into the shofar — the nostrils of Adam — as He placed the *neshamah* into Adam HaRishon. When Hashem blows a *neshamah* from Himself into someone else, we can be certain that this *neshamah* is pure, holy, and totally good, without any evil.

Furthermore, this first *tekiyas shofar* in history, when Hashem blew the *neshamah* into Adam, took place on the first Rosh Hashanah in history, as Adam was created on Rosh Hashanah.

When the second Shofar sounded, it was at Har Sinai, when Hashem gave us the Torah. Hashem told the Bnei Yisrael the first two Commandments, and, upon hearing the voice of Hashem, their *neshamos* left them. Hashem had to then breathe new souls into them. And then the world reverted to the perfect idyllic state, as it was prior to the sin of Adam HaRishon. Why? Because once again Hashem Himself blew the *neshamah* into them, just as He had done on the very first Rosh Hashanah to Adam HaRishon. This was an exact replica of how Hashem created Adam. And when Hashem breathes a perfectly *kadosh* and pure *neshamah* into a person, all evil vanishes.

⤷ *The Shofar of L'asid Lavo*

Finally, we come to the Shofar of *L'asid Lavo*. This is also not a simple shofar; it will be the Shofar of *Techiyas HaMeisim*! *Neshamos* will once again be blown, giving life, in the purest and holiest form — without any evil. Hashem will once again, for the third time, perform וַיִּפַּח בְּאַפָּיו נִשְׁמַת חַיִּים.

It is not simply blowing the horn of a ram that results in all the evil vanishing and being replaced by *Tov*. It is the power of the Jewish *neshamah* being fused with the *guf*, being blown into the body by Hashem. As the *Chasam Sofer* writes,[22] a Jew's *neshamah* is holier than the Torah itself. Whenever the *neshamah* enters a *guf* directly from Hashem, that *neshamah* causes all evil to vanish.

Each of these three incredible moments, when Adam was created, when the Torah was given, and when Mashiach will come, is marked by Hashem blowing life, blowing a holy and pure *neshamah*, into a *guf*, an action that destroys all evil.

In perfect symmetry, we were *zocheh* to both of these monumental horns at the time of *Akeidas Yitzchak*. *Pirkei D'Rabbi Eliezer*[23] writes that when Avraham Avinu raised the knife, fully intending to slaughter his son Yitzchak, Yitzchak Avinu actually died; his *neshamah* left his body. When Avraham was told to not harm his son, Yitzchak experienced *Techiyas HaMeisim*, and he came back to life. Yitzchak realized that he had experienced *Techiyas HaMeisim*, and he then recited a *berachah*: Baruch Atah Hashem Mechayeh HaMeisim!

The idyllic state of the world is always ushered in by the blowing of the Shofar. At the time of Adam HaRishon, it was ushered in with וַיִּפַּח בְּאַפָּיו נִשְׁמַת חַיִּים. At the Giving of the Torah, it was ushered in when the Jews had to be revivified and given new *neshamos*. This is also what will happen *L'asid Lavo*, when

Mashiach comes, and *Techiyas HaMeisim* takes place, with *neshamos* being restored into those who have passed away.

The shofar that we blow on Rosh Hashanah has the power of *Mattan Torah* and *Techiyas HaMeisim*. Every year, on Rosh Hashanah, on some level, Hashem is instilling into every Jew a new dimension of his *neshamah*, a purer soul, a holier soul. A soul that has more energy and a greater capacity to overcome the *yetzer hara* and come closer to Hashem. We are *mispallel* that the Ribbono shel Olam give us *siyata d'Shmaya* that our blowing of the shofar should instill within us a *neshamah kedoshah v'tehorah*. We should all be *zocheh* to the *biyas goel tzedek* and hear the שׁוֹפָר גָּדוֹל לְחֵרוּתֵנוּ, *bimheirah veyameinu, amen.*

ENDNOTES

1. ראש השנה טז, א-ב.
2. ראש השנה טז, ב.
3. שם טז, ב.
4. שולחן ערוך ורמ"א אורח חיים סימן תקפ סעיף ז.
5. ביאור הגר"א שם.
6. פרקי דרבי אליעזר פרק לא.
7. מאמר החכמה לרבי משה חיים לוצאטו.
8. נפש החיים שער א פרק ו.
9. ביאורי חכמה, עמוד קמח-קמט, פירוש של הרב דוד כהן על המאמר החכמה.
10. עיני ישראל, עמוד פה, מאת הרב ישראל ווינטראב.
11. דעת תבונות עמוד 322.
12. בראשית רבה יד, ו.
13. רמח"ל דרך ה, חלק ב פרק ד.
14. שם קן-קנא.
15. ביאורי חכמה עמוד קמא; יסוד ושורש העבודה שער האחד עשר שער האיתון פרק שלישי.
16. שיח יצחק, דרוש תוכחת מוסר עמוד נד.
17. נפש החיים שער א' פרק י"ב.
18. שפתי חיים מועדים א עמוד קמה.
19. הובא בספר עיני ישראל עמוד פו.
20. יערות דבש דרוש א.
21. ראש השנה יום א, סד.
22. תורת משה כי תצא עמוד מג.
23. פרקי דרבי אליעזר פרק לא.

Start the New Year With Rav Yonasan Eibeshutz and Be Prepared for the War of Rosh Hashanah

❧ The Centrality of the Akeidah

Avraham Avinu was instructed by Hashem to take his son Yitzchak, whom he had eagerly awaited for 100 years, and from whom he had been told his legacy would continue, and offer him as a *korban* to Hashem. Avraham Avinu passed this test, displaying great zeal and alacrity, placing the love of Hashem above his human emotions.

Akeidas Yitzchak is central to many of the *minhagim* and *tefillos* of Rosh Hashanah. It is the *zechus* we most invoke on the *Yom HaDin*. Let us present a number of examples.

❧ Tekiyas Shofar

The only *mitzvah d'Oraisa* specific to Rosh Hashanah is the mitzvah of *tekiyas shofar*. The Gemara[1] says that the reason we blow the shofar of a ram is to remind Hashem of *Akeidas*

Yitzchak. Hashem gives us an assurance that when we do so, He will view it as if we personally sacrificed ourselves at the *Akeidah.*

❧ *Zichronos*

In Mussaf of Rosh Hashanah we recite the *berachah* of *Zichronos*, asking Hashem to remember us for our favor. Here, too, the mention of the *Akeidah* is front and center.

אֱלֹקֵינוּ וֵאלֹקֵי אֲבוֹתֵינוּ, זָכְרֵנוּ בְּזִכָּרוֹן טוֹב לְפָנֶיךָ, וּפָקְדֵנוּ בִּפְקֻדַּת יְשׁוּעָה וְרַחֲמִים מִשְּׁמֵי שְׁמֵי קֶדֶם, וּזְכָר לָנוּ ה׳ אֱלֹקֵינוּ אֶת הַבְּרִית וְאֶת הַחֶסֶד וְאֶת הַשְּׁבוּעָה אֲשֶׁר נִשְׁבַּעְתָּ לְאַבְרָהָם אָבִינוּ בְּהַר הַמֹּרִיָּה. וְתֵרָאֶה לְפָנֶיךָ עֲקֵדָה שֶׁעָקַד אַבְרָהָם אָבִינוּ אֶת יִצְחָק בְּנוֹ עַל גַּבֵּי הַמִּזְבֵּחַ, וְכָבַשׁ רַחֲמָיו לַעֲשׂוֹת רְצוֹנְךָ בְּלֵבָב שָׁלֵם, כֵּן יִכְבְּשׁוּ רַחֲמֶיךָ אֶת כַּעַסְךָ מֵעָלֵינוּ.

Our God and the God of our forefathers, remember us with a favorable remembrance before You, recall us with a recollection of salvation and mercy from the primeval, loftiest heavens. Remember for us, Hashem, our God, the covenant, the kindness, and the oath that You swore to our father Avraham on Mount Moriah. Let there appear before You the Akeidah when Avraham, our father, bound Yitzchak, his son, upon the altar and he suppressed his mercy to do Your will wholeheartedly. So may Your mercy suppress Your anger from upon us.

We then conclude, כִּי זוֹכֵר כָּל הַנִּשְׁכָּחוֹת אַתָּה הוּא מֵעוֹלָם, וְאֵין שִׁכְחָה *For it is You* לִפְנֵי כִסֵּא כְבוֹדֶךָ, וַעֲקֵדַת יִצְחָק, לְזַרְעוֹ הַיּוֹם בְּרַחֲמִים תִּזְכֹּר, *Who eternally remembers all that is forgotten, and there is no forgetfulness before Your Throne of Glory, and may You mercifully remember today the Akeidah of Yitzchak for the sake of his offspring.* בָּרוּךְ אַתָּה ה׳, זוֹכֵר הַבְּרִית, *Blessed are You, Hashem, Who remembers the covenant [made with Avraham Avinu at the Akeidah].*

When we ask Hashem to recall merit on our behalf, it is the *Akeidah* that we focus on more than any other *zechus* that Klal Yisrael may have. The *berachah* of *Zichronos* is centered around the *Akeidah*, asking Hashem to remember the exceptional self-sacrifice of our forefathers as a merit on our behalf.

Throughout our illustrious history there were numerous *tzaddikim* who also performed mitzvos and exhibited personal sacrifice in the service of the Ribbono shel Olam. What is special and unique about the *Akeidah* that it stands alone as the paragon of merit that we invoke on Rosh Hashanah? Moshe Rabbeinu likewise accomplished numerous spiritual achievements on behalf of Klal Yisrael. Why do we not invoke any of his *maasim tovim* as a *zechus* for us on the *Yom HaDin*? Why do we not remind Hashem, for instance, that Moshe Rabbeinu taught us all the entire Torah? Why is the *Akeidah* the central event that we invoke as cause for Hashem to be merciful in His judgment on Rosh Hashanah?

✍ Kerias HaTorah

The subject of the Torah reading of the second day of Rosh Hashanah is the *Akeidah*. The Gemara[2] teaches that on the first day of Rosh Hashanah we *lein*, וַה׳ פָּקַד אֶת שָׂרָה כַּאֲשֶׁר אָמָר, *Hashem remembered Sarah as He had said …* (Bereishis 21:1) which is the opening *pasuk* heralding the birth of Yitzchak, and on the second day we *lein* וַיְהִי אַחַר הַדְּבָרִים הָאֵלֶּה וְהָאֱלֹקִים נִסָּה אֶת אַבְרָהָם, *And it happened after these things that God tested Avraham…* (ibid., 22:1), which are the opening words of the *parashah* of the *Akeidah*. Rashi[3] explains that we *lein* this *parashah* so that Hashem recalls *Akeidas Yitzchak* as a merit for us on the *Yom HaDin*.

✍ Tashlich

The *minhag* on Rosh Hashanah to recite *Tashlich*** at a body of water is another instance when we invoke the merit of *Akeidas Yitzchak*. The Rema[4] codifies that we go to the water to recite the *pasuk,* וְתַשְׁלִיךְ בִּמְצֻלוֹת יָם כָּל חַטֹּאתָם, *and cast into the depths of the sea all of our sins.* We spent hours *davening* in shul; why

---

* One should remember that when one goes to *Tashlich* on Rosh Hashanah, he must not throw bread to the fish or birds, as the halachah forbids one to feed non-domestic animals on Yom Tov.

could we not spend a few more moments and add this *pasuk* to the *davening*? Why must we go down to the river to recite this *pasuk*?

The *Mishnah Berurah*[5] explains that is it based on the *Midrash* that states that when Avraham Avinu went to perform the *Akeidah*, the *Satan* tried various methods to prevent him from fulfilling Hashem's decree. One tactic employed by the *Satan* was that he created a river to block Avraham's path. Avraham was neck-deep in the water, crying out to Hashem, הוֹשִׁיעֵנִי אֱלֹקִים כִּי בָאוּ מַיִם עַד נָפֶשׁ, *Save me, for water has reached my soul*, before he was able to pass through.

Thus, *Tashlich* is yet another custom of Rosh Hashanah which we perform to invoke the great merit of the *Akeidah*.

∾ *Eating the Head of a Ram*

The *Shulchan Aruch*[6] writes that it is customary to eat the head of a ram on Rosh Hashanah as a *siman*, a portent and prayer, "*she'nihiyeh l'rosh v'lo l'zanav*, that we be as the head and not as the tail." Why the head of a ram? The *Shulchan Aruch* explains: It is to remember the ram that Avraham used as a replacement at *Akeidas Yitzchak*.

∾ *Tefillah of the Baal Tokeiah*

Prior to blowing the shofar, the *baal tokeiah* recites a special *tefillah*. In this prayer he states: וְתִמָּלֵא עַל עַמְּךָ רַחֲמִים וְתִסְתַּכֵּל בְּאֶפְרוֹ שֶׁל יִצְחָק אָבִינוּ הַצָּבוּר עַל גַּבֵּי הַמִּזְבֵּחַ וְתִתְנַהֵג עִם בָּנֶיךָ בְּמִדַּת הָרַחֲמִים וְתִכָּנֵס לָהֶם לִפְנִים מִשּׁוּרַת הַדִּין וּזְכוֹר לָהֶם עֲקֵדַת יִצְחָק לְזַרְעוֹ, *May You be filled with mercy upon Your people, and may You contemplate the ashes of Yitzchak, our forefather, that are heaped upon the Altar. May You deal with Your children with the Attribute of Mercy and may You overstep for them the line of the law. Remember for their sake the Akeidah of Yitzchak for his offspring* …. Here, too, the *Akeidah* receives unique prominence, in that no other event from our collective national history is mentioned in his prayer — only the *Akeidah*.

There are various customs as to what item should be used in the performance of *kapparos*. The *Rema*[7] mentions the use of a chicken, while the *Mishnah Berurah*[8] states that a fish may be used if a chicken is not available. A third *minhag* is to use money.[9] The *Meiri*, however, maintains that the original custom was to use an *ayil*, a ram. The use of a ram, explains the *Meiri*,[10] allows us to understand the mechanism of the ritual of *kapparos*. The ritual of *kapparos* is a *zecher*, remembrance, of the *Akeidah*.

When Avraham was told not to harm Yitzchak, he caught sight of a ram that he then offered in lieu of his son. Every action Avraham performed on the ram he did with the express intent that Hashem should consider it as if he were performing it on his dear son Yitzchak. "*Yehi ratzon*, may it be Your will, that this should be as if I am bringing Yitzchak as a *korban*." He repeated this *tefillah* with each step of the *avodah*. Thus, Avraham Avinu performed the very first *kapparos*.

The purpose of *kapparos*, the *Meiri* explains, is that it is a re-enactment of *Akeidas Yitzchak*! In fact, the *Meiri* mentions that *kapparos* was originally practiced on Rosh Hashanah itself.

We have identified seven different practices of Rosh Hashanah that are performed to invoke the great merit of the *Akeidah*. Let us discover why the *Akeidah* is so central to Klal Yisrael having a successful outcome on the *Yom HaDin*.

≈ מִי שֶׁעָנָה לְאַבְרָהָם אָבִינוּ —
When Did Avraham Avinu Daven?

Toward the end of *Selichos*, we state, מִי שֶׁעָנָה לְאַבְרָהָם בְּהַר הַמּוֹרִיָּה, הוּא יַעֲנֵנוּ, *the One Who answered Avraham Avinu on Har HaMoriah, He should answer us [as well]*. Which *tefillah* is referenced here? When Avraham Avinu was proceeding with the *Akeidah*, we don't find that he davened for anything at that time. Avraham was focused on performing exactly what Hashem had instructed him to do. What are we referring to when we say that

Hashem, Who answered Avraham on Har HaMoriah, should answer us?

❧ When Did the Akeidah Take Place?

One may argue that the centrality of the *Akeidah* to Rosh Hashanah is because Rosh Hashanah is the day that the *Akeidah* took place. Is that in fact so? Let us explore. When did the *Akeidah* take place? Interestingly, the Torah does not tell us when the *Akeidah* actually happened. The *Mishnah* and the Gemara also do not give us an indication as to when these events transpired.

The *Pesikta Rabasi*[11] says that when Hashem instructed Avraham to offer Yitzchak as a *korban*, Avraham could have challenged this unusual command. Hashem had told him כִּי בְיִצְחָק יִקָּרֵא לְךָ זָרַע, *Since through Yitzchak will offspring be considered yours* (*Bereishis* 21:12); how could that be reconciled with this new directive: to bring Yitzchak as an offering to Hashem? However, Avraham refrained from challenging Hashem. He remained silent; he had no reaction other than to actually perform the *tzivui* with outstanding *zerizus*. וַאֲנִי כְחֵרֵשׁ לֹא אֶשְׁמָע וּכְאִלֵּם לֹא יִפְתַּח פִּיו, *But I am like a deaf man, I do not hear, like a mute who does not open his mouth* (*Tehillim* 38:14). Avraham, however, did ask Hashem to repay him in kind. When the descendants of Yitzchak would be judged by Hashem *bayom hazeh*, on this day, then, Avraham asks, Hashem should disregard the prosecutors and accusers who may rise up with claims against Klal Yisrael. Regardless of how numerous they may be, just as I remained quiet when instructed to perform the *Akeidah*, so too should You, Hashem, remain silent and not prosecute Klal Yisrael when accusations are hurled against Yitzchak's descendants.

This *Midrash* is revealing to us that Avraham actually did offer a prayer at the *Akeidah*. Avraham beseeched Hashem that just as he was silent and did not challenge Hashem's command, so too — on this day — Hashem should remain silent and not prosecute Klal Yisrael. Avraham's reference to "this day" clearly indicates that the *Akeidah* took place on the *Yom HaDin*, on Rosh Hashanah.

The *Midrash* then continues, and tells us the name Avraham gave to the place where the *Akeidah* took place. שֵׁם אַבְרָהָם וַיִּקְרָא הַמָּקוֹם הַהוּא ה' יִרְאֶה אֲשֶׁר יֵאָמֵר הַיּוֹם בְּהַר ה' יֵרָאֶה, *And Avraham called the name of that place* ה' יִרְאֶה, *as it is said this day, on the mountain Hashem will be seen* (*Bereishis* 22:14). To what does הַיּוֹם, *this day*, in this *pasuk* refer? The *Midrash* then explicitly asserts that it was Rosh Hashanah when the *Akeidah* took place, and Hashem acceded to Avraham's request. He would remain silent when the accusing angels would prosecute the Bnei Yisrael, and He would disregard their accusations.

Avraham then asked Hashem to swear that He would honor His commitment, and in fact Hashem swore, as the *pasuk* states, וַיֹּאמֶר בִּי נִשְׁבַּעְתִּי נְאֻם ה', *And he [the angel] said, "By Myself I swear—the word of Hashem* (ibid., 22:16). The *Midrash* explains that this is why the Torah says that Rosh Hashanah takes place "*Bachodesh Hashvi'i.*" It refers not only to the seventh month, but also to the "month of the *shevuah*, oath," the oath that Hashem took that He will ignore the prosecutors.

One may suggest that the *Akeidah* is central to the service of Rosh Hashanah because it happened on Rosh Hashanah. But upon further analysis, is this really a satisfactory rationale? Just because Rosh Hashanah is the anniversary of the *Akeidah*, should the *Akeidah* now become the central theme of Rosh Hashanah? Furthermore, as we are about to learn, it is far from unanimous that the *Akeidah* even took place on Rosh Hashanah in any case.

❧ *Different Opinions as to the Date of the Akeidah*

The *Yalkut Reuveini*,[12] an ancient compilation of *midrashim*, records that the *Akeidah* took place on Yom Kippur, not on Rosh Hashanah. Likewise, *Derashos Even Shva'ib* [13] states that we can make a *kal vachomer*, an *a fortiori* argument. Non-Jews are *arlei lev*, their hearts are uncircumcised. Their hearts are not as perceptive of spirituality as the heart of a Jew. Yet, they can do teshuvah and return to God. *Kal vachomer*, certainly, Jews, who are *malei lev*, who are soft-hearted and perceptive to teshuvah, should definitely do teshuvah. Especially on this holy day, on Yom Kippur, which is designated for our teshuvah, as it received many added, enhanced *kedushos*. He writes that it is the day on which Avraham Avinu was circumcised, **it is the day of the *Akeidah***, it is the day on which we received the second *Luchos*, and it is the day that we were forgiven for the *Cheit HaEigel*. Clearly, he, too, is of the opinion that the *Akeidah* took place on Yom Kippur.

According to the opinions that the *Akeidah* happened on Yom Kippur, we still do not blow the shofar of a ram on Yom Kippur or perform any other ritual on Yom Kippur to recall *Akeidas Yitzchak*. Clearly, the remembrance of the *Akeidah* is unrelated to the day on which it transpired.

There is even an opinion that the *Akeidah* did not take place in Chodesh Tishrei. *Midrash Rabbah*[14] expounds upon the *pasuk* הַחֹדֶשׁ הַזֶּה לָכֶם (*Shemos* 12:2), which refers to Chodesh Nissan. Many great events took place in Nissan. Hashem chose the Jewish people in Nissan, and He will ultimately redeem us in Nissan. Yitzchak was born in Nissan, and, according to this *midrash*, *Akeidas Yitzchak* took place in Nissan as well. And yet, according to this opinion, there is no commemoration of *Akeidas Yitzchak* in the month of Nissan. Evidently, the centrality of the *Akeidah* to Rosh Hashanah is not a matter of commemorating the anniversary of the *Akeidah*. The merit of the *Akeidah* must be fundamental to the very essence of the *Yom HaDin*. Let us try to uncover the essential connection of the *Akeidah* to Rosh Hashanah.

◈ The Unique Perspective of Rav Yonasan Eibeshutz

Rav Yonasan Eibeshutz offers an outstanding insight into what actually transpires on Rosh Hashanah that will open up for us a new dimension of understanding why the *Akeidah* is so essential to our *avodah* on the *Yom HaDin*.

The *pasuk* states, מָה אֱנוֹשׁ כִּי תִזְכְּרֶנּוּ וּבֶן אָדָם כִּי תִפְקְדֶנּוּ, *What is frail man that You should remember him, and the son of mortal man that You should be mindful of him? (Tehillim 8:5).* The Gemara[15] explains that this question was asked of the Ribbono shel Olam at the time that He created Man.

When Hashem wanted to make Man, He first created a group of angels. He then queried these *malachim,* "Should I make Man in My image?" The *malachim* asked what Man was, and Hashem explained how Man would act, how he would conduct himself.

When the *malachim* understood the nature of Man, they were perplexed. They asked Hashem, "If this is Man, why would You want to create him? מָה אֱנוֹשׁ כִּי תִזְכְּרֶנּוּ וּבֶן אָדָם כִּי תִפְקְדֶנּוּ? Creating Man does not seem to be a good idea."

Hashem extended His small finger and burned all the *malachim*. He then created another group of *malachim* and the process repeated itself. They, too, expressed their incomprehension that Hashem would want to create Man. The second group was similarly destroyed.

When Hashem then queried a third group of *malachim* whether or not to create Man, their answer was, "It is Your world; do as You please." Man was then created.

Many years passed; eventually the *Dor HaMabul,* Generation of the Flood, and the subsequent *Dor HaHaflagah,* Generation of the Dispersion, arrived. The *malachim* saw how corrupt and destructive these generations were and turned to Hashem, suggesting that the first two groups of angels appear to have been correct in their assessment of the desirability of Man's creation.

Hashem responded to the *malachim* with the following words, וְעַד זִקְנָה אֲנִי הוּא וְעַד שֵׂיבָה אֲנִי אֶסְבֹּל, which can be translated, *Until I am old, I am He; until I get old I will tolerate him* (*Yeshayah* 46:4). Hashem states, "Although Man may be bad now, one day he will be good, and I will patiently tolerate him until he is." What is the meaning of Hashem's response?

‎∾ *The War in Shamayim on Rosh Hashanah*

Although the *malachim* advised Hashem against it, Hashem created Man, on Rosh Hashanah. Rav Yonasan Eibeshutz[16] teaches us that this process is repeated annually. On every Rosh Hashanah since that initial creation, Hashem recreates Man all over again.

We believe that the calendar is not linear, progressing onward continually, but rather it is circular, a living cycle that repeats itself every year. Every year on Rosh Hashanah, Hashem re-creates Man for the upcoming year. Hashem created Adam on the first Rosh Hashanah, and He recreates Man every year on Rosh Hashanah. Each and every one of us is being re-created annually.

As Hashem embarks on His annual creation of Man, the *malachim* once again challenge Him and try to persuade Hashem that creating Man is not a wise choice. They are *mikatreig* annually, attempting to prevent Hashem from repeating what they consider to have been a mistake in the first place. On the very first Rosh Hashanah, the *malachim* asked Hashem, מָה אֱנוֹשׁ כִּי תִזְכְּרֶנּוּ וּבֶן אָדָם כִּי תִפְקְדֶנּוּ, and every year they again ask Hashem this question. They point out our flaws and the numerous *aveiros* that we committed, and they advise Hashem to not repeat the mistake of creating Man.

Every Rosh Hashanah there is a war in heaven! All the angels cry out to Hashem, "Don't do it! Perhaps proceed with the re-creation of the entire universe, of the world and all its animal and plant inhabitants — but don't create Man! Man is corrupt. Man is destructive. Man is evil. Don't make him again."

A fascinating *Zohar*[17] explains the *pasuk,* וּלְאָדָם לֹא מָצָא עֵזֶר כְּנֶגְדּוֹ (*Bereishis* 2:20), which literally refers to the fact that Man could not find a mate. The *Zohar* explains it in a novel way. He says that Adam could not find any עֵזֶר , *help*, among Creation as every creation tried to dissuade Hashem from making Man! The trees, the animals, the birds, the fish, the angels — everything in Creation — shouted out to God that creating Man was a bad idea. Thus, וּלְאָדָם לֹא מָצָא עֵזֶר כְּנֶגְדוֹ refers to the fact that Man did not have anyone to help him, anyone to promote his cause and defend his right to be created.

We come to shul on Rosh Hashanah dressed in our Yom Tov finery, feeling that we have a clean slate and are getting a fresh start. However, Rav Yonasan Eibeshutz writes that if only we understood what was transpiring in *Shamayim* on Rosh Hashanah — that tremendous efforts were being expended to prevent us from being re-created, working to end our existence — we would not be able to eat, drink, sleep, or dress, for fear of losing the war with the *malachim*. There are myriads of angels fighting with Hashem, striving to convince Him to end the existence of Man.

The *Sfas Emes*[18] presents the same idea. This challenge of the *malachim* resurfaces annually on Rosh Hashanah. Part of the *din* on Rosh Hashanah is defending against this *kitrug*, defending our right as humans to exist. Rosh Hashanah is thus a very fearsome day.

❧ *How Do We Answer the Claim of the Angels?*

How can we hope to be victorious against the *malachim* and their claim that Man's actions have clearly demonstrated that he does not deserve to be re-created? Can we truly claim that we are "prime examples" of what Hashem had in mind when He made Man?

The *Midrash Tanchuma*[19] states that when Hashem wanted to create the world, the angels told Him that He should not ruin His beautiful world by creating Man. The angels scanned the future history of Mankind and declared, מָה אֱנוֹשׁ כִּי תִזְכְּרֶנּוּ. Hashem responded that they were looking at the wrong generation! The angels were looking at the generation of אֱנוֹשׁ, when the sin of idolatry was introduced, when they in fact should be looking elsewhere. "You are looking at the generation of the *Mabul*," Hashem tells them, "Let me direct your attention to a different time, a different generation, so that you will see the type of behavior that more than justifies the creation of Man." Hashem then showed the *malachim* Avraham Avinu taking his beloved son Yitzchak, and bringing him to the *Akeidah* with *zerizus* and *simchah* to fulfill the word of Hashem. Avraham allowed his love for Hashem to transcend the love he had for his long-awaited, most-beloved son. It is with the merit of the *Akeidah* that Hashem silences all the angels and all the naysayers who did not want Him to create Man.

As noted above, the *Pesikta* teaches that Avraham Avinu had implored Hashem that just as he, Avraham, had remained silent in the face of the *nisayon* of the *Akeidah*, so too should Hashem maintain His silence in the face of our accusers. In his *tefillah*, Avraham Avinu referred to this annual war between Hashem and the angels about allowing the re-creation of Man. Avraham implored Hashem to recall his self-sacrifice for every Rosh Hashanah to come, and to maintain His defense for the right for Man to be created yet again.

The response to the *malachim*, the answer as to why Hashem created Man, with all his many flaws and deficiencies, is to observe Avraham Avinu and see the level he achieved. Our right to be created against the accusations of those who seek to undermine the value of our existence comes only through the *Akeidah*.

❧ *The Akeidah: Critical to Our Defense on the Yom HaDin*

Rav Dovid Cohen,[20] the Rosh Yeshivah of Chevron, explains that this concept clarifies why the *Akeidah* plays such a central role to our service on Rosh Hashanah. The *Akeidah* is the one defense we have against the warring angels, against the prosecutors and accusers who readily point out our flaws and beseech Hashem not to make the same mistake again, not to give mankind a new lease on life. The *Akeidah* is proof that Man can transcend his *taavos*, can put his physical and emotional desires aside in the service of Hashem, that Man can achieve the spiritual levels that will justify his existence.

We repeatedly invoke the *zechus* and the message of the *Akeidah*, reminding Hashem of the event that provides a definitive answer to their claim, silencing them and allowing us to be granted a favorable *din*. True, Man can be destructive and corrupt, but Man can take another direction as well. Man can perform such an act of selfless sacrifice as Avraham did, that, in doing so, he has the potential to rise to a *madreigah*, spiritual level, that supersedes that of even the *malachei ha'shareis*, ministering angels.

When the angels look down from *Shamayim* and see Man achieve a level such as Avraham did at the *Akeidah*, they are filled with tearful emotion from witnessing so profound an act being performed by a human being. That is why the central focus of the Rosh Hashanah service is *Akeidas Yitzchak*. It is the merit of the *Akeidah* that will literally save the day.

∾ *The Merciful Old Man*

After witnessing the *Dor HaMabul* and *Dor HaHaflagah*, the *malachim* expressed their opinion that it had been a mistake to have created Man. Hashem answered, וְעַד זִקְנָה אֲנִי הוּא וְעַד שֵׂיבָה אֲנִי אֶסְבֹּל, I will tolerate him until I get old. What does Hashem mean? Mortals age, people get older from year to year. But Hashem is immortal; He does not age!

The *Maharsha*[21] explains that Hashem sometimes appears to the *neviim*, prophets, in different guises. For example, at *Krias Yam Suf*, Klal Yisrael saw Hashem as an *ish gibor milchamah*, a mighty warrior. At Har Sinai, when the Jewish nation was in a prophetic state, Hashem appeared to them as a *zakein malei rachamim*, an elderly person who was filled with compassion.

Hashem agreed with the angels that then, during the *Dor*

HaMabul and *Dor HaHaflagah*, Mankind is undeserving of existence. But, says Hashem. I will wait around, I will be patient, until I am an old man — until the time when I will appear to Klal Yisrael as an old man at the time of *Mattan Torah*. Hashem said that even though at that moment in time Man did not deserve to live, the day will come that he will justify his existence. On the day of the Giving of the Torah you will see Klal Yisrael in a new light, you will see Man who is worthy of existence.

‿ *Which Is It? Akeidah or Mattan Torah?*

However, this interpretation of the Gemara is at odds with the *Midrash Tanchuma's* account of Hashem's response to the *malachim*. The Midrash explains that Hashem's answer to the *malachim's* protest, questioning Man's right to exist, is the *Akeidah*. Looking at Avraham Avinu and the level he achieved at the *Akeidah* provides all the necessary justification for Man's existence. The Gemara, on the other hand, presents a different justification for Man's existence: Man deserves to exist because the day will come when the Bnei Yisrael will receive the Torah.

Which is the true justification for Man's existence? Avraham Avinu at the *Akeidah*, or the Giving of the Torah on Har Sinai?

When Avraham was commanded not to sacrifice Yitzchak, he found an *ayil* nearby that he offered in his stead. *Pirkei D'Rabbi Eliezer*[22] brings a *midrash* that the ram's left horn was preserved and blown by the Ribbono shel Olam at *Mattan Torah*, on Har Sinai. The horn of the very animal that was sacrificed in lieu of Yitzchak Avinu was sounded at the giving of the Torah. The right horn of that ram was longer than the left, and is referred to as the *Shofar Gadol*, the Great Shofar. That horn will be blown *L'asid Lavo*, at the End of Days, at the time of the ingathering of all the Jews from exile. As the *pasuk* says, וְהָיָה בַּיּוֹם הַהוּא יִתָּקַע בְּשׁוֹפָר גָּדוֹל וּבָאוּ הָאֹבְדִים בְּאֶרֶץ אַשּׁוּר וְהַנִּדָּחִים בְּאֶרֶץ מִצְרָיִם וְהִשְׁתַּחֲווּ לַה' בְּהַר הַקֹּדֶשׁ בִּירוּשָׁלָם, *It shall be on that day that a great shofar will be blown, and those who are lost in the land of Assyria and those cast away in the land of Egypt will come [together], and they will prostrate themselves to Hashem on the holy mountain in Jerusalem* (*Yeshayah* 27:13).

Why did Hashem save the horns of this specific ram for these two occasions? Couldn't the horns of a different ram, a ram that was alive at the time of those events, be sufficient? Surely there was no shortage of rams at the time of *Mattan Torah* and there will be no shortage at the time of *L'asid Lavo*. There must be some connection between the horn of *Kabbalas HaTorah* and the horn of *L'asid Lavo*, and this connection seems to also be related to *Akeidas Yitzchak*.

❧ *What the Shofar Accomplishes*

The Ramchal,[23] in his commentary to the *davening* of Rosh Hashanah, presents a profound and fundamental idea.* He seeks to explain the purpose of blowing the shofar on Rosh Hashanah. After all, we spend many hours reciting the various *tefillos* of Rosh Hashanah. What is the purpose of also blowing a ram's horn? What does it add to what we seek to accomplish on the *Yom HaDin*?

The Ramchal says that the purpose of the shofar is to magnify the forces of good in this world, and to simultaneously diminish the forces of evil. Why must we do this? It is because when Adam HaRishon committed the *aveirah* of eating from the *Eitz HaDaas* on Rosh Hashanah, evil was infused into the fabric of the world. The forces of evil grew so strong that they completely overpowered and conquered the forces of good. Evil's triumph over the world was pervasive. These forces of evil dragged Man down and ultimately led to the *Dor HaMabul* and *Dor HaHaflagah*.

When evil has the forces of good in its grasp, holding it hostage, then goodness can never accomplish in This World. Hashem therefore decided that it was time to allow the forces of good to be released from the clutches of evil. This re-instatement

---

* For a complete discussion of this Ramchal, see "The Ramchal Reveals the Universal Reverberations of the Shofar," page 138.

of the forces of good in the world took place at Har Sinai, when the Torah was given. The forces of good were able to free themselves of the forces of evil, and they were able to assert themselves to a great extent. However, they were not, as yet, able to completely subdue the forces of evil. The Ramchal writes that the spiritual power of the shofar is what triggered this incredible comeback of the forces of good while it simultaneously quells the forces of evil.

The first time this happened was at the Giving of the Torah, when the forces of good freed themselves and began to assert themselves. But the process was incomplete. This first blowing of the shofar was unable to effect a complete eradication of evil; it could not provide goodness with complete dominion over the world.

When will the forces of good be able to fully assert themselves throughout the world, and in so doing completely conquer and destroy the forces of evil? It will be when the Great Shofar is blown *L'asid Lavo*, in the End of Days. This is why the shofar that will be blown then is referred to as the *Shofar Gadol*, the Great Shofar. The shofar of *Mattan Torah* did not complete the task, but the shofar of *L'asid Lavo*, *im yirtzeh Hashem*, will complete the task.

When we blow the shofar on Rosh Hashanah, and when we recite *pesukim* about the shofar of Sinai, we are not merely reciting *pesukim* that contain references to the shofar. We are amplifying what that shofar achieved; we are furthering the *koach* of good in the world and are bridging the gap to the final, ultimate shofar that will be blown at the End of Days. We are bringing the shofar of *L'asid Lavo* ever closer.

∾ Why Did These Shofaros Have to Come From the Ayil of Akeidas Yitzchak?

With this understanding of the function of the shofar, it is clear why the shofar of Har Sinai and the shofar of *L'asid Lavo* come from the same animal. But why did they have to come from the ram that was sacrificed in lieu of Yitzchak Avinu at the *Akeidah*?

The *Midrash*[24] says that the Man, the *Adam*, that Hashem had in mind when he created the original Man, was Avraham Avinu, and Avraham Avinu should have been the first Man to be created. However, Hashem was concerned. If Avraham, the ultimate man, had been created first and he made a mistake, there would be no one else who could have rectified his mistake. Instead, Hashem made Adam first, and this way, if he were to sin, Avraham would come and correct it.

Avraham Avinu is the paragon Man whom God intended when He said *Naaseh Adam*. When did Avraham demonstrate that he is the archetypical of Man, that he is the quintessential Man, whom Hashem considered the pinnacle of Creation? He demonstrated this when he passed the final and ultimate test, the tenth *nisayon*: *Akeidas Yitzchak*.

The Ramchal[25] writes that Adam sinned on that very first day of his creation, eating from the *Eitz HaDaas*. Hashem exhibited tolerance and patience. He knew that Adam would not be able to return to his original spiritual level immediately. Hashem set out to establish a time frame in which it could realistically be expected for Man to regain the same level of potential that he had prior to the *aveirah* of the *Eitz HaDaas*, at the time Adam was initially created.

Hashem established the time frame and then made a stipulation. If, within this predetermined window of time, a man would rise to the occasion and demonstrate that he can be the prototypical Man whom Hashem had intended to create, then he would achieve, for all his descendants, the ability for them to always return to that lofty level of *Adam HaRishon kodem hacheit*, Adam before the sin. This man's descendants would possess this tremendous potential. One who does not achieve this level during this time frame, on the other hand, will have descendants who for all eternity will be subject to remain less than ideal. They would never be able to restore themselves to the level of *Adam HaRishon kodem hacheit*.

The time frame that Hashem established was from Adam HaRishon until Avraham Avinu. During this period, there were *tzaddikim*, righteous people, exceptional people, but it was not until Avraham Avinu that anyone achieved the level of the ultimate Man. In doing so, Avraham received the guarantee that his descendants would always retain the ability to return to the *madreigah* of *Adam HaRishon kodem hacheit*.

The Ramchal offers the metaphor of a tree. Only branches of the tallest and sturdiest tree can expect to be as strong and sturdy as the tree trunk. Branches of weaker trees cannot achieve this same strength. In order for a man to hope that one day he can achieve the level of Adam HaRishon before he sinned, he must be a branch of the tree that established itself as epitome of what Man can accomplish — that of Avraham Avinu. The growth of the other nations of the world is stymied by their ancestors' lack of initiative in achieving the greatness that would have benefited their descendants for time immemorial. Only Klal Yisrael, descendants of Avraham Avinu, have this privilege, because Avraham rose to the occasion. He did not squander the opportunity. No matter how low we may fall, or how far we may stray, we always retain this incredible ability not only to come back, but to return to the loftiest level that is possible: *Adam HaRishon kodem hacheit*. We can anticipate that *L'asid Lavo*, when the Great Shofar sounds, we will all be reinstated to that extraordinary *madreigah*.

The nations of the world can graft themselves onto our tree, as it were, by becoming members of Klal Yisrael. If a non-Jew undergoes *geirus*, converting to *Yiddishkeit*, he can then reap the benefits eligible to those who are descendants of Avraham Avinu and then he, too, can achieve the ultimate level. All members of humanity do have an opportunity: They can remove themselves from the tree of their ancestors and graft themselves onto our tree, joining us as descendants of Avraham Avinu. This is alluded to in the words of the *pasuk,* וְנִבְרְכוּ בְךָ כֹּל מִשְׁפְּחֹת הָאֲדָמָה, which can be translated, *and can be grafted onto you all the families of the world* (Bereishis 12:3). *Geirus* affords the non-Jew the potential to reach the loftiest of levels.

ᔍ Hashem's Answer to the Malachim

When the angels came to Hashem and challenged His desire to make Man, pointing out the capacity for destruction that Man has, Hashem's response encapsulates both the answer of the *midrash* and the answer of the Gemara: Avraham Avinu and *Mattan Torah*. They are not a contradiction, but rather two components of a single answer. The spiritual level Avraham Avinu achieved at the *Akeidah* allowed for the spiritual elevation that was later experienced at Har Sinai. This is indicated by the fact that the shofar of *Kabbalas HaTorah* originated from the *ayil* of the *Akeidah*, the ram of Yitzchak Avinu.

When Avraham Avinu performed the *Akeidah*, he established for his descendants, for all time, the unlimited potential that Man has within him. The first time these extraordinary capabilities were displayed was at the Giving of the Torah, when the shofar was blown, enabling the forces of good to free themselves from the forces of evil. Good asserted itself in the world, but the task was incomplete. To complete the task of unleashing the forces of good and fully eradicating evil, we blow the shofar annually on Rosh Hashanah that will ultimately lead to the *Shofar Gadol* of *L'asid Lavo*. Then the task will be complete.

This great mission of Mankind, introduced by Avraham Avinu, expressed at *Kabbalas HaTorah*, and which will further be expressed at the time of *L'asid Lavo*, was all earned through the merit of Avraham Avinu.

Every year on Rosh Hashanah, says Rav Yonasan Eibeshutz, there is a war, a battle, with the angels who are screaming and clamoring, מָה אֱנוֹשׁ כִּי תִזְכְּרֶנּוּ, fighting against our right to exist. Then we sound the shofar, and we remind the Ribbono shel Olam, and remind ourselves that Hashem continues to pay attention to Man due to the infinite potential we all have. We can rise even above the heavenly angels, to soar to the heavens and cling to our Creator. That is our *zechus* on Rosh Hashanah for a blessed year.

May the Ribbono shel Olam bless us with a year of good

health and success, a year of growth in *ruchniyus* and of coming closer to the Ribbono shel Olam. May we be *zocheh* to hear the sound of the Shofar *Gadol bimheirah v'yameinu, Amen.*

ENDNOTES

1. ראש השנה טז, ב.
2. מגילה לא, א.
3. רש״י שם. ע׳ במטה אפרים סימן תקצח ס״ק ה, ומשנה ברורה סימן שכד ס״ק לא.
4. או״ח סימן תקפג סעיף א.
5. משנה ברורה שם ס״ק ח.
6. או״ח סימן תקפג סעיף ג.
7. או״ח סימן תרה.
8. משנה ברורה שם ס״ק ד.
9. חיי אדם כלל קמד, ד.
10. חיבור התשובה
11. פסיקתא רבתי פרשה מ אות ח.
12. ילקוט ראובני, וירא.

13. ספר דרשות אבן שועיב, דרש ליו״כ.
14. שמות רבה פרשה טו, יא.
15. סנהדרין לח, ב.
16. יערות דבש חלק ב דרוש ה עמוד פג.
17. זוהר הקדוש חלק א׳ כח.
18. שפת אמת לסוכות תרמו ד״ה בעינין דברים page 208.
19. מדרש תנחומא פרשת וירא כג, יח.
20. מאמרי חכמה מאמר ז עמוד שכא.
21. מהרש״א סנהדרין לח עמוד ב.
22. פרקי דרבי אליעזר פרק לא.
23. מאמר החכמה, רמח״ל.
24. בראשית רבה יד, ו.
25. דרך ה׳, חלק ב פרק ד אות ג.

Rav Shlomo Kluger Uncovers the Annual Lottery of Rosh Hashanah

ﮯ May Hashem's Malchus Be Revealed and Recognized

In the *berachah* of *Kedushas HaYom* of Rosh Hashanah, we recite:

אֱלֹקֵינוּ וֵאלֹקֵי אֲבוֹתֵינוּ, מְלוֹךְ עַל כָּל הָעוֹלָם כֻּלּוֹ בִּכְבוֹדֶךָ, וְהִנָּשֵׂא עַל כָּל הָאָרֶץ בִּיקָרֶךָ, וְהוֹפַע בַּהֲדַר גְּאוֹן עֻזֶּךָ עַל כָּל יוֹשְׁבֵי תֵבֵל אַרְצֶךָ, וְיֵדַע כָּל פָּעוּל, כִּי אַתָּה פְּעַלְתּוֹ, וְיָבִין כָּל יְצוּר, כִּי אַתָּה יְצַרְתּוֹ, וְיֹאמַר כֹּל אֲשֶׁר נְשָׁמָה בְאַפּוֹ: ה' אֱלֹקֵי יִשְׂרָאֵל מֶלֶךְ, וּמַלְכוּתוֹ בַּכֹּל מָשָׁלָה, *Ribbono shel Olam, rule over the whole world in Your honor. Elevate Yourself over the entire land in Your Glory. Reveal Yourself in the majesty of Your might, etc.*

We ask Hashem that His sovereignty and dominion should become manifest over the whole world. Every creation should recognize its Creator. We ask that Hashem's *Malchus* be evident throughout all of Creation.

This is somewhat of a strange request. What does Rosh Hashanah have to do with Hashem's sovereignty being recognized throughout the world? We know that the day will

eventually come when all will recognize God's *Malchus*. וְהָיָה ה׳
לְמֶלֶךְ עַל כָּל הָאָרֶץ בַּיּוֹם הַהוּא יִהְיֶה ה׳ אֶחָד וּשְׁמוֹ אֶחָד, on that day the
world will recognize His *Malchus*.

Will that day be on Rosh Hashanah? We have no tradition
that Mashiach will come on Rosh Hashanah, so why do we ask
— on Rosh Hashanah — that Hashem's *Malchus* be recognized
globally? We should mention that we, Klal Yisrael, recognize
Hashem and His *Malchus*, and that should suffice for what we
are striving to accomplish on Rosh Hashanah, the *Yom HaDin*,
as Hashem, our King, judges us.

❧ *Approach of the Ramchal*

The Ramchal authored *Maamar HaChachmah*, a compendium
on the *tefillos* of the Yamim Noraim, in which he explains[1] that
on Rosh Hashanah Hashem stands as King over the whole
world, manifest as the Ruler of all existence on this day. Since
as its King He is judging the world on Rosh Hashanah, it is
fitting to *daven* that one day He should be recognized by all.
This would then lead to *tikkun*, rectification, of all of Creation.
As the Ramchal writes, even though this request is not directly
connected to Rosh Hashanah, we mention that we hope that one
day the whole world will recognize this, since it is the day when
Hashem functions as the King of the universe.

The question remains: If this is not an event connected to
Rosh Hashanah and is not an event that will transpire on Rosh
Hashanah, why include it in our Rosh Hashanah *davening*? Let
us try to discover how the revelation of Hashem's sovereignty in
the world is fundamental to our aspirations on Rosh Hashanah.

❧ *Festive Dress and Meals*
on the Day of Judgment?

The Tur[2] writes that the *minhag* is to prepare for Rosh Hashanah
by taking a haircut, trimming one's nails, and wearing fresh white
clothing. On Yom Tov itself, we eat, drink, and rejoice.

Now let us consider: If someone were to be charged with a capital offense, and their life were on the line, this type of behavior would seem out of place. They would not have the emotional wherewithal to don their nicest clothing, bathe, and shave. They would be focused on and worried about their upcoming trial. Personal grooming and dressing in finery would be the furthest thing from their mind. With their life being in jeopardy, they would not be partaking in festive meals, replete with numerous delicacies and fine wine!

Yet, on the *Yom HaDin*, on a day that the Books of Life and Death are open before Hashem as He proceeds to judge us, we do just that! We dress up and have a festive meal. Why? The Tur explains that this is because we are confident that Hashem will perform a miracle for us and save us.

This Tur is presenting an idea that seems to be antithetical to our understanding of the process of judgment on Rosh Hashanah! The Gemara[3] states that the *omek hadin*, the depth of judgment, is hidden from us. The scrutiny is beyond our ability to fathom. Hashem looks at each person individually, and He carefully probes and analyzes every action and thought. Can anyone confidently say that his mitzvos outweigh his *aveiros*!

In *Selichos* we recite that the number of *aveiros* we've committed is more numerous than the hairs on our head. As such, no person can confidently state that he will emerge victorious in judgment in the eyes of Hashem. Even the angels melt in awe of Hashem's judgment, as the *tefillah* of *Nesaneh Tokef* states, "*malachim yechafeizun, chil u're'adah yocheizun.*"

If, *chas v'shalom*, a person has more *aveiros* than mitzvos, then when he is judged on Rosh Hashanah, he is immediately given the guilty verdict and sentenced to death.

How can the Tur write that we are happy and self-assured on Rosh Hashanah? Why would confidence in the outcome of the *din* be an appropriate sentiment?

Typically, we try to engender *eimas hadin*, fear of [the outcome of] the judgment. In fact, the reason we don't say *Hallel* on Rosh Hashanah is because of our fear at this awesome time, when the

Books of Life and Death are open before the Ribbono shel Olam. If, as the Tur writes, we are so confident with regard to a positive outcome, so assured that a miracle will be invoked to save us, perhaps we should say *Hallel*?

Understanding this Tur will allow us not only to achieve a deeper understanding of Rosh Hashanah, but it also will serve to clarify the progression we undergo in the days from Rosh Hashanah through the *Aseres Yemei Teshuvah*, Yom Kippur, and Succos.

๏ Even Remnants of Mitzvos Are Powerful

The Gemara[4] states that the *shiyarei*, residual parts, of a mitzvah restrain punishment. *Tenufah*, waving a *korban*, although it is considered a residual part of a mitzvah and not the mitzvah itself, has the power to prevent harmful *ruchos*, winds, and harmful dew. Rava adds that the same can be said of the *lulav*. The main mitzvah of the *lulav* is to hold it, to perform *netilah*, lifting, of the *lulav*. Once someone picks up the *lulav*, he has discharged his obligation of the mitzvah of *lulav*. Yet, we do *naanuim*, waving the *lulav* in all six directions as we perform the mitzvah, as it, too, prevents bad winds and bad dew. Even though the mitzvah has been completed with merely picking up the *lulav*, the *shiyarei mitzvah* are potent merits and serve to ward off the evil winds and the evil dew. Rav Acha bar Yaakov waved his *lulav* back and forth, simultaneously proclaiming that his *lulav* is an arrow in the eye of the *Satan*. However, the Gemara concludes, when *shaking* the lulav one should not do this, since such statements will only serve to incite the *Satan*.

๏ Why Incite the Satan With the Lulav?

Of all the mitzvos to use in taunting the *Satan*, Rav Acha bar Yaakov used the *lulav*. Why? Why wouldn't he blow the shofar and tell the *Satan* that *this* mitzvah is an arrow in his eye? Or why not use any other item used for a mitzvah?[5]

❧ Understanding the Timing of the Naanuim on Succos

On Succos, we shake the *lulav* three times during *Hallel*. The first is when we recite *Hodu L'Hashem*, the second when we say *Ana Hashem*, and the third when we once again recite *Hodu L'Hashem*.

Perek 117 of *Tehillim* states: הַלְלוּ אֶת ה׳ כָּל גּוֹיִם שַׁבְּחוּהוּ כָּל הָאֻמִּים. כִּי גָבַר עָלֵינוּ חַסְדּוֹ וֶאֱמֶת ה׳ לְעוֹלָם הַלְלוּקָה. The following *perek*, 118, starts with הוֹדוּ לַה׳ כִּי טוֹב כִּי לְעוֹלָם חַסְדּוֹ. In the middle of this *perek*, *pasuk* 25, we reach the *pasuk* אָנָּא ה׳ הוֹשִׁיעָה נָּא. *Pasuk* 29 then repeats הוֹדוּ לַה׳ כִּי טוֹב כִּי לְעוֹלָם חַסְדּוֹ.

Tosafos[6] wonders why Beis Hillel maintains that we shake the *lulav* and *esrog* when we say אָנָּא ה׳ הוֹשִׁיעָה נָּא, which is right in the middle of the *perek*. *Tosafos* understands shaking the *lulav* when we say the first and final *pesukim* of the *perek*. But why shake it when saying a *pasuk* that is in the middle?

Tosafos explains that the reason for shaking at that point is based on *I Divrei HaYamim* 16: 32-35: יִרְעַם הַיָּם וּמְלוֹאוֹ יַעֲלֹץ הַשָּׂדֶה וְכָל אֲשֶׁר בּוֹ. אָז יְרַנְּנוּ עֲצֵי הַיָּעַר מִלִּפְנֵי ה׳ כִּי בָא לִשְׁפּוֹט אֶת הָאָרֶץ. הוֹדוּ לַה׳ כִּי טוֹב כִּי לְעוֹלָם חַסְדּוֹ. וְאִמְרוּ הוֹשִׁיעֵנוּ אֱלֹקֵי יִשְׁעֵנוּ וְקַבְּצֵנוּ וְהַצִּילֵנוּ מִן הַגּוֹיִם לְהֹדוֹת לְשֵׁם קָדְשֶׁךָ לְהִשְׁתַּבֵּחַ בִּתְהִלָּתֶךָ, *The sea and its fullness will roar; the field and everything in it will exult; then all the trees of the forest will sing with joy—before Hashem, for He will have come to judge the earth. Give thanks to Hashem for He is good; for His kindness endures forever. Say, "Save us, O God of our salvation; gather us and deliver us from the nations, to give thanks to Your holy Name, to glory in Your Praise.* The exultation of Hashem's creations is an allusion to the shaking of the *lulav*, the *naanuim*. This will happen when Hashem comes to judge the world. This seems to imply that the *naanuim* are in response to the *Yom HaDin*. When is it אָז יְרַנְּנוּ עֲצֵי הַיָּעַר, when do we shake the trees of the forest? מִלִּפְנֵי ה׳ כִּי בָא לִשְׁפּוֹט אֶת הָאָרֶץ, when Hashem comes to judge the land.

The shaking then happens when the next *pasuk* is recited: הוֹדוּ לַה׳ כִּי טוֹב כִּי לְעוֹלָם חַסְדּוֹ. The *pasuk* in *Divrei HaYamim* continues and tells us when the second set of *naanuim* is to be performed: וְאָמְרוּ הוֹשִׁיעֵנוּ אֱלֹקֵי יִשְׁעֵנוּ – when we say that Hashem should save us — when we recite, אָנָּא ה׳ הוֹשִׁיעָה נָּא. Thus, says *Tosafos*, the opinion of Beis Hillel is rooted in the verses in *Divrei HaYamim*.

However, if these *pesukim* are teaching us the timing of the *naanuim*, why does the *pasuk* interject the words, מִלְּפְנֵי ה׳ כִּי בָא לִשְׁפּוֹט אֶת הָאָרֶץ? What is the connection between the timing of shaking the *Arba Minim* and the *Yom HaDin*? The *pasuk* could simply say אָז יְרַנְּנוּ עֲצֵי הַיָּעַר, at *Hodu* and *Ana*[7]!? As mentioned, these *pesukim* indicate that the *naanuim* are a response to the days of judgment. Let us explore the connection.

❧ Two Judgments on Rosh Hashanah

The *Netziv*,[8] the Volozhin Rosh Yeshivah, reveals to us that really two judgments take place on Rosh Hashanah. He also posits the idea that the shofar has two dimensions to it.

One judgment is the individual *din* of each and every person on his own. Each person is judged for life and for his livelihood, as the *pasuk* states, כִּי חֹק לְיִשְׂרָאֵל הוּא (*Tehillim* 81:5); חֹק refers to livelihood. Hashem judges Jew and non-Jew alike on Rosh Hashanah, and every person is assessed as an individual. Mitzvos and *maasim tovim* are tallied up and are weighed against a person's *aveiros*. Hashem then determines a person's health, livelihood, and success. Every detail of a person's personal life — for that year — is decided on Rosh Hashanah.

The second judgment involves the entirety of the Bnei Yisrael, as we are judged against the nations of the world. There is a war, a *milchamah*, that takes place between the angels of the nations of the world and Klal Yisrael. Hashem comes to rest His *Kavod*, His Glory, on the Bnei Yisrael, as we proclaim Him as the King. The other nations work to hinder this effort, and they strive to prevent Hashem from having His *Kavod* rest on Klal Yisrael. By proclaiming that the whole world will recognize Hashem's *Malchus*, we are victorious over the *koach hadin*, in the communal judgment of the *tzibbur* of Klal Yisrael.

✑ Two Dimensions of the Shofar

The shofar also has two distinct *dinim*, two different dimensions to it.

The shofar functions as a wake-up call, stirring us to arouse from the narcotic of complacency. עוּרוּ יְשֵׁנִים מִשְּׁנַתְכֶם, *Arouse, you slumberers, from your sleep!*[9] This is the function of the shofar on the personal level, for each and every person individually.

On the national level, the shofar functions as the clarion call to battle, since we are at war with the angels of the nations of the world on Rosh Hashanah. Hashem is coming to have His *Shechinah* dwell on us, and these angels are working to instigate against us. We fight with them, and the way we are victorious is by proclaiming Hashem to be King of the universe.

We are well aware of the first aspect of Rosh Hashanah. There is an individual *din*, a personal judgment, for each of us, during which Hashem scrutinizes our behavior and judges us based on our actions. He utilizes our personal merits and demerits in deciding our fate — as individuals — for the upcoming year.

But what does the *Netziv* mean when he says there is a war on Rosh Hashanah against the ministering angels of the world[10]? How are we fighting a war? And what does he mean, "Hashem is coming to rest His Glory on the Bnei Yisrael, and the nations of the world work to hinder these efforts"? In what way do the nations of the world try to intervene against Hashem resting His *Shechinah* on Klal Yisrael?

✑ Klal Yisrael vs. Umos HaOlam

Tehillim 16:11 states, נְעִמוֹת בִּימִינְךָ נֶצַח, *the delights that are in Your right hand for eternity.* This is one of the phrases we recite between paragraphs of *Hoshanos* on Hoshana Rabbah. The *midrash*[11] teaches that this *pasuk* can be understood with a parable about two people who enter a court to stand before the judge. We have no idea in whose favor the judge will decide and who will be victorious. When the litigants exit, the one who raises the flag is the one who has prevailed, who emerges victorious. Likewise, the Jewish people and the *umos ha'olam*, the nations of the world, come before Hashem on Rosh Hashanah, where they stand on trial. Here too, the victor is not clear. When Klal Yisrael emerges from the court after the *Yemei HaDin* raising the flag — the *lulav*, *esrog*, *hadassim*, and *aravos* — it is clear to all that we have emerged victorious. Holding the *Arba Minim* in our hands demonstrates our status as triumphant victors.

Once again, we are baffled by the point of discussion. What court case is there between the Bnei Yisrael and the *umos ha'olam*? In what sense is Rosh Hashanah a judgment between the Jews and the nations of the world? Aside from each person being judged on his own personal level for health, welfare, *parnassah*, etc., is there a national competition between the Jewish people and the rest of the world? What do we win when we emerge with the *Arba Minim*?

The *Midrash* and the *Netziv* are both teaching us that on Rosh Hashanah there is some sort of conflict, some type of war, taking place between Klal Yisrael and the *umos ha'olam*. It is unclear what the point of conflict is, or why it is a major aspect of the judgment on Rosh Hashanah. Rav Shlomo Kluger advances an idea that will revolutionize our understanding of what actually transpires on Rosh Hashanah.

⌇ *The Celestial Lottery*

The *pasuk* states, בְּהַנְחֵל עֶלְיוֹן גּוֹיִם בְּהַפְרִידוֹ בְּנֵי אָדָם יַצֵּב גְּבֻלֹת עַמִּים, לְמִסְפַּר בְּנֵי יִשְׂרָאֵל. כִּי חֵלֶק ה' עַמּוֹ יַעֲקֹב חֶבֶל נַחֲלָתוֹ *When the Supreme One gave the nations their inheritance, when He separated the children of man, He set the borders of the peoples, according to the number of the Children of Yisrael. For Hashem's portion is His people; Yaakov is the measure of His inheritance (Devarim* 32: 8-9).

These *pesukim* are explained in an astounding fashion by *Targum Yonasan ben Uziel* and *Pirkei D'Rabbi Eliezer*.[12] In the times of *Migdal Bavel*, the Tower of Babel, Hashem was displeased with mankind as a single unit and He decided to divide the people of the world into individual nations. Since there would eventually be seventy people who would go down to Mitzrayim with Yaakov Avinu, Hashem chose to make seventy different nations.

בְּהַפְרִידוֹ בְּנֵי אָדָם — Says Hashem: I am going to separate mankind;

יַצֵּב גְּבֻלֹת עַמִּים — I am going to establish the boundaries of people.

How many?

לְמִסְפַּר בְּנֵי יִשְׂרָאֵל — Based on the number of the Jewish people, which is seventy.

Hashem then gathered all the ministering angels together, and embarked on a lottery of sorts. Each angel would choose one nation that they would be responsible for and oversee. Hashem entered seventy-one names into the lottery, and each angel picked one.

When it came time for Hashem to choose His nation, he picked Avraham and his descendants: כִּי חֵלֶק ה' עַמּוֹ יַעֲקֹב חֶבֶל נַחֲלָתוֹ. Hashem selected Klal Yisrael! And Hashem was overjoyed with His pick in the lottery! As the *pasuk* says, חֲבָלִים נָפְלוּ לִי בַּנְּעִמִים, *My share is a pleasant share* (Tehillim 16:6).

The *malach Michael* then congratulated Hashem on His choice. After all the seventy nations were chosen, Hashem gave each nation a different language, each nation had its *malach*, and Klal Yisrael became the חֶבֶל, *portion*, of Hashem.

❧ Two Judgments on Rosh Hashanah Explained

Rav Shlomo Kluger[13] writes that there are in fact two separate processes occurring simultaneously on Rosh Hashanah.

The first process occurs as Hashem is judging each and every individual, and no single person can possibly anticipate the outcome. Rosh Hashanah is referenced in the *pasuk*, בַּכֶּסֶה לְיוֹם חַגֵּנוּ (Tehillim 81:4). It is a day that is hidden. What is hidden about it? Certainly, the moon is hidden, since it is the very beginning of the lunar month and the moon is not yet visible. Rav Shlomo Heiman[14] adds another hidden element of Rosh Hashanah. On every Rosh Hashanah, each Jew is given an undisclosed verdict by the Ribbono shel Olam, as if in a box that is sealed shut and whose contents are unknown. We likewise have no idea of the outcome of the *din* and what the year has in store for us. The *din* is completely hidden. This is the first aspect of the *din* of Rosh Hashanah: personal judgment on each and every individual. Regarding this personal *din*, there can be no confidence in the judgment, no assurances that someone will have a good year. Without exception, we all but tremble in trepidation on Rosh Hashanah from the *eimas hadin*.

What then does the Tur mean by stating, as noted above, that we are confidently dressed in our finest, partaking of festive meals, and enjoying fine wine because we know Hashem will perform a miracle for us?

Rav Shlomo Kluger explains that this Tur is referring to the second process of *din* that takes place on Rosh Hashanah.

Every year on Rosh Hashanah, the *malachim* clamor before Hashem, imploring Him to recast the celestial lottery. They want to change the nations for which they are responsible. Each *malach* wants a chance to be the one who has Klal Yisrael. Hashem acquiesces annually, and He gathers His court together to redistribute the nations of the world among the *malachim*. Every year there is a *din*, and Hashem then decides if Klal Yisrael will continue to be His nation, or if we will be given to one of the other angels. He judges annually whether or not we will continue to be the *chelek Hashem*.

The good news is that in regards to this *din*, we know that Hashem will make a miracle for us, and He will ensure that we remain His nation. We rest assured that the outcome of this *din* will be in our favor. We are confident that we will continue to be עַמּוֹ וְצֹאן מַרְעִיתוֹ, *His nation and the sheep of His pasture* (*Tehillim* 100:3).

Why then do we wear our finest clothing on Rosh Hashanah? If a person's personal life is on the line, why does the confidence in the collective *din*, that Hashem will once again choose us as His lot, deem it appropriate for us to bathe, take haircuts, look our best, and partake in festive meals?

Rav Shlomo Kluger compares our situation on Rosh Hashanah to someone who receives a phenomenal gift, a priceless commodity, while simultaneously receiving a small degree of *agmas nefesh*, a small inconvenience. For instance, someone is gifted the winning lottery ticket to a multimillion-dollar drawing, contingent on which is his having to make the long trek to the bank. The inconvenience that he has to undergo is so minimal and insignificant compared to the exceptional windfall he is receiving that his celebration over his victory is not mitigated in the slightest.

Our personal lives and circumstances are in jeopardy, and no one can be confident that he will emerge victorious. We need to be very concerned about this, and we must strive our utmost to increase the likelihood that we will in fact emerge victorious in *din*. However, the overwhelming happiness, the phenomenal thrill at knowing that we will once again emerge from the celestial lottery as the nation of Hashem supersedes this concern to such a degree that our concerns naturally fall by the wayside. We are confident that Hashem will once again select us to be His, and this gives us such incredible joy and *simchah* that it completely overrides any *agmas nefesh* we might have in anticipation of our personal *din*. Rejoicing in this collective victory of Klal Yisrael is therefore appropriately celebrated, and we dress in our finest *bigdei* Yom Tov and partake in festive meals.

This allows us to understand and appreciate the meaning of the Tur. We are *batuach* and *sameiach* in the collective, national *din*, despite the fact that the personal *din* is still undecided.

∾ *The Victory Lap With the Arba Minim*

We carry our *Arba Minim* on Succos, and we openly display our victory, we publicly proclaim that we won. We are not celebrating that each individual had a favorable outcome in his personal judgment, for, as we said, no one knows what verdict he received. Rather, we are celebrating our victory at once again being selected as Hashem's nation. Hashem revisited the great court case as to who will be His *am*, His nation, His *chelek*, His lottery pick. The lottery, the court case against all the angels of the nations of the world, is not rigged, and there is no predetermined outcome. Yet, we are able to raise our *lulavim* in triumphant victory, confident that this was one court case from which we emerged victorious.

This is the meaning behind the shaking of the *lulav* and the *esrog*. We were victorious over the *umos haolam* in that we have once again been *zocheh* to the greatest *berachah* in the world: to be considered the *am Hashem*.

Tosafos[15] quoted above, discusses the timing of the *naanuim*. The recitation of certain *pesukim* is accompanied by the *naanuim*, and the source for the *pesukim* is from *I Divrei HaYamim*. אָז יְרַנְּנוּ עֲצֵי הַיָּעַר, when do we do the *naanuim*, when will the trees of the forest shake? מִלִּפְנֵי ה' כִּי בָא לִשְׁפּוֹט אֶת הָאָרֶץ, when Hashem comes to judge the world. To which judgment does this refer? To the judgment as to which nation will be the *am Hashem*, who will be the *chelek Hashem*. Then we pick up the *lulav, esrog, hadassim*, and *aravos*, and we declare, הוֹדוּ לַה' כִּי טוֹב כִּי לְעוֹלָם חַסְדּוֹ. We thank Hashem for emerging victorious in that *din*. We shake again when we say the words *ana Hashem hoshiah na*, as we ask Hashem to save us from the verdict we fear: the individual judgment of whose outcome we are unsure, praying and relying on the mercy of HaKadosh Baruch Hu.

This is what the *Netziv*[16] is referring to when he writes that Rosh Hashanah is a day of a *milchamah* for Klal Yisrael. It is a war between us and the ministering angels of the other nations of the world. None of these angels have any legitimate claim or challenge against any single individual Jew. Rather, the *milchamah* is between them and the Jewish nation as a whole. They don't want Klal Yisrael to enjoy the privilege of being guided by Hashem.

～ *The Song: We Are Your Lot*

During Mussaf on Yom Kippur we sing, כִּי אָנוּ עַמֶּךָ וְאַתָּה אֱלֹקֵינוּ. אָנוּ בָנֶיךָ וְאַתָּה אָבִינוּ. אָנוּ עֲבָדֶיךָ וְאַתָּה אֲדוֹנֵנוּ, וְגו׳, *We are Your people, and You are our God. We are Your children, and You are our Father, etc.*

At first glance, it seems curious that this *tefillah* is included in the *davening* of Yom Kippur. What does our relationship with Hashem, however it is manifest, have to do with Yom Kippur? The focus of Yom Kippur is asking Hashem to forgive us — סְלַח לָנוּ. מְחַל לָנוּ. כַּפֶּר לָנוּ — so why do we change course and state that we are the share, the portion, the lot of Hashem?

This *tefillah* is declaring another significant element of the Yamim Noraim. Aside from our personal judgment, there is another *din*, a communal evaluation. It is regarding this second *din*, in which Hashem is challenged by the ministering angels of all seventy nations, that we are confident and can comfortably declare as a congregation, אָנוּ עַמֶּךָ, אָנוּ בָנֶיךָ, אָנוּ עֲבָדֶיךָ, אָנוּ קְהָלֶךָ, אָנוּ נַחֲלָתֶךָ .... We are Yours, and about this we are certain.

～ *What Is the Chelek of Hashem?*

What does it mean to be the *chelek* of Hashem? We are God's lottery prize, His portion. What does this truly signify?

Let us study a very fundamental Ramban[17] that will deepen our understanding of the *pasuk,* כִּי חֵלֶק ה׳ עַמּוֹ יַעֲקֹב חֶבֶל נַחֲלָתוֹ. The Honorable God created everything, and He placed the power to govern what exists in this world through the upper spheres. Every nation, in its land, has a certain constellation that is the intermediary between God on High and that specific nation. Even though Hashem runs the world and is in control, neverthe-less there is somewhat of a hierarchy. Hashem delegates what happens to the *umos ha'olam* through one of His subordinates: the *kochavim,* the *mazalos.* Every nation has its own constel-lation, a *malach,* an intermediary assigned to it to act as a go-between between it and Hashem.

However, Klal Yisrael is different. Eretz Yisrael is the *nachalah* of Hashem, and there is no angel to function in the role of intermediary. Hashem refers to Klal Yisrael with the phrase, וִהְיִיתֶם לִי סְגֻלָּה מִכָּל הָעַמִּים, *You shall be to Me the most beloved treasure of all peoples* (*Shemos* 19:5) and וִהְיִיתֶם לִי לְעָם וְאָנֹכִי אֶהְיֶה לָכֶם לֵאלֹקִים, *You will be a people unto Me and I will be a God unto you* (*Yirmiyahu* 30:22). The implication is clear: Hashem will not deal with Klal Yisrael through an intermediary; He will care for and protect us personally, as it were. There is no go-between — just God and the Jewish people, unlike all the other nations of the world. This is what the *pasuk* means by כִּי חֵלֶק ה' עַמּוֹ, we are the *chelek* of HaKadosh Baruch Hu.

This idea can give us a very profound understanding of the mitzvah of *succah* as well.

∞ *Why Isn't Succos in Nissan?*

When Klal Yisrael left Mitzrayim, we were accompanied by the *Ananei HaKavod*. These Clouds of Glory came to us on the fifteenth day of Nissan. The Tur poses the question that if the *Ananei HaKavod* came to the Bnei Yisrael in Nissan, we ought to be commemorating this fantastic event in Nissan! Why do we celebrate in Tishrei?

The Vilna Gaon[18] answers this question, teaching us that the celebration of Succos is not about the original arrival of the *Ananei HaKavod*, but rather is a commemoration of the *Ananei HaKavod* returning to us after we forfeited our right to them because of the *Cheit HaEigel*.* After the sin of the Golden Calf, the *Ananei HaKavod* departed, and so did Hashem's Presence. In His place, a *malach* was dispatched to lead the Jewish people. After Moshe Rabbeinu *davened*, and Klal Yisrael was forgiven, Hashem fully reinstated our unique relationship with Him. The *Ananei HaKavod* returned, symbolic of the fact that the close and

---

* For a complete discussion on the approach of the Vilna Gaon, see "The Return of the Clouds of Glory: The Vilna Gaon Revolutionizes Succos," page 278.

personal relationship that we enjoyed with Hashem prior to the *Cheit HaEigel* had been completely restored.

When Klal Yisrael stood at Har Sinai, Hashem had "fired" the *Malach HaMaves*, telling him that he had no jurisdiction over the Jewish nation. He is a *malach* and, said Hashem, the Jewish people are Mine, and are not under the control of a *malach*. They are My *chelek*, as the *Midrash* cited above states: בְּהַנְחֵל עֶלְיוֹן גּוֹיִם בְּהַפְרִידוֹ בְּנֵי אָדָם יַצֵּב גְּבֻלת עַמִּים לְמִסְפַּר בְּנֵי יִשְׂרָאֵל. כִּי חֵלֶק ה' עַמּוֹ יַעֲקֹב חֶבֶל נַחֲלָתוֹ. The Jews are My *chelek*, and you, as a *malach* cannot touch them.[19] Every other nation of the world required a *malach*, except for Klal Yisrael, whose personal relationship directly with Hashem was unique and did not allow for an intermediary.

Klal Yisrael had achieved an incredible feat at Har Sinai, when Hashem rescinded the *Malach HaMaves's* jurisdiction over the Jewish people. This exceptional achievement was lost due to the *Cheit HaEigel*.

∽ The Cheit HaEigel Resulted in an Intermediary Between Hashem and Klal Yisrael

By committing the sin of the *Eigel*, the Bnei Yisrael violated this relationship with Hashem. They demonstrated that they did want an intermediary; they did want a go-between to intervene between them and Hashem. They indicated that they wanted to be like the other nations of the world.

Hashem's response was that if this was what they wanted, then they were welcome to have a *malach* function in the capacity of an intermediary, and Hashem left, leaving a *malach* in His stead. Just as the other nations of the world utilize a *sar* as their connection to Hashem, so too would Klal Yisrael.

When Moshe Rabbeinu implored Hashem to forgive Klal Yisrael, he was not satisfied with merely achieving a state where Hashem would not punish the Bnei Yisrael for the *aveirah*. He did not rest until Hashem agreed to restore our relationship with Him to how it had been, without an intermediary, saying, אִם אֵין פָּנֶיךָ הֹלְכִים אַל תַּעֲלֵנוּ מִזֶּה, *If Your Presence does not go along, do not bring us forward from here* (*Shemos* 33:15). Rabbeinu Yonah[20] writes that for *tzaddikim* it does not suffice to be atoned and forgiven. They want to achieve the level that had been theirs previously; חַדֵּשׁ יָמֵינוּ כְּקֶדֶם. They want the relationship to be renewed as if nothing had ever happened to disturb it.

It was Moshe Rabbeinu who had *davened* for the *Ananei HaKavod* to return. וְנִפְלִינוּ אֲנִי וְעַמְּךָ, *and I and Your people will be made distinct* (*Shemos* 33:16). Moshe Rabbeinu beseeched Hashem to maintain Klal Yisrael's unique status, in which we exist without an intermediary, without a *malach* between us and Hashem. Hashem answered Moshe in the affirmative, and the *Ananei HaKavod* returned — on the first day of Succos.

The Gemara[21] states that Moshe Rabbeinu was still not satisfied. He wanted more, and his requests were granted. Hashem not only acceded to his request for the *Shechinah* to once again rest on Klal Yisrael, Moshe also requested that the *Shechinah* NOT rest on the *umos ha'olam*, and this was granted as well. It was not enough that Klal Yisrael should not have an intermediary; Moshe Rabbeinu wanted this relationship to be unique to Klal Yisrael, and he wanted no other nation in the world to have the same special relationship.

✎ *What Does Sitting in the Succah Commemorate?*

When we sit in the *succah*, we are commemorating that even though at the time of the *Cheit HaEigel* we lost the privilege of being Hashem's personal nation, the one people in the world who enjoyed a direct relationship with Him, we were able to receive a total reprieve and reinstatement of this unique connection to Hashem. Furthermore, we celebrate that Hashem did not offer this special relationship to any of the other nations of the world.

When we sit in the *succah,* we acknowledge and celebrate that we and only we are the *Chelek Hashem*. Basking in the Divine shade of the *succah*, we enjoy our direct relationship with Hashem as our personal Protector.

✣ Two Processes of the Yamim Noraim

As stated above, throughout the Yamim Noraim there are really two processes.

Each and every person traverses this awesome time of year as an individual. As an individual, this is a frightening and daunting process. After all, who could truly say that he is righteous, a virtuous *tzaddik* in the eyes of Hashem?

There is a second process that involves Klal Yisrael in its entirety. Another court case takes place, seeking to determine if we will be able to remain the *Chelek Hashem* — something we had lost on 17 Tammuz as a result of the *Cheit HaEigel*. When we shake the *lulav* we display and proclaim that we were victorious, and that it is we, and we alone, who are privileged to be the *Chelek Hashem*. We are confident that the outcome of this second, collective, *din* is favorable for us and is a triumphant victory that has to be celebrated.

We can now suggest an explanation as to why Rav Acha bar Yaakov specifically chose the *lulav* with which to incite the *Satan*. All the other mitzvos in the Torah are personal mitzvos, each one signifying that the individual performing it is an *eved Hashem*. This does not frighten the *Satan*, who can access the life recordings of each individual, impugning our worthy status calling into question our right to be called a true *eved Hashem*.

There is one mitzvah, however, that does frighten the *Satan*; one mitzvah is an arrow in his eye. That is the mitzvah of *lulav*, which is evidence of the *tzibbur's* victory. *Lulav* indicates that it is not I as an individual who is a worthy *eved Hashem*. Rather, it signifies that Klal Yisrael collectively is the *Chelek Hashem*.

This is an untouchable concept that the *Satan* cannot challenge. There is nothing about this that the *Satan* can successfully undermine. Just as we are confident that Hashem will choose us, the *Satan* knows this as well.

The one constant in this universe is נֵצַח יִשְׂרָאֵל לֹא יְשַׁקֵּר, the eternity of the Jewish people as the nation of Hashem. God always actively selects and chooses Klal Yisrael, כִּי חֵלֶק ה' עַמּוֹ יַעֲקֹב חֶבֶל נַחֲלָתוֹ.

The way we strengthen this, the way we achieve this, and the way in which we are victorious in this judgment, is we *daven*, "Ribbono shel Olam, please manifest Your *Malchus* over the whole world. We are Your Nation, Your people, Your ambassadors in the world. We are the ones who can declare that Your *Malchus* should be recognized in the whole world."

This is why one of the focal points of the *tefillah* on Rosh Hashanah is this added dimension of *davening* that not only is Hashem the *Melech*, but that His *Malchus* should be recognized throughout the world. This approach is indicated by the words of the *Netziv* cited above.

This is an important way to understand the progression from Rosh Hashanah to Yom Kippur and Succos.

We *daven* and hope that just as we are confident of the outcome of the *din* in regard to maintaining our status as the *Chelek Hashem*, so too may each one of us emerge victorious in our personal *din*, and may we all be blessed with a year of *berachah v'hatzlachah ad bias goel tzeddek*.

ENDNOTES

1. מאמר החכמה - רמח"ל.
2. טור או"ח סימן תקפא.
3. פסחים נד, ב.
4. סוכה לו, ב-לח, א.
5. דרושים ולקחי מוסר חלק ב', תלמיד של הגאון רבי מרדכי בנט, עמוד עו.
6. תוס' סוכה לו, ב.
7. דרושים ולקחי מוסר, שם, עמוד עז.
8. הרחב דבר נציב, פרשת, כ"ג:כ"ד.
9. רמבם ספר יד החזקה.
10. ירח למועדים ימים נוראים מאמר מז.
11. ויקרא רבה ל, ב.
12. תרגום יונתן בן עוזיאל, דברים לב, ח-ט, פרקי דרבי אליעזר פרק כד.
13. חכמת שלמה או"ח סימן תקפ"א.
14. חידושי ר' שלמה אמרו קצרות אות' נט בשם ר"י בלאזר.
15. תוס' סוכה לו, ב.
16. עיין בעמק דבר אחרי מות טז, כט.
17. רמב"ן פרשת אחרי מות יח, כה.
18. עבודת הגרשוני שיר השירים.
19. שמות רבה לב, ח.
20. שערי תשובה שער א אות מב.
21. ברכות ז, א.

ASERES
YEMEI TESHUVAH

The Urgency of Teshuvah

∾ *Human Nature*

An interesting phenomenon generally occurs when we hear words of inspiration that we feel are powerful and poignant. It is human nature to think, "If only so-and-so had heard this; he could have really used this type of *mussar*." We have the ability to deflect all criticism, believing that it does not apply to us. The wise man, however, is able to listen carefully to *divrei hisorerus* and apply them to himself for the sake of self-improvement.

∾ *Blessings vs. Curses*

Life is serious and we have to make some very difficult choices in this world. This is dramatically depicted in *Parashas Re'eh*, which begins with the *pasuk*, רְאֵה אָנֹכִי נֹתֵן לִפְנֵיכֶם הַיּוֹם בְּרָכָה וּקְלָלָה, *See, I present before you today a berachah, blessing, and a klalah, curse (Devarim 11:26)*. These are the two options. If you follow the Torah, you will receive blessing, and if you don't uphold the mitzvos, *klalah* will befall you. It's that simple.

∾ *Life vs. Death*

However, let's take a look at *Parashas Netzavim*, where there is a very similar *pasuk*: רְאֵה נָתַתִּי לְפָנֶיךָ הַיּוֹם אֶת הַחַיִּים וְאֶת הַטּוֹב וְאֶת

הַמָּוֶת וְאֶת הָרָע, *See — I have placed before you today the life and the good, and the death and the evil* (*Devarim* 30:15). Suddenly, the stakes are much higher. Earlier, Hashem had simply said that if you follow the Torah, things will be good and you'll have a life of *berachah*. If you do not follow the Torah, things won't be as good for you. Suddenly, the contrast is much starker — now we are talking about life and death. Why have the stakes been raised? First, it was *berachah* and *klalah*, and now it is life and death; why the change?

✑ The Rambam

In *Hilchos Teshuvah*,[1] the Rambam tells us that just as they weigh the merits and sins of a person — his mitzvos and *aveiros* — at the time he passes away, to determine whether or not he deserves *Olam Haba*, so too are all people judged on the Yom Tov of Rosh Hashanah. One who has more mitzvos than *aveiros* is considered a *tzaddik* and is sealed in the Book of Life. One who has more *aveiros* than mitzvos is considered a *rasha* and is sealed for *misah*, death. And one who is a *beinoni* — neither a *tzaddik* nor a *rasha* — his judgment remains suspended until Yom Kippur.

Hashem waits until Yom Kippur to judge one who is a *beinoni*. As the Rambam continues, If he does teshuvah, he will be inscribed for life. Thus, we see that doing teshuvah tips the scales in favor of merit, and he will earn life. But, the Rambam states, if a person does not do teshuvah, then his fate will be sealed *l'misah*, for death.

✑ Who Is a Beinoni?

Let us define the term *beinoni* to identify who is included in that category. Since the Rambam defines a *tzaddik* as someone who has more mitzvos than *aveiros* and a *rasha* as vice versa, clearly the Rambam's opinion must be that a *beinoni* is someone who has an equal number of mitzvos and *aveiros*; i.e., his merits and demerits are perfectly balanced. A *beinoni* is fifty-fifty, and this is indeed how the Raavad understands the Rambam. But Rav Yitzchak Blazer, the author of *Sheilos U'Teshuvos Pri Yitzchak*, affectionately known as Rav Itzele Peterburger, and one of the primary disciples of Rav Yisroel Salanter, raises a fundamental question regarding the Rambam's way of understanding the *beinoni*.

～ Why Does the Beinoni Need Teshuvah?

Rav Itzele asks why the Rambam states that if a *beinoni* does teshuvah he will live, and if he doesn't do teshuvah he won't. Why is the *beinoni* required to do teshuvah? After all, if a *beinoni's* mitzvos and *aveiros* are perfectly balanced — fifty-fifty — then all he should have to do is one more mitzvah in order to tip the scales of justice in his favor. Why does the Rambam insist that he do teshuvah in order to earn a positive judgment? By doing any mitzvah, however big or small, the *beinoni* will no longer be in that category; he will have tipped the scales in his favor and he will be ruled a *tzaddik* who merits life. Let the *beinoni* put on *tzitzis* or *tefillin*, let him learn Torah for five minutes, or let him give *tzedakah*. Any of these actions will tip the scales and render him a *tzaddik*! Why does the Rambam write that doing teshuvah is the only way to tip the scales in his favor?

On Rosh Hashanah, if someone has one hundred and one mitzvos, and one hundred *aveiros*, he will immediately be sealed for life. The same should apply to the *beinoni* who does one additional mitzvah to tips the scales in his favor. So why is teshuvah necessary?

～ The Three Open Books

The Rambam's description of the judgment of Rosh Hashanah is sourced in the Gemara,[2] which states that three books are open before Hashem on Rosh Hashanah: One for the completely righteous, one for the completely wicked, and one for those who are *beinonim*; i.e., in-between. The completely righteous will be sealed for life immediately, while the completely wicked will be sealed for death immediately. However, the judgment of the *beinonim* is suspended from Rosh Hashanah until Yom Kippur. Thus far the Gemara seems identical to the description of the Rambam.

However, the Gemara continues, if the *beinoni* merits, he will be written for life; if he does not merit, he will be written for death.

The Gemara does not indicate in any way that the *beinoni* must do teshuvah in order to earn a judgment for life. Rather, all the Gemara says is that if the *beinoni* merits, he will tip the scales in his favor. Simply understood, all the *beinoni* must do is one more mitzvah in order to merit life. The message of the Gemara is clear and cogent: the judgment depends on the balance of *zechusim* and *aveiros*. Tipping the scale can occur by adding any mitzvah to the side of mitzvos.

Why, then, does the Rambam state that the only way for the *beinoni* to succeed in judgment is to do teshuvah? Why can't he simply do one more mitzvah to tip the scales? This is the compelling question of Rav Itzele Peterburger.[3]

✑ *The Dire Sin of Not Doing Teshuvah*

To answer this question, Rav Itzele leads us on a remarkable journey exploring new vistas in the world of teshuvah. Rav Itzele poses the following questions: If one does not do teshuvah, is it just a lost opportunity? Is it just a gift that was not utilized? Rav Itzele explains that not doing teshuvah is more than just a lost opportunity or not taking advantage of a gift from the Ribbono shel Olam. If a person does not do teshuvah, then not only must he pay for the sin that was committed in the first place, but he now also has to pay for the sin of not doing teshuvah.

✑ *The Bandit Who Did Not Escape*

This concept is illustrated by Rabbeinu Yonah,[4] who describes one who postpones doing teshuvah, preferring to defer doing teshuvah until he is an old man. One who does this, says

Rabbeinu Yonah, incurs the wrath of Hashem every single day that he delays and does not do teshuvah. This is analogous to a band of thieves who were caught and imprisoned by the king. In the dark of the night, the bandits dug an underground tunnel that eventually reached outside the walls of the prison and they escaped. When the prison guard entered the cell the next morning, he saw the tunnel and realized that the band of thieves had escaped. Only one prisoner remained in the cell. The guard began to beat the remaining bandit. "You fool!" the guard shouts. "The tunnel was right in front of you and you could have escaped easily. The fact that you didn't flee shows that you are not afraid of the king. If you truly feared the king, you would have done anything in your capacity to avoid punishment."

So, too, says Rabbeinu Yonah, one who sins incurs the wrath of Hashem. If the person truly fears Hashem, he will do anything in his power to avoid punishment. Of course, there is no actual escaping from the Ribbono shel Olam. But there is teshuvah, which can help a person avoid punishment. One who does not do teshuvah, who does not seize this opportunity to escape his fate, will ultimately have to pay for the sin that he committed, and he will also receive punishment for disparaging the honor of Hashem by not doing teshuvah.

Rav Itzele points out that we learn from Rabbeinu Yonah that not only is it a mitzvah to do teshuvah, it is an *aveirah* to not do teshuvah.

✒ The Obligation to Do Teshuvah

Rav Itzele cites a Gemara[5] that *geirim*, converts, endure suffering because they delayed in coming under the wings of Hashem. What shall we say, then, about a Jew who actually *is* obligated to keep all the mitzvos in the Torah? If he sins, he is obligated to do teshuvah. If he delays in doing teshuvah, then he will surely be held accountable for the delay, incurring severe repercussions.

Rav Itzele further explains that one has an obligation to do teshuvah the entire year, and any delay in doing so is a *cheit*.

However, during the *Aseres Yemei Teshuvah*, the Ten Days of Repentance between Rosh Hashanah and Yom Kippur, the obligation to do teshuvah rises to an entirely new level.

∾ Mitzvos and Aveiros: Not Created Equal

Two people can both perform the same exact mitzvah, yet one person will receive more reward than the other. How is this possible? Each receives the reward for the mitzvah itself, but *lefum tzaara agra*, the reward is commensurate with the effort. The one who puts more effort into doing the mitzvah will be rewarded not only for the mitzvah but also for the extra effort he expended to perform it.

The same principle holds true for punishment. If one fails to perform a mitzvah, he will receive an *onesh*, punishment. The failure to perform one mitzvah may be more severe than the failure to perform a different mitzvah. For instance, in the times of the Beis HaMikdash, the strings of *tzitzis* were required to be made in two colors. Some needed to be white while others were blue, dyed with *techeiles*. If one were lax in procuring strings for his *tzitzis*, would the *aveirah* be more severe if they were white strings or blue strings?

The Gemara[6] says that it is more reprehensible to be missing white strings than it is to be missing blue strings. This is because it is so much easier to obtain white strings. Their increased availability makes them less costly, and therefore there is less of an excuse not to have them. Certainly, it would have been a sin to not have the blue strings, but it would have been more excusable because it was harder to acquire them.

Rav Itzele stresses that the same concept applies to the mitzvah of teshuvah. Throughout the entire year we are obligated to do teshuvah, and it is problematic to delay, but at least we can say that there is a mitigating factor, that it is not easy to do teshuvah. However, during the *Aseres Yemei Teshuvah*, teshuvah is much easier to do, and therefore during the *Aseres Yemei Teshuvah* we have no excuse for not repenting our sins.

⮾ Hashem's Enhanced Availability

The Gemara[7] presents a contradiction between two *pesukim*. One *pasuk* states, "כַּה' אֱלֹקֵינוּ בְּכָל קָרְאֵנוּ אֵלָיו", *As is Hashem, our God, Who is close to us at all times*" (*Devarim* 4:7). The other *pasuk* reads, "דִּרְשׁוּ ה' בְּהִמָּצְאוֹ", seek out Hashem when He can be found" (*Yeshayah* 55:6), which implies that Hashem is not always available. It seems that there are times when Hashem can be found, and there are times when He cannot. The Gemara answers that the first *pasuk* refers to a *tzibbur*, community, while the second is discussing a *yachid*, individual. To a *tzibbur*, to a *minyan*, Hashem is always available. To an individual, however, at times Hashem is available and at times He is not available. When is Hashem available to an individual? Says Rabbah bar Avuha, these are the ten days between Rosh Hashanah and Yom Kippur. During the *Aseres Yemei Teshuvah*, Hashem makes Himself available, so to speak, to each individual.

During the course of the year, when Hashem is not readily available to an individual, it may be hard for him to do teshuvah. However, during the *Aseres Yemei Teshuvah* Hashem is available; He is close by. דִּרְשׁוּ ה' בְּהִמָּצְאוֹ. That is when teshuvah is much easier to accomplish.

The Rambam[8] writes that even though teshuvah and crying are always appropriate and beneficial, during the *Aseres Yemei Teshuvah* they are even more effective, and they are immediately accepted.

Thus, says Rav Itzele, since teshuvah is so much easier to achieve during the *Aseres Yemei Teshuvah*, the punishment for someone who does not avail himself of this opportunity is so much greater.

⮾ No Excuses When Teshuvah Is Easier: Rav and the Butcher

Rav Itzele then takes this idea to a frightening conclusion. The ramifications of this idea should cause any sensitive person to shudder. The Gemara recounts that whenever anyone would insult or otherwise hurt R' Z'eira, R' Z'eira would intentionally pass near that person, making himself available so that it would be easier for the other person to ask for *mechilah* for his wrongdoing.

The Gemara[9] illustrates this concept by relating an episode concerning Rav. A certain butcher had wronged Rav. Certainly, the butcher should have come to Rav before Yom Kippur to ask for forgiveness. However, the butcher did not do so, and Rav decided to go to appease the butcher. On his way to the butcher, Rav met Rav Huna, who asked Rav where he was heading, and Rav told him that he was going to be reconciled with the butcher. Rav Huna told Rav that he would not succeed in repairing his relationship with the butcher, but rather he would kill the butcher.

Nevertheless, Rav went to the butcher's shop and found him engaged in the process of cleaving open the skull of an animal. The butcher saw Rav and told him to leave. "I have nothing to do with you," he said. While he was chopping the bones, a piece of bone flew up and struck the butcher in the throat, killing him.

Obvious questions arise: The halachah demands that if one hurts or insults another person, he must ask for *mechilah*, forgiveness, from the injured party. But the halachah does not say that the person who was hurt should go out of his way to make it easy for the other person to ask for *mechilah*. In regard to the case of Rav and the butcher, we can also ask, isn't it beneath Rav's dignity to go to the butcher? It seems to be a lack of *kavod HaTorah*; where did Rav learn this behavior? Additionally, what is the meaning of Rav Huna's response when he said that Rav would kill the butcher?

◠ *Emulating Hashem*

Says Rav Itzele: Rav learned this behavior from HaKadosh Baruch Hu Himself! This is exactly how Hashem conducts Himself with one who transgresses. Hashem knows that a sinner is really obligated to come to Him and do teshuvah, throughout the year. But perhaps that is too difficult for him; maybe I am too far from him, says Hashem, and it is too overwhelming a challenge for the sinner to do teshuvah.

Hashem therefore opts to go to man, to come to us, and be more readily available for us to ask *mechilah* of Him. Hashem gifts us ten days of the year during which He makes Himself available to us. He gives us ten days each year during which it is easier to do teshuvah, because He is right here, before us, in very close proximity.

If it is not beneath Hashem's dignity to go to the sinner in order to make it easier for the sinner to do teshuvah, then it was not beneath the dignity of Rav or R' Z'eira. They learned this behavior from Hashem!

Rav Itzele continues. The ramifications of this Gemara are quite frightening. Just look at what happened to this butcher. Had Rav not gone out of his way to make it easy for the butcher to ask for forgiveness, it is likely that nothing would have happened to the butcher. Even if the butcher had chanced upon Rav in the street, the butcher might not have been punished as severely. But because Rav went out of his way to make it easy for the butcher to ask for forgiveness, and still the butcher did not take advantage of this opportunity, the butcher suffered a terrible death.

That is why Rav Huna told Rav that he would kill the butcher. He was saying that if Rav stayed away and the butcher did not ask him for forgiveness, then things would not be as bad for the butcher. But, if Rav were to make it easy for him to ask for *mechilah* and he still refused, then that would be the death of the butcher.

This was the fate of a butcher who did not ask forgiveness from Rav, a *basar v'dam*, a human being, when Rav made it easy for him to do so. What then, says Rav Itzele, will be the fate of a person who doesn't avail himself of the opportunity to do teshuvah during the *Aseres Yemei Teshuvah*, when Hashem, the *Melech Malchei HaMelachim*, comes close to him and makes it easy to do teshuvah!? We can only imagine what his fate will be! And then Yom Kippur arrives, and the Ribbono shel Olam is even closer and more available to us than at any other time of the year. If we still don't do teshuvah, the consequences are frightening.

❧ *Shehechiyanu … We Hope*

At the start of Yom Kippur, everyone stands in shul during *Kol Nidrei*, and together recites the *berachah* with tremendous emotion: שֶׁהֶחֱיָנוּ וְקִיְּמָנוּ וְהִגִּיעָנוּ לַזְּמַן הַזֶּה, Thank You, Hashem, for having granted us the privilege of surviving to reach this day, a day when it is easier to do teshuvah. Rav Meir Simchah, the *Meshech Chochmah*,[10] stirringly says that perhaps some people would have been better off not having lived until Yom Kippur. True, Yom Kippur is an incredible opportunity, but this is only if you take advantage of it, only if you utilize the opportunity. If you do not take advantage of it, then, *chas v'shalom*, it is as Rav Huna told Rav: "Do you know where you are going? You are going to kill the butcher. If that butcher is going to forgo this opportunity that has made teshuvah so easy, the consequences will be devastating." And so they were. If that is what happens when you don't ask a human being for *mechilah*, imagine what may happen if one does not repent to Hashem.

❧ *Alone on the Road*

The *Mishnah*[11] says in the name of R' Chanina ben Chachinai: A person who is up at night and one who walks alone on the road and diverts his attention endanger their lives. The *Noda B'Yehudah*, Rav Yechezkel Landau, offers an incredible explanation.[12] "One who is up at night" refers to one who is up at night during the days of *Selichos*, during the *Aseres Yemei Teshuvah*, when we rise in the dark of night to beseech the Ribbono shel Olam. "And one who walks alone on the road" is also a reference to the *Aseres Yemei Teshuvah*. Throughout the year, Hashem is readily available only to a *minyan* of Jews, but during the *Aseres Yemei Teshuvah* Hashem makes Himself available even to a *yachid*, even to someone who is traveling along the road of teshuvah by himself. "One who diverts his attention" implies that if at a time like this, when it is so easy to do teshuvah, a person preoccupies himself and does not take advantage of the opportunity, then he "endangers his life."

≫ Understanding the Rambam

Says Rav Itzele, now we can understand the Rambam cited above regarding a *beinoni* whose mitzvos and *aveiros* are equal, who, the Rambam writes, must do teshuvah in order to tip the scales in a favorable direction.

If a person does not do teshuvah, he can learn Torah, he can *daven*, he can give *tzedakah*, he can do hundreds, even thousands of mitzvos, but the *aveirah* of not doing teshuvah during the *Aseres Yemei Teshuvah* is so overwhelming that it will outweigh any merits a person would manage to accomplish. During the *Aseres Yemei Teshuvah*, and especially on Yom Kippur, teshuvah becomes so much easier, since the Ribbono shel Olam makes Himself so available. Not taking advantage of this opportunity is a transgression so severe that no mitzvah can counterbalance it.

Before Rosh Hashanah, there is also an obligation to do teshuvah. But if someone does not do teshuvah at that time, it is like any other *aveirah*. As long as a person has more mitzvos than *aveiros*, he will be inscribed for life. But once a person comes to the *Aseres Yemei Teshuvah* as a *beinoni*, there is a dramatic change. Now there is only one option, only one road to salvation. Says the Rambam, if he does teshuvah, he will be sealed for life; if not, he will be sealed for death.

Teshuvah is a great gift, but when the Ribbono shel Olam makes it easy, we would be wise to take advantage. By not utilizing the *Aseres Yemei Teshuvah*, we are acting like the butcher who did not take advantage of the opportunity that Rav gave him.

✑ Understanding the Pesukim

In *Parashas Re'eh* (*Devarim* 11:26) the Ribbono shel Olam tells Klal Yisrael that there are two options before them from which they must choose. Follow the Torah, receive *berachah*, and your life will be good. But if you don't follow the Torah, then you will be subject to *klalah* and life will be more difficult. Then, in *Parashas Nitzavim* (ibid., 30:15) Hashem changes the choice to life and death. What had changed in the interim between these *parshiyos*?

The *Meshech Chochmah*[13] explains that what changed, what caused this dramatic shift, was that Hashem introduced the mitzvah of *teshuvah*.

The Torah tells us in *Parashas Nitzavim,* כִּי הַמִּצְוָה הַזֹּאת אֲשֶׁר אָנֹכִי מְצַוְּךָ הַיּוֹם לֹא נִפְלֵאת הִוא מִמְּךָ וְלֹא רְחֹקָה הִוא. לֹא בַשָּׁמַיִם הִוא לֵאמֹר מִי יַעֲלֶה לָּנוּ הַשָּׁמַיְמָה וְיִקָּחֶהָ לָּנוּ וְיַשְׁמִעֵנוּ אֹתָהּ וְנַעֲשֶׂנָּה. וְלֹא מֵעֵבֶר לַיָּם הִוא לֵאמֹר מִי יַעֲבָר לָנוּ אֶל עֵבֶר הַיָּם וְיִקָּחֶהָ לָּנוּ וְיַשְׁמִעֵנוּ אֹתָהּ וְנַעֲשֶׂנָּה. כִּי קָרוֹב אֵלֶיךָ הַדָּבָר מְאֹד בְּפִיךָ וּבִלְבָבְךָ לַעֲשֹׂתוֹ, *For this commandment that I command you today—it is not hidden from you and it is not distant. It is not in heaven, [for you] to say, "Who can ascend to heaven for us and take it for us, so that we can listen to it and perform it?" Nor is it across the sea, [for you] to say, "Who can cross to the other side of the sea for us and take it for us, so that we can listen to it and perform it?" Rather, the matter is very near to you — in your mouth and in your heart — to perform it* (*Devarim* 30:11-14): This "mitzvah" to which the Torah refers is the mitzvah of teshuvah — the opportunity to repent and obtain forgiveness for our *aveiros* — there are no longer only *berachos* and *kelalos*. Now the stakes are much higher. Now it is either *chaim* or *maves* — life or death!

✑ The Power of Each Day of the Aseres Yemei Teshuvah

We should consider the ramifications of the Ribbono shel Olam Himself coming to us during the *Aseres Yemei Teshuvah* and literally begging us to do teshuvah. It is an opportunity we must utilize. These days are the most important days of our lives! In the *sefer Yaaros Devash*[14] Rav Yonasan Eibeshutz says that each of the seven days between Rosh Hashanah and Yom Kippur can repair and rectify the corresponding day of the week for the entire preceding year.

For instance, if a person does teshuvah on the Sunday of the *Aseres Yemei Teshuvah*, then he can be absolved of all the *aveiros* done on the Sundays of the year. Doing teshuvah on Monday of the Ten Days of Repentance will rectify all the Mondays of the year, and so on.

Teshuvah does not mean that we must correct all of our failings at once. But we must begin. We must choose one area in which we can make improvements. Our improvements may seem like a small change in the scheme of things, but even a small change has enormous significance. As we know, *mitzvah goreres mitzvah*, one mitzvah leads to another mitzvah, so perhaps one small change will lead to teshuvah *sheleimah*, complete and total teshuvah.

Teshuvah has the power to usher in the ultimate *Geulah Sheleimah*, the Ultimate Redemption, may we merit to see it in our days.

ENDNOTES

1. רמב״ם הלכות תשובה פרק ג הלכה ג.

2. ראש השנה טז, א.

3. ספר כוכבי אור סימן ה.

4. שערי תשובה לרבינו יונה פרק א אות ב.

5. גמרא יבמות מח, ב.

6. מנחות מג, א.

7. ראש השנה יח, א, יבמות מט, א.

8. רמב״ם הלכות תשובה פרק ב.

9. יומא פז, א.

10. משך חכמה פרשת נצבים, ל, כ.

11. פרקי אבות ג, ה.

12. דרושי הצל״ח דרוש כ׳ לעשרת ימי תשובה.

13. משך חכמה פרשת נצבים ל, יא.

14. יערות דבש דרוש א׳, הובא במשנה ברורה סימן תכג ס״ק ב.

How to Desire — Rosh Hashanah Through Succos, As Seen Through the Lens of Rav Yonasan Eibeshutz

Part 1: The Ten Days of Teshuvah and the Ten Commandments

✎ *Yoma Arichta — One Long Day*

The two days of Rosh Hashanah are referred to as a *Yoma Arichta*, one long day. This terminology and concept are unique to Rosh Hashanah and is not used in reference to other Yamim Tovim. The *kedushah* of the two days of Rosh Hashanah is considered *kedushah achas*, one sanctity. All other Yamim Tovim have two days in *Chutz LaAretz*, yet they are not considered one day; they are viewed as two separate days of Yom Tov. This distinction has halachic ramification as well. For example, if an egg is laid on the first day of any other Yom Tov, it may not be eaten on that day, but it can be eaten on the second day of Yom Tov. This allowance is based on the following argument: *Mi-ma nifshach*, Either way you look at it, if the first day was really Yom Tov, then the second day is *chol*, and there is no reason one cannot eat the egg. If the second day is Yom Tov, then the first day was *chol* and the egg was in fact laid on a weekday, making it permissible. However, the *Mishnah Berurah* in *Hilchos Rosh Hashanah*[1] states that if an egg is laid on the first day of Rosh Hashanah, it is prohibited to be eaten on the second day, because both days of Rosh Hashanah are considered to have one *kedushah*, holiness. In *Hilchos Yom Tov* the *Mishnah Berurah*[2] similarly states that the two days of Rosh Hashanah are deemed one *kedushah*, and are considered to be one long day.

❧ Why Are the Two Days Viewed as One?

How do we understand this concept, that what we know to be two separate days are looked at halachically as one long day? If it is meant to be one day, then just make Rosh Hashanah one day, and if it is supposed to be two days, then the sanctity of each day should be separate. What is the underlying rationale of this novel concept that both days are considered to be one *kedushah*?

❧ The Ten Days Correspond to the Ten Commandments

Rav Yonasan Eibeshutz[3] introduces us to a revolutionary concept: Aside from the *Aseres Yemei Teshuvah* being spiritual tools that are *mesugal*, capable, of helping us correct our *aveiros*, these ten days of teshuvah correspond to the *Aseres HaDibros*, the Ten Commandments.

Moshe Rabbeinu ascended to *Shamayim* on Rosh Chodesh Elul, and he returned forty days later, on Yom Kippur, with the second *Luchos*, which contained the *Aseres HaDibros*. In fact, the *sefer Elef Kasav*[4] quotes Rav Daniel Prustitz, a contemporary of the Chasam Sofer. He writes that on each day of the *Aseres Yemei Teshuvah* another one of the *Aseres HaDibros* was inscribed.

When they were all complete, Moshe brought the second *Luchos* down to Klal Yisrael.

The first day of Rosh Hashanah parallels the first commandment, אָנֹכִי ה' אֱלֹקֶיךָ, *I am Hashem, your God* (*Shemos* 20:2). In *Keshes Yehonasan*, Rav Yonasan Eibeshutz explains the appropriateness of this equivalency. On Rosh Hashanah we use the shofar and the *pesukim* of *Malchiyos*, Kingship, and *Zichronos*, Remembrance, to proclaim Hashem's sovereignty over us. This is a most fitting ritual for the first day of Rosh Hashanah, since it is the day that corresponds to אָנֹכִי ה' אֱלֹקֶיךָ, the declaration of Hashem's Kingship. We blow the shofar to coronate Hashem as our King.

❧ Why Yoma Arichta?

The second day of Rosh Hashanah corresponds to the second of the *Aseres HaDibros*, לֹא יִהְיֶה לְךָ אֱלֹהִים אֲחֵרִים, *You shall not recognize the gods of others* (ibid., v. 3). We know that the first two *Dibros* were said by Hashem *b'dibur echad*, in one utterance. Hashem spoke once and we heard two statements; therefore, the two days of the year that correspond to them are considered to be one long day. That is the underlying rationale for why we reckon Rosh Hashanah a *Yoma Arichta*.

❧ Rav Yonason Eibeshutz Continues the Analogy

In *Yaaros Devash*,[5] Rav Yonasan elaborates on the specific connection between לֹא יִהְיֶה לְךָ אֱלֹהִים אֲחֵרִים, *You shall not recognize the gods of others,* the second of the *Aseres HaDibros* and the second of the *Aseres Yemei Teshuvah*. Initially, the second day of Rosh Hashanah was observed only in *Chutz LaAretz*, not in Eretz Yisrael, and the Gemara[6] states that one who resides outside of Eretz Yisrael is considered to be worshiping a foreign deity. Thus, says Rav Yonasan, the second day of the *Aseres Yemei Teshuvah* corresponds to the second of the *Aseres HaDibros*: לֹא יִהְיֶה לְךָ אֱלֹהִים אֲחֵרִים, *You shall not recognize the gods of others.*

The third day of Tishrei is the date on which we commemorate the murder of Gedaliah. Thus, the third of Tishrei corresponds to the sixth Commandment, לֹא תִרְצָח, *You shall not kill* (*Shemos* 20:13). Shabbos Shuvah corresponds to the fourth of the Ten Commandments: זָכוֹר אֶת יוֹם הַשַּׁבָּת לְקַדְּשׁוֹ, *Remember the Sabbath day to sanctify it* (ibid., v. 8).

✎ *A Well-Documented Teaching*

This concept that the Ten Days of Repentance correspond to the *Aseres HaDibros* is repeatedly documented in our classic sources. This idea is mentioned in several places in the *Sfas Emes*.[7] It is also brought in the *Sefer Likkutei Yehudah*, by the *Sfas Emes's* grandson, Reb Yehudah Aryeh Leib Heina. He writes that he heard from his grandfather that the *Aseres Yemei Teshuvah* correspond to the *Aseres HaDibros*, and adds the point mentioned above that because the first two *Dibros* were spoken by Hashem in one utterance, Rosh Hashanah's two days are considered one long day.

He discusses a curiosity in the order of the first two commandments. Usually we first purify an object by performing *taharah*, purification; only then can the item be sanctified. Thus, generally *taharah* precedes *kedushah*, holiness. Something that is *tamei*, impure, cannot be sanctified. In line with this, the first commandment, accepting Hashem as our God, seemingly should really have been taught second. First, we should have to forsake all other deities and commit to not worshiping any *avodah zarah*; only then would we be able to accept the *kedushah* of Hashem upon ourselves.

Hashem displayed kindness to us by enabling us to believe in Him and thereby to jump into *kedushah*, even before we had cleansed ourselves from the *tumah* of *avodah zarah*.

✎ *Erev Yom Kippur: Lo Signov*

On Erev Yom Kippur, an important task that is emphasized is *V'heishiv es hagezeilah*, to return any item that one may have stolen. This helps ensure that when one enters into Yom Kippur, the only *aveiros* that remain are *bein adam laMakom*, since one has already rectified the *aveiros bein adam lachaveiro*. Thus, Rav Yonason Eibishutz teaches that Erev Yom Kippur corresponds to the *Dibur* of לֹא תִגְנֹב, *Lo Signov*, You shall not steal.[8]

Because of the special concern that we may have items in our possession that do not belong to us, it is customary to perform *kapparos* with a chicken. *Chazal* explain that chickens are not fit to be used as *korbanos*, because their innards contain *gezeilah*, theft. Since chickens peck their food from the ground regardless of the owner, they are representative of the sin of stealing. As we do *kapparos*, we ask Hashem to exchange any decrees that should have devolved on *ganavim*, and instead allow them to devolve on the chicken. This, says Rav Yonasan Eibeshutz, is a deeper dimension to the mitzvah of *kapparos*.

❧ Uncovering the Source of the Connection Between the Aseres HaDibros and the Aseres Yemei Teshuvah

From where did the *Acharonim* derive the concept that the *Aseres HaDibros* correspond to the *Aseres Yemei Teshuvah*? The *Tanna D'Vei Eliyahu Zuta*[9] teaches us an incredible concept. Why does Hashem give us so much *nachas ruach* during the *Aseres Yemei Teshuvah*? As we know, there are many benefits that accrue to the Bnei Yisrael at this time of the year. On each of the seven days between Rosh Hashanah and Yom Kippur, one can be *mesaken*, rectify, the corresponding day of the week for all infractions that were committed on that day throughout the prior year. Furthermore, although the rest of the year Hashem readily accepts only the prayers *davened* with a *minyan*, during the *Aseres Yemei Teshuvah* Hashem readily accepts even *tefillos* said in private. Why did Hashem give us this special gift that we know as the *Aseres Yemei Teshuvah*?

The *Tanna D'Vei Eliyahu* answers that we receive this gift in the merit of the *asarah nisyanos*, ten tests, that Avraham Avinu underwent and over which he triumphed. It is also, says the *Tanna D'Vei Eliyahu*, in the merit of Klal Yisrael having accepted the *Aseres HaDibros*. This is one of the early sources from which the *Acharonim* have derived that the Ten Days of Repentance correspond to the *Aseres HaDibros*.*

⟋ *Source in the Pesikta*

The *Pesikta*[10] discusses the ten *korbanos*, offerings, brought on Rosh Hashanah in the Beis HaMikdash. They include פַּר בֶּן בָּקָר אֶחָד אַיִל אֶחָד כְּבָשִׂים בְּנֵי שָׁנָה שִׁבְעָה ... וּשְׂעִיר־עִזִּים אֶחָד חַטָּאת, *one young bull, one ram, seven male lambs ... [and] one male of the goats for a sin-offering (Bamidbar 29:2, 5)*. The *Pesikta* writes that these ten offerings correspond to the ten days of the *Aseres Yemei Teshuvah*. When we do teshuvah throughout the ten days from Rosh Hashanah to Yom Kippur Hashem promises that He will cleanse us and re-create us as a new entity. The *Pesikta* also mentions that the Ten Days of Repentance correspond to the Ten Commandments; thus, we have another early source for this concept that we have been discussing.

Interestingly, the *Pesikta* continues, that in the Haftarah we read on Shabbos Chazon (*Yeshayah* 1:16-17), we find another *remez* to the *Aseres Yemei Teshuvah* and Yom Kippur. The *navi* begins, רַחֲצוּ הִזַּכּוּ וְכוּ', *Wash yourselves, purify yourselves*, etc., and in total lists nine actions that one must perform to please Hashem; he concludes with a tenth statement: לְכוּ נָא וְנִוָּכְחָה יֹאמַר ה'. אִם יִהְיוּ חֲטָאֵיכֶם כַּשָּׁנִים כַּשֶּׁלֶג יַלְבִּינוּ אִם יַאְדִּימוּ כַתּוֹלָע כַּצֶּמֶר יִהְיוּ, *Come, now, let us reason together, says Hashem. If your sins are like scarlet, they will become white as snow; if they have become red as crimson, they will become [white] as wool (ibid., v. 18)*. These nine activities correspond to the first nine days of teshuvah. If we merit to complete these achievements during the first nine days of the Ten Days of Repentance, then we will merit that Hashem will cleanse us of our sins on the tenth day, Yom Kippur.

---

* See also the *Pesikta* below.

~ Aseres Yemei Teshuvah: A Gift in the Merit of Yaakov Avinu

The Chida uncovers an interesting allusion to the *Aseres Yemei Teshuvah* in the *pesukim* In *Parashas Vayeitzei*. The *pasuk* states that Yaakov vowed, וַיִּדַּר יַעֲקֹב נֶדֶר לֵאמֹר אִם יִהְיֶה אֱלֹקִים עִמָּדִי וּשְׁמָרַנִי בַּדֶּרֶךְ הַזֶּה אֲשֶׁר אָנֹכִי הוֹלֵךְ וְנָתַן לִי לֶחֶם לֶאֱכֹל וּבֶגֶד לִלְבֹּשׁ וְשַׁבְתִּי בְשָׁלוֹם אֶל בֵּית אָבִי וְהָיָה ה׳ לִי לֵאלֹקִים — וְהָאֶבֶן הַזֹּאת אֲשֶׁר שַׂמְתִּי מַצֵּבָה יִהְיֶה בֵּית אֱלֹקִים וְכֹל אֲשֶׁר תִּתֶּן לִי עַשֵּׂר אֲעַשְּׂרֶנּוּ לָךְ, *"If God will be with me, will guard me on this way that I am going; will give me bread to eat and clothes to wear; and I return in peace to my father's house, and Hashem will be a God to me — then this stone that I have set up as a pillar shall become a house of God, and, whatever You will give me, I shall repeatedly tithe to You"* (*Bereishis* 28:20-22).

The literal translation of עַשֵּׂר אֲעַשְּׂרֶנּוּ לָךְ is "tithe I shall tithe to You," so that two "tens" are mentioned in the verse. The two tens to which Yaakov alludes, posits the *Chida*, are the *Aseres Yemei Teshuvah* and the *Aseres HaDibros*, the former given in the *zechus* of the latter.

The *Midrash* says that the road Yaakov is referring to with the words וּשְׁמָרַנִי בַּדֶּרֶךְ הַזֶּה, *and guard me on this way that I am going*, is the road of the service of Hashem. The *road* alludes to the three major *aveiros* for which, rather than violate the prohibition, one is required to sacrifice his life; i.e., *avodah zarah*, *gilui arayos*, and *shefichas damim* — idolatry, illicit relations, and murder.

The *Chida* explains the *pasuk* as follows:

אִם יִהְיֶה אֱלֹקִים עִמָּדִי, *if Hashem will be with me*, He will be my God; this fulfills the first two *Dibros*, *Anochi Hashem Elokecha* and *Lo Yihyeh Lecha*.

וּשְׁמָרַנִי, *and He will guard me*, from violating the three major *aveiros*, which are included in three of the *Aseres HaDibros*; this fulfills the *Dibros Anochi Hashem*, *Lo Sinaf*, and *Lo Sirtzach*, וְנָתַן לִי, *and Hashem will give to me*, so that I will not have stolen; this fulfills the eighth *Dibur*, *Lo Signov*.

לֶחֶם לֶאֱכֹל וּבֶגֶד לִלְבֹּשׁ, *He will provide just the most basic needs — bread and simple clothing*, without luxury. I will not covet, and I will not desire more. This is the fulfillment of the tenth *Dibur*, *Lo Sachmod*.

וְשַׁבְתִּי, *and I will return*; i.e., *I will keep Shabbos*, as the word *Shabbos* is found in this word. This is the *remez* to the fulfillment of the fourth *Dibur*, *Zachor Es Yom HaShabbos Lekadsho*.

אֶל בֵּית אָבִי, *to my father's house*, indicating that he will fulfill the fifth *Dibur*, *Kabeid Es Avicha V'es Imecha*.

וְהָיָה ה', *and Hashem will be*; this implies the commandment not to take Hashem's Name in vain, since one who is provided for by the King will not swear falsely in His Name; this hints to the fulfillment of the third *Dibur*, *Lo Sisa*.

לִי לֵאלֹקִים, *for me as a God*; since Hashem is my God, I will not testify falsely; this fulfills the ninth *Dibur*, *Lo saanah b'reiacha eid sheker*. Note that the Yerushalmi[11] states that the Ten Commandments are alluded to in *Krias Shema*, with the *Ani Hashem Elokeichem* at the end of *Shema* corresponding to *Lo Saana*.

Thus, we see that in his vow, Yaakov accepted upon himself — and then proceeded to fulfill — all of the *Aseres HaDibros*. He ended by saying, וְכֹל אֲשֶׁר תִּתֶּן לִי עַשֵּׂר אֲעַשְּׂרֶנּוּ לָךְ. The Ribbono shel Olam responds, if you keep the *Aseres HaDibros*, you will receive the gift of the *Aseres Yemei Teshuvah*. The two mentions of ten allude to our concept that the Ten Days of Repentance are a gift to Klal Yisrael as a reward for the Ten Commandments that Yaakov Avinu accepted upon himself and subsequently fulfilled.

❧ The Ten Days Correspond to the Ten Utterances

Rav Yonasan Eibeshutz makes another interesting correlation that just as the Ten Days of Repentance correspond to the Ten Commandments, they also correspond to the Ten Utterances through which Hashem created the world. The Gemara[12] counts the number of times Hashem "voiced" an utterance to cause a new creation to occur, and totals only nine; however, the Gemara further states that the word *Bereishis* itself is also a *maamar*, utterance, that served to create. Unlike the other nine *amiros*, which are explicitly written in the text, this *maamar* is concealed.

Bereishis, the first *dibur* that served to create, corresponds to the first day of Rosh Hashanah. Since the *maamar* is concealed, so too is Rosh Hashanah בְּכֶּסָא, concealed, at the time of the month when the moon is not visible.[13]

Part 2:
Yom Kippur and Lo Sachmod

◦ *Yom Kippur Corresponds to Lo Sachmod*

Following the pattern that the ten *Dibros* parallel the ten days of the *Aseres Yemei Teshuvah*, Yom Kippur, the most awesome and powerful day of the year, thus corresponds to the last of the *Aseres HaDibros*, לֹא תַחְמֹד, *You shall not covet* (ibid., v. 14). This is a surprising connection, as we may have thought that Yom Kippur seemingly corresponds to the most stringent *aveirah* in the Torah. However, this connection can be explained by an awe-inspiring comment made by the Vilna Gaon. The Gra writes, all *aveiros* and *chataim* are rooted in *chemdah*, desire. As the whole Torah is encompassed in the Ten Commandments, and the Ten Commandments are encompassed in the final commandment, *Lo Sachmod*, it is quite compelling that the holiest and most important day of the year corresponds to *Lo Sachmod*, which encompasses the whole Torah.

◦ *The End Is Connected to the Beginning*

The *Chida*[14] cites Rav Yonason Eibeshutz, who further elaborates on this concept. They invoke the concept that נָעוּץ סוֹפָן בִּתְּחִילָתָן, the end, the conclusion, of a Torah segment is rooted in the beginning. The last *Dibrah, Lo Sachmod*, and the first, *Anochi Hashem*, are interconnected, and thus, so is Yom Kippur to Rosh Hashanah. One who is accustomed to following the urgings of desire and lust will ultimately come to deny *Anochi Hashem*. The way to ensure that *Anochi* is preserved is by controlling one's desires and fulfilling *Lo Sachmod*. If one allows his desires to overpower him, then Anochi is in jeopardy of receding.

ҩ *Why Do We Read About Arayos on Yom Kippur?*

Rav Shaul Brach[15] and Rav Chananya Yom Tov Lipa Kish[16] teach that this connection between Yom Kippur and *Lo Sachmod* illuminates the logic of reading the *parashah* of *arayos* during Minchah on Yom Kippur. Since on Yom Kippur we strive to overcome our *taavah*, desire, and *chemdah*, craving, for illicit relationships, it is most appropriate to read the portion of the Torah that discusses *arayos*.

ҩ *The Derashah of Rav Yosef Engel*

Rav Yosef Engel[17] recorded an extensive *derashah* for Shabbos Shuvah centering on the concept that the *Aseres Yemei Teshuvah* correspond to the *Aseres HaDibros*. Rav Engel states that although this idea is based on *Tanna D'Vei Eliyahu*, Rav Yonasan Eibeshutz said it of his own accord and this *chiddush* illuminates many difficult areas of Torah.

ҩ *Lo Sachmod? But I Want It!*

Rav Engel begins with the question that the Ibn Ezra raises in his commentary on the *Aseres HaDibros*.[18] He asks how one can be commanded to not want something that he sees and finds appealing. A person can be told to hold back from doing an action or from performing an activity. But if one sees an item that he really likes, he will desire it. Isn't it a natural reaction? I see it, I like it, I want it. A person can stop himself from acting on that desire, but how does he stop himself from having the yearning for the possessions of another?

In response, Rav Yosef Engel advances an ingenious approach. He says that since *Lo Sachmod* corresponds to Yom Kippur, the Torah is saying that on this one day of the year we should eliminate all physical desires, *taavah*, and lust. The *lav*, negative commandment, then, is primarily meant for Yom Kippur, the only day of the year on which it would be possible to eradicate lust in its entirety, a day on which *chemdah* is removed from the human heart, and the one day a year that the *Satan* is not operational. A day, *the Pirkei D'Rav Eliezer* teaches us, that we are like the angels who have no *chemdah* and *taavah*. It is the one day a year that lust, *taavah*, ceases. Therefore, on that day we have the ability to fulfill *Lo Sachmod*!

But does Torah say that *Lo Sachmod* is limited to one day a year? It is one of the Ten Commandments to be fulfilled every day of one's life! Rav Yosef Engel suggests that what the prohibition of *Lo Sachmod* means is that one should curb physical desires during the entire year so that when Yom Kippur comes around, he can fulfill it completely. Truthfully, there is only one day a year on which it is possible to fulfill the *lav* completely, in its fullest and truest sense. But one can only achieve this level on Yom Kippur if throughout the year he lives with discipline. Then, when Yom Kippur arrives, and we are like *malachim* who have no *taavah*, *Lo Sachmod* can be achieved the way it was meant to be.

⮞ *The Satan Has a Day Off*

The Gemara[19] reveals that on Yom Kippur, the *Satan* has no authority to instigate, to persuade us to sin, and to prosecute. On this day, it is as if the *Satan* is off duty. This is derived from the *Satan's* name, "הַשָּׂטָן," which has the *gematria* 364. For 364 days of the year the *Satan* has permission to prosecute, but on Yom Kippur he is not permitted to do so.

Two questions arise: What is meant by stating that on Yom Kippur the *Satan* cannot instigate and prosecute? Unfortunately, people sometimes still do *aveiros* even on Yom Kippur. Furthermore, asks Rav Yosef Engel, the name of the *Satan* is שטן, which has the numerical value of 359, not 364. His name is not *HaSatan*. The *hei* is only added as a title, **HaSatan**, **the** *Satan*. Why do we include the letter *hei* when calculating the *gematria* of his name?

∾ *Satan vs. HaSatan*

Rav Yosef Engel explains that there are two ways the *Satan* operates, and thus there is a difference between *Satan* and *HaSatan*. There is the outright blatant *Satan*, and there is the internal, subconscious *Satan*. Throughout the course of the year, the *Satan* employs two basic tactics to cause people to sin. On the one hand, he coaxes, encourages, directs, and orders a person to act even against clear halachah. The person who succumbs is listening to **the** *Satan's* instruction when he commits the *aveirah*. This is the *Satan* acting as *HaSatan*: the obvious, blatant *Satan*.

Most of the time, however, the *Satan* does not work this way. Most of the time the *Satan* employs some form of subterfuge, confusing a person, and then convincing him that not only is it acceptable to perform the *aveirah*, but that even, perhaps just in this case, it is a mitzvah to do this action.

The Gemara[20] teaches that the *Satan* has seven names. One of these names is *Tzefoni*, Hidden. He is hidden inside us and cloaks his intentions to the point where we may come to think that he is actually the *yetzer tov*.

This explains a *pasuk* in *Yirmiyahu* in a novel fashion. *Yirmiyahu* 1:14 states, וַיֹּאמֶר ה׳ אֵלַי מִצָּפוֹן תִּפָּתַח הָרָעָה עַל כָּל יֹשְׁבֵי הָאָרֶץ, *Hashem said to me, "From the North the evil will be released upon all the inhabitants of the land."* The usual understanding of this verse is that "the evil starts from the north [of Eretz Yisrael]," but we can also understand it to mean that "the evil always starts from the hidden"; i.e., the verse is referring to the hidden *Satan*.

On a daily basis, we must fight both the blatant, open *Satan*, and the internal, hidden *Satan*. While the open *Satan*, known as *HaSatan*, does not perform his function on Yom Kippur, the hidden *Satan* is operational 365 days a year; he never takes a break.

∾ The Tenth Commandment — Chemdah and Taavah

In *Parashas Yisro*, the Torah articulates the tenth *Dibur* with the following words: לֹא תַחְמֹד בֵּית רֵעֶךָ לֹא תַחְמֹד אֵשֶׁת רֵעֶךָ וְעַבְדּוֹ וַאֲמָתוֹ וְשׁוֹרוֹ וַחֲמֹרוֹ וְכֹל אֲשֶׁר לְרֵעֶךָ, *You shall not covet your fellow's house. You shall not covet your fellow's wife, his manservant, his maidservant, his ox, his donkey, nor anything that belongs to your fellow* (*Shemos* 20:14). Thus, in *Yisro*, the words *Lo sachmod* are stated twice. In *Parashas Va'eschanan*, however, the tenth commandment reads differently: וְלֹא תַחְמֹד אֵשֶׁת רֵעֶךָ וְלֹא תִתְאַוֶּה בֵּית רֵעֶךָ שָׂדֵהוּ וְעַבְדּוֹ וַאֲמָתוֹ שׁוֹרוֹ וַחֲמֹרוֹ וְכֹל אֲשֶׁר לְרֵעֶךָ, *And you shall not covet your fellow's wife, you shall not desire your fellow's house, his field, his slave, his maidservant, his ox, his donkey, or anything that belongs to your fellow* (*Devarim* 5:18). The phrase וְלֹא תִתְאַוֶּה is added; *taavah*, desire, is one facet of the tenth Commandment. Thus, Yom Kippur corresponds to both *chemdah*, coveting, and *taavah*, desiring. Somehow, the root of all evil, which must be corrected on Yom Kippur, is rooted in these two human phenomena.

∾ Chemdah, Taavah, and Lashon Hara — The Three Main Categories of Sin

Rav Yosef Engel demonstrates how from time immemorial *chemdah* and *taavah* have been at the root of all sin. Look no further than the first sin in the Torah. The sin of Adam and Chavah consisted of three elements.

First, the *nachash*, serpent, came to Chavah and spoke *lashon hara* about *HaKadosh Baruch Hu*, telling Chavah that Hashem ate from the *Eitz HaDaas* and then created the entire world.

Then, the Torah tells us about the second and third parts of their *aveirah*: וַתֵּרֶא הָאִשָּׁה כִּי טוֹב הָעֵץ לְמַאֲכָל וְכִי תַאֲוָה הוּא לָעֵינַיִם וְנֶחְמָד הָעֵץ לְהַשְׂכִּיל, *And the woman perceived that the tree was good for eating and that it was a delight to the eyes, and that the tree was desirable as a means of wisdom…* (*Bereishis* 3:6). Thus we find that their *aveirah* consisted of both תַאֲוָה, *taavah,* and נֶחְמָד , *chemdah.*

Thus, the sin of Adam and Chavah, the root of all *aveiros,* is itself based on three bad traits: *lashon hara, taavah,* and *chemdah. Taavah* refers to *arayos,* adultery, and *chemdah* refers to *gezeilah,* theft.

These three sins are often found grouped together in the teaching of *Chazal.* For example, the Gemara states,[21] "Most people steal [which is rooted in *chemdah*], some people commit sins of adultery [which is rooted in *taavah*], and everyone violates *avak lashon hara.*" These three primary categories of sin are all rectified on Yom Kippur. *Lashon hara* is rectified by the Kohen Gadol's offering of the *ketores,* incense-offering, which atones for the sins of speech. Theft and illicit relations are rectified as Yom Kippur is the one day of the year without *chemdah* and *taavah.* Thus, Yom Kippur atones for these three main categories of *aveiros: lashon hara, chemdah,* and *taavah.*

◈ *Another Yoma Arichta*

In the same way that Rosh Hashanah is considered *Yoma Arichta,* one long day, there are two more days that can also considered to be *Yoma Arichta.* The Gemara[22] states that one who eats on 9 Tishrei, Erev Yom Kippur, is considered to have fasted on both the ninth and the tenth. The ninth and tenth of Tishrei are thus considered to be one long day.

As noted, Yom Kippur corresponds to *Lo Sachmod,* and the 9th of Tishrei corresponds to the ninth Commandment, לֹא תַעֲנֶה בְרֵעֲךָ עֵד שָׁקֶר, *you shall not bear false witness against your fellow* (*Shemos* 20:13). The Gemara associates bearing false witness with the *aveirah* of *lashon hara. Pesachim*[23] quotes Rav Sheishes in the name of Rav Elazar ben Azariah, who states that one who speaks *lashon hara*, one who accepts *lashon hara*, and one who testifies falsely deserve to be thrown to the dogs. This curious grouping is intended to teach us that testifying falsely is synonymous with violating the sin of *lashon hara*.

Thus, since 9 Tishrei corresponds to לֹא תַעֲנֶה בְרֵעֲךָ עֵד שָׁקֶר, which includes distancing oneself from *lashon hara*, and 10 Tishrei corresponds to the *Dibur* prohibiting *chemdah* and *taavah*, Rav Yosef Engel teaches[24] that this is why these two days are considered one long fast day: It is because these two days together can correct the three *aveiros* that as a group are the root of all sin, evidenced by the sin of Adam and Chavah, which incorporated *chemdah*, *taavah*, and *lashon hara*.

The ninth and tenth of Tishrei form a dynamic pair that helps us eradicate the three primary *aveiros*, and thereby we overcome all iniquity.

Part 3:
Succos — Channeling Our Desires

ֶ *Succos: Rishon L'Cheshbon Avonos*

The first day of Succos is called *Rishon L'Cheshbon Avonos*[25] because it is the first day on which a person has an opportunity to sin after Yom Kippur. On Yom Kippur, we are given the spiritual energy to overcome *chemdah* and *taavah*. This boost remains with us for another four days as we prepare for the Yom Tov of Succos. As we arrive at Succos, it is the first opportunity to be challenged by the human tendency toward lust and desire. This is the deeper reason, explains Rav Yosef Engel, that Succos is called *Rishon L'Cheshbon Avonos*. This would seem to be a very tenuous time as we must be vigilant to ensure that *chemdah* does not creep back in to our daily lives. How can we be equipped to face this challenge?

The Ribbono shel Olam, in His infinite kindness, gives us an incredible gift: the Yom Tov of Succos, through which we can repurpose our *chemdah* by harnessing the *middah* of *chemdah* to do mitzvos. The three mitzvos of Succos transform the *middah* of *chemdah* into a tool that can be used for performing the mitzvos of *HaKadosh Baruch Hu* with desire.

✑ *Nisuch HaMayim*

On Succos we have a special mitzvah of *Nisuch HaMayim*, Pouring of the water on the *Mizbei'ach* in the Beis HaMikdash. There are many instances in the Torah where we find that *mayim*, water, is symbolic of *taavah*. Throughout Tanach, Yishmael is often associated with water. This is because Yishmael was steeped in *taavah*, symbolized by water.

Rav Yosef Engel directs us to the Rambam to further demonstrate that *mayim* represents *taavah*. The Rambam[26] writes that the moon affects the water. When there is a full moon, the rivers and lakes rise. When the moon is not visible, then the water in the lakes and rivers recedes. The currents, tides, and waves are affected by the gravitational force of the moon. When the moon is full, the water beneath the ground gravitates upward, and there is more water in the rivers and oceans. The *Ibn Ezra*[27] writes that the *Aseres HaDibros* correspond to the ten celestial bodies. The celestial body that corresponds to *Lo Sachmod* is the moon! Incredibly, the moon, which corresponds to lust, is the celestial body that impacts the water, which is likewise symbolic of *taavah*.

✑ *The Aseres HaDibros Correspond to the Celestial Bodies*

Therefore, on Succos, after striving to overcome *chemdah*, we are now prepared to harness the *middah* of *chemdah* for a positive purpose. We take *mayim*, which represents *taavah*, and use it as part of the *avodah* in the Beis HaMikdash. This service of *Nisuch HaMayim* is illustrative of our channeling our *taavah* in the service of Hashem.

On Rosh Hashanah, the moon has to be בְּכֶסָא, concealed, because on Rosh Hashanah we are not yet equipped to deal with *taavah*. But Succos takes place during the full moon, because we are now on the spiritual level at which we can harness *taavah*, through the *avodah* of *Nisuch HaMayim* and utilize it for good. After experiencing Yom Kippur, when we achieve atonement from our sins of *chemdah*, we can now attain mastery over the *middah* and control it to be used for *avodas Hashem*. Perhaps this is alluded to by the fact that we recite *Kiddush Levanah* on Motza'ei Yom Kippur; i.e., only after we achieve mastery over *chemdah* are we ready to sanctify the moon that represents *taavah*.

∾ *The Esrog, a Desirable Fruit*

The most important of the *Arba Minim* is the *esrog*. The other three species are bound together, but the *esrog* is uniquely special and it is held separately. The Ramban writes[28] that at the *cheit* of the *Eitz HaDaas*, the Torah tells us, וְנֶחְמָד הָעֵץ, *and the tree was desirable* (*Bereishis* 3:6). The word נֶחְמָד, *nechmad*, is translated by *Targum*[29] as *umerageg*, the same *lashon* as the word *esrog*. Thus, the Ramban states that the word *esrog* means *chemdah*, desire. It is a desirable fruit, and that is why it is called a *pri eitz hadar*; *hadar* here is translated as *desirable*.

When we take the *esrog* on Succos, we express our desire for *kedushah*, for mitzvos, for serving Hashem. Prior to Yom Kippur, we could not take the *esrog*, since we were not yet ready to channel our desires toward *avodas Hashem*. Only after eradicating *chemdah* and *taavah* through Yom Kippur — albeit only temporarily — can we now begin to utilize *chemdah* and *taavah* for mitzvos.

On Succos we can achieve a new level of spirituality and we are able to use the *mayim* of *taavah* and the *esrog* of *chemdah* in the service of Hashem.

Shir HaShirim 2:3 states, כְּתַפּוּחַ בַּעֲצֵי הַיַּעַר כֵּן דּוֹדִי בֵּין הַבָּנִים בְּצִלּוֹ חִמַּדְתִּי וְיָשַׁבְתִּי וּפִרְיוֹ מָתוֹק לְחִכִּי, *Like the fruitful, fragrant apple among the barren trees of the forest, so is my Beloved among the* gods. *In His shade I delighted and [there] I sat, and the fruit of his Torah was sweet to my palate.* צל, *shade,* is another concept that is described with the term *chemdah.* Shade is desirable. Our sitting in the *succah* on Succos is another way we channel our desire toward mitzvos.

Rav Yosef Engel[30] writes that the entire year we work to overcome *chemdah,* and it is only on Yom Kippur itself that we can completely overcome it, but not eradicate it. After Yom Kippur we are now equipped to harness it. We have learned to direct our desires, our *taavos,* to the performance of mitzvos. We are then able to harness our lust and utilize it for *ruchniyus.*

Just as when one sees a luxurious item, he wants it, so too when you see a *masechta,* you must yearn for it, desire it, and have a *cheshek* to master it. As one enjoys consuming a mouthwatering delicacy, so too should one learn to experience that same delicious flavor with *limud HaTorah.*

❧ Summary: How Does One Develop Chemdah for Ruchnius?

The *avodah* during the *Aseres Yemei Teshuvah* and Tishrei is to work on developing our ability to channel and harness our innate desires, lusts, and *taavos* into *avodas Hashem.* It all starts on Rosh Hashanah when we coronate *HaKadosh Baruch Hu* by accepting Hashem as our King. We blow the shofar: *Anochi Hashem Elokecha.* Then, on the second day of Rosh Hashanah, we commit to לֹא יִהְיֶה לְךָ אֱלֹהִים אֲחֵרִים. The third day, לֹא תִּרְצָח. On Shabbos Shuvah we strengthen ourselves regarding Shabbos. On Erev Yom Kippur we atone for לֹא תַעֲנֶה בְרֵעֲךָ עֵד שָׁקֶר and for *lashon hara.* On Yom Kippur we do teshuvah for לֹא תַחְמֹד. Then, once we have been able to achieve angelic status for one day, we can reset *chemdah,* and tell Hashem, through the mitzvah of *Nisuch HaMayim,* that now our *taavah* is for Him.

When Hashem split the water into celestial water and earthly water, the water that was on earth protested, stating that it too wanted to be in *Shamayim,* near Hashem. Hashem told the earthly water that it would receive the mitzvah of *Nisuch HaMayim,* which represents the *taavah* to be closer to the Presence of Hashem, closer to HaKadosh Baruch Hu.

Then, on Succos, we take the *esrog,* the *targum* of which is *chemdah,* and utilize it in the service of Hashem. And finally, we sit in the shade of the *succah,* as the *pasuk* says בְּצִלּוֹ חִמַּדְתִּי וְיָשַׁבְתִּי, desiring to sit in the shade of Hashem.

May Hashem strengthen us all, that through the *avodah* of the Yamim Noraim, we will be able to overcome our physical drives, and we will elevate ourselves so that our *chemdah* and *taavah* are directed toward yearning for Hashem and His Torah.

ENDNOTES

1. משנה ברורה סימן תר ס"ק א.
2. משנה ברורה סימן תקיג ס"ק יד.
3. יערות דבש חלק א דרוש ה עמוד קיט.
4. אלף כתב אות תשס"א ותת"ד, הובא במגדים חדשים עמוד רכב.
5. יערות דבש חלק ב דרוש א עמוד ד-ה.
6. כתובות קי, ב.
7. שפת אמת ראש השנה תרלב, תרלג.
8. יערות דבש עמוד ה.
9. תנא דבי אליהו זוטא פרק כב.
10. פסיקתא רבת בחודש השביעי רשבע.
11. ירושלמי ברכות א, ה.
12. ראש השנה לב, א.
13. ליקוטי יהודה לראש השנה.
14. דברים אחדים דרוש כ' לשבת שובה, וכן בחדרי בטן שבת שובה עמוד שער־ שעז, ועניני ראש השנה עמוד שנז.
15. הבה תמים - ליום קדוש - (רב שאול בראך) - רכ"ח.

16. פתיל חיי -ב - עמוד ק.
17. אוצרות יוסף דרשה לשבת שובה עמוד 32-33.
18. אבן עזרא יתרו , יד.
19. יומא כ, א.
20. סוכה נב, א.
21. בבא בתרא קסה, א.
22. יומא פא, ב.
23. פסחים קיח, ב.
24. אוצרות יוסף, דרשה לשבת שובה עמוד 37.
25. מדרש תנחומא אמור אות ל.
26. מורה נבוכים ב:י.
27. אבן עזרא יתרו כ, יד.
28. רמבן פרשת אמור כג, מ.
29 תרגום אונקלוס בראשית ג, ו.
30. אוצרות יוסף, דרשה לשבת שובה עמוד 34-35.

YOM KIPPUR

The Divine Purity
of the Name of Hashem
That Manifests as Yom Kippur

⌇ Why Not State the Date Immediately?

Parashas Acharei Mos begins with the Torah's instructions to be delivered to Aharon regarding his *Avodah* on Yom Kippur. However, the *pesukim* omit a crucial detail. In discussing the various *korbanos* and other aspects of the Service, the Torah does not mention that this *Avodah* is to be performed on the tenth of Tishrei! It is only at the very end of the *parashah* that the Torah finally states the date:

וְהָיְתָה לָכֶם לְחֻקַּת עוֹלָם בַּחֹדֶשׁ הַשְּׁבִיעִי בֶּעָשׂוֹר לַחֹדֶשׁ תְּעַנּוּ אֶת נַפְשֹׁתֵיכֶם וְכָל מְלָאכָה לֹא תַעֲשׂוּ הָאֶזְרָח וְהַגֵּר הַגָּר בְּתוֹכֲכֶם. כִּי בַיּוֹם הַזֶּה יְכַפֵּר עֲלֵיכֶם לְטַהֵר אֶתְכֶם מִכֹּל חַטֹּאתֵיכֶם לִפְנֵי ה׳ תִּטְהָרוּ, *This shall remain for you an eternal decree: In the seventh month, on the tenth of the month, you shall afflict yourselves and you shall not do any work, neither the native nor the proselyte who dwells among you. For on this day he shall provide atonement for you to cleanse you; from all your sins before Hashem shall you be cleansed (Vayikra 16: 29-30).*

This is the one Yom Tov for which the Torah first provides the instructions for the *Avodah* of the festival, and only later relates when to do it. This anomaly is pointed out by the *Bnei Yissaschar*,[1] who asks why the Torah departs from its normal practice of discussing a Yom Tov after telling us when it is to be celebrated. It seems that the Torah telling us the date of Yom Kippur is an afterthought.

✑ *A Time of Anger*

Rabbeinu Sherira Gaon authored a historical compendium of events, with a special focus on the lives of the Geonim who preceded him. He writes[2] that in the year תתכ״ב, Rav Achai b'rei d'Raba bar Avuha — namely, Rav Achai Gaon — passed away on Yom Kippur at a time of anger, followed four years later, in the year תתכ״ו, by the *petirah* of Rav Tachna and Mar Zutra ben Rav Chinana. This addition — that Rav Achai Gaon passed away at a time of anger — is a deviation from his standard writing style. When recording the passing of the other Geonim, he merely states the dates without commenting that they were "times of anger." Why does he add this description to the passing of Rav Achai Gaon[3]?

✑ *Avoiding the Name "Yom HaKippurim"*

In years gone by, observes the *Bnei Yissaschar*,[4] *chassidim* and *anshei maaseh*, pious individuals, referred to Yom Kippur by the title *Yom HaKadosh*, the holy day. Why, asks the *Bnei Yissaschar*, wasn't it simply referred to by its proper name, Yom HaKippurim? Furthermore, he asks, the *masechtos* that deal with our holy days are titled *Shabbos, Rosh Hashanah, Succah, Pesachim*. Why isn't there a *Maseches Yom HaKippurim*? The *masechta* that discusses Yom Kippur is called *Yoma*, the Day.

✑ *Yom Kippur, the Physical Manifestation of the Shem HaMeforash!*

The *Bnei Yissaschar* advances a dramatic idea. Yom Kippur is a day that comes from a hidden realm; it is, in fact, the Name of Hashem materializing and crystallizing as a day of the year. It is the *Shem Hashem* that manifests as a day. There is a Divine energy and power inherent in Yom Kippur. עִיצוּמוֹ שֶׁל יוֹם, the essence of the day, is *kadosh* and powerful, so much so that we dare not utter its name, which is a manifestation of the *Shem Hashem*. Therefore, we even call the *masechta* discussing Yom Kippur by the name *Yoma*. It is from a different realm altogether, as if it were beyond the Torah itself, and therefore the date is not mentioned in the Torah until the very end of the *parashah*. Hashem allows His Name to become a day — and therefore we are reluctant even to verbalize the name of the day — because it is tantamount to saying the Name of Hashem. Out of respect we refer to Yom Kippur by a pseudonym: *Yom HaKadosh*. From here we see that there is a supernatural quality to the day of Yom Kippur itself; it is the manifestation of the Name of Hashem.

✑ *Hashem vs. BaShem*

The *sefer Az Yashir*,[5] written by a dear friend and noted *talmid chacham*, Rav Moshe Schwerd, cites Rav Yoshe Ber Soloveitchik, who advances the same concept. He quotes the *Bnei Yissaschar* as he expands the idea further. During the *Avodah* of Yom Kippur, the Kohen Gadol says the *Vidui*, Confession, three times. First, he recites the *Vidui* for himself and his household. Next, he says *Vidui* for all of the Kohanim. Third, he recites *Vidui* for all of Klal Yisrael.

The *Mishnah*[6] describes the procedure as the Kohen Gadol recites *Vidui* for himself and his family, in which he says, "*Ani u'beisi*, I and my household." The text that the Kohen Gadol recites includes two sentences that both begin with the words, "*Ana Hashem*, please, Hashem": First, "*Ana Hashem*, we have sinned," followed by "*Ana Hashem*, forgive us." The Mishnah subsequently[7] describes the *Vidui* recited by the Kohen Gadol for himself, for his family, and for all the Kohanim. The same two sentences are recited, and both sentences begin with *Ana*

Hashem. However, the third iteration of the *Vidui*, the one for all of Klal Yisrael, is slightly different.[8] The second sentence begins with the words, *Ana BaShem*.

The *Tosafos Yom Tov*[9] makes note of this, wondering why the language has changed, and if, in fact, the version recorded is correct. He concludes that the correct text is actually for all three iterations to begin the second sentence with "*Ana BaShem*."

Rav Soloveitchik addresses this question of the *Tosafos Yom Tov*.[10] The relationship that Klal Yisrael enjoys with Hashem is unique and multifaceted. On the night of Yom Kippur, our relationship with Hashem is especially distinctive. On that night, Hashem serves as our Mother. The *kittel* we wear is comparable to a mother who swaddles her child in white. When an infant soils his garments, the mother cleans him and changes his clothing.

On the night of Yom Kippur we are like the soiled infant, with *aveiros* sullying our pure *neshamos*. Hashem, our Mother, yearns to help us. He cleanses us, He swaddles us, and He dresses us in white. It is not beneath Hashem's dignity for Him to personally clean up our mess.

The process Hashem utilizes to cleanse us, as it were, is to take the *Shem Hashem* and manifest it as a day: the day of Yom Kippur.

We know that אֱלֹקִים נִצָּב בַּעֲדַת קֵל, Hashem stands where there are three *dayanim*, where a *beis din* is being convened. At the onset of Yom Kippur, we want to bring the *Shechinah* to us, so we convene a *beis din*. This *beis din* does much more than just annul the vows in the form of *Kol Nidrei*; it serves as the conduit through which the *Shechinah* can come to forgive our sins. When the *beis din* is in place, the *Shechinah* comes down from the seventh *Raki'a*, the loftiest level of *Shamayim*. Hashem approaches each and every one of us to cleanse the filth that has polluted our *neshamos*.

Hashem accomplishes the cleansing process with the *Yom*, the Day, which is the manifestation of the *Shem Hashem*, the Name of Hashem. Therefore, says Rav Soloveitchik, the *Tosafos Yom*

Tov is correct: The *kapparah* we seek — for the Kohen Gadol, for the Kohanim, and for Klal Yisrael — is the *kapparah* that is brought about *BaShem*, **with** the Name of Hashem. That is why we say, "*Ana BaShem, kapper na*, please, **with** Your Name, atone for me.

≈ The Correct Way to Read the Tefillah

The *tefillah* should be read as follows: *Ana*, Please, *BaShem*, with Your Name, *kapper na*, please atone! (And not as it is commonly read – *Ana BaShem*, Please, Hashem, *kapper na* ….) We are asking that through the power of the *Shem* of Hashem, He should cleanse us of all sin.

The source of the *kedushah* of Yom Kippur and the power of the *kapparah* of Yom Kippur are fueled by its manifestation as the *Shem Hashem*, by the Name of Hashem descending to us and concretizing as the day of Yom Kippur. Uttering the name *Yom Kippur* is considered to be akin to stating the *Shem HaMeforash*, the Name of Hashem. Therefore, it was customary not to refer to Yom Kippur by name, but rather to call it *Yom HaKadosh*, the holy day.

≈ Why Do We Say, "Hashem Hu HaElokim," Seven Times?

During the final moments of Yom Kippur, we repeat the phrase "*Hashem Hu HaElokim*" seven times, thereby affirming that *Hashem, He is God*. What is the significance of these words and why do we say them as Yom Kippur is drawing to a close? When Yom Kippur is over, the *Shechinah* departs, so to speak, and Hashem re-ascends the *Seven Rakios*. We recite, "*Hashem Hu HaElokim*," seven times to escort, so to speak, the *Shechinah* to the highest heavens.

Hashem is *mechapper* our *aveiros* with His Name. As the Name of Hashem ascends the *Seven Rakios*, so too, the Day slips away.

❧ BaYom, Explained

כִּי בַיּוֹם הַזֶּה יְכַפֵּר עֲלֵיכֶם לְטַהֵר אֶתְכֶם מִכֹּל חַטֹּאתֵיכֶם לִפְנֵי ה' תִּטְהָרוּ.

This *pasuk* is only one of six places in Tanach where the word בַיּוֹם is vocalized with a *patach* under the *beis* rather than a *shva*. In fact, in this context, the word should really be *b'yom*, not *baYom*. *B'yom* means "during the day," and *baYom* means "with *the* day." It would seem more logical for the verse to state, "In the course of this day, Hashem will atone for you." The *shva* seems to fit the meaning of the *pasuk* much better than the *patach*.[11] *B'yom* implies that the *kapparah* takes place on the day of Yom Kippur; *baYom*, on the other hand, implies that the Day *itself* is the tool with which the *kapparah* is effected. *BaYom*, it is *with* the Day, utilizing the Day, that the *kapparah* happens. In light of what we have learned, we can explain this vocalization. The word *baYom* is employed to indicate that the atonement does not merely transpire during the course of the day, but *Itzumo shel Yom mechapper*, the very essence of the day inherently atones. *BaYom*, with the day itself, which is the manifestation of the Name of HaKadosh Baruch Hu, Hashem atones for our sins.

❧ Shedding Tears on Yom Kippur

Parenthetically, the words כִּי בַיּוֹם הַזֶּה יְכַפֵּר contain a *remez* to an important *avodah* of Yom Kippur. The *roshei teivos* of these words, when rearranged, spell the word בְּכִיָּה, crying, conveying the importance of shedding tears on Yom Kippur. The *roshei teivos* of the words מִכֹּל חַטֹּאתֵיכֶם לִפְנֵי ה' תִּטְהָרוּ, when rearranged, form the word *chamalti*, I was merciful. Rav Chaim Palagi writes[12] that if a person cries, shedding tears on Yom Kippur, he will merit mercy and forgiveness for his sins.

❧ Does Yom Kippur Need Teshuvah?

From the above we see the unique atonement power of the day of Yom Kippur itself. However, it would seem that this is not our halachic conclusion, because if someone fasts for the entire duration of Yom Kippur, but he does not do teshuvah, his Yom Kippur has accomplished nothing for him. We rule as the *Chachamim* do[13]: *Ein Yom Kippur mechapper bli teshuvah*, Yom Kippur does not atone unless it is accompanied by repentance. Rebbe, however, differs with the *Chachamim*; he maintains that the very essence of Yom Kippur serves to atone for one's *aveiros*, and this atonement is effected even if one does not do teshuvah. Thus, "עִיצוּמוֹ שֶׁל יוֹם מְכַפֵּר, *the very essence of the day [inherently] atones*" refers to this concept.

Despite the fact that we do not *pasken* according to Rebbe, the Rambam employs the expression, "*Itzumo shel Yom mechapper.*"[14] This shows that this terminology does have halachic standing. The Rambam is teaching us that although Yom Kippur alone is not *mechapper*, and one must also do teshuvah to achieve atonement, nevertheless, the atonement does not come solely from one's teshuvah. Rather, once one does teshuvah, then the *itzumo shel Yom* can in fact be *mechapper*. The process of teshuvah activates the power inherent in the day of Yom Kippur that allows one to be forgiven for his wrongdoings. However, it is interesting to note, as we shall present below, that there are some instances where we seem to *pasken*, like Rebbe, that *itzumo shel Yom* is *mechapper*.

✍ Kippurim, in the Plural

The full and proper name of this Yom Tov is Yom HaKippurim. Why use the plural form? Why not use the singular, as we usually refer to it, Yom Kippur? The *Darchei Moshe*[15] explains that not only is Yom Kippur a day of *kapparah* for those who are alive, it is also a day of atonement for those who have passed away. The plural form refers to the atonement of these two groups.

How can the day be a *kapparah* for those who already have passed away? As mentioned above, we *pasken* like the *Chachamim* that *ein Yom Kippur mechapper bli teshuvah*, and one who is no longer among the living cannot do teshuvah. So how can Yom Kippur effect *kapparah* for the deceased? If they cannot do teshuvah, then Yom Kippur cannot atone for them.

Rav Yaakov Orenstein, the *Baal Yeshuos Yaakov*,[16] explains that most people do not pass away immediately after Yom Kippur, but rather some time during the course of the year. In that case, how do those people achieve atonement and forgiveness? Any sin that may have been committed between the previous Yom Kippur and the day he was *niftar* will not have been privy to the awesome forgiving power of Yom Kippur. How is atonement for these final months achieved? The answer is in the name Yom Kippurim. The Yom Kippur following one's demise is *mechapper* for *aveiros* committed during the final months of one's life, from the day after Yom Kippur until the day of *petirah*. This unique *kapparah* is effective even without teshuvah.

When we rule that the essence of Yom Kippur is not *mechapper* without teshuvah, that ruling applies only to one who is able to do teshuvah. If one is unable to do teshuvah, then the essence of the day can be *mechapper*, and the next Yom Kippur will effect a *kapparah* for the sins that may have been committed between the prior Yom Kippur until the *petirah*. Thus, for someone who cannot do teshuvah, we do *pasken* that *itzumo shel Yom* is *mechapper*.

☙ Attending Rebbe's Levayah Guaranteed Olam Haba

There is another illustration of the concept that *itzumo shel Yom* is manifest. The Gemara[17] relates that at the time that Rebbe was *niftar*, a Heavenly voice proclaimed that anyone who had attended the *levayah* of Rebbe is *mezuman*, prepared, for *chayei Olam Haba*, life in the World to Come. A launderer had missed the *levayah*, and when he heard what was declared from Heaven, he jumped off the roof in despair. A *Bas Kol* then declared that he, too, merited *Olam Haba* even though he had not attended the funeral.

What was so unique about Rebbe's *levayah* that anyone

who attended was *mezuman l'chayei Olam Haba*? Rav Yitzchak Elchanan Spector gives an incredible answer.[18]

❧ Why Do We Read About the Ten Martyrs on Yom Kippur?

Why do we read about the *Asarah Harugei Malchus* during the *tefillos* that we recite during Mussaf on Yom Kippur?

Chazal ask why the death of Miriam is juxtaposed to the instructions about the *Parah Adumah*. They answer that it is to teach us that just as the *Parah Adumah* is *mechapper*, so too the death of the righteous also provides *kapparah*. Miriam's passing away was *mechapper* for the Bnei Yisrael. That is why we read about the *Asarah Harugei Malchus* on Yom Kippur: Their deaths provided *kapparah* for the Jewish people.

We stated earlier that Rebbe and the Rabbanan disagreed about whether or not Yom Kippur itself is *mechapper*, or if one must do teshuvah in order to activate the *kapparah* of Yom Kippur. Rebbe held that *itzumo shel Yom*, the essence of the day, is itself enough to provide atonement. The Rabbanan disagreed and maintained that it is only with teshuvah that Yom Kippur can provide atonement.

Extrapolating based on this *machlokes*, advances Reb Yitzchak Elchanan, Rebbe and the Rabbanan would also disagree whether the death of a *tzaddik* on its own can provide atonement even without teshuvah. Rebbe maintained that it does, while the Rabbanan stated that the passing of a *tzaddik* can atone only if the person also did teshuvah and repented.

There is a mystical concept that on the day of an eminent sage's *petirah*, we *pasken* in accordance with his opinions in halachah. Thus, on the day that Rebbe passed away, we *paskened* as he did: One need not do teshuvah in order to acquire the atonement that can be achieved with the passing of *tzaddikim*. Therefore, a message was received from *Shamayim* stating just that. Today, in accord with Rebbe's *shitah*, opinion, all in attendance receive automatic atonement through his passing, even without having done teshuvah. In honor of Rebbe, on the day he passed away, the halachah was that *itzumo shel Yom* was *mechapper*, and all in attendance were *mezuman l'chayei Olam Haba*.

Even though we must do teshuvah to activate the *kapparah*, the day itself has great power to be *mechapper: ki baYom hazeh yechaper*, because *with this day*, Hashem forgives us.

≈ *When Does the Kapparah Happen?*

We have begun to uncover the extraordinary power inherent in the day of Yom Kippur itself. The Gemara[19] says that if one passes away on Erev Yom Kippur it is an evil portent because he lost out on the atonement of Yom Kippur. However, if he passes away on Motza'ei Yom Kippur, the Gemara states that it is a good *siman* that his sins were all completely forgiven. What about someone who passes away on Yom Kippur itself? Is that a good or evil omen?

This question really hinges on whether the atonement of Yom Kippur takes place incrementally as the day progresses, or does it atone only at its conclusion? If it takes place incrementally, one who passes away on Yom Kippur at least achieved a degree of atonement. However, if the atonement is achieved only upon its conclusion, it would be a bad sign to pass away on Yom Kippur. Rav Elchanan Wasserman explains[20] that Rav Sherira Gaon clearly held that Yom Kippur does not atone until the day is over, which would make it a bad sign to pass away on Yom Kippur.

Therefore, when he recorded the passing of Rav Achai Gaon, which happened on Yom Kippur, he was afraid that it would reflect poorly on Rav Achai Gaon, for he was *niftar* before the conclusion of Yom Kippur, and he had not yet been granted the *kapparah* that Yom Kippur would have afforded him had he lived another few hours. This would have led to a *p'gam*, defect, in the honor of Rav Achai Gaon. Therefore, to explain why Rav Achai Gaon did not live to the conclusion of Yom Kippur, Rav Sherira Gaon wrote that it was "a time of anger" to convey the message that the *petirah* of Rav Achai Gaon was prompted by Hashem's anger toward the entire generation, rather than, *chas v'shalom*, a negative judgment that did not allow Rav Achai Gaon to achieve the *kapparah* of Yom Kippur.

❧ The Petirah of Rabbi Akiva

This same idea can also be applied to the *petirah* of Rabbi Akiva, who, we are taught by *Yalkut Shimoni*,[21] was killed on Yom Kippur. In fact, it is suggested[22] that we even recite a hidden *hesped* for Rabbi Akiva on Yom Kippur. On the night of Yom Kippur, our *davening* begins with *Kol Nidrei*, which starts with the phrase, "*Ohr zarua latzaddik u'l'yishrei leiv simchah*, Light is sown for the righteous; and for the upright of heart, gladness" (*Tehillim* 97:11). Why do we begin the *davening* on the Yom HaKadosh with this sentence from *Tehillim*? It is suggested that the reason we start this way is because the *pasuk* "אוֹר זָרֻעַ לַצַּדִּיק וּלְיִשְׁרֵי לֵב שִׂמְחָה" spells, with its *sofei teivos*, "Rabbi Akiva" (ר׳ עקיבה). Just as Rav Elchanon explained regarding Rav Achai Gaon, the death of Rabbi Akiva was not a *siman ra*, negative portent; rather, it was also a time of anger, as evidenced by the harsh decrees the Roman promulgated against us.

❧ The Source of the Power of Atonement of Yom Kippur

There is an inherent power of Divine atonement in the day of Yom Kippur. *Bnei Yissaschar* writes[23] that the day of Yom Kippur and the concept of teshuvah come from a special, remote, and hidden place.

The *Yalkut Shimoni* teaches[24] that Hashem asked *Chochmah* (Wisdom) what should happen to one who sins. *Chochmah* responded that the offender deserves the death penalty. The *neviim* (prophets) were asked the same question, and they offered the same response. Hashem asked the *malachim*, and once again the response was that the offenders deserve to be punished by death. Even when the Torah was asked, the only suggestion given was to bring an offering to gain atonement, but the possibility of teshuvah was not offered.

Only HaKadosh Baruch Hu could conceive the idea of teshuvah. It was beyond the scope of *Chochmah*, the *neviim*, and the *malachim* to comprehend that a sinner could be given a second chance.

The day of Yom Kippur comes from *Olam Haba*,[25] from the hidden World to Come. When Yom Kippur begins, it is as if *Olam Haba* itself is coming down to This World. As in *Olam Haba*, Yom Kippur is a day, without eating or drinking, and we conduct ourselves like the Heavenly angels. And since it comes from a hidden source, the date of the Yom Tov is hidden until the very end of the Torah's discussion about it, when it is finally revealed so we will know when to observe it.

May we always be *zocheh* to taste the Divine quality of this day that emanates from *Olam Haba* and may we return to Hashem with *teshuvah sheleimah* and merit a *chasimah tovah*.

ENDNOTES

1. בני יששכר מאמר חדש תשרי מאמר ח אות ב.

2. אגרת דרבינו שרירא גאון חלק ג פרק ד.

3. כמוצא שלל רב, ימים נוראים עמוד שסח.

4. בני יששכר מאמר חדש תשרי מאמר ח אות ב.

5. אז ישיר עמוד קפא-קפב.

6. יומא פרק ג משנה ח.

7. יומא פרק ד משנה ב.

8. יומא פרק ו משנה ב.

9. תוספות יום טוב, יומא פרק ו משנה ב.

10. נפש הרב עמוד כה-כו.

11. קול בן לוי עמוד 247, הובא בכמוצא שלל רב שם.

12. פני חיים אחרי מות.

13. יומא פז, א.

14. הלכות תשובה פרק א הלכה ג.

15. דרכי משה סימן תרכ"א, וגם הובא ברוקח.

16. ישועת יעקב סימן תרכא.

17. כתובות קג, ב.

18. נחל יצחק פתיחה אות ו, שי לתורה ראש השנה יום כיפור עמ׳ ער׳ בשם רבי ישראל סאלנטר.

19. כתובות דף קג, ב.

20. קובץ הפרדס אלול תרצב, והובא בקובץ עניינים על מסכת חולין.

21. ילקוט שמעוני משלי פרק ט.

22. רבי שמואל מאיר שליט"א הובא בכמוציא שלל רב עמוד שדמ.

23. בני יששכר, שם.

24. ילקוט שמעוני תהלים רמז תשב, ע׳ ירושלמי מכות ב, ו.

25. של"ה מסכת יומא אות קלח.

Kapparah
Through Limud HaTorah

⮰ Ki HaMitzvah Hazos —
What Is "This Mitzvah"

The Torah states, כִּי הַמִּצְוָה הַזֹּאת אֲשֶׁר אָנֹכִי מְצַוְּךָ הַיּוֹם לֹא נִפְלֵאת הִוא מִמְּךָ וְלֹא רְחֹקָה הִוא. לֹא בַשָּׁמַיִם הִוא לֵאמֹר מִי יַעֲלֶה לָּנוּ הַשָּׁמַיְמָה וְיִקָּחֶהָ לָּנוּ וְיַשְׁמִעֵנוּ אֹתָהּ וְנַעֲשֶׂנָּה. וְלֹא מֵעֵבֶר לַיָּם הִוא לֵאמֹר מִי יַעֲבָר לָנוּ אֶל עֵבֶר הַיָּם וְיִקָּחֶהָ לָּנוּ וְיַשְׁמִעֵנוּ אֹתָהּ וְנַעֲשֶׂנָּה. כִּי קָרוֹב אֵלֶיךָ הַדָּבָר מְאֹד בְּפִיךָ וּבִלְבָבְךָ לַעֲשֹׂתוֹ, *For this commandment (mitzvah) that I command you today — it is not hidden from you and it is not distant. It is not in heaven, [for you] to say, "Who can ascend to the heaven for us and take it for us, so that we can listen to it and perform it?" Nor is it across the sea, [for you] to say, "Who can cross to the other side of the sea and take it for us, so we can listen to it and perform it?" Rather, the matter is very near to you—in your mouth and in your heart—to perform it* (Devarim 30:11-15).

In summary, the Torah says that הַמִּצְוָה הַזֹּאת, *this mitzvah*, is very close to you.

⮰ "This Mitzvah" Refers to Teshuvah

What is הַמִּצְוָה הַזֹּאת? What is *"this* mitzvah? The Ramban states[1] that הַמִּצְוָה הַזֹּאת is the mitzvah of teshuvah.

The Torah earlier mentioned teshuvah. In *Devarim* 30:2, the Torah says, וְשַׁבְתָּ עַד ה' אֱלֹקֶיךָ, *And you will return to Hashem, your God.* Therefore, says the Ramban (and this is the opinion of the *Sforno* and the *Abarbanel* as well), when the Torah says that *this mitzvah* is not distant, it is referring to the mitzvah of repentance.

≈ *"This Mitzvah" Is Talmud Torah*

However, while these illustrious *Rishonim* have offered us an explanation stating that הַמִּצְוָה הַזֹּאת refers to the mitzvah of teshuvah, the Gemara relates something entirely different. The Gemara[2] states, רָבָא אָמַר לֹא בַשָּׁמַיִם הִוא, *Rava says, What does the Torah mean when it says that it is not in heaven?* לֹא תִמָּצֵא בְּמִי שֶׁמַּגְבִּיהַּ דַּעְתּוֹ עָלֶיהָ כַּשָּׁמַיִם *This teaches that [Torah scholarship] will not be found in one who believes his mind towers over it like the heavens.* And what does it mean when the Torah says, וְלֹא מֵעֵבֶר לַיָּם הִוא? The Gemara answers, וְלֹא תִמָּצֵא בְּמִי שֶׁמַּרְחִיב דַּעְתּוֹ עָלֶיהָ כַּיָּם, *nor will it be found in one who believes his mind is as broad as the ocean in relation to it, i.e., he believes his mind is sufficiently large to accommodate the Torah with ease.*

The Gemara continues, רַבִּי יוֹחָנָן אָמַר לֹא בַשָּׁמַיִם הִוא לֹא תִמָּצֵא בְּגַסֵּי רוּחַ, *R' Yochanan says that this is teaching us that the Torah is not in the heavens; i.e., you will not find it in the haughty.* וְלֹא מֵעֵבֶר לַיָּם הִוא לֹא תִמָּצֵא לֹא בְּסַחֲרָנִים וְלֹא בְּתַגָּרִים, *And it is not across the ocean; this teaches that [Torah scholarship] will not be found in traveling businessmen nor with peddlers.* What does it mean when the Torah says that it is not across the ocean? It means that it will not be found in businessmen and merchants who are continually traveling over the seas.

The Gemara tells us very explicitly, as codified very clearly in the Rambam,[3] that when the Chumash says, כִּי הַמִּצְוָה הַזֹּאת לֹא בַשָּׁמַיִם הִוא וְלֹא מֵעֵבֶר לַיָּם הִוא, it is not referring to the mitzvah of teshuvah, but rather it is referring to the mitzvah of learning Torah. Why, then, do the Ramban, *Sforno*, and *Abarbanel* say that the *pesukim* are referring to the mitzvah of teshuvah if the Gemara says explicitly that it is referring to the mitzvah of learning Torah?

≈ *Which Is It? Torah or Teshuvah?*

Another difficulty pertains to the *Haftarah* of Shabbos Shuvah, which is excerpted from *Sefer Hoshea*. Hoshea begins his prophecy by saying, שׁוּבָה יִשְׂרָאֵל עַד ה' אֱלֹקֶיךָ כִּי כָשַׁלְתָּ בַּעֲוֹנֶךָ, *Return, Yisrael, unto Hashem your God, for you have stumbled in your iniquity* (Hoshea 14:2). First the *Navi* warns Klal Yisrael to do teshuvah, and then continues, קְחוּ עִמָּכֶם דְּבָרִים וְשׁוּבוּ אֶל ה', *Take words with you and return to Hashem …* (ibid.).

In *Parashas Haazinu*, the Sifri explains the words of this *pasuk*, קְחוּ עִמָּכֶם דְּבָרִים, as a reference to Torah. "*Ein devarim ela Torah;* There are no "words" except Torah. The word *devarim* must refer to Torah, as the Torah states, אֶת הַדְּבָרִים הָאֵלֶּה דִּבֶּר ה' אֶל כָּל קְהַלְכֶם בָּהָר מִתּוֹךְ הָאֵשׁ הֶעָנָן וְהָעֲרָפֶל, *These words [devarim] Hashem spoke to your entire congregation on the mountain, from the midst of the fire, the cloud, and the thick cloud* (Devarim 5:19).

Rav Shlomo Wahrman[4] questions what the *Navi* Hoshea is trying to tell us. First he cries out to the Bnei Yisrael to do teshuvah, and then he says קְחוּ עִמָּכֶם דְּבָרִים, *go learn Torah*. What does the *Navi* want us to do? Should we do teshuvah or should we learn Torah?

≈ *Four Classes of Aveirah*

Rav Aharon Kotler, the founder and Rosh Yeshivah of the Lakewood Yeshivah, Beis Medrash Govoha, who had a significant hand in building Torah in America, teaches us a very fundamental principle.

We know from the Rambam that teshuvah has four parts:

1) *Azivas HaCheit*: abandoning the sin, ceasing to commit the *aveirah*.
2) *Kabbalah al HeAsid*: committing to never violating the transgression again.

3) *Charatah*: regretting having sinned.

4) *Vidui*: confessing to having committed the sin.

Rav Aharon expounds that even though these are the four parts of teshuvah, the *Navi* quoted above teaches us that there is another aspect of teshuvah. *Prat nosaf b'mitzvas teshuvah*, there is an additional element in doing teshuvah; that added component is the mitzvah of *talmud Torah*. Learning Torah is an added aspect of teshuvah. Yes, the Navi is telling us to do teshuvah. And, he adds, קְחוּ עִמָּכֶם דְּבָרִים, *learn Torah*, because learning Torah is a part of the teshuvah process.

✍ Limud HaTorah: Part of Doing Teshuvah

The idea that part and parcel of doing teshuvah is learning Torah is also set forth by Rav Gamliel Rabinovich.[5] In fact, Rav Gamliel cites the *Midrash*[6] that seems to present this idea very clearly. The *Midrash* asks, What should a person do if he has transgressed an *aveirah* for which he is liable to receive the death penalty, either at the hand of *beis din* or *misah b'yedei Shamayim*? What can one do to ensure that he can live?

The *Midrash* answers that if the sinner had been accustomed to learning one *blatt* of Gemara each day, he should now learn two *blatt* daily. If he generally learned one *perek* every day, he should now increase his learning to two *perakim* daily.

This *midrash* is clearly reinforcing the *yesod* of Rav Aharon Kotler: *Limud HaTorah* is a very important component of teshuvah.

✍ Why Is Learning Torah an Aspect of Teshuvah?

However, why should learning Torah be a part of teshuvah? *Talmud Torah* is its own independent mitzvah! Why, then, and how, is *talmud Torah* part of the mitzvah of teshuvah?

Rav Aharon explains that we must understand the purpose of teshuvah. To Whom are you returning? One who does teshuvah is returning to Hashem; in fact, the goal of teshuvah is *hiskarvus l'Hashem*, drawing close to Hashem. As the *pasuk* says, שׁוּבָה יִשְׂרָאֵל עַד ה' אֱלֹקֶיךָ. With teshuvah, one returns all the way עַד ה', he comes close to Hashem.

גְּדוֹלָה תְּשׁוּבָה שֶׁמַּגַּעַת עַד כִּסֵּא הַכָּבוֹד, Teshuvah is great because it reaches all the way to the Throne of Glory.[7] And the most effective way to come close to Hashem is through learning Torah, as the Mishnah says in *Pirkei Avos*,[8] "*Afilu echad [she'oseik baTorah], Shechinah imo*, Even if only one person learns Torah, Hashem is with him."

Learning Torah is the best way to accomplish the goal of teshuvah, which is closeness to Hashem. Therefore, the *Navi* tells us, שׁוּבָה יִשְׂרָאֵל, *Do teshuvah, Klal Yisrael!* How do we do teshuvah? קְחוּ עִמָּכֶם דְּבָרִים; i.e., the best way to do teshuvah is by learning Torah!

Rav Wahrman explains that the Ramban, who says that כִּי הַמִּצְוָה הַזֹּאת is referring to the mitzvah of teshuvah, is not contradicting the Gemara that says the *pasuk* refers to the mitzvah of learning Torah. Learning Torah is not only its own independent mitzvah, but it is also an important component of the mitzvah of teshuvah.

❧ The Chida's Revolutionary Chiddush

One of the most prolific Jewish authors and Torah giants of all time is the *Chida*, Rav Chaim Yosef Dovid Azulai. He introduces a momentous concept that redefines our concept of teshuvah.

The Gemara[9] outlines the various categories of *aveiros*, and states how effective teshuvah is for each category. The Gemara quotes Rav Yishmael, who taught that just as there are four categories of sins, there are *daled chelkei kapparah*, four divisions of atonement.

❧ The Four Categories of Sin Require Different Atonements

1. The first category is failing to fulfill a *mitzvas asei*, a positive commandment. If one does not say *Shema*, does not put

on *tefillin*, or eats a meal outside of the *succah* on Succos, he transgresses a *mitzvas asei*. If a person does teshuvah for this *aveirah*, there is immediate atonement. "עָבַר עַל עֲשֵׂה וְשָׁב אֵינוֹ זָז מִשָּׁם עַד שֶׁמּוֹחֲלִין לוֹ, One who transgresses a *mitzvah asei* and atones does not even move from there before he is forgiven." *Teshuvah* atones at once, and he is forgiven on the spot.

2. The second category is one who transgresses a *lav*, a prohibitive commandment. Examples include wearing a garment that contains *shaatnez*, speaking *lashon hara*, and eating *tereifah*. If one commits an *aveirah* in this category and then does teshuvah, that does not suffice. Teshuvah alone cannot atone for the *aveirah*. Something more must be done. The Gemara says, "תְּשׁוּבָה תּוֹלָה וְיוֹם הַכִּפּוּרִים מְכַפֵּר, *Teshuvah suspends the punishment, and then Yom Kippur provides atonement.*" Teshuvah alone is not sufficient; the sinner also needs Yom Kippur in order to be forgiven.

3. The third category is an *aveirah* that carries a penalty of *kareis* or *misas beis din*, for which the courts can sentence the transgressor to capital punishment, such as violating the Shabbos. "עָבַר עַל כְּרֵיתוֹת וּמִיתוֹת בֵּית דִּין וְעָשָׂה תְּשׁוּבָה וְיוֹם הַכִּפּוּרִים תּוֹלִין וְיִסּוּרִין מְמָרְקִין, If one does teshuvah for an *aveirah* in this category, *teshuvah and Yom Kippur can cause the punishment to be suspended.*" For this category of sin, however, even teshuvah with Yom Kippur are not enough to purge the *aveirah*. For this category of sin, a person needs *yissurim, afflictions and difficulties, to atone for the sin.*

4. The final category of sin is the most severe. This is the *aveirah* of causing a *chillul Hashem*, desecration of the Name of Hashem. As the Gemara states, "אֲבָל מִי שֶׁיֵּשׁ חִילּוּל הַשֵּׁם בְּיָדוֹ אֵין לוֹ כֹּחַ בִּתְשׁוּבָה לִתְלוֹת וְלֹא בְיוֹם הַכִּפּוּרִים לְכַפֵּר וְלֹא בְיִסּוּרִין לְמָרֵק, *If someone committed the sin of desecrating the Name of Hashem, teshuvah cannot suspend, Yom Kippur cannot atone, and even afflictions and tzaros cannot purge the sin.*" "אֶלָּא כּוּלָן תּוֹלִין וּמִיתָה מְמָרֶקֶת, *Rather, the combined influence of all*

three causes the sin to be suspended, and only death purges the sin and provides atonement."

This is quite a frightening Gemara, for we are informed that there are sins that are not rectifiable simply by doing teshuvah.

~ *The Incredible Power of Limud HaTorah!*

However, the *Chida* comes to offer us a significant *pesach tikvah*, a wondrous ray of hope. He writes[10] that these four categories of sin that need teshuvah, or the addition of Yom Kippur, or suffering, or even death in order to achieve forgiveness, don't apply to everyone. They apply only to a person who is not involved in learning Torah. One who learns Torah *lishmah*, for its own sake, however, doesn't need Yom Kippur, *tzaros*, or *misah* to be forgiven. If one who commits an *aveirah* learns Torah in the proper way accompanied by teshuvah, then his teshuvah combines with his Torah learning and he needs nothing more to achieve forgiveness!

The *Chida* adds that this incredible *chiddush* is actually alluded to in *Shemoneh Esrei*, which we say three times a day. We *daven* for forgiveness and we say: הֲשִׁיבֵנוּ אָבִינוּ לְתוֹרָתֶךְ. *Bring us back, our Father, to Your Torah,* and if we return to learning Torah, then וְהַחֲזִירֵנוּ בִּתְשׁוּבָה שְׁלֵמָה לְפָנֶיךָ, *and influence us to return in perfect repentance before You.* Learning Torah is the surest and most direct way to do teshuvah.

The *Bnei Yissaschar*[11] makes an astounding comment on these words of the *Chida*. He writes that even though there are *sug-yas* that put this *chiddush* into question, nevertheless, once this giant, namely the *Chida*, has *paskened* down here in this world that learning Torah alone can atone for all sin, that is how they *pasken* in the *Beis Din shel Maalah*.

Teshuvah is a voyage to the *Kisei HaKavod*, it is a journey back to Hashem, and for certain types of *aveiros* a person needs more powerful fuel. Sometimes one's teshuvah may need a boost from Yom Kippur. Sometimes one may need an even stronger boost in the form of *yissurim*. At times it may even require *misah*. But the power of Torah is very strong. It is such powerful fuel, it has such powerful energy, that when a person's teshuvah voyage back to Hashem is powered by Torah, then no added boost it needed. Torah can fuel teshuvah for any *aveirah*.

❧ *The Source of the Koach of Yom Kippur*

We may even add that we all know that the greatest Day of Atonement in the entire year is the *Yom HaKadosh*, Yom Kippur. Where does Yom Kippur derive its *koach*? What lies in the soul of the day that gives it the power to atone?

Perhaps we can suggest the origin for the power of Yom Kippur based on a Gemara[12] that tells us that Yom Kippur is the day of atonement because it is the day on which the second set of *Luchos* were given to Klal Yisrael. Yom Kippur is the day on which we received the Torah, that gives it the *koach* to serve as a day of atonement.

But didn't we receive the Torah on Shavuos? Didn't Moshe Rabbenu bring the *Luchos* down on Shavuos? Yes; however, those *Luchos* were shattered because of the *Cheit HaEigel*. The Torah that we have today was in fact received on Yom Kippur, when Hashem forgave the sin of the Golden Calf. Therefore, since Yom Kippur is the day on which we received the Torah, it is the *koach haTorah* that has made Yom Kippur into a Day of Atonement.

❧ *Lighting a Ner on Yom Kippur*

The following *minhag*, practiced on Erev Yom Kippur, serves as a further demonstration of our discussion.

There is a well-known *minhag*, brought down by the *Rema*,[13] to light a *yahrtzeit* candle in memory of a deceased parent before Yom Kippur. The candle is referred to as a *ner neshamah*, and it functions as a form of *kapparah*, atonement, for the deceased parent. The *Mishnah Berurah*[14] writes that it would seem that one candle would be sufficient for both one's parents. This *minhag* is certainly well known, yet there is another, lesser-known *minhag*:

In addition to the *yahrtzeit* candle, one should light additional candles. The *Rema*[15] writes that it is customary to light a candle on behalf of every man in the house, and clearly states that this is done for the men, and not the women. The *Mishnah Berurah*[16] adds that nowadays we light a candle only for those men in the household who are married. In addition to a *yahrtzeit* candle when relevant, every married man should light a candle for himself before Yom Kippur.

This additional candle is called a *gezunte licht*, a candle of health or well-being. What is the reason for this candle and why do only men light this candle? The *Magen Avraham*[17] provides an explanation, stating that the Torah, in the form of the second *Luchos*, was given on Yom Kippur. Torah is compared to a *ner*, a candle, as the *pasuk* says, כִּי נֵר מִצְוָה וְתוֹרָה אוֹר, For a mitzvah is a lamp and the Torah is light (*Mishlei* 6:23). As a way of signifying that this is the day on which we received the Torah, the ultimate *ner*, we have the *minhag* to light a *ner*. The *Elya Rabbah*[18] explains that since women are not obligated in the mitzvah of *talmud Torah*, they therefore do not have the *minhag* to light this candle.

Once again, we find that the backbone and soul of Yom Kippur is the fact that it is the day on which the Torah was given.

❧ Why FIVE Inuyim?

There are *chamishah inuyim*, five afflictions, with which we are afflicted on Yom Kippur. We abstain from eating, bathing, anointing with oil, wearing leather shoes, and marital relations. What is the meaning of specifically five restrictions on Yom Kippur?

The *Elya Rabbah*[19] explains that these *chamishah inuyim* correspond to the *Chamishah Chumshei Torah*, the Five Books of the Torah. What is the connection between the Five Books of Torah and the afflictions of Yom Kippur? The *Elya Rabbah* explains that Yom Kippur was the day on which we received the Five Books of the Torah, and therefore on the anniversary of that date

Hashem gave us five corresponding *inuyim*. In light of what we have learned — that the driving force of Yom Kippur is the Torah — we understand the connection between the five afflictions that bring us atonement and the five Books of the Torah, for it is the *koach* of the Torah that fuels Yom Kippur's power to atone for our sins.

What we are learning is that *limud HaTorah* is the most powerful boost we can give to our teshuvah.

As the *Chida* taught, teshuvah together with Torah learning does not necessitate Yom Kippur, *yissurim*, or *misah* to accompany it. This is an amazing concept: By devoting oneself to focused and intense learning and applying oneself to understand the teachings of the Torah, one protects himself from difficulties and *tzaros*. The very essence of Yom Kippur is powered by the fact that it is the day on which the Torah was given.

May HaKadosh Baruch Hu strengthen us in dedicating ourselves to His holy Torah and thereby achieve the great *berachos* of *selichah*, *mechilah*, and *kapparah*.

ENDNOTES

1. רמב״ן דברים ל, יא.

2. עירובין נד, א.

3. רמב״ם הלכות תלמוד תורה פרק ג הלכה ח.

4. אורות ימי הרחמים סימן ל.

5. טיב המועדים אלול־תשרי עמוד שעה.

6. ויקרא רבה כה, א.

7. יומא פו, א.

8. פרקי אבות פרק ג משנה ו.

9. יומא פו, א.

10. כסא דוד דרוש ט, עמוד קנח, בשם ספר עיר בנימין.

11. מאמרי חדש תשרי מאמר ה דרוש יד אות מ.

12. תענית ל, ב.

13. משנה ברורה סימן תרי סעיף ד.

14. משנה ברורה שם ס״ק יב.

15. משנה ברורה סימן תרי סעיף ד.

16. משנה ברורה שם ס״ק יא.

17. מגן אברהם סימן תרי ס״ק ג.

18. אליה רבה סימן תרי.

19. אליה רבה שם.

succos

Teshuvah: Reclaiming Stolen Goods From the Dark Side and the Joy of Succos

∾ Before Doing Teshuvah, Mitzvos Are Snatched Away

The Rambam[1] declares the incredible value of teshuvah, and contrasts the status of the *baal teshuvah* prior and subsequent to his doing teshuvah. Yesterday, says the Rambam, this person's sins caused a separation between him and Hashem, to the point that his cries and pleas for help went unheeded and unanswered, as the *pasuk* states, גַּם כִּי תַרְבּוּ תְפִלָּה אֵינֶנִּי שֹׁמֵעַ, *Even if you were to intensify your prayer, I will not listen* (*Yeshayahu* 1:15). Prior to doing teshuvah, when one did a mitzvah, "they grab it away from before him," as the *pasuk* says, כִּי תָבֹאוּ לֵרָאוֹת פָּנָי מִי בִקֵּשׁ זֹאת מִיֶּדְכֶם רְמֹס חֲצֵרָי, *When you come to appear before Me, who sought this from your hand, to trample My courtyards?* (ibid. 1:12).

How are these words of the Rambam to be understood? What is meant by "when one did a mitzvah, they grab it away from before him"? Who are "they"? And why would anyone grab away his mitzvah? Even the mitzvos of the worst *rasha* are ascribed to him and would still bring him some merit. As the Gemara states,[2] "אֵין הַקָּדוֹשׁ בָּרוּךְ הוּא מְקַפֵּחַ שְׂכַר כָּל בְּרִיָּה", *Hashem does not deprive any creature of its reward*, so we know that a *rasha* will be rewarded for every good deed that he does. What does the Rambam mean that the mitzvah will be grabbed away from him? Further, what does the Rambam mean that the mitzvah will be grabbed away "from before him"? Why not simply say that it will be grabbed away?

❧ The Gra Explains

In the *Shemoneh Esrei* of Mussaf on Yom Tov, we recite the *tefillah*, אַתָּה בְחַרְתָּנוּ מִכָּל הָעַמִּים אָהַבְתָּ אוֹתָנוּ וְרָצִיתָ בָּנוּ. The Vilna Gaon (*Siddur HaGra*)* explains that these three phrases refer to the *Shalosh Regalim*. אַתָּה בְחַרְתָּנוּ מִכָּל הָעַמִּים, *You selected us from among all the nations*, refers to Pesach, when Hashem chose us as His nation and took us out of Mitzrayim. אָהַבְתָּ אוֹתָנוּ, *You showed Your love to us*, is a reference to Shavuos, when Hashem openly demonstrated His love for us by giving us the Torah on Har Sinai. וְרָצִיתָ בָּנוּ, *and You desired us*, refers to Succos.

We can clearly understand that the first two phrases refer to the first two *Regalim*. But how does וְרָצִיתָ בָּנוּ, *and You desired us*, indicate a reference to Succos? What is it about the Yom Tov of Succos that shows that Hashem wanted us? How does this phrase capture the essence of the Yom Tov?

❧ A Rasha's Mitzvos Are Detrimental

The *Be'er Heitev*[3] makes a cryptic comment that is very difficult to understand. He writes that all the good deeds that a *rasha* does, and all the Torah that he learns before he does teshuvah, provide added strength to the *kelipos*, shells (i.e., *sitra achra*, the dark side), until he does teshuvah. The mitzvos he performed and the Torah he learned prior to doing teshuvah are not only

---

* The approach of the Vilna Gaon is discussed in "The Return of the Clouds of Glory," page 278, but we offer another approach here.

not considered meritorious, but they, in fact, strengthen the forces of evil. What does the *Ba'er Heitev* mean?

A *pasuk* in *Tehillim* seems to express a similar idea: וְלָרָשָׁע אָמַר אֱלֹקִים מַה לְּךָ לְסַפֵּר חֻקָּי וַתִּשָּׂא בְרִיתִי עֲלֵי פִיךָ, *But to the wicked, Hashem said, "To what purpose do you recount My decrees and bear My covenant upon your lips?"* (*Tehillim* 50:16). Hashem is telling the *rasha* that his learning is not appreciated, desired, or valued.

The *Ba'er Heitev* and, in fact, the simple reading of the *pasuk* seem to be saying that if a person who has not done teshuvah performs a mitzvah, then his mitzvos are not beneficial. His mitzvos, for some reason, make things worse for him; his mitzvos are detrimental. The *rasha* empowers the dark side by doing mitzvos.

This seems to be what the Rambam means when he writes that prior to doing teshuvah a person's sins are grabbed away. When a *rasha* does a mitzvah or learns Torah, the *sitra achra* or the accusers grab it away and use it to aid the side of evil. The *Beis HaLevi*,[4] in fact, quotes this idea of the *Ba'er Heitev*, using it to explain the words of the Rambam. How can we relate to this startling concept?

∽ Why Is a Rasha Rewarded in This World?

The ramifications of this idea are even more far-reaching. The *Chida*[5] discusses the concept that a *tzaddik* who commits an *aveirah* may receive his punishment in This World so that he will not have to be punished in *Olam Haba*. On the other hand, if a *rasha* does a mitzvah or two, he may receive his reward in This World, so that he does not receive reward in *Olam Haba*. The *Chida* questions why Hashem, the *Av HaRachaman*, would not allow the *rasha* to receive his reward in *Olam Haba*, where the benefits would be more fully enjoyed.

The *Chida* explains that really the *rasha* should not receive any reward for the mitzvos he performs. When a *rasha* does a mitzvah, not only is it not counted as mitzvah, but it benefits the *sitra achra*. The *Chida* writes that the mitzvos a *rasha* performs are classified as *aveiros* for him! When a *rasha* shakes a *lulav*, when he blows *shofar*, when he keeps Shabbos, not only are these actions not true mitzvos, but it is, in fact, as if he were doing *aveiros*. Since the *rasha* thus does not have any mitzvos, there is no reward for him to receive in *Olam Haba*. It is precisely because Hashem has mercy on him that he receives anything at all as a reward in This World. Because his actions add strength to the *sitra achra*, he is not truly entitled to any reward at all.

∽ L'Shem Yichud: In Order to Unify [the Holy Name of Hashem]

There is a dispute among the *poskim* whether mitzvos *tzerichos kavannah*, require intent, or if mitzvos *ein tzerichos kavannah*, do not require intent. That is, is it incumbent on a person to have the specific *kavannah* that he is performing that particular mitzvah while doing so? The *Shulchan Aruch*[6] rules that the performance of a mitzvah does require *kavannah*, while other *Rishonim* disagree. Even those who maintain that mitzvos do need *kavannah* agree that there is no obligation to articulate the intention by stating, "*l'Shem yichud*," prior to performing a mitzvah. After all, it is stated that mitzvos require *kavannah*, not mitzvos require *amirah*, speech. In addition, mitzvos *tzerichos kavannah* means that one must have *kavannah* to do a mitzvah, yet a person need not have *kavannah* as to what the mitzvah accomplishes.

Why, then, do many people recite a *l'Shem yichud tefillah* before performing a mitzvah? Rav Zorach Eidelitz[7] (a contemporary of the Noda B'Yehudah in Prague) explains the reasoning for reciting *l'Shem yichud*. He cites the above-mentioned teaching that mitzvos performed by a *rasha* are hijacked by the *sitra achra*, which they empower, and that their mitzvos may actually be considered *aveiros* because they fuel the dark side. But there is a way to ensure that the *sitra achra* cannot steal his mitzvos. He must stipulate the following condition: He declares that he wants to fulfill the mitzvah only if it will be *mekadesh Shem Shamayim* and sanctify the Name of Hashem. But, if for some reason, he is classified as a *rasha* and any mitzvah he performs will be attributed to the *sitra achra*, then, he says, he hereby has intention *not* to fulfill the mitzvah. Hence, *l'Shem yichud*, may my mitzvah be effective only if it will not be grabbed away and used by the *sitra achra*, but rather will sanctify the Name of Hashem.

This stipulation must be uttered aloud, because *malachim* cannot ascertain what a person is thinking. This *tenai*, condition, prevents the *malachim* of the *sitra achra* from hijacking one's mitzvos. The *tenai* is effective because everyone — even those who maintain that mitzvos do not need *kavannah* — agrees that having negative *kavannah*, having *kavannah* **not** to perform a mitzvah, is enough to ensure that the mitzvah will not be fulfilled, or, in this case, only be fulfilled in a way that will bring the person merit.

Rav Zorach Eidelitz's understanding is that reciting the *tefillah "l'Sheim yichud"* is intended to prevent one's mitzvos from going to the dark side. It is a *tenai* that allows the mitzvah to not be fulfilled if fulfilling it would cause it to go to the dark side.

The *pasuk* states, רָחַשׁ לִבִּי דָּבָר טוֹב אֹמֵר אָנִי מַעֲשַׂי לְמֶלֶךְ לְשׁוֹנִי עֵט סוֹפֵר מָהִיר, *My heart is astir with a good theme, I say, "My works are for a king, my tongue is like the pen of a skillful scribe"* (*Tehillim* 45:2). The *Yismach Moshe*[8] explains this *pasuk*, saying that David HaMelech is articulating the very same idea proffered by Rav Zorach Eidelitz. אֹמֵר אָנִי, *I say*, מַעֲשַׂי לְמֶלֶךְ, *my works*, i.e., my mitzvos, should be *l'Sheim yichud*, just for Hashem, *the King* of all kings. Furthermore, says the *Yismach Moshe*, when the *mekatregim*, prosecutors, hear a person make the *tenai*, the condition that he specifically does not want to be *yotzei* the mitzvah if it will not go directly to Hashem, they immediately back off, because they won't be able to grab a mitzvah with which the doer is not being *yotzei* in any case. This, then, actually works to the benefit of the person doing the mitzvah, because now the mitzvah is free and clear to go up to Hashem, since the *mekatregim* are no longer trying to grab it. The *pasuk* goes on to say, לְשׁוֹנִי עֵט סוֹפֵר מָהִיר, *therefore my tongue says divrei Torah*, and, because of the *tenai* that I made, I no longer have to worry about the *mekatregim*.

❧ Should a Rasha Do Mitzvos?

This seems to be a demoralizing concept. Based on this idea, there is seemingly no reason for a *rasha* to do mitzvos, as it may be an *aveirah*, not a mitzvah at all.

However, this idea does not seem reasonable from an intellectual perspective. Why would a *rasha's* mitzvos be viewed as sins? Mitzvos and *aveiros* don't cancel each other out, so just because someone has committed *aveiros* should not mean that his mitzvos are not mitzvos. A sinner's mitzvos should enable him to enjoy the benefits of performing good deeds.

In the time of the Rambam, there were communities who, under threat of death, were forcibly converted to Islam. As a monotheistic religion, Islam is not *avodah zarah*; nevertheless, many of the rabbanim of those communities instructed those who had converted to no longer perform any mitzvos. These rabbanim were of the opinion that those who had converted were *reshaim*, and a *rasha's* mitzvos are considered to be *aveiros*.

The Rambam wrote *Iggeres HaShmad* (also known as the *Maamar Kiddush Hashem*), a letter to these communities, combatting this attitude. In this letter he refutes the concept that a *rasha* who performs mitzvos is actually performing an *aveirah*.[9]

One refutation he brings is from Achav ben Amri, who was someone who denied the existence of Hashem, and who worshiped *avodah zarah*. Yet, when he fasted for two and a half hours, he was rewarded for his efforts. The *gezeirah* decreed upon him became void, and his life was spared (*I Malachim* 21:25-29). How can he have been rewarded if he was a *rasha*? It is clear that Hashem valued his *taanis* even though he was a *rasha*. Clearly, the mitzvos of a *rasha* are not considered to be *aveiros*, or he would not have been answered by having his life extended.

Eglon, the king of Moav, was a *rasha* who was a source of sorrow to Klal Yisrael (*Shoftim* Ch. 3). Yet when Ehud came to him, telling him that he had the word of Hashem to convey, he stood up out of respect for Hashem. This one act was rewarded, and he merited to be the progenitor of Rus and, subsequently, David and Shlomo HaMelech. Thus, we see that the good deeds of a *rasha* are deemed mitzvos and are rewarded as such

Nevuchadnetzar, another *rasha*, actually destroyed the first Beis HaMikdash and killed as many Jews as there is sand on the shore. Yet, when he took four steps to show honor and respect toward Hashem, he was rewarded with a reign of forty years.

Eisav HaRasha is another example. The *Navi* tells us that Hashem loathed Eisav, וְאֶת עֵשָׂו שָׂנֵאתִי, *But I hated Eisav* (*Malachi* 1:3). The Gemara describes the extent of his wickedness[10]: on a single day he committed five *aveiros*. He committed murder, served *avodah zarah*, had relations with a married woman, denied the existence of *Techiyas HaMeisim*, and rejected the *bechorah*, birthright. Yet, in the *zechus* of his having performed the mitzvah of *kibbud av*, honoring his father, the Rambam holds that Rome rules the world until *Techiyas HaMeisim*. Even though Eisav was a true *rasha*, he was still rewarded for the sterling mitzvah he performed, setting the bar for the performance of *kibbud av*.

Thus, the *Rambam* says, since we see that Hashem rewards the good deeds of these exceptionally wicked people, He most assuredly will also reward the mitzvos of Jews who were forced to convert publicly but who continued to do mitzvos in secret. The people who were compelled to convert should certainly continue to do as many mitzvos as possible.

Those who are of the opinion that a *rasha* who does a mitzvah is tantamount to doing an *aveirah* understand the following *pasuk* in a unique fashion. The *pasuk* says, כִּי שְׁתַּיִם רָעוֹת עָשָׂה עַמִּי, *For My people have committed two evils* (*Yirmiyah* 2:13); they understand this to refer to people such as these forced converts who first committed an *aveirah* by converting, and then subsequently added another *aveirah* when they performed a mitzvah.

The Rambam says that this reasoning is mistaken, for Hashem definitely rewards each person who does a mitzvah, regardless of whether or not he is a *rasha*. No matter how low a person may sink spiritually or how evil a person may be, his mitzvos are still mitzvos.

◈ Understanding the Concept: A Rasha's Mitzvos Are Not Merits

How, then, do we understand the *Ba'er Heitev*, who said that when a person who is a *rasha* performs a mitzvah it goes to the dark side? How do we understand the *Chida*, who writes that a *rasha* who does a mitzvah is considered to be doing an *aveirah*? How do we understand the reason of Rav Zorach Eidelitz of saying *l'Sheim yichud* in order to salvage one's mitzvos in case he happens to be considered a *rasha*?

◈ Contradiction in the Rambam

We may be tempted to simply explain that the Rambam argues with the *Ba'er Heitev* and the *Chida*, as he states that even a *rasha* is rewarded for doing a mitzvah. This, however, would not be possible, as the Rambam we quoted earlier states, *Prior to his doing teshuvah, when someone would do a mitzvah, "they grab it away from before him."* This implies that when a *rasha* does a mitzvah, the mitzvah is taken away from him. Thus, the Rambam seems to be contradicting himself. How do we reconcile this apparent contradiction?

◈ The Noda B'Yehudah's Approach to the Rambam

The *Noda B'Yehudah*[11] explains that the Rambam does in fact reject the simple understanding of this concept, maintaining that a *rasha* will definitely be rewarded for any mitzvah he does. When he then writes that a *rasha's* mitzvos are "grabbed away from before him" this means that they are taken from him in *Olam Haba*. The *rasha* is rewarded for his mitzvos only in This

World, but not in the World to Come. That is why the Rambam added the word *befanav* — *before him*; i.e., in This World.

☙ *The Yalkut*

The *Beis HaLevi*[12] quotes a cryptic *Yalkut*[13] stating that one who has committed an *aveirah* and is embarrassed to do teshuvah should exchange it for *maasim tovim* and then do teshuvah. This is similar to someone who has bad coins. In an effort to obtain good coins, he gives his coins to a moneychanger along with a few extra coins, and the moneychanger then gives him good coins.

What does the *Yalkut* mean? If one is embarrassed to do teshuvah, what does he exchange for *maasim tovim*? And how is this similar to someone exchanging coins?

The *Beis HaLevi* cites the words of the Rambam that if a *rasha* does a mitzvah, that mitzvah is grabbed away. He also quotes the concept of the *Ba'er Heitev*, that the mitzvos performed by a *rasha* give power to the *sitra achra*. He then builds on these ideas to explain the *Yalkut*.

☙ *The Beis HaLevi Explains the Yalkut*

If a *rasha* wants to do teshuvah, what should be his first step? Should he do teshuvah on his *aveiros*, or should he begin to do mitzvos? With the understanding we have developed in the words of the Rambam and *Ba'er Heitev*, it would seem reasonable that the *rasha's* first step must be to do teshuvah, since mitzvos performed prior to doing teshuvah will not count as *zechusim*, but actually are regarded as sins and are given over to the *sitra achra*. Without first doing teshuvah, the mitzvos don't accomplish anything! First achieve the *sur mei'ra*, turn [away] from evil, and only then the *asei tov*, do good [deeds].[14]

The *Beis HaLevi* posits that the *Yalkut* is teaching us that this approach is incorrect. Even though a *rasha's* mitzvah is grabbed away, and even though his mitzvos reinforce the *koach* of the *sitra achra*, the first step of teshuvah still must be to perform mitzvos and do *maasim tovim*. Then, when a person eventually does teshuvah, his teshuvah not only eradicates the *aveiros* he did, but it also serves to reinstate the mitzvos that the *sitra achra* grabbed. The mitzvos he performed while still a *rasha*, before having done teshuvah, will ultimately be credited back to him retroactively when he does teshuvah.

If someone were to choose not to do any *maasim tovim*, any mitzvos, until he gets around to doing teshuvah, then when that day finally arrives, he will be left bereft of mitzvos. His teshuvah will alleviate the effects of the *aveiros*, but it will not provide him with *zechusim* that he may have earned had he opted to do mitzvos all along, even prior to doing teshuvah.

Thus, says the *Beis HaLevi*, even a *rasha* is obligated to do all the mitzvos, even though he has not yet done teshuvah. He definitely must work toward doing teshuvah, and even though right now he may be embarrassed and not ready to do teshuvah, he should engage in performing all the mitzvos he can. Then, when he eventually does do teshuvah, he will be able to exchange those mitzvos — which were performed while he was a *rasha* — for mitzvos that truly are a credit and a *zechus* for him. This is the meaning of the *Yalkut*.

The *Yalkut's* parable of the coins is thus explained as well. If someone has bad coins, he should pay the moneychanger a few extra coins and he will receive good coins in exchange. If the person did not have any coins, then he would have nothing to exchange, and he would not be able to receive anything from the moneychanger. Thus, while he is still a *rasha*, it is better to collect mitzvos — "bad coins" —and have something to exchange for good coins once he does teshuvah rather than having no coins at all, lest, when he wants to pay the "moneychanger" — with teshuvah — the "moneychanger" will not have anything to give him. But if he continues to do mitzvos before doing teshuvah, his bad coins will then be regarded as good coins.

The *Beis HaLevi's yesod* is that even though a *rasha's* mitzvos are stolen from him, they will be returned to him when he does teshuvah. What a windfall teshuvah then becomes! An entire year, the mitzvos being performed by the *rasha* are not entered into his spiritual bank account. They are held in spiritual escrow for him, to be made available at a later date. When a person then does teshuvah, not only does he remove the sins and the blemishes from his *neshamah*, but now this bank account is instantaneously flooded with the *zechusim* and mitzvos that had been held for him and that now are returned to him. It's like an instantaneous clearance of all debt held against him, and simultaneously winning the lottery.

‿ *Rav Yitzchak Elchanan Spector's Approach Introduces Exceptions to the Rule*

Rav Yitzchak Elchanan Spector[15] writes that certain mitzvos that a *rasha* does are untouchable, and they will not be grabbed away. They are exempt from being hijacked, and remain for the person who did the mitzvah, even though he was a *rasha* at the time the mitzvah was performed. Mitzvos that were performed *lishmah* are not taken away from a *rasha*. A mitzvah done *lishmah* goes straight to one's secure account in *Shamayim* and cannot be touched.

Earlier we stated that a source of this idea, that mitzvos performed by a *rasha* are taken away by the *sitra achra*, is the *pasuk*[16] that reads, וְלָרָשָׁע אָמַר אֱלֹקִים מַה לְּךָ לְסַפֵּר חֻקָּי וַתִּשָּׂא בְרִיתִי עֲלֵי פִיךָ, *But to the wicked, Hashem said, "To what purpose do you recount My decrees and bear My covenant upon your lips?"* Hashem tells the *rasha* that his learning is not appreciated, desired, or valued. Rav Yitzchak Elchanan explains that this applies only to mitzvos that are merely עֲלֵי פִיךָ, only on your mouth. The Torah existing only on the mouth indicates that the Torah is just superficial, and not *lishmah*. The very *pasuk* that teaches us that Hashem does not want the mitzvos of a *rasha* applies this solely to mitzvos that are not performed *lishmah*.

The *pasuk* states,[17] לֹא תוֹסִיפוּ הָבִיא מִנְחַת שָׁוְא קְטֹרֶת תּוֹעֵבָה הִיא לִי חֹדֶשׁ וְשַׁבָּת קְרֹא מִקְרָא לֹא אוּכַל אָוֶן וַעֲצָרָה, *Bring your worthless meal-offering no longer, it is incense of abomination to Me. As for the*

New Moon and Shabbos, and your calling of convocations, I cannot abide mendacity with solemn assembly. Don't bring Hashem mitzvos that are not *lishmah*, that are not genuine; He does not want those mitzvos. But mitzvos done with pure intention are always desired by Hashem.

Rav Yitzchak Elchanan adds that if a mitzvah performed *lishmah* is untouchable by the *sitra achra*, then the mitzvah of *tzedakah* is also untouchable. He explains that the mitzvah of *tzedakah* differs from other mitzvos in the Torah. Other mitzvos — such as *succah, shofar, tefillin*, eating matzah — the objective of the mitzvah is the action that must be performed. The act of sitting in the *succah* is the mitzvah. The act of eating the matzah is the mitzvah. However, *tzedakah* is different. The mitzvah is that the *ani*, the pauper, should receive assistance from you. But the actual physical action of reaching into your wallet, removing a dollar bill, and handing it to the *ani* is not inherently an action that is a mitzvah. Rather than the mitzvah being in the act itself, it lies in the outcome of the action: The poor person now can buy food.

For this type of mitzvah, in which the action is not the mitzvah, but rather the effect, the outcome, it does not matter whether it is *lishmah*. The pauper does not care at all what the donor's intentions were; the bottom line is that he now has money to buy food for his family. The effect, the food that his family eats, tastes exactly the same, whether or not it was given *lishmah*. The *totzaah*, result, is what is important in regard to the mitzvah of *tzedakah*, and the *totzaah* of the mitzvah does not depend on the *kavannah*, on whether it was performed *lishmah*.

Since only the outcome is important, and this outcome is unaffected by a person's *kavannah*, giving *tzedakah* in any fashion — *lishmah* or not — will be equivalent to doing another mitzvah *lishmah*. Therefore, *tzedakah* is another untouchable mitzvah that the *sitra achra* can never take away from the *rasha* who gives the *tzedakah*.

This, says Rav Yitzchak Elchanan, would mean that even though we maintain that *mitzvos tzerichos kavannah*, the mitzvah of *tzedakah* may not require *kavannah*; it would be an exception, since the *ikkur* is not the *maaseh* but rather the *totzaah*.[18]

◦ *Achav's Untouchable Zechusim*

The Gemara[19] states that Achav was very philanthropic; he gave away much of his fortune, and therefore Hashem overlooked his *aveiros*. Rav Yitzchak Elchanan is troubled by how Hashem could overlook his *aveiros* because of the mitzvos he had done. Achav had done the mitzvos when he was a *rasha*, and his mitzvos should not count as a *zechus* for him until he did teshuvah! However, using the aforementioned principle, since *tzedakah* is an untouchable mitzvah, Achav would have the *zechus* of his *tzedakah* to help overcome his *aveiros*, even though the *tzedakah* had been given while he was a *rasha*.

◦ *Another Approach: Sin Extinguishes a Mitzvah*

Earlier, we quoted the Rambam in *Iggeres HaShmad*, that every single mitzvah a person does will be justly rewarded. Even Achav, Nevuchadnetzar, and Eisav were rewarded for the mitzvos they had done. And yet the Rambam writes that a *rasha* who does a mitzvah has his mitzvah grabbed away. Based on a Gemara, Rav Yitzchak Elchanan offers a novel interpretation of the Rambam. As we will see, the person will still be rewarded, but an *aveirah* dulls the positive effects the mitzvah would have otherwise had on him and on his *neshamah*.

The Gemara[20] relates that sin extinguishes a mitzvah; מִצְוָה מְכַבֶּה עֲבֵירָה. This is another way to understand how the mitzvos a person performs prior to doing teshuvah are grabbed away. Every mitzvah has a certain light that shines on a person's *neshamah*. Some mitzvos also provide "side benefits," such as protecting the person who had done the mitzvah. Mitzvos are also beneficial in the sense that the reward for doing one mitzvah is the chance to perform another mitzvah. As the Mishnah teaches, מִצְוָה גּוֹרֶרֶת מִצְוָה,[21] one mitzvah leads to another mitzvah.

There are many spiritual and mystical benefits that come from doing a mitzvah, and these benefits may be reaped in *Olam Hazeh* or in *Olam Haba*.

A *rasha* who performs a mitzvah will most assuredly be rewarded for his mitzvah performance, just as is a *tzaddik*. However, doing an *aveirah* dulls the mitzvos the person has done. The sin dims the spiritual light of the mitzvah, and the side benefits will not be available to the person. It is to these side benefits that the Rambam refers when he writes that the mitzvos of a *rasha* are grabbed away.

ᴒ *Torah Can Never Be Taken*

That Gemara also states that while sin extinguishes mitzvos, it cannot extinguish Torah. Rav Yitzchak Elchanan explains that since Achav was using his money to support *talmidei chachamim*, his sins did not extinguish the mitzvos he had done in the support of Torah. This concept further limits the type of mitzvos that can be grabbed away by the *sitra achra*. Torah learning and the support one provides to those learning Torah cannot be grabbed away, as supporting Torah study is equivalent to learning Torah oneself.

Therefore, says the *Shem MiShmuel*,[22] the *Rambam* writes specifically that when the *rasha* does a **mitzvah**, they grab it from before him. The Rambam does not say that if a *rasha* learns Torah it is grabbed away, since Torah study would not be grabbed from him.

ᴒ *The Steipler's Understanding*

The Steipler Gaon was asked about the teaching of the Rambam that "*osin mitzvah v'chotfin befanav.*" He writes,[23] *Chas v'shalom* to say that the mitzvos of a *rasha* are not considered mitzvos. The truth is that even someone who is a murderer, thief, adulterer — or even someone who is guilty of every *aveirah* in the Torah — will receive the same reward as a *tzaddik* for the mitzvos he does perform. The idea posited that the mitzvos of a *rasha* are taken away, hijacked, by the *sitra achra*, is a separate concept that we cannot understand without knowing kabbalah. Every mitzvah a person does has a certain *hashpaah*, influence on the *neshamah*. The *neshamah* is then drawn to do more mitzvos, and the now-illuminated soul is more connected to Hashem. While a *rasha* does receive reward for doing the mitzvos he performs, his *neshamah* will not receive a stronger connection to Hashem, and the mitzvah will not have the same *hashpaah* on his soul. Then, when a person does teshuvah, he retroactively will receive all the benefits that he could have received from having done the mitzvah unsullied by sin.

৵ *Rav Isaac Sher's Understanding*

Rav Isaac Sher, Rosh Yeshivah of Slabodka and son-in-law of the Alter of Slabodka, offers another insight into understanding the Rambam.[24] Another teaching in that Gemara is that mitzvos are *meigin* and *matzil*: They protect a person and they rescue a person. But these apply only to a person who is not a *rasha*. A *rasha* will be rewarded for the mitzvos he performs, but he will not receive the protection, shelter, and salvation that a mitzvah would otherwise provide.

In summation, the Rambam's position in *Iggeres HaShmad* is therefore upheld: A *rasha* who does a mitzvah will be rewarded for the mitzvah, but he will lose out on other aspects that would normally positively impact the person doing the mitzvah. Whether it be the light, or the protection, or the *hashpaah*, these added benefits will not be available to the *rasha* who does a mitzvah, until he does teshuvah.

Shulchan Aruch HaRav[25] brings this idea as *halachah l'maaseh*. Even a *rasha* who does not accept the yoke of Torah can do mitzvos — but his mitzvos will add strength to the *kelipos*. Ultimately, when the person does teshuvah, be it in this lifetime or in a future *gilgul*, the mitzvos and *zechusim* will all be reinstated.

‌ *The Bas Kol of Motza'ei Yom Kippur*

Tosafos[26] quotes a *midrash* stating that on Motza'ei Yom Kippur a *bas kol* calls out *"Lech echol b'simchah lachmecha*, Go, eat your bread with joy." However, *Tosafos* does not quote the entire *pasuk*, which reads, לֵךְ אֱכֹל בְּשִׂמְחָה לַחְמֶךָ וּשֲׁתֵה בְלֶב טוֹב יֵינֶךָ כִּי כְבָר רָצָה הָאֱלֹקִים אֶת מַעֲשֶׂיךָ, *Go, eat your bread with joy and drink your wine with a glad heart, for God has already approved your deeds*.[27] The *pasuk* concludes that because Hashem already desires your deeds, Hashem is already pleased with you.

The Rambam, in the very same halachah where he states that a *rasha's* mitzvos are not desired by Hashem, and they are grabbed away from before him, also discusses the status of mitzvos performed after a person does teshuvah. The person who has done teshuvah, writes the Rambam,[28] is connected and attached to the *Shechinah*, and his *tefillos* will be answered even before they are petitioned, and his mitzvos are received by Hashem with pleasure and joy, as the *pasuk* says כִּי כְבָר רָצָה הָאֱלֹקִים אֶת מַעֲשֶׂיךָ. The Rambam quotes this very *pasuk*, which *Tosafos* states a *bas kol* cries out on Motza'ei Yom Kippur.

The *Shem MiShmuel*[29] elucidates the words כִּי כְבָר רָצָה הָאֱלֹקִים אֶת מַעֲשֶׂיךָ, *for Hashem has already approved your deeds*. Why does the *pasuk* say כְבָר, *already*, if it was not until now, after Yom Kippur, when we have done teshuvah, that Hashem desires our actions? We did not do teshuvah prior to today, Yom Kippur, so the *pasuk* ought to say *hayom*, for *today* Hashem has approved your deeds.

When a person does teshuvah, as we have explained above, it is not only from now on that Hashem wants the repentant's mitzvos. When a person does teshuvah, all the mitzvos he has ever done now retroactively find favor in the eyes of Hashem! Hashem always loved the actions that are now mitzvos.

On Motza'ei Yom Kippur, Hashem is telling us via the *bas kol* that we should go eat bread *b'simchah*, go drink wine *b'simchah*. Why? Says Hashem, because not only do I now love your mitzvos, but retroactively I always loved all the mitzvos you performed over the past year.

The *Shem MiShmuel* thus explains *Tosafos*, that Hashem is telling us on Motza'ei Yom Kippur that the person who did teshuvah gets back all his mitzvos; they are all returned to him retroactively.

✑ *Zman Simchaseinu*

Succos is *Zman Simchaseinu*, a time of extreme happiness. What is the cause of this exuberance? We can now gain an original insight into the joy of Succos. The entire year a person does mitzvos, but since he has also done *aveiros*, the mitzvos he performed are not available to him. He cannot reap their full benefit. As long as a person is still sinning, he cannot maximize the benefits of the mitzvos. But now that he has done teshuvah on Yom Kippur, retroactively the benefits of all the mitzvos that had been sitting in escrow are now available for him to enjoy. This calls for celebration, and is something that should engender abundant *simchah*. This joy, we have learned, is generated by the *bas kol* that declares כִּי כְּבָר רָצָה — because Hashem *already* wanted, *already* approved our actions.

וְרָצִיתָ בָּנוּ ✑

Is it no wonder then that Succos is alluded to and is captured succinctly by two words in our *tefillah*: וְרָצִיתָ בָּנוּ! We go into Succos, immediately on the heels of Yom Kippur, celebrating the fact that Hashem already wanted our actions, already desired our deeds retroactively, וְרָצִיתָ בָּנוּ — and You showed us favor, You desired our actions, as we heard Hashem proclaim to us on Motza'ei Yom Kippur, כִּי כְּבָר רָצָה הָאֱלֹקִים אֶת מַעֲשֶׂיךָ.

Pesach is וְרָצִיתָ בָּנוּ. Succos is אָהַבְתָּ אוֹתָנוּ Shavuos is אַתָּה בְחַרְתָּנוּ, Pesach is — Ribbono shel Olam, You showed us favor — not only from now on, but even retroactively, as all our mitzvos come back into our account.

↶ Protection of the Mitzvos, Symbolized by the Succah

Until a person does teshuvah, he is not able to benefit fully from the mitzvos he does. He cannot receive the shelter, protection, and salvation that the mitzvos would otherwise provide. Now we arrive at Motza'ei Yom Kippur, and Hashem tells us that He now loves all our mitzvos, and therefore at this time we can receive the shelter and protection of the mitzvos. We go straight into Succos, where we sit directly in the shelter of Hashem, which, perhaps, is symbolic of the fact that because we have done teshuvah we can receive the shelter and protection of the mitzvos.

Shem MiShmuel teaches that *Perek* 124 in *Tehillim* references the *din* of Rosh Hashanah and Yom Kippur: לוּלֵי ה׳ שֶׁהָיָה לָנוּ בְּקוּם עָלֵינוּ אָדָם: *Had Hashem not protected us* when all those *mekatregim* were standing against us on Rosh Hashanah and Yom Kippur, אֲזַי חַיִּים בְּלָעוּנוּ בַּחֲרוֹת אַפָּם בָּנוּ, *they would have swallowed us alive.* בָּרוּךְ ה׳ שֶׁלֹּא נְתָנָנוּ טֶרֶף לְשִׁנֵּיהֶם, *Blessed is Hashem Who did not present us as prey for their teeth* when they took away our mitzvos. But now that we did teshuvah, עֶזְרֵנוּ בְּשֵׁם ה׳ עֹשֵׂה שָׁמַיִם וָאָרֶץ, *we are assisted with the Name of Hashem, Maker of Heaven and Earth.* The *Yud Kei Vav Kei* is the Name of Hashem associated with Heaven; *Alef Daled Nun Yud* is the Name of Hashem associated with the Earth. Likewise, *Shem MiShmuel* teaches, the *succah*, which has the *gematria* 91, is numerically equivalent to the sum of two of the Names of Hashem (*Yud Kei Vav Kei* and *Alef Daled Nun Yud*).

The *succah* is our refuge from all those *mekatregim*, and the *simchah* of Succos is not merely the fact that we were forgiven, but that the *kapparah* of Yom Kippur retroactively allows us to access the multitudes of mitzvos from throughout the year from which we had not previously been able to benefit.

May we be *zocheh* to do *teshuvah sheleimah* and to be able to access the full glory of all the mitzvos we have done and merit a true *zman simchaseinu.*

ENDNOTES

1. רמב״ם הלכות תשובה פרק ז הלכה ז.
2. בבא קמא לח, ב.
3. באר היטב אורח חיים סימן תקע.
4. הקדמה לבית הלוי על התורה.
5. חיד״א דברים אחדים דרוש כ לשבת שובה עמוד שפג-שפד.
6. שלחן ערוך סימן ס ס׳ ד.
7. אור לישרים עמוד מח-מט.
8. ישמח משה פרשת כי תשא, עמוד תשג-תשד.
9. אגרת השמד או מאמר קדוש ה׳ עמוד מו-מט.
10. בבא בתרא טז, ב.
11. אהבת ציון דרוש שני.
12. הקדמת בית הלוי על התורה.
13. ילקוט הושע (רמז תקבט).
14. תהילים לד, טו.
15. נחל יצחק על חושן משפט פתח שער חלק ב.
16. תהילים נ, טז.
17. ישעיה א, יג.
18. עיין אתוון דאורייתא כלל יג אות א, וכלי חמדה קונטרס אחרון אות ו p.6.
19. סנהדרין קב, ב.
20. סוטה כא, א.
21. פרקי אבות ב, ג.
22. שם משמואל ראש השנה עמוד סט.
23. קריינא דאגרתא חלק א אות קו.
24. לקט שיחת מוסר.
25. שלחן ערוך הרב הלכות תלמוד תורה פרק ד הלכה ג.
26. תוספות יומא פז עמוד ב.
27. קהלת ט, ז.
28. רמבם הלכות תשובה פרק ז הלכה ז.
29. שם משמואל ראש השנה עמוד קד-קה.

The Return of the Clouds of Glory: The Vilna Gaon Revolutionizes Succos

✑ Booths or Clouds of Glory

The *pasuk* states, לְמַעַן יֵדְעוּ דֹרֹתֵיכֶם כִּי בַסֻּכּוֹת הוֹשַׁבְתִּי אֶת בְּנֵי יִשְׂרָאֵל בְּהוֹצִיאִי אוֹתָם מֵאֶרֶץ מִצְרָיִם אֲנִי ה' אֱלֹקֵיכֶם, *So that your generations will know that I caused Bnei Yisrael to dwell in booths [succos] when I took them out of the land of Mitzrayim; I am Hashem, your God* (*Vayikra* 23:43). What does the word *succos* refer to in this verse? In what type of booths did Hashem "cause the Bnei Yisrael to dwell"?

The Gemara[1] cites a *machlokes* between Rabbi Eliezer and Rabbi Akiva as to the identity of these *succos*. Rabbi Eliezer says they were Clouds of Glory and Rabbi Akiva says they were actual booths. The definitive explanation seems to be the opinion of Rabbi Eliezer: Clouds of Glory. Rashi here states that the *succos* to which the *pasuk* refers are the *Ananei HaKavod*, the Clouds of Glory, that surrounded and protected the Jewish people as they traveled through the *Midbar*. It is interesting to note that typically Rashi's modus operandi is to tell us *peshuto shel mikra*, the simple explanation of the verse. Why does he deviate from his usual practice here? In this case, the straightforward translation of the *pasuk* would seem to be actual *succos*, yet Rashi writes that the word *succos* refers to the *Ananei HaKavod*.

The *Mizrachi* explains that Rashi selected the *pshat* of *Ananei HaKavod* because it is a more grammatically correct interpretation of the *pasuk*, which states, בְּסֻכּוֹת הוֹשַׁבְתִּי, *I caused Bnei Yisrael to sit in the succos*. This implies that Hashem created the *succos* and placed Bnei Yisrael into them. Physical *succos* would have been constructed by the people themselves, rather than by the Ribbono shel Olam. Therefore, Rashi's reading truly is the simplest interpretation indicated by the words of the verse: *Ananei HaKavod*.

The Targum similarly translates the verse to mean, *in the shade of clouds I situated Bnei Yisrael when I took them out of Mitzrayim*. So we see that Targum, too, agrees with Rashi that the *succos* in the *pasuk* refer to the *Ananei HaKavod*.

✑ Halachic Ramifications

This is not merely a matter of aggadata, but it has halachic ramifications as well. Interestingly, one of the few *simanim* in the *Shulchan Aruch*[2] that has only one *se'if*, subsection, and, uniquely, has no title, quotes the *pasuk* stating that there is an obligation to sit in a *succah* for seven days, because Hashem housed the Jewish people in *succos* when He took them out of Mitzrayim. The *Shulchan Aruch* then adds that the *succos* mentioned in the verse refer to the Clouds of Glory that enveloped Bnei Yisrael and protected them from the heat and the sun when Hashem took them out of Mitzrayim.

Rav Yosef Caro, the author of the *Shulchan Aruch*, was a *posek;* however, this *siman* merely translates the *pasuk*, and does not seem to include any halachah. Of what halachic significance is it that the *succos* in the *pasuk* refer to the *Ananei HaKavod*? The Bach[3] explains that the mitzvah of *succah* differs from most other mitzvos. When it comes to other mitzvos, we perform them because Hashem told us to do them, without our having to be cognizant of the reason. The mitzvah of *succah* is one of three unique mitzvos where the Torah specifically utilizes the word לְמַעַן, *so that,* * indicating the reason for the mitzvah. In this case, the *pasuk* states, לְמַעַן יֵדְעוּ דֹרֹתֵיכֶם כִּי בַסֻּכּוֹת הוֹשַׁבְתִּי אֶת בְּנֵי יִשְׂרָאֵל בְּהוֹצִיאִי אוֹתָם מֵאֶרֶץ מִצְרָיִם, *So that your generations will know that I caused Bnei Yisrael to dwell in booths [succos] when I took them out of the land of Mitzrayim* (Vayikra 23:43). Thus, the reason is so that all generations will know that when Hashem took us out of Mitzrayim, He caused us *to dwell in succos*.

The Bach further explains: In order to fulfill the mitzvah of *succah*, one must have this reason in mind while he is in the *succah*. That is, if one sits in the *succah* and does not contemplate the fact that he is to recall the *succos* in which Hashem placed us while we were in the *Midbar*, then he has not fulfilled the mitzvah of *succah* properly. It is not enough to have *kavannah* to perform the mitzvah of sitting in the *succah*; one also has the additional obligation to remember the *reason* behind the mitzvah.

Therefore, the *Shulchan Aruch* deviates from its normal practice and explains that the verse refers to the *Ananei HaKavod*, because unless we have this concept in mind while we are sitting in the *succah*, it will compromise our fulfillment of the mitzvah.

⁓ *Why Is Succos Celebrated in Tishrei?*

The Tur, similar to the *Shulchan Aruch*, states[4] that we sit in the *succah* to remember the *Ananei HaKavod*. The Tur then raises a basic question: We left Mitzrayim in Nissan and it was at this time that the *Ananei HaKavod* were given to protect us. It would seem only logical that we should celebrate Succos at the time of the year that it happened.

---

* The other two mitzvos are *tefillin*: לְמַעַן תִּהְיֶה תּוֹרַת ה' בְּפִיךָ, so that Hashem's Torah may be in your mouth (Shemos 13:9), and *tzitzis*: לְמַעַן תִּזְכְּרוּ וַעֲשִׂיתֶם אֶת כָּל מִצְוֹתָי וִהְיִיתֶם קְדֹשִׁים לֵאלֹקֵיכֶם, So that you may remember and perform all My commandments and be holy to your God (Bamidbar 15:40).

The Tur answers that leaving one's home in Nissan to go into a temporary hut does not make it clear that one is performing a mitzvah. It is usually comfortable to eat and sleep outdoors at that time of year. It would not be obvious that your intent in entering the *succah* is to fulfill the mitzvah; in fact, bystanders could assume you are going out to enjoy the weather. Even though you may think, "*L'maan yeidu...*" as you sit in the *succah*, clearly doing the mitzvah for its own sake, your intent is not clear to passersby; thus, we do not celebrate Succos in Nissan. In Tishrei, however, when it is cold and the rainy season is about to begin, it is not as pleasant outside. Sitting in the *succah* at that time sends a clear message that you are sitting in the *succah* solely to follow the will of Hashem.

This answer, however, is not fully satisfying. We are accustomed to commemorating events at the time of the year that they occurred. Nowhere else is the date changed due to a concern about what people will think! Why is it different here?

☙ Why Do We Commemorate the Ananei HaKavod?

The Gemara[5] teaches us that there Klal Yisrael were provided with their basic needs while they were in the *Midbar* in the merit of three illustrious people: Moshe Rabbeinu, Aharon HaKohen, and Miriam HaNeviyah. In the *zechus* of Moshe Rabbeinu, we were given the *mahn*, in the *zechus* of Aharon HaKohen we were given the *Ananei HaKavod*, and in the *zechus* of Miriam HaNeviyah we were given the *Be'er*, well of water. No mitzvah or festival was established to commemorate the *mahn* or the *Be'er*. The *Chida* asks[6]: Why, then, do we have a Yom Tov to commemorate the *Ananei HaKavod*.

☙ Sefer Shemos: Chag HaAsif

In *Sefer Shemos*, the Yom Tov of Succos is mentioned twice, but it is not referred to as by that name; instead, it is referred to as *Chag HaAsif*, the Festival of the Ingathering or as the Festival of the Harvest.

1. In *Parashas Mishpatim*: וְחַג הָאָסִף בְּצֵאת הַשָּׁנָה בְּאָסְפְּךָ אֶת מַעֲשֶׂיךָ מִן הַשָּׂדֶה, *and the Festival of the Ingathering at the close of the year, when you gather in your work from the field* (*Shemos* 23:16).

2. In *Parashas Ki Sisa*: וְחַג הָאָסִיף תְּקוּפַת הַשָּׁנָה, *and the Festival of the Harvest shall be at the changing of the year* (ibid., 34:22).

It is not until *Parashas Emor* that the Torah refers to Succos by that name: דַּבֵּר אֶל בְּנֵי יִשְׂרָאֵל לֵאמֹר בַּחֲמִשָּׁה עָשָׂר יוֹם לַחֹדֶשׁ הַשְּׁבִיעִי הַזֶּה חַג הַסֻּכּוֹת שִׁבְעַת יָמִים לַה׳, *On the fifteenth day of this seventh month is the Festival of Succos, a seven-day period for Hashem* (*Vayikra* 23:34). Why is it that in *Sefer Shemos* — which relates the Exodus and the sojourn in the *Midbar* — there is no mention of the name Succos with regard to the Yom Tov that commemorates the *succos* provided by Hashem?

❧ Why Are the Ananei HaKavod Mentioned Last?

We encounter another difficulty in the *Midrash*[7] that lists the numerous miracles that were performed for Bnei Yisrael in the *Midbar*: the *mahn*, the *slav* (quail), *Be'er Miriam*, the *Mishkan*, the Presence of the *Shechinah*, the *Kehunah*, *Malchus*, and the *Ananei HaKavod*. Why does the *Midrash* mention the Clouds of Glory last? They were present from the moment Bnei Yisrael left Mitzrayim, and logically, therefore, they should be mentioned first. All of the above questions indicate that there must be something more to the phenomenon of the *Ananei HaKavod* that warrants the celebration of a Yom Tov.

❧ We Don't Commemorate Every Miracle, So Why Do We Celebrate Succos?

The Vilna Gaon, in his commentary on *Shir HaShirim*,[8] offers an illuminating answer to the Tur's question, stating that the objective of the Yom Tov of Succos cannot possibly be merely to celebrate the fact that we were protected by the Clouds of Glory in the *Midbar*. As noted, numerous miracles occurred in the *Midbar* but we do not commemorate them with a Yom Tov. A miracle in and of itself does not warrant being commemorated by a celebration. The Yom Tov of Succos, then, must be celebrating something in addition to the miracle of the *Ananei HaKavod*.

The Gaon explains that while we were journeying through the *Midbar*, Hashem provided us with protection in the form of the *Ananei HaKavod*. However, after the sin of the *Eigel HaZahav*, Golden Calf, Hashem took away the *Ananei HaKavod*, and Bnei Yisrael thus lost their protection. Instead, Hashem said He would send a *malach* to protect and guide them. The Torah states, הִנֵּה אָנֹכִי שֹׁלֵחַ מַלְאָךְ לְפָנֶיךָ לִשְׁמָרְךָ בַּדָּרֶךְ וְלַהֲבִיאֲךָ אֶל הַמָּקוֹם אֲשֶׁר הֲכִנֹתִי, *Behold! I send an angel before you to protect you on the way, and to bring you to the place that I have made ready* (Shemos 23:20). The *malach* was to be the intermediary, the go-between for Hashem and Bnei Yisrael. Klal Yisrael was devastated. On Rosh Chodesh Elul, Moshe Rabbeinu ascended to *Shamayim*, where he *davened* to Hashem to forgive Bnei Yisrael for the *Cheit HaEigel*. While in *Shamayim*, Moshe inscribed a new set of *Luchos*. He then came down on Yom Kippur, and Hashem said, "סָלַחְתִּי כִּדְבָרֶךָ, *I have forgiven because of your word*" (Bamidbar 14:20). Although Hashem forgave the Bnei Yisrael, since they were still deprived of the *Ananei HaKavod*, they felt they were severely lacking. They wanted more than to be forgiven, they wanted their relationship to revert to what it had been prior to the Sin, when Hashem openly demonstrated His love for us by providing us with the *Ananei HaKavod*.

Klal Yisrael missed the Presence of the Ribbono shel Olam. More than forgiveness, they wanted the *Shechinah*, symbolized by the *Ananei HaKavod*, to return. Moshe, as representative of the people, said, אִם אֵין פָּנֶיךָ הֹלְכִים אַל תַּעֲלֵנוּ מִזֶּה, *If Your Presence does not go along, do not bring us forward from here* (Shemos 33:15). They did not want a *malach*, they wanted the *Shechinah*. They had been forgiven, but they felt that Hashem's love had not returned. Their relationship with Hashem had been diminished from what it had been previously, and they wanted to feel that Hashem wants them, that He loves them. Bnei Yisrael remained devastated and distraught. They wanted *ritzui*; they wanted Hashem to want and desire them as He had done prior to the sin of the *Eigel*.

‫ ‬ *The Lost Clouds Return!*

On 11 Tishrei, the day after Yom Kippur, Bnei Yisrael received the commandment to build the *Mishkan*. The people brought donations to begin construction of the *Mishkan*. The Torah then tells us, וְהֵם הֵבִיאוּ אֵלָיו עוֹד נְדָבָה **בַּבֹּקֶר בַּבֹּקֶר**, *But they continued to bring him free-willed gifts morning after morning* (Shemos 36:3). For the next two mornings, 12 and 13 Tishrei, the people continued to bring *nedavos*, donations, for the *Mishkan*. On 14 Tishrei, says the Vilna Gaon, נָטְלוּ כָּל חֲכַם לֵב מִמּשֶׁה אֶת הַזָּהָב בְּמִנְיָן וּבְמִשְׁקָל, the *chacham lev*, the wise men, gathered together and weighed all that was brought.* On 15 Tishrei, construction com-

---

* This is the version of the chronology brought in the ביאור הגר"א on *Shir HaShirim*. Rav Shlomo Brevda (brought in ליקוטי הגרא עמוד תי"ג־תי"ד) points out that this calculation, however, is problematic for the following reason. The Gemara [Shabbos 86b] states that all agree that the Torah was given on Shabbos. Thus, Yom Kippur on the following year was on Tuesday, and the commandment to build the *Mishkan* was given on Wednesday. The people then brought their donations on Thursday and Friday. How, then, could these donations have been weighed on the following day, which was Shabbos, when *melachah* is prohibited? Rav Shlomo Brevda posits that a more accurate account is the one brought in *sefer* עבודת הגרשוני שיר השירים, which states that what occurred on the 14th of Tishrei was, וַיְצַו מֹשֶׁה וַיַּעֲבִירוּ קוֹל בַּמַּחֲנֶה לֵאמֹר אִישׁ וְאִשָּׁה אַל יַעֲשׂוּ עוֹד מְלָאכָה לִתְרוּמַת הַקֹּדֶשׁ וַיִּכָּלֵא הָעָם מֵהָבִיא, *Moshe commanded that they proclaim throughout the camp, saying, "Man and woman shall not do more work toward the gift for the Sanctuary!" And the people were restrained from bringing* (Shemos 36:6). *Shabbos* 96b learns from this verse that it is prohibited to carry on Shabbos. According to the account of עבודת הגרשוני, there was no weighing on the 14th; all that occurred were the proclamation and the cessation of donations. This is also consistent with the Vilna Gaon's commentary in *Seder Olam* 6.

menced on the *Mishkan*. It was on this day, as construction of the *Mishkan* commenced, that the *Ananei HaKavod* returned. Hashem returned His Presence to Bnei Yisrael on 15 Tishrei, the first day of Succos.

∾ *Succos: What Are We Really Celebrating?*

Succos is not only a celebration of a miracle, of the miraculous *Ananei HaKavod* that protected us in the *Midbar*. We are celebrating that after Klal Yisrael did teshuvah the Clouds of Glory were returned and we were thus able to reinstate the initial love that Hashem had for us and He Himself once again led Bnei Yisrael. The *kapparah* was achieved on Yom Kippur, and the *ritzui* on Succos!

∾ *Succos MUST Be in Tishrei*

Knowing the chronology of the departure of the *Ananei HaKavod* and their ultimate return in the month of Tishrei, it becomes clear why Succos must be commemorated during this time of the year. On the anniversary of the return of the *Ananei HaKavod*, we celebrate the re-establishment of our close, loving relationship with Hashem! We are commemorating that the *Chibah HaRishonah*, the initial love that Hashem had for us, was reinstated as a result of the teshuvah for the *Cheit HaEigel*. The power of teshuvah was so great that it restored our relationship with Hashem to its previous state.

The Vilna Gaon writes[9] that as the *Mishkan* was being built, the *tefillah* that was said was, וִיהִי נֹעַם הי אֱלֹקֵינוּ עָלֵינוּ וּמַעֲשֵׂה יָדֵינוּ כּוֹנְנָה עָלֵינוּ וּמַעֲשֵׂה יָדֵינוּ כּוֹנְנֵהוּ, *May the pleasantness of the Lord, our God, be upon us; our handiwork, establish for us; our handiwork, establish it* (*Tehillim* 90:17). The very next *pasuk* reads, יֹשֵׁב בְּסֵתֶר עֶלְיוֹן בְּצֵל שַׁקַּי יִתְלוֹנָן, *Whoever sits in the refuge of the Most High, he shall dwell in the [protective] shade of the Almighty* (ibid., 91:1). Thus we see that Hashem's Presence returned when we began to build the *Mishkan*, demonstrating the restoration of our original relationship.

◈ *The True Desire of Tzaddikim*

Rabbeinu Yonah[10] explains. When two friends quarrel, they may eventually resolve their differences and reconcile. But their relationship usually does not return to the same state as it was prior to their disagreement. However, when we do teshuvah, hoping to reconcile with Hashem, we are not content with mere *kapparah*, forgiveness. We are not only seeking atonement to spare us from *yissurim*, tribulations, and other punishments. We *daven* that Hashem should go much further; we pray that He will want us, desire us, find favor in us, and have the same affection toward us as if we had never sinned. As Elihu stated, יֶעְתַּר אֶל אֱלוֹקַ וַיִּרְצֵהוּ, *[One] entreats God, and He accepts him (Iyov* 33:26). Rabbeinu Yonah adds that it is possible for an *aveirah* to be forgiven and for the sinner to be freed of any *yissurim*, yet Hashem may still not desire that person and will not desire his offerings (i.e., his mitzvos). This was the status of the Bnei Yisrael on 11 Tishrei, when Hashem had forgiven the sin of the *Eigel* but no longer desired such a close relationship with them.

A *tzaddik's* greatest desire, writes Rabbeinu Yonah, is to gain the favor of Hashem, so that Hashem desires him. For when Hashem wants a person, true eternal life ensues, and one can bask in the warm glow of *Olam Haba* even while still residing in this world. As the *pasuk* says, חַיִּים בִּרְצוֹנוֹ, *Life results from His favor* (*Tehillim* 30:6).

We are not satisfied by simply receiving *kapparah* and *selichah*. We need more than that. We need to return to the way it was before we sinned. *Chazal* say, [11] אֵין לָנוּ אֶלָּא הַאֲרָת פָּנֶיךְ, Ribbono shel Olam, we want to feel that Your countenance is illuminating us, and we want to bask in Your glory. We want *ritzui* — to be desired by Hashem. This is a level that can be achieved only if one can reacquire the same status he enjoyed prior to sinning. This is the level Klal Yisrael achieved on Succos after repenting for the *Cheit HaEigel*. The *succah*, which represents the *Ananei HaKavod*, is the testament that we have achieved not only *kapparah*, but also *ritzui*, and that can only happen after the *kapparah* of Yom Kippur. Thus, Succos must fall in Tishrei rather than in Nissan.

❧ The Vilna Gaon's Explanation of אַתָּה בְחַרְתָּנוּ:

In Yom Tov *davening* we say, אַתָּה בְחַרְתָּנוּ מִכָּל הָעַמִּים אָהַבְתָּ אוֹתָנוּ וְרָצִיתָ בָּנוּ וְרוֹמַמְתָּנוּ מִכָּל הַלְּשׁוֹנוֹת וְקִדַּשְׁתָּנוּ בְּמִצְוֹתֶיךָ וְקֵרַבְתָּנוּ מַלְכֵּנוּ לַעֲבוֹדָתֶךָ וְשִׁמְךָ הַגָּדוֹל וְהַקָּדוֹשׁ עָלֵינוּ קָרָאתָ. The Vilna Gaon explicates these words as follows.

אַתָּה בְחַרְתָּנוּ מִכָּל הָעַמִּים — You chose us from among all the nations of the world. This statement refers to Pesach, when Hashem took us out of Mitzrayim to become His nation and selected us as His people.

אָהַבְתָּ אוֹתָנוּ — You loved us. This occurred on Shavuos, when Hashem gave us the Torah.

וְרָצִיתָ בָּנוּ — And You desired us. Even though we sinned, You still showed that You wanted us. This refers to the Yom Tov of Succos, at which time Hashem restored the *Ananei HaKavod*, demonstrating that His love, affection, and desire for us were reinstated, even after the sin of the *Eigel*. These two words, וְרָצִיתָ בָּנוּ, beautifully capture the true essence of Succos. After severing our connection to God, we achieved forgiveness and ultimately, we were welcomed back into the protection of the *Ananei HaKavod*, as Hashem demonstrated His eternal desire for us as His people.

According to the Vilna Gaon, it is this joy at the return of the *Shechinah* that is the reason that the Yom Tov of Succos specifically is referred to as *Zman Simchaseinu*. We rejoice over the fact that not only were we forgiven, but that Hashem has clearly shown that our relationship with Him was restored to what it had been, as if we had never sinned. This *ritzui* is what we are celebrating, captured succinctly in the words, וְרָצִיתָ בָּנוּ.

❧ Chag HaAsif, Chag HaSuccos

Rav Meir Simchah of Dvinsk[12] uses this Vilna Gaon to explain why the Torah refers to Succos as *Chag HaAsif*, and not as

Succos. The *pesukim* in *Shemos* were written even before the *Cheit HaEigel* and the subsequent departure of the *Ananei HaKavod*. At that time there was no "*Chag HaSuccos*"; it was only after Klal Yisrael's teshuvah was accepted and the Clouds of Glory returned that there became a reason to celebrate Succos by that name. Until then the Yom Tov was referred to as *Chag HaAsif*, a harvest festival in celebration of gathering in all the produce from the fields. But in *Sefer Vayikra* — after the *Cheit HaEigel*, subsequent teshuvah, and the return of the *Ananei HaKavod* — Hashem gave instructions for a transformed seven-day Yom Tov called *Chag HaSuccos*.

❧ *Ananei HaKavod Listed Last*

In *Parashas Re'eh*, Rav Yitzchak HaKohen Huberman writes[13] that this explains why the *Midrash* quoted above places the *Ananei HaKavod* at the end of the list. The miracle of the *Ananei HaKavod* that is significant to us is when they were returned, rather than when they were given initially. Therefore, they are enumerated last.

❧ *But the Ananei HaKavod NEVER Left?*

The *pasuk* states, וְאַתָּה בְּרַחֲמֶיךָ הָרַבִּים לֹא עֲזַבְתָּם בַּמִּדְבָּר אֶת עַמּוּד הֶעָנָן לֹא סָר מֵעֲלֵיהֶם בְּיוֹמָם לְהַנְחֹתָם בְּהַדֶּרֶךְ וְאֶת עַמּוּד הָאֵשׁ בְּלַיְלָה לְהָאִיר לָהֶם וְאֶת הַדֶּרֶךְ אֲשֶׁר יֵלְכוּ בָהּ, *And You, in Your great compassion, did not forsake them in the Wilderness; the pillar of cloud did not turn away from them by day to lead them on the way, nor the pillar of fire by night to provide illumination upon them and upon the way they were to travel* (Nechemiah 9:19). According to this verse, the *Ananei HaKavod* never left Bnei Yisrael throughout the time they were in the *Midbar*. How can the Vilna Gaon's explanation that the *Ananei HaKavod* were taken away and then returned be reconciled with this *pasuk* that explicitly states that they never left?

❧ The Ananei HaKavod Always Sheltered the Women

Tosafos asks[14] why women are not obligated in the mitzvah of *succah*. The principle "אַף הֵן הָיוּ בְּאוֹתוֹ הַנֵּס, *although they too were a part of the miracle,*" obligates women in *Arba Kosos* on Pesach, in *Mikrah Megillah* on Purim, and in *neiros* Chanukah. As beneficiaries of the miracles, they too must participate and fulfill those mitzvos. When the Bnei Yisrael were in the *Midbar*, all the people, including the women, were protected by the *succos* of the *Ananei HaKavod*. Therefore, logically, they too should be obligated in the commemoration of the *neis*, and they should be required to sit in the *succah*. *Tosafos* answers that the principle of אַף הֵן הָיוּ בְּאוֹתוֹ הַנֵּס applies only to *mitzvos d'Rabbanan*, not to *mitzvos d'Oraisa*.

According to the Vilna Gaon, however, we can answer *Tosafos's* question differently. Succos is not merely a celebration of being the beneficiaries of the *Ananei HaKavod*, a miracle that the women enjoyed just as much as the men. Succos is actually a celebration of the *return* of the *Ananei HaKavod*, heralding the return of the special relationship Klal Yisrael enjoys with Hashem.

The *Cheit HaEigel*, which precipitated the departure of the *Ananei HaKavod*, was perpetrated by the men of Klal Yisrael, not the women. The Tur states [15] that originally Rosh Chodesh was given as a Yom Tov to all twelve *Shevatim*, men and women, but the Yom Tov was taken from the men. Rosh Chodesh remained as a Yom Tov for women because they never served the *Eigel*. Likewise, Rav Akiva Eiger[16] notes, regarding the custom not to wear gold jewelry on Yom Kippur, because it is reminiscent of the *Eigel HaZahav*,* that women, who did not participate in the *Cheit HaEigel*, MAY wear gold jewelry on Yom Kippur.

Therefore, the *Chasam Sofer* explains[17] that since the women

---

* This concept is based on the principle, *ein kateigor naaseh saneigor*, a prosecutor cannot become an advocate for the defense.

did not participate in the *Cheit,* they were never excluded from the *Ananei HaKavod* and their relationship with Hashem neither faltered nor wavered. Thus, since they never lost the shade and protection of the *Ananei HaKavod* the women are not obligated to commemorate the return of the Clouds. Only the men were deprived of the *Ananei HaKavod*; the women enjoyed the protection of the Clouds of Glory continually, without interruption. The women are therefore not included in the celebration of their return, and that is why they are *pattur* from sitting in the *succah.*

We can suggest that this can explain the *pasuk* in *Nechemiah* as well. The *Navi* states that the *Ananei HaKavod* never left, and, in fact, this is true. For the women, the *Ananei HaKavod* remained present continuously throughout the time the Bnei Yisrael were in the *Midbar.* The men were excluded from *Ananei HaKavod* because of the *Cheit HaEigel,* and were allowed back in on Succos, but the Clouds themselves never left.

✑ Why Is Simchas Torah Connected to Succos?

Thus, Succos is the celebration of the *tikkun,* rectification, of the *Cheit HaEigel,* the return of Hashem's full desire for Bnei Yisrael, as it was prior to the *Cheit.* Succos is followed by Shemini Atzeres, which the Vilna Gaon describes as the Yom Tov that has the greatest *simchah* of all the Yamim Tovim. Shemini Atzeres is followed by Simchas Torah. Why does Simchas Torah follow Succos? Would it not be more logical to celebrate Simchas Torah on Shavuos?

The *Sforno* (*Ki Sisa* 32:19) teaches that when Moshe Rabbeinu came down from Har Sinai carrying the *Luchos,* he witnessed the Jews worshiping the *Eigel.* He continued to descend the mountain, *Luchos* intact. But when he saw Jews dancing around the *Eigel,* he threw down the *Luchos* and shattered them. We see that it was the dancing that prompted him to break the *Luchos.*

When one does an *aveirah,* explains the *Sforno,* he can always mend his ways by doing teshuvah. But if someone derives much *hanaah,* pleasure, from doing an *aveirah,* remedying that sin becomes much more difficult. *Simchah* is present when someone truly enjoys something to his core, and when this is displayed for an *aveirah*, the possibility of doing teshuvah becomes more remote.

As stated, on Succos we celebrate because we were able to atone for the *Cheit Eigel* and do such complete teshuvah that we reclaimed our relationship with Hashem. But there is still one more step. When the Bnei Yisrael served the *Eigel,* they danced and sang around the Calf. We still must show that we are rectifying this misplaced joy as well. In order to show that we have so completely eradicated any connection to the *Eigel* that not only would we never worship it, but we would only use *simchah* for the Torah, we sing and dance with the *Sefer Torah*, demonstrating happiness and joy in celebration of the Torah. Celebrating Simchas Torah is the ultimate rectification for the sin of the *Eigel*.

❧ My Daughter, My Sister, My Mother

The *Meshech Chochmah*[18] brings a *midrash*[19] stating that the Ribbono shel Olam loves Klal Yisrael so much that first He refers to us as *biti,* My daughter. Hashem then says that He loves Klal Yisrael even more, referring to us as *achosi*, My sister. Finally, Hashem says that His love for Klal Yisrael is even greater, and He calls us *imi*, My mother.

The *Meshech Chochmah* explains this cryptic *midrash*. We have three Yamim Tovim: Pesach, Shavuos, and Succos. Klal Yisrael did not do anything to merit the Yom Tov of Pesach. Quite the contrary; Klal Yisrael had descended to the forty-ninth level of *tumah*. We worshiped idols just as the Egyptians did. Although we were completely undeserving, Hashem came to rescue us. This is analogous to a parent providing for a child. The child does not do anything to earn the parent's affection or the numerous provisions he receives from his parent. Hashem calling Bnei Yisrael "My Daughter" is a reference to His rescue of us from Mitzrayim on Pesach, providing for us without our having earned it.

Next comes Shavuos, for which Bnei Yisrael did purify themselves and prepare for three days, elevating themselves to be able to say *Naaseh V'Nishma*. Recognizing our efforts, Hashem came down to Har Sinai and gifted us the Torah. This is similar to a mutual relationship between siblings, with each party doing for the other; thus, Hashem calls us "My sister" in the context of the Yom Tov of Shavuos.

On Succos, however, our relationship achieved a new level. Here, it was Klal Yisrael who took the full initiative to rectify the rift in our relationship with Hashem. We did complete teshuvah and rectified the *Cheit HaEigel* so that Hashem's *ratzon* completely returned to us as it had been initially. Now the roles are reversed, so to speak, and we are the parent, so to speak. Hashem calls us "My mother."

We know that the more work one puts into something, the more happiness he experiences from it. Something that one gets without effort does not provide the same level of joy as those for which he toils. Succos is the Yom Tov for which we worked the hardest, and therefore it is the one Yom Tov that we refer to as *Zman Simchaseinu*. Hashem saw our efforts and our desire to restore our cherished relationship with Him, and Hashem responded not only סָלַחְתִּי כִּדְבָרֶךָ, but also with the words we were yearning for, וְרָצִיתָ בָּנוּ, I want you.

ENDNOTES

1. סוכה יא, ב.

2. אורח חיים סימן תרכ"ה.

3. שם.

4. טור אורח חיים סימן תרכ"ה.

5. תענית, ט.

6. חיד"א ראש דוד עה"ת פרשת אמור, הובא בספר ענני הכבוד, כח, בית אלקים שער היסודות פרק לז.

7. שמות רבה פרשה ב אות ה.

8. ביאור הגר"א שיר השירים פרק א פסוק ד.

9. ליקוטי הגר"א עמוד תיג-תיד.

10. שערי תשובה שער א אות מב.

11. מדרש תהלים מזמור פ.

12. משך חכמה פרשת משפטים פרק כג פסוק טז.

13. בן לאשרי, הובא בספר ענני הכבוד עמוד עח.

14. תוספות פסחים קח עמוד ב ד"ה היו.

15. טור אורח חיים סימן תיז.

16. הגהות רע"א סימן תר.

17. דרשות חתם סופר שנת תקצה עמוד 106.

18. משך חכמה פרשת ואתחנן פרק ה פסוק טו.

19. חזית שיר השירים סוף פרק ג.

The Sanctity of the Beis HaMikdash in the Succah

✍ Why Is לְשַׁכֵּן שְׁמוֹ שָׁם Omitted from Succos?

Analyzing the *pesukim* regarding the *Moadim* we encounter an anomaly that warrants exploration. Regarding Pesach, the verse states, וְזָבַחְתָּ פֶּסַח לַה׳ אֱלֹקֶיךָ ... בַּמָּקוֹם אֲשֶׁר יִבְחַר ה׳ לְשַׁכֵּן שְׁמוֹ שָׁם, *You shall slaughter the pesach-offering to Hashem, your God ... in the place where Hashem will choose to rest His Name* (*Devarim* 16:2). The Torah tells us here that the Beis HaMikdash served as a place for the *Shechinah*, the Presence of Hashem, to rest. The Torah continues, commenting about the Yom Tov of Shavuos: וְשָׂמַחְתָּ לִפְנֵי ה׳ אֱלֹקֶיךָ ... בַּמָּקוֹם אֲשֶׁר יִבְחַר ה׳ אֱלֹקֶיךָ לְשַׁכֵּן שְׁמוֹ שָׁם, *You shall rejoice before Hashem, your God…in the place that Hashem, your God, will choose to rest His Name* (ibid., 16:11). Again, the Torah is telling us that the Beis HaMikdash is the location that Hashem selected for *hashra'as HaShechinah*. Finally, we come to the commandment regarding the Yom Tov of Succos, which states, שִׁבְעַת יָמִים תָּחֹג לַה׳ אֱלֹקֶיךָ בַּמָּקוֹם אֲשֶׁר יִבְחַר ה׳ כִּי יְבָרֶכְךָ ה׳ אֱלֹקֶיךָ בְּכֹל תְּבוּאָתְךָ וּבְכֹל מַעֲשֵׂה יָדֶיךָ וְהָיִיתָ אַךְ שָׂמֵחַ, *A seven-day period shall you celebrate to Hashem, your God, in the place that Hashem, your God, will choose, for Hashem will have blessed you in all your crop and in all your handiwork, and you will be completely joyous* (ibid., 16:15). The *Meshech Chochmah*[1] points out that while here the Torah identifies the Beis HaMikdash as "the place that Hashem ... will choose," the *pasuk* does not mention that the Beis HaMikdash serves as the resting place of the *Shechinah*. The words שָׁם שְׁמוֹ לְשַׁכֵּן are conspicuously absent.

Why does the Torah deviate from the terminology established in the verses regarding Pesach and Shavuos?

⌖ Becoming Hashem's Partner in Creation

The Mahari Vayil[2] writes that one who fulfills the mitzvah of *succah* becomes Hashem's partner in the creation of the world. How is the Yom Tov of Succos connected to *Maaseh Bereishis*, the Creation of the world? Why does the mitzvah of *succah* render us Hashem's partners in Creation?

⌖ Vayechulu — Partnering With Hashem

The Gemara[3] records another means whereby a person can be a partner with Hashem in *Maaseh Bereishis*. Rav Hamnuna states that one who recites the *pesukim* of וַיְכֻלּוּ, *Vayechulu*, on Friday evening is considered to be Hashem's partner in Creation. The Maharsha[4] explains that unless people affirm that Hashem created the world, mankind would not be aware that Hashem did so. Therefore, reciting *Vayechulu* testifies that Hashem created the world, publicizing that Hashem did in fact do so. In performing this significant ritual, one becomes Hashem's partner in Creation. In addition, says the Maharsha, Hashem created the world with speech; as the *pasuk* says, בִּדְבַר ה' שָׁמַיִם נַעֲשׂוּ, *By the word of Hashem the heavens were made* (*Tehillim* 33:6). But Hashem's declaration serves as only one witness, and we know that we need at least two witnesses for testimony to be accepted by *beis din*. Therefore, by reciting *Vayechulu* one serves as the required second witness.

We can understand, then, how reciting *Vayechulu* elevates one to the level of a partner with Hashem. But how does fulfilling the mitzvah of *succah* render one a partner of Hashem in Creation?

❧ Guard Your Tongue —
Especially in the Succah

The *Mishnah Berurah*[5] states that since the *kedushah* in the *succah* is exceptionally glorious, it behooves us to limit the mundane conversations we have in the *succah*. We should try to speak only *divrei Torah* and other *divrei kedushah*. We should certainly be extremely careful not to speak *lashon hara, rechilus*, or any other form of forbidden speech within the walls of the *succah*.

Although we know that one should also minimize speaking *divrei chol* while wearing *tefillin*, only transgressing the laws of speech in the *succah* is mentioned in the *Mishnah Berurah*. Why is the *succah* specifically singled out to admonish us from discussing *divrei chol* in it?

The *Shaarei Tzion* states[6] that the *Mishnah Berurah's* source is found in the *Shelah HaKadosh*, who writes[7] that his father's custom was to speak only *divrei Torah* in the *succah*. The *Shelah* explains that the *succah* has extraordinary *kedushah*, as evidenced by the fact that the wood used for the *succah* (e.g., the *schach*) is prohibited from being used for a mundane purpose all seven days of Succos. The sanctity of the material components of the *succah* is not derived from their being used for the mitzvah. Rather, the *kedushah* is an intrinsic part of the *succah* during the days of Succos, even when no one is in the *succah*. The Gemara[8] teaches that the source of this *kedushah* is the *pasuk,* חַג הַסֻּכֹּת תַּעֲשֶׂה לְךָ שִׁבְעַת יָמִים, *You shall make the festival of Succos for a seven-day period* (*Devarim* 16:13).

The rationale and understanding behind the inherent *kedushah* of the *succah* are interesting. We know that there is a difference between *tashmishei mitzvah*, items such as *tzitzis* or a *shofar* that are used in the performance of a mitzvah, and *tashmishei kedushah*, items such as a *Sefer Torah* or *tefillin* that have inherent *kedushah*, even when not in use. *Tashmishei mitzvah* are articles that provide us with a medium through which we can perform a mitzvah, but they do not have any inherent *kedushah*.

For example, *m'ikar hadin*, halachically, a pair of *tzitzis* and a *shofar* can be disposed of in any way one chooses; they do not require burial. During the seven days of Yom Tov, even when the *succah* is not in use, the *succah* structure itself is conceptually different from a *shofar* or a *tallis*.

ঔ The Shechinah Rests on the Succah

Rav Yerucham Olshin, Rosh Yeshivah of Lakewood, brings a beautiful array of sources to illuminate this subject.[9] He cites the incredible explanation that is brought in the *sefer Chessed L'Avraham*[10] and in the *Sfas Emes*.[11] The halachah taught in the *mishnah* in *Succah*[12] that the minimum height of a *succah* is ten *tefachim*, handbreadths, is predicated on the teaching of the Gemara[13] that the *Shechinah* never descends within ten *tefachim* from the ground. Thus, the *succah* has this height requirement so that the *Shechinah* may attach itself to it. This is the deeper explanation for what the Gemara teaches us, that just as the *Shem Shamayim* attaches itself to the *korban chagigah*, it likewise does to the *succah*.

This facet of the mitzvah of *succah* requires further analysis. There is no other *mitzvah d'Oraisa* that must be performed at a height of at least ten *tefachim* from the ground so that the *Shechinah* can rest on the mitzvah item.* Let us determine why this *cheftzah shel mitzvah*, the *succah*, is specifically intended to be the resting place of the *Shechinah*.

ঔ Hashem, Please Rebuild the Fallen Succah of David

On Succos we recite an additional *HaRachaman* in *Birchas HaMazon*, asking Hashem to rebuild *Succas David hanofeles*, the fallen *Succah* of David HaMelech, a reference to the Beis HaMikdash. Why is this added to the *bentching* on Succos?

---

* A similar explanation is needed for the minimum-height requirement for the position of the Chanukah menorah.

There is no obvious connection between the Yom Tov of Succos and the rebuilding of the Beis HaMikdash. The *HaRachaman* we add on Shabbos is most appropriate because Shabbos is considered *me'ein Olam Haba*, a semblance of the World to Come. We therefore add the request that Hashem bequeath to us the day that is totally Shabbos and peace forever, referring to *Olam Haba*. The *HaRachamans* that are added on Yom Tov, Rosh Chodesh, and Rosh Hashanah are all *m'inyanei d'yoma*, requests that reflect the characteristic of the day. On Succos, however, this request for the rebuilding of the Beis HaMikdash does not seem to be connected to the essence of the Yom Tov.

To explain this difficulty as well as to illuminate the unique spiritual quality of Succos, the *Shem MiShmuel*[14] introduces us to a concept that is fundamental to our understanding of this Yom Tov. The *succah*, he writes, is a *dugmah*, model, of the Beis HaMikdash. This small structure that we construct outside of our homes is itself a microcosm of the *Mishkan* and the Beis HaMikdash.

❧ *The Succah:*
A Microcosm of the Mishkan and the Mikdash

The Beis HaMikdash is referred to as the *chadar*, chamber, of the King, as the *pasuk* states, הֱבִיאַנִי הַמֶּלֶךְ חֲדָרָיו נָגִילָה וְנִשְׂמְחָה בָּךְ, *The King has brought me into His chambers; we will rejoice and be glad in You* (*Shir HaShirim* 1:4). Therefore, the *succah*, a microcosm of the Beis HaMikdash, is likewise rendered the *chadar* of the *Melech*, King. This gives us a new insight into why Succos is *Zman Simchaseinu*, as entering the King's *chadar* brings intense joy: נָגִילָה וְנִשְׂמְחָה בָּךְ.

The *Sfas Emes* adds[15] that the *pasuk* states, שָׂמַחְתִּי בְּאֹמְרִים לִי בֵּית ה' נֵלֵךְ. *I rejoiced when they said to me, "Let us go to the House of Hashem"* (*Tehillim* 122:1). The *succah* is a spark, a glimmer, of the Beis HaMikdash upon which the *Shechinah* rests; therefore, it is especially fitting for Succos to be called *Zman Simchaseinu*.

This dimension of the mitzvah of *succah* can help explain a difficult halachah. The halachah is that one can fulfill the mitzvah of *shofar* even with a stolen *shofar*, and yet a stolen *succah* is *pasul*. The *Shem MiShmuel* elucidates that since we know that stolen items could not be used in the building of the Beis HaMikdash, as the *Shechinah* will not reside in a home constructed with stolen materials, the *succah*, which is a *dugmah* of the Beis HaMikdash, is *pasul* if it is built with stolen materials, and the *Shechinah* will not dwell there.

The *mukabalim* teach that the concept that the *succah* is a *dugmah* of the Beis HaMikdash has practical ramifications as well. The *Arizal* writes[16] that a table used in the *succah* should have four legs (and a bed should also be placed in the *succah*). The furniture in the *succah* should be arranged with the table to the south and the lamp, the menorah, in the north. The reason is that one is supposed to arrange the *succah* in a fashion reminiscent of how the *keilim* were arranged in the Beis HaMikdash, with a four-legged table in the south and the candelabra in the north.[17] Once again, we see that the *succah* is in the likeness of the Beis HaMikdash.*

∾ Taking Leave of the Succah, Our Miniature Beis HaMikdash

This concept, that the *succah* is a microcosm of the Beis HaMikdash, will help us understand a beautiful *minhag* that has been codified by the Rama.[18] It is *minhag Yisrael* that when the mitzvah of *succah* has been completed, we don't simply stop sitting in the *succah*; we actually say goodbye to the *succah*, offering a prayer that was codified by the Rama, יְהִי רָצוֹן . . . כְּשֵׁם שֶׁקְיַמְתִּי וְיָשַׁבְתִּי בְּסֻכָּה זוֹ, כֵּן אֶזְכֶּה לְשָׁנָה הַבָּאָה לֵישֵׁב בְּסֻכַּת עוֹרוֹ שֶׁל לִוְיָתָן, *May it be Your will that just as I have fulfilled [the mitzvah] and dwelled in this succah, so may I merit in the coming year to dwell in the succah of the skin of Livyason*. The question is, why do we have to

---

* Note that this is what our *nusach* of the *Arizal* states; however, in the Beis HaMikdash the *Shulchan*, Table, was in the north, and the *Menorah* was in the south.

say goodbye to the *succah*? When we finish blowing the *shofar* on Rosh Hashanah, we don't say goodbye to the *shofar*; we just put it away until the next year. Likewise, when Succos is over, we don't take leave of the *lulav* and *esrog*. Says Rav Hutner,[19] in the times of the Beis HaMikdash, there was a mitzvah of לִינָה, that is, sleeping in Yerushalayim after the *Shalosh Regalim*, taking leave of the Beis HaMikdash, as it were, to show that we find it difficult to part with it. Likewise, since the *succah* is a microcosm of the Beis HaMikdash, we have the custom of not simply exiting the *succah* but we take leave of it and we pray that it be the will of Hashem that we will sit in the shade of the *Livyason*.

❧ From Yom Kippur to Succos

On Yom Kippur we fervently pray for the rebuilding of the Beis HaMikdash. Rav Shlomo Kluger[20] writes that by giving us the Yom Tov of Succos, Hashem tests us to see if our Yom Kippur *davening* for the Beis HaMikdash was genuine, which is demonstrated when we reside in the *succah*. If one performs the mitzvah of *succah* properly, then Hashem considers his *tefillos* for the Beis HaMikdash as sincere and without ulterior motive. However, if one does not fulfill the mitzvah of this *dugmah* of the Beis HaMikdash properly, then it is clear that he is not truly yearning for the rebuilding of the Beis HaMikdash.

❧ Sanctity of a Beis HaKnesses in the Succah

There is yet another dimension of the mitzvah of *succah*, which is understood in light of what we have learned. The *Pele Yo'etz* writes [21] that the *kedushah* of a *succah* is analogous to the sanctity ascribed to a shul. Therefore, one must be very careful to conduct himself with proper dignity and decorum in the *succah*. The *poskim* teach that just as with a *beis haknesses*, one is not permitted to use a *succah* as a shortcut.[22] This concept is understood in light of the fact that the *succah*, like the shul, is a *mikdash me'at*, miniature Beis HaMikdash,

Thus, the *succah*, in addition to being a *tashmishei mitzvah*, is also a *dugmah* a microcosm, of the Beis HaMikdash. The *Shechinah* therefore rests on the *succah*, giving its structure inherent *kedushah* and necessitating that it be at least ten *tefachim* in height.

❧ *The True Objective of Succos*

Let us explore the source of the concept that the *succah* is a microcosm of the Beis HaMikdash and discover the basis for this comparison. Having established that the *kedushah* of the *succah* is a paradigm of the sanctity of the Beis HaMikdash, let us probe further to discover why indeed the *succah* has this sanctity. As we learned in the previous essay, the Vilna Gaon[23] teaches us that the objective of the Yom Tov of Succos must be to celebrate something in addition to the miracle of the *Ananei HaKavod*. We celebrate Succos, as the Vilna Gaon explains, to commemorate the reinstatement of the *Ananei HaKavod*, which had no longer afforded protection after the sin of the *Eigel HaZahav*. On Rosh Chodesh Elul, Moshe Rabbeinu ascended to *Shamayim* for the third time, where he *davened* to Hashem to forgive Bnei Yisrael for the *Cheit HaEigel*, and on Yom Kippur Hashem said, "סָלַחְתִּי כִּדְבָרֶךְ, I have forgiven because of your words" (*Bamidbar* 14:20). Although Hashem forgave Bnei Yisrael, they were still deprived of the *Ananei HaKavod*, and they therefore felt that forgiveness alone did not suffice. They wanted more than to be forgiven, they wanted *ritzui*, to know that their relationship had been restored to what it had been prior to the Sin. It was only when the construction of the Mishkan had begun that Hashem openly demonstrated His love for us by again providing us with the *Ananei HaKavod*. This *ritzui* took place on the fifteenth day of Tishrei. Thus, we can understand why the *succah* has the sanctity of the Beis HaMikdash, as it commemorates the return of the *Ananei HaKavod* and the resting of the *Shechinah* upon the *Mishkan* at this very time of the year.

Thus, the *succah*, in which we sit on the anniversary of the date the *Shechinah* came down to join Klal Yisrael, is considered a *mikdash me'at*. The *schach* must be at a height at which the *Shechinah* can come to dwell on the *succah*; i.e., no less than ten *tefachim* from the ground. This, then, is the ultimate commemoration of what took place on that date so many years ago: וְעָשׂוּ לִי מִקְדָּשׁ וְשָׁכַנְתִּי בְּתוֹכָם.

⚫ *Buy Arba Minim Now,*
but Wait to Build the Succah!

Our insight into the sanctity of the *succah* helps us resolve an apparent discrepancy in the halachah. The *Mateh Ephraim*[23] writes that one should purchase the *Arba Minim* before Yom Kippur, as doing so enables one to amass more *zechusim* prior to the *Yom HaDin*. However, elsewhere, the *Mateh Ephraim* writes[24] that one should build his *succah* immediately after Yom Kippur— beginning on Motza'ei Yom Kippur — so as to go *mei'chayil el chayil*, from strength to strength. Building the *succah* right after Yom Kippur allows one to transition from one mitzvah to another. But why not reverse the order? Build the *succah* prior to Yom Kippur, since that will increase *zechusim* as we head into Yom Kippur, and then demonstrate going from one mitzvah to another by purchasing the *Arba Minim* right after Yom Kippur?

According to the insights of the Vilna Gaon cited above, though, we can understand the *Mateh Ephraim*. True, we try to collect as many *zechusim* as possible prior to Yom Kippur so as to increase our chances for a favorable outcome in *din*; therefore, we seek to purchase the *Arba Minim* prior to Yom Kippur. However, the mitzvah of *succah* is an exception to the objective of collecting *zechusim* prior to Yom Kippur. It must wait, because the *tzivui*, command, of וְעָשׂוּ לִי מִקְדָּשׁ was said only after Bnei Yisrael had received *mechilah*, immediately after Yom Kippur.

Since the *succah* symbolically reenacts the fulfillment of וְעָשׂוּ לִי מִקְדָּשׁ, we follow the same timeline, with Yom Kippur and *mechilah* first, followed by construction of our *mikdash me'at*.

Only after *mechilah* can we expect to experience the reenactment of the next part of the *pasuk* — וְשָׁכַנְתִּי בְּתוֹכָם — the *ritzui* seen as the *Shechinah* joins us in the *succah*. It was only after Yom Kippur that Hashem's desire for us returned to its previous level, as represented by the return of the *Ananei HaKavod*. Thus, it is most appropriate to build the *succah*, which is a *dugmah* of the *Mishkan*, after Yom Kippur.

❧ The World: A Prototype of the Mishkan

The *Midrash*[25] is bothered by the wording used in the *pasuk* that states, וַיְהִי בְּיוֹם כַּלּוֹת מֹשֶׁה לְהָקִים אֶת הַמִּשְׁכָּן, *And it was on the day that Moshe finished erecting the Mishkan* (Bamidbar 7:1). Why does the Torah write לְהָקִים אֶת הַמִּשְׁכָּן, when it would have sufficed to have written לְהָקִים הַמִּשְׁכָּן? What is the word אֶת coming to include? The *Midrash* explains that it includes another "*Mishkan*" that was completed at the same time.

The *Midrash* tells us that until the *Mishkan* was erected, the world was unstable, and the *Mishkan* served to provide a solid base and foundation for the world. Thus, the *Mishkan* lent stability to the entire world, and it is the entire world that is included in the *pasuk* as having been erected at the same time as the *Mishkan*. The *Midrash*[26] then expounds upon this concept and demonstrates numerous ways in which the *Mishkan* is comparable to the world.

1) Both the *Mishkan* and the entire world are referred to as an *Ohel*, since they both are covered with *yerios*, curtains. The world has *yerios* on it; as the *pasuk* says, נוֹטֶה שָׁמַיִם כַּיְרִיעָה, *stretching out the heavens like a curtain* (Tehillim 104: 2); so, too, the *Mishkan* had *yerios* on it, as the *pasuk* states, וְעָשִׂיתָ יְרִיעֹת עִזִּים לְאֹהֶל עַל הַמִּשְׁכָּן, *You shall make curtains of goat hair or a Tent over the Mishkan* (Shemos 26:7).

2) Just as the *Shamayim* is *mavdil*, separates, so, too, the *Paroches*, Partition, in the *Mishkan* was *mavdil*; it provided separation.

3) On the third day of Creation, the waters no longer covered

the whole world, instead gathering together in the oceans. Similarly, in the *Mishkan*, the *Kiyor*, Laver, constituted the gathering of the water into one place.

4) There are luminaries in the sky that provide light. Similarly, the *Mishkan's Menorah* provided light.

5) The world has birds that spread their wings to fly; so, too, the *Mishkan* housed *Keruvim*, Cherubim, whose wings were spread wide.

6) The terminology used at the completion of the Creation of the World (וַיְכַל אֱלֹהִים, *Hashem completed* [*Bereishis* 2:1]) is the same as that used when the *Mishkan* was completed (וַיְכַל מֹשֶׁה, *Moshe completed* [*Shemos* 40:22]): וַיְכַל.

7) Just as when Creation was completed Hashem offered a blessing (וַיְבָרֶךְ אֱלֹקִים [בראשית ב:ג]), so too, Moshe offered a blessing upon the completion of the *Mishkan* (וַיְבָרֶךְ אֹתָם [שמות לט:מג]).

◈ *The Succah: Becoming a Partner in Creation*

The *Mishkan* thus serves as a prototype of the entire world. The Gemara says[27] that Betzalel knew how to combine the letters that were used to create the world. The Torah tells us this to indicate the connection between the world and the *Mishkan*. Since the building of the *Mishkan* gave the world a more stable foundation, it was not enough for Betzalel to know only the skills needed to make the *Mishkan* itself, but he also had to know how to combine the letters that were utilized in the creation of the world. To make the *Mishkan*, he also had to know how to build a world. The *Mishkan* and Mikdash give the world its stability and strengthen its foundation. As we build our *succah*, a microcosm of the *Mishkan*, we reinforce the stability of all of creation; thus, we become a partner with Hashem in *Maaseh Bereishis*, the Creation of the world.

◈ *The Succah Is the Answer to Our Tefillos*

On the Yamim Noraim there are many instances where we ask

Hashem to rebuild the Beis HaMikdash. We mention that when this happens, "וּבְכֵן צַדִּיקִים יִרְאוּ וְיִשְׂמָחוּ, *And the tzaddikim will see the Beis HaMikdash and they will rejoice.*" We also say, "וְהַרְאֵנוּ בְּבִנְיָנוֹ וְשַׂמְּחֵנוּ בְּתִקּוּנוֹ, *We will see its construction and we will rejoice in its establishment.*" We can perhaps suggest that Hashem answers our *tefillos;* even though we have not yet been *zocheh* to the rebuilding of the Beis HaMikdash, Hashem gives us the mitzvah of *succah,* a *dugmah* of the Beis HaMikdash. By sitting in our *succos* and rejoicing in the happiness of the Yom Tov, on some level this is a fulfillment of the *tefillah* וּבְכֵן צַדִּיקִים יִרְאוּ וְיִשְׂמָחוּ.

❧ *Yaakov Avinu Is the Counterpart of Succos*

The Tur writes[28] a fascinating comment in the name of his brother, stating that Avraham Avinu is *kneged* Pesach, as he hosted the *malachim* on Pesach. Yitzchak Avinu is *kneged* Shavuos, as the *shofar* of Har Sinai came from the ram of Yitzchak. Yaakov Avinu is *kneged* Succos. The Belzer Rebbe explains that Yaakov Avinu symbolizes Succos because he was the only person who was able to achieve *kedushas Beis HaMikdash* in a location other than the Har HaBayis. When Yaakov went to sleep, the *Makom HaMikdash* came to him and he achieved *kedushas haMikdash shelo b'mikomo.* This is exactly what the *succah* is: *Kedushas Mikdash* in a location other than the Har HaBayis.

❧ *Why Is* לְשַׁכֵּן שְׁמוֹ שָׁם *Omitted on Succos?*

Utilizing this new perspective of the *succah,* Rav Yitzchak Hutner[29] and Rav Yerucham Olshin[30] answer the question of the *Meshech Chochmah* that we asked above. Why, when teaching us about Pesach and Shavuos, does the Torah tell us that the Beis HaMikdash serves לְשַׁכֵּן שְׁמוֹ שָׁם, *so that Hashem can dwell there,* while in the discussion of Succos this phrase is omitted? It is because on Succos the Mikdash is not a requirement for *hashra'as haShechinah,* because the *Shechinah* is present in our own *succah*! The *succah* is a *dugmah* of the Mikdash, and therefore לְשַׁכֵּן שְׁמוֹ שָׁם applies to our own *succah*! As long as the *succah* is kosher and the *schach* is no less than ten *tefachim* from the ground, then the *Shechinah* rests in the *succah*. We still go to the Mikdash for the mitzvah of *aliyah l'regel* and to bring *korbanos*, but the שָׁם שְׁמוֹ לְשַׁכֵּן does not apply to Succos, since that can be achieved at home, in our very own *succah*.

With this understanding, it is clear why the most appropriate *tefillah* on Succos is that Hashem should build *succas David hanofeles*. We were *zocheh* to build a *mikdash me'at*, the *succah* in which Hashem dwells and which is a *dugmah* of the Mikdash. We *daven* that in the *zechus* of our efforts, the Ribbono shel Olam should bless us to see the restoration of the ultimate Mikdash, the Third Beis HaMikdash, שֶׁיִּבָּנֶה בֵּית הַמִּקְדָּשׁ בִּמְהֵרָה בְיָמֵינוּ, אָמֵן.

ENDNOTES

1. משך חכמה ראה פרק טז פסוק ב.
2. שו"ת מהר"י וייל סימן קצא; הובא בבאר היטב סימן תרל"ט ס"ק א.
3. שבת קיט, ב.
4. מהרש"א שבת קיט עמוד ב.
5. משנה ברורה סימן תרלט ס"ק ב.
6. שם ס"ק.
7. של"ה הקדוש מסכת סוכה, הובא ג"כ בספר ראשית חכמה שער קדושה פרק יד אות לד.
8. סוכה ט, א.
9. ירח למועדים מאמר כ"ג.
10. חסד לאברהם מעין ד' נהר נח.
11. שפת אמת סוכות תרמ"ב.
12. סוכה ב, א.
13. סוכה ה, א.
14. שם משמואל סוכות תרעח עמוד קסד; סוכות תרעט עמוד קעא; סוכות תרעב עמוד קלד ועמוד קלח.

15. שפת אמת סוכות תרס.
16. אבן השוהם סימן תכלט ס"ק ד.
17. פיתוחי חותם סימן תכלט ס"ק ד.
18. אורח חיים סימן תרס"ז סעיף א
19. מאמרי פחד יצחק סימן קיט.
20. קהלת יעקב סוכות דרוש כד.
21. פלא יועץ - סוכה.
22. שו"ת משנת יעקב חלק ב סימן תרל, הובא בירח למועדים סוכות עמוד קצ.
23. מטה אפרים סימן תרג סעיף ה.
24. מטה אפרים סימן תרכד סעיף טו.
25. במדבר רבה יב, יא.
26. במדבר רבה יב, יג.
27. ברכות נח, א.
28. טור אורח חיים סימן תי"ז.
29. מאמרי פחד יצחק סימן קיט
30. ירח למועדים סוכות מאמר כג.

The Borders of Eretz Yisrael Encompassed in Your Succah: The Abarbanel's Revolutionary Approach to Succos

✍ Shivas HaMinim in the Succah

There is a custom[1] to display in the *succah* samples of the *shivas haminim*, seven species, with which Eretz Yisrael is praised. The origin of this custom is not readily identified, but as all *minhagei Yisrael* are rooted in holy sources, let us endeavor to discover the meaning of this practice.

✍ Sit in a Succah and You Will Be Zocheh to Sit in It Again

The *pasuk* tells us, חַג הַסֻּכֹּת תַּעֲשֶׂה לְךָ שִׁבְעַת יָמִים בְּאָסְפְּךָ מִגָּרְנְךָ וּמִיִּקְבֶךָ, *You shall make the Festival of Succos for a seven-day period, when you gather in from your threshing floor and from your wine cellar (Devarim 16:13).* The letter ת as the prefix to a *shoresh*, word root, adds the directive "you shall" to the action mentioned.* Usually, when the Torah employs this prefix, it is to issue a command, a mitzvah that we are directed to do. Thus, the *pasuk* can be read as an instruction from the Torah. However, this prefix can also be interpreted not as a directive, but as a declaration that you will do it.

The *sefer Yaffeh LaLev*,[2] by Rav Chaim Palagi, quotes a *Pesikta* that interprets this *pasuk* using both interpretations. The *pasuk* could have written the instruction beginning with the word *asei*, make, without using the prefix ת. The fact that the ת is added tells us that the *pasuk* means, "You are to make the *succah*, and if you do, you have a *havtachah*, assurance, from Hashem that you will continue to do so for years to come." It is both a command to celebrate the Yom Tov and a *berachah* that if you do keep the Yom Tov, you will be enabled to continue to keep the Yom Tov in years to come. The *Kaf HaChaim*,[3] Rav Yaakov Chaim Sofer, quotes this *Pesikta*, including the promise of being blessed to continue to sit in the *succah* in the future.

The Abarbanel[4] also quotes this *derashah* of the *Pesikta*. When Yitzchak Avinu was born, Avraham Avinu made a *seudah* at his bris (*Bereishis* 21:8). The *Midrash Rabbah* states that the *malachim*, in the guise of men, attended the *seudah*. The Abarbanel points out that the *pasuk* makes no mention of the *malachim* having attended this *seudah*. How, then, does the *Midrash* know that the *malachim* attended? He explains that the source is the *malachim's* response when Avraham welcomed them into his home and invited them to partake in a meal. He told them, "יֻקַּח נָא מְעַט מַיִם וְרַחֲצוּ רַגְלֵיכֶם וְהִשָּׁעֲנוּ תַּחַת הָעֵץ. וְאֶקְחָה פַת לֶחֶם וְסַעֲדוּ לִבְּכֶם אַחַר תַּעֲבֹרוּ כִּי עַל כֵּן עֲבַרְתֶּם עַל עַבְדְּכֶם, Let some water be brought and wash your feet, and recline beneath the tree. I will fetch a morsel of bread that you may sustain yourselves, then go on — inasmuch as you have passed your servant's way" (*Bereishis* 18:4-5). The *malachim's* response to his invitation was, "כֵּן תַּעֲשֶׂה כַּאֲשֶׁר דִּבַּרְתָּ,

---

* It is one of the איתן letters that, when added to a *shoresh*, describe who will be performing the said action: א: *I will*, י: *he will*, ת: *you will*, נ: *we will*.

Do so, just as you have said" (ibid., v. 5). Based on the prefix ת, *Chazal* interpret this to mean that they were saying "do this now" — i.e., feed us now — "and you will feed us again in a year." They were predicting that they would come to the *seudah* to celebrate Yitzchak's *bris milah*. Says the Abarbanel, this is similar to how the *Pesikta* interprets the *pasuk* חַג הַסֻּכֹּת תַּעֲשֶׂה לְךָ, on which the *Midrash* says, "אִם עָשִׂיתָ כֵּן עַכְשָׁיו, יְהִי רָצוֹן שֶׁתַּעֲשֶׂה כֵּן לְשָׁנָה אַחֶרֶת, *If you do so now, may it be the will of Hashem that you will also be able to do so in the following year.* This is also found in the Ran[5] in *Parashas Vayeira.*

Interestingly, despite the *Pesikta* being quoted by several sources, this explanation is actually absent from the text of the *Pesikta* that is available to us. This lost passage has been pre-served for posterity by the Abarbanel and the Ran, and we can invoke the statement, "בָּרוּךְ הַמָּקוֹם שֶׁמָּסַר עוֹלָמוֹ לְשׁוֹמְרִים, *Blessed is the Omnipresent [Hashem], Who entrusted His world to guard-ians."[6]*

ஜ *Succah: A Segulah for a Long Life*

This *midrash* is teaching that the mitzvah of the *succah* carries with it a special *berachah* for *arichas yamim*, longevity. Each year that a person fulfills the mitzvah of *succah*, he is granted a new *havtachah* that he will survive at least another year to fulfill the mitzvah again.

The *pasuk* states, בַּסֻּכֹּת תֵּשְׁבוּ שִׁבְעַת יָמִים כָּל הָאֶזְרָח בְּיִשְׂרָאֵל יֵשְׁבוּ בַּסֻּכֹּת, *You shall dwell in succos [booths] for a seven-day period; every ezrach [native] in Israel shall dwell in booths* (Vayikra 23:42). The term *ezrach* is unique to the mitzvah of dwelling in the suc-cah. Rav Naftali of Ropshitz[7] teaches that this word is used here to convey a message. The word *ezrach* refers to an elderly per-son. Hashem is thus promising that one who keeps the mitzvah of dwelling in the *succah* will, in fact, live to a ripe old age and will merit to fulfill the mitzvah of *succah* even as a *zakein*, elder. The *gematria* of the word אֶזְרָח is numerically equivalent to the *gematria* of the word גְּבוּרָה, as both equal 216. The significance of this is that the *pasuk* states, יְמֵי שְׁנוֹתֵינוּ בָהֶם שִׁבְעִים שָׁנָה וְאִם בִּגְבוּרֹת שְׁמוֹנִים שָׁנָה, *The days of our years among them are seventy, and if with might, eighty years* (*Tehillim* 90:10). Sitting in the *succah* is a *segulah* that one will live to be an *ezrach*, which is achieved at the age of *gevurah*: Sit in the *succah* and you'll live to be at least eighty.

❧ *Succah = Chai*

Rav Chaim Palagi[8] quotes the *Zohar*, who says that the *succah* resembles the letter ב, *beis*. A *succah* must have three walls, as does the letter ב. The letter ב is composed of three ו's, *vavs*, and is thus numerically equivalent to eighteen, the value of the word חי, *chai*, life. The mitzvah of *succah* shields and protects us, and taking refuge in the shade of Hashem's *emunah* gives us longevity. In the merit of fulfilling the mitzvah of *succah*, we will be *zocheh* to *arichas yamim*, as alluded to by the fact that the *succah* resembles the letter *beis*.

❧ *Why Is the Succah a Segulah for Longevity?*

Why is fulfilling the mitzvah of *succah* a *segulah* for a long life? There are many very significant mitzvos that we do not find provide a person with this gift. What is unique about the mitzvah of *succah* so that one who sits in the *succah* is promised a long life?

❧ *What About the Promise of V'heiveisi?*

Hashem promised the Jewish people that He would save them from Mitzrayim: וְהוֹצֵאתִי, I will take you out of Egypt; וְהִצַּלְתִּי, I will rescue you from Egypt; וְגָאַלְתִּי, I will redeem you; וְלָקַחְתִּי, I will take you for My own, as My people; וְהֵבֵאתִי, I will bring you into Eretz Yisrael (see *Shemos* 6:6-8). The first four promises were fulfilled, and Hashem saved us from Egypt. He gave us the Torah and acquired us as His chosen nation.

However, *Tiferes Shlomo*[9] points out that the fifth promise,

וְהֵבֵאתִי, did not come true with regard to the generation to whom it was promised. Seemingly, Hashem fulfilled only four out of these five promises to the *Yidden* who were enslaved in Egypt. Hashem promised that generation that He would bring them into Eretz Yisrael. But this did not take place.

◇ Why Does Hashem State אֲנִי ה׳ אֱלֹקֵיכֶם Here?

In the instructions regarding the Yom Tov of Succos, the Torah tells us, לְמַעַן יֵדְעוּ דֹרֹתֵיכֶם כִּי בַסֻּכּוֹת הוֹשַׁבְתִּי אֶת בְּנֵי יִשְׂרָאֵל בְּהוֹצִיאִי אוֹתָם מֵאֶרֶץ מִצְרָיִם אֲנִי ה׳ אֱלֹקֵיכֶם. *So that your generations will know that I caused Bnei Yisrael to dwell in booths when I took them from the land of Egypt; I am Hashem, your God* (*Vayikra* 23:43). The last phrase of the *pasuk* seems superfluous. We all know that Hashem is our God. Why does the Torah feel the need to remind us that Hashem is our God specifically amid the commandments of Succos?

The Gemara[10] discusses what factor enables one to live a long life. R' Yochanan was told there were elderly men living in Bavel. R' Yochanan responded that this cannot be true, since the *pasuk* states, לְמַעַן יִרְבּוּ יְמֵיכֶם וִימֵי בְנֵיכֶם עַל הָאֲדָמָה אֲשֶׁר נִשְׁבַּע ה׳ לַאֲבֹתֵיכֶם לָתֵת לָהֶם כִּימֵי הַשָּׁמַיִם עַל הָאָרֶץ, *In order to prolong your days and the days of your children upon the Land that Hashem has sworn to your forefathers to give them, like the days of Heaven over the earth* (*Devarim* 11:21). Living long is therefore a feature of הָאֲדָמָה, the Land of Eretz Yisrael! R' Yochanan infers that one who is not in Eretz Yisrael cannot expect to live long! Thus, it cannot be that old people live in Bavel. However, after R' Yochanan was informed that these elderly people came to shul early and left shul late, he agreed that in this *zechus* there could be old people in Bavel. R' Yehoshua ben Levi instructed his son to come early to shul and to stay later afterward so that he would live long.

The Maharsha is troubled by this Gemara. R' Yochanan provides a *pasuk* to prove that longevity can occur only in Eretz Yisrael; how does one's shul attendance counter the inference of the *pasuk*? The Maharsha's novel conclusion is that a shul must be considered as having the equivalent spiritual status of Eretz Yisrael. In the future, when Mashiach comes, the shuls will be transported to Eretz Yisrael. Since they will eventually be there, the shuls already have the status of Eretz Yisrael. Therefore, one who spends a long time in shul will live long. Staying in shul and breathing the air is tantamount to actually breathing in the air of Eretz Yisrael.*

Rav Dovid Shapiro (the son of the Bnei Yissaschar) writes[11] that the *pasuk* לְמַעַן יֵדְעוּ דֹרֹתֵיכֶם כִּי בַסֻּכּוֹת הוֹשַׁבְתִּי אֶת בְּנֵי יִשְׂרָאֵל בְּהוֹצִיאִי אוֹתָם מֵאֶרֶץ מִצְרָיִם אֲנִי ה' אֱלֹקֵיכֶם teaches us that just as a shul has the same status as Eretz Yisrael, so too does the *suc- cah*! Sitting in a *succah* is equivalent to sitting in *kedushas* Eretz Yisrael, the holiness of Eretz Yisrael!

There is a fundamental difference between Eretz Yisrael and all the other countries in the world. Every other land has an inter- mediary between it and the Ribbono shel Olam; it has a minister- ing angel that serves as a go-between, connecting Hashem and the people. The Jews in Eretz Yisrael, however, enjoy a unique relationship directly with Hashem. There is no intermediary. This explains the Gemara[12] that states that one who resides in Eretz Yisrael is considered to have a God, while someone who dwells in *chutz l'Aretz* is considered to be Godless.

The purpose of the *succah* is for us to sit in the direct shade of Hashem: *b'tzila d'm'heimenusa*. This direct connection to Hashem and His Presence is reminiscent of living in Eretz Yisrael, where the inhabitants continuously enjoy this direct relationship with Him.

As Bnei Yisrael left Mitzrayim, Hashem enveloped them in the protection of Clouds of Glory, representative of Eretz Yisrael, so that the Jewish people would already have the benefits of liv- ing in the Land; as we know, the Gemara states, "the air of Eretz Yisrael makes a person wise."[13] We commemorate this concept

---

* Parenthetically, a fascinating *she'eilah* based on this *yesod* suggests that fruit planted inside a shul may be obligated in *terumah* and *maaser* (ע בספר אהל משה עניני המקדש והגלות עמ' קעט-קפ).

by dwelling in *succos* that will give us the same benefit: a direct and personal relationship with Hashem.

That is why the *pasuk* concludes with the words, *"I am Hashem, your God."* The *pasuk* is stating that when you sit in a *succah*, which is equivalent to sitting in Eretz Yisrael, it will be considered that you indeed have a God. At least during the week of Succos, one who dwells in a *succah* will achieve the level of closeness to Hashem as those who live in Eretz Yisrael, since the *succah* itself is a microcosm of Eretz Yisrael, with all its *kedushah*.

With regard to residing in Eretz Yisrael, the Torah relates, לְמַעַן יִרְבּוּ יְמֵיכֶם וִימֵי בְנֵיכֶם עַל הָאֲדָמָה אֲשֶׁר נִשְׁבַּע ה' : You will prolong your days in Eretz Yisrael. By extension, one who resides in the *succah*, a microcosm of Eretz Yisrael, will also merit long life. Sitting in the virtual Eretz Yisrael will provide the same *berachah* as residing in the actual Eretz Yisrael.

◎ *Two Unique Mitzvos*

The Vilna Gaon[14] writes that there are only two mitzvos in the Torah that one fulfills with his entire body, with all 248 limbs: dwelling in *Eretz Yisrael* and sitting in the *succah*. These are the only two mitzvos during which our entire body enters into the *cheftzah* of the mitzvah. This is hinted at in the *pasuk* that states, וַיְהִי בְשָׁלֵם סֻכּוֹ וּמְעוֹנָתוֹ בְצִיּוֹן, *Then His Tabernacle [*סֻכּוֹ*] was in Jerusalem [*בְשָׁלֵם*], and His Dwelling in Tzion (Tehillim* 76:3). When can you do a mitzvah *b'shleimus*, with the entirety of your being? Only in the *succah* or in *Tzion*, Eretz Yisrael. Furthermore, a person is not considered *shaleim*, complete, until he has fulfilled these two mitzvos.

One might find this concept troubling, however, since one might think that immersing in a *mikveh* is yet another mitzvah that one enters into with his entire body[15]! However, the Ran explains (in the name of the Ramban) that immersing in the *mikveh* is, in itself, not a mitzvah. It is only *machshirei mitzvah*, the preparation to a mitzvah. In addition, the *Kesef Mishnah*[16] writes that one becomes *tahor* only upon exiting the *mikveh*, not upon entering it, and therefore the fulfillment of the *tevilah* is not when one enters or is immersed in the *mikveh*, but upon emerging.

❧ How Do We Know That the Avos Observed Succos?

We know that the *Avos* kept the entire Torah. The Vilna Gaon[17] was asked how we know that the *Avos* observed Succos. He replied that we know it from the *pasuk*, וְאַבְרָהָם זָקֵן בָּא בַּיָּמִים וַה' בֵּרַךְ אֶת אַבְרָהָם בַּכֹּל, *Now Avraham was old, well on in years, and Hashem had blessed Avraham with everything* (*Bereishis* 24:1). The word בַּכֹּל stands for the three phrases in the Torah that discuss the mitzvah of *succah*:

בַּסֻּכֹּת תֵּשְׁבוּ שִׁבְעַת יָמִים (*Vayikra* 23:42)

כָּל הָאֶזְרָח בְּיִשְׂרָאֵל יֵשְׁבוּ בַּסֻּכֹּת (ibid.)

לְמַעַן יֵדְעוּ דֹרֹתֵיכֶם כִּי בַסֻּכּוֹת הוֹשַׁבְתִּי אֶת בְּנֵי יִשְׂרָאֵל (ibid., v. 43)

The mitzvah of *succah* is hinted at with the word *bakol*, with everything, because it is one of the two mitzvos that can be fulfilled with all of your body![18] Your *bakol*, your entire being, can fulfill the mitzvah of *succah*; therefore, since the mitzvah of *succah* is performed with the entire *guf* and all the *eivarim*, it is only fitting that it is hinted to with the word *bakol*.

The *Bnei Yissaschar*[19] calculates the *gematria* of the word סוּכָּה with the letters spelled *b'milui*, in full. Using this format, the letters of *succah* are spelled סמ"ך, וי"ו, כ"ף, ה"א. The total is 248, the number of limbs we use to fulfill the mitzvah.

❧ Succah Fulfills Both

Sitting in the *succah* not only allows one to fulfill one of the two mitzvos that can be performed with the entirety of a person. Since, as noted above, the *succah* is considered to be a part of Eretz Yisrael, by sitting in the *succah* a person simultaneously fulfills **both** mitzvos that uniquely are performed with one's entire body: living in Eretz Yisrael and sitting in the *succah*!

We can thus interpret the *pasuk* וַיְהִי בְשָׁלֵם סֻכּוֹ וּמְעוֹנָתוֹ בְצִיּוֹן to mean that if one wants to perform a mitzvah with *sheleimus*, he should sit in the *succah*. Why? Because וּמְעוֹנָתוֹ בְּצִיוֹן , sitting in the *succah* is tantamount to living in Eretz Yisrael.[20]

⤳ *The Promise of V'heiveisi*

The *succos* in which Bnei Yisrael lived during their sojourn in the *Midbar* were microcosms of Eretz Yisrael; as we have seen, dwelling in the *succos* is considered as if they were living in Eretz Yisrael. Thus, the *succos* themselves are the fulfillment of the promise of *V'heiveisi*! Bringing Bnei Yisrael into their *succos* was equivalent to bringing them into Eretz Yisrael, as Hashem had promised.

דִירַת עֲרַאי ⤳

The *succah* is termed a דִירַת עֲרַאי, *temporary dwelling*.[21] There is profound hidden meaning in this phrase. The borders of Eretz Yisrael are listed in the Gemara[22]: רֶקֶם, *Rekem*, in the east; אַשְׁקְלוֹן, *Ashkelon*, in the south; עַכּוֹ, *Acco*, in the north. Rashi[23] states that the western border is the יָם, the Mediterranean Sea. The Rambam[24] writes that these are the borders of Eretz Yisrael with regard to all halachos that pertain to Eretz Yisrael. Rav Shem Klingberg reveals that the *roshei teivos*, initial letters, of the four borders of Eretz Yisrael spell the word עֲרַאי! The *succah* is considered a דִירַת עֲרַאי because sitting in it is tantamount to sitting within the boundaries of Eretz Yisrael.[25]

Rav Klingberg adds[26] that by giving us the mitzvah of sitting in the *succah*, the temporary dwelling, Hashem demonstrates His love for us. By fulfilling the mitzvah of *succah*, we are sitting in His Land, in Eretz Yisrael, where the *Shechinah* dwells. Incredibly, the *gematria* of דִירַת עֲרַאי is the same as that of הַבּוֹחֵר בְּעַמּוֹ יִשְׂרָאֵל בְּאַהֲבָה (*Ahavas Olam*).*

---

* דִירַת עֲרַאי is also numerically equivalent to the phrase אֶת סֻכַּת דָוִד, an allusion to the fact that the *succah* is also a microcosm of the Beis HaMikdash, a concept that is explored in the "Sanctity of the Beis

This is an incredible gift that Hashem bestows on us: He gives us the mitzvah of *succah*, which, when performed anywhere in the world, is equivalent to actually living in Eretz Yisrael and encompasses the *berachos* of Eretz Yisrael, such as longevity!

✷ Zman Simchaseinu

This concept also helps us understand why Succos is referred to as זְמַן שִׂמְחָתֵנוּ, *the time of our rejoicing*.

Rav Meir Shapiro states [27] that there is no *simchah* comparable to that of entering Eretz Yisrael. This is hinted at in the Torah in the *pasuk,* וְהָיָה כִּי תָבוֹא אֶל הָאָרֶץ, *And it will be when you enter the Land* [Eretz Yisrael] (*Devarim* 26:1). The *Ohr HaChaim* teaches that the term *vehayah* is a reference to *simchah*, to a time of joy and happiness. Coming to Eretz Yisrael is the ultimate *simchah*.

We also see this in *Sefer Bereishis*. When Yaakov Avinu left Eretz Yisrael, the *pasuk* says that he poured oil,[28] whereas when he returned to Eretz Yisrael he poured both oil and wine.[29] As we know, וְיַיִן יְשַׂמַּח לְבַב אֱנוֹשׁ, *wine rejoices the heart of man*; thus, his utilizing wine on his return was symbolic of the exceptional *simchah* he experienced as he entered Eretz Yisrael.

In our *davening* on Yom Tov we also refer to this when we say, "וַהֲבִיאֵנוּ לְצִיוֹן עִירְךָ בְּרִנָּה. וְלִירוּשָׁלַיִם בֵּית מִקְדָּשְׁךָ בְּשִׂמְחַת עוֹלָם".

Succos is called זְמַן שִׂמְחָתֵנוּ, *the time of our rejoicing*, because the *succah* is a microcosm of Eretz Yisrael. Entering the *succah* is tantamount to entering Eretz Yisrael, and it is therefore a time of great joy.

✷ Succos Corresponds to Yaakov Avinu

The Tur teaches that the Yom Tov of Succos corresponds to Yaakov Avinu. The Belzer Rebbe explains the depth of this analogy. When Yaakov left Eretz Yisrael and passed the *makom HaMikdash*, the future site of the Beis HaMikdash, Hashem moved the *makom* to Yaakov's location. This incident is an

---

HaMikdash in the *Succah*," page 293.

example of the *kedushah* of Eretz Yisrael being situated some-where other than its actual space. This is exactly what takes place in the *succah*: The *kedushah* of Eretz Yisrael joins us wher-ever we build our *succah*.

❧ *Why Are There Three Regalim?*

Let us add one precious nugget that will deepen our under-standing of this exhilarating concept. The Abarbanel[30] writes that Hashem gave us *Shalosh Regalim* to correspond to three amazing kindnesses that He showered upon us. The Yamim Tovim allow us to display *hakaras hatov*, gratitude, to Hashem for these kindnesses.

The three extraordinary gifts that Hashem gave the Bnei Yisrael are *Yetziyas Mitzrayim*, *Mattan Torah*, and Eretz Yisrael. Pesach is a Yom Tov of gratitude toward Hashem for having taken us out of Egypt. On Shavuos, we display *hakaras hatov* toward Hashem for having given us the Torah. Succos is the Yom Tov when we show our appreciation to Hashem for having given us Eretz Yisrael and its produce.

We may suggest that on Succos, which is when we collec-tively thank Hashem for having given us Eretz Yisrael, Hashem elevates our *succah* to the status of Eretz Yisrael. Furthermore, writes the Abarbanel, the reason Succos has seven days is to celebrate the *Shivas HaMinim,* seven species, with which Eretz Yisrael is blessed. This is a possible explanation for the custom to display the *Shivas HaMinim* in the *succah*.

May we be *zocheh* to the *berachah* of *Chag HaSuccah Taaseh Lecha* and in the merit of sitting in the *succah* this year, may we be *zocheh* to sit in the *succah* again, for many years to come.

ENDNOTES

1. בחצרות החיים מד- בטאון ארגון
   החוברות דחסידי צאנז, עמ' ק.
2. יפה ללב חלק ב' או"ח סימן תרס"ז.
3. כף החיים או"ח סימן תרס"ז.
4. אברבנאל פרשת וירא.
5. פירוש הר"ן וירא י"ח, א-כ"ו.
6. כמוצא שלל רב סוכות עמוד קל"ו.
7. זרע קודש לקוטים לסוכות ולהושענא
   רבא.
8. מועד לכל חי סימן כ' אות נ'.
9. תפארת שלמה לסוכות.
10. ברכות ח, א.
11. ספר צמח דוד ליקוטי אמרים לחג
    הסוכות; שו"ת תירוש ויצהר סימן
    קי"ד.
12. כתובות קא, ב.
13. בבא בתרא קנח, ב.
14. המאור הגדול - תהלים עמוד תס"ד.
15. אוצרות התורה סוכות עמוד ס"ב:

16. דברים יא, כא.
17. דברי אליהו, פרשת חיי שרה.
18. כמוצא שלל רב, סוכות עמוד קל"ה.
19. אגרא דכלה וישלח עמוד של"ד.
20. שו"ת תירוש ויצהר סימן קיד.
21. סוכה ב, א.
22. גיטין ב, א.
23. רש"י גיטין ב.
24. רמב"ם הלכות תרומות פרק א' הלכה
    ז.
25. אהלי שם על המועדים עמוד צ"א (רב
    שם קלינברג).
26. שם.
27. ניצוצי אור המאיר, רב מאיר שפירא,
    עמוד 258.
28. ויצא כח, יח.
29. וישלח לג, יד.
30. אברבנאל פרשת ראה עמוד קמ"ח.

Praying for Rain — Praying for the "Fallen Succah"

≫ How Is Succos Connected to Rebuilding the Beis HaMikdash?

During Succos, we add a special *HaRachaman* into *Bircas HaMazon*: הָרַחֲמָן, הוּא יָקִים לָנוּ אֶת סֻכַּת דָּוִד הַנּוֹפָלֶת, *May the Merciful One establish for us the fallen succah of David HaMelech*. The phrase סֻכַּת דָּוִד הַנּוֹפָלֶת refers to the Beis HaMikdash. Hence, this is a request to HaKadosh Baruch Hu to rebuild the Beis HaMikdash. Why do we make this request on Succos? How is the building of the Third Beis HaMikdash a central theme of this Yom Tov?

≫ No Lashon Hara in the Succah

The *Mishnah Berurah*[1] states that since the *kedushah* of the *succah* is so profound, one should try to minimize idle conversation in the *succah*. One should attempt to discuss there only *kedushah* and Torah. Certainly, the *Mishnah Berurah* cautions, one must be extremely careful to avoid speaking *lashon hara*, *rechilus*, or other forms of forbidden speech while in the *succah*.

Why must the Chofetz Chaim tell us that we cannot speak *lashon hara* or *rechilus* in the *succah*? They are never permitted to be spoken! And if the Chofetz Chaim is stressing the importance of maintaining the *kedushah* of the *succah*, why mention only these *aveiros* to avoid while in the *succah*? Why not state that one should not wear *shaatnez* or eat *tereifah* — or do any other *aveirah* — in the *succah*? What is the reason these sins of speech are specifically mentioned as being prohibited in the *succah*?

✑ Why Do We Daven for Rain on Succos?

The topic of our *tefillos* on the last day of Succos is *geshem*, rain. We pray for rain. Why do we *daven* for rain on Succos? We don't want it to rain now! In fact, rain on Succos is a sign of a *kelalah*, curse. The Gemara states that on Shemini Atzeres we sit and eat in the *succah*, but we don't make the *berachah Leisheiv baSuccah*. Why not wait to *daven* for rain until after Succos, when we are no longer obligated to sit in the *succah*?

How is the request for rain connected to the Yom Tov of Succos to the extent that we *daven* for rain although we do not yet want it to rain?

✑ What Is the Origin of Rain?

We know that rain is caused by evaporation, condensation, and precipitation. These are the three components of the water cycle, as the wind moves the clouds from over the oceans to the land where the rain is needed.

However, this is only a scientific and physical explanation. The Chasam Sofer[2] reveals that beneath the surface there is a spiritual process that transpires and produces rain. The Chasam Sofer amazingly teaches that rain actually comes from clouds that are produced from the hot air, the vapor, that is released as people speak.

Thus, if mankind speaks inappropriately or sinfully — such as when *lashon hara* and *rechilus* are spoken — hot air that is full of sin will then produce rain that is imbued with *zuhamah*, grime; it will have been sullied by sin. The food that would then be grown due to that rain would subsequently be *tamei* and would contaminate whoever ate it. The people who eat this food would become further sullied and would then produce even more detrimental speech. The ensuing rain would then be even more toxic and poisonous. This cycle would continue to repeat itself, and seemingly there would be no remedy for this cycle of contamination.

≥ How Can We Restore Order?

The only way to break this vicious cycle is to stop the poisonous rain from ruining the next crop. A drought is the perfect way to restore the water cycle to its proper mode: Break the cycle by withholding rain until the people humble themselves and realize that they must change their ways.

The early rains are referred to as *yoreh* and the late rains as *malkosh*. The Gemara in *Mesechta Taanis*[3] states that the late rains are referred to as *malkosh*, "שֶׁמָּל קַשִׁיוּתֵיהֶן שֶׁל יִשְׂרָאֵל, *because they circumcise* — i.e., sever — *the obstinacy of the Jewish people.*"

≥ The Curse of Yehoshua bin Nun

The Gemara[4] tells of the curse that Yehoshua bin Nun placed upon anyone who would rebuild the city of Yericho (*I Melachim* 6:26). The curse was that whoever rebuilt Yericho would lose his children. His children would die as the building process progressed, and the builder would lose his last child as the city was being completed.

Nevertheless, a man by the name of Chiel embarked on the rebuilding of Yericho (*I Melachim* 16:34). His children died, and Eliyahu HaNavi and King Achav both came to be *menachem avel*. They discussed why the tragedy had occurred. Eliyahu remarked that the reason for Chiel's loss was the aforementioned curse of Yehoshua. Achav, an evil king, said to Chiel: "Now then, the curse of Moshe Rabbeinu did not come to pass; do you really think the curse of his student Yehoshua will come true?"

Moshe Rabbeinu had told Klal Yisrael:

הִשָּׁמְרוּ לָכֶם פֶּן יִפְתֶּה לְבַבְכֶם וְסַרְתֶּם וַעֲבַדְתֶּם אֱלֹהִים אֲחֵרִים וְהִשְׁתַּחֲוִיתֶם
לָהֶם. וְחָרָה אַף ה' בָּכֶם וְעָצַר אֶת הַשָּׁמַיִם וְלֹא יִהְיֶה מָטָר וְהָאֲדָמָה לֹא תִתֵּן אֶת
יְבוּלָהּ וַאֲבַדְתֶּם מְהֵרָה מֵעַל הָאָרֶץ הַטֹּבָה אֲשֶׁר ה' נֹתֵן לָכֶם.

*Beware for yourselves, lest your heart be seduced and you turn
astray and serve gods of others and prostrate yourselves to them.
Then the wrath of Hashem will blaze against you; He will restrain
the heaven so there will be no rain and the ground will not yield
its produce; and you will be swiftly banished from the goodly Land
that Hashem gives you (Devarim 11:16-17).*

Hashem promised that if Bnei Yisrael were to worship idols,
then the moisture in the heavens would be constrained and no
rain would fall. The nation would quickly be forced to abandon
a parched Eretz Yisrael.

Achav told Chiel, "I have erected an idol in each furrow in the
land of Eretz Yisrael, and the rain is so abundant that it does not
allow me to go worship my idols!" Achav implied that Moshe's
curse had not been not realized, and he reasoned that Yehoshua's
curse would also not materialize; thus, he said, Chiel should not
believe that the curse caused his children's death.

◁ *Eliyahu Takes Control*

Eliyahu HaNavi heard this conversation and immediately
vowed that there would no longer be any more dew or rain, כִּי
אִם לְפִי דְבָרִי, *except by my word (I Melachim 17:1)*. He intended to
activate the curse of Moshe Rabbeinu.

Eliyahu then *davened* to be given the "key" that controls
rain. The Gemara[5] teaches that there are three "keys" of which
Hashem retains sole possession: the key of childbirth, the key of
Techiyas HaMeisim, and the key of rain. Until this point, no other
entity, not even a *malach*, had ever been given control of any of
these keys. Because Eliyahu intended to uphold the honor of
Hashem, an exception was made and Hashem gave him the key
of rain. Eliyahu then withheld the rain, causing a drought.

Because Eliyahu suspended the rains, Achav wanted to kill
him. Hashem instructed Eliyahu to escape eastward and hide in

the valley of Kris. While Eliyahu, as a fugitive from Achav, was in hiding, ravens sustained him during the drought with bread and meat for a year.

Eliyahu now witnessed the suffering of the people: After a year without rain, there was no food, and they were starving and dying. Hashem instructed Eliyahu to go to Tzarfas, where a widow would feed him. He remained in Tzarfas for a year, after which the widow's young son became ill and *there was no more breath left in him* (ibid., v. 17). Eliyahu had extraordinary gratitude toward the widow, and he wanted to revive the boy. In order to perform *Techiyas HaMeisim*, Eliyahu would have to acquire the second of the three keys: the key of *Techiyas HaMeisim*, which was retained by Hashem. However, it would be inappropriate for Eliyahu to control two of the special keys while Hashem retained control over only one of them. For Eliyahu to bring the child back to life, he would have to relinquish the key of rain. Eliyahu made the exchange, and he was able to revive the boy.

Now that Hashem again controlled the rainfall, we would expect the clouds to gather and the rain to fall, but this is not the way the events unfolded. In the third year of the drought, obeying the command of Hashem, Eliyahu gathers everyone — including the prophets of Baal — to Har HaCarmel (ibid., Chapter 18), where he challenged the prophets of Baal to demonstrate the power of their god. When they failed, Eliyahu proved that Hashem is the true God, whereupon all of Klal Yisrael cried out, "הי הוא הָאֱלֹקים הי הוּא הָאֱלֹקים!" The *Navi* then tells us that a tiny cloud, about the size of a hand, appeared, and then *there was a great rain* (ibid., v. 45).

✍ *The Chasam Sofer's Four Questions:*

1. The Chasam Sofer[6] finds the words that Eliyahu used curious. Why say that it should rain "כּי אִם לְפִי דְבָרִי, *only by my word*"? Why not say that the rain should fall only "by Hashem's word"?

2. Furthermore, asks the Chasam Sofer, Achav's claim seems to be correct — why, in fact, didn't Moshe Rabbeinu's curse come to pass? Why was there still rain while idol worship was rampant?

3. He also asks why it rained only after Eliyahu arranged this spectacle that included all of Klal Yisrael and the prophets of Baal.

4. Finally, what is the significance of the small hand-shaped cloud that descended from *Shamayim*?

As we see in the above *pesukim* from *Devarim*, Hashem presented Bnei Yisrael with two options: either וְעָצַר אֶת הַשָּׁמַיִם, *He will restrain the heaven* and withhold the rain, or וַאֲבַדְתֶּם מְהֵרָה, *you will be swiftly banished*. The Chasam Sofer understands this as a choice, rather than that both will happen. In the times of Achav, the people were so sullied and contaminated that constraining the heavens and withholding rain would not have been sufficient. Hashem was going to have to banish them, in fulfillment of the *pasuk*, וַאֲבַדְתֶּם מְהֵרָה. But when Achav mocked Eliyahu, Hashem held back the rain to indicate that Eliyahu was a true prophet of Hashem and that Moshe Rabbeinu's curse was valid.

At this point, since the every day speech was so sinful, the rain would have been incredibly toxic, and the cycle would have continued, making matters even worse. Eliyahu therefore stated that there would be rain only לְפִי דְבָרִי — only through *my words*. He was not saying that it would rain due to his command; rather, he was saying that the words of the *reshaim* would stop producing clouds, and that only his words — his righteous words — would continue to produce clouds, and the rain that then would fall as a result of his words would be pure and holy. Their holiness would ensure that the crops would be wholesome.

Eliyahu was concerned that *his* words alone would not suffice. He therefore gathered together all the *Yidden* and had them *daven* together, chanting in unison, "*Hashem Hu HaElokim*," over and over again, creating a cloud of *kedushah* and *taharah*.

When Klal Yisrael came together and *davened*, their words of *tefillah* created a small cloud, shaped like a hand, that descended and portended the heavy rains that followed.

❧ *The Source of Rain Is Our Words!*

From this episode, the Chasam Sofer draws the conclusion that rain's origin is not based on a physical phenomenon; rather, it comes from our words — from the vapor that issues from our mouths! If we speak *divrei Torah*, *divrei kedushah*, *tefillah*, words of encouragement, kind words, then we will produce kosher rain, which will in turn result in the growth of beautiful, sweet, holy fruits, which can further elevate all who consume them. On the other hand, if we speak *devarim assurim*, forbidden words, specifically *lashon hara*, the result will be a poisonous, toxic rain cycle.

❧ *Clouds That Block Tefillos*

The Gemara[7] states that Rava would never authorize a fast on a cloudy day, because he felt that the clouds will hold back the *tefillah*. As the *pasuk* states, סַכּוֹתָה בֶעָנָן לָךְ מֵעֲבוֹר תְּפִלָּה, *You wrapped Yourself in a cloud that prayer cannot pierce* (*Eichah* 3:44). Rav Yonasan Eibeshutz[8] asks, What is this cloud that prevents our *tefillos* from passing through? He explains that this cloud is made up of the hot air and mist that issues from our mouths each day, words that often contain words of deceit, *lashon hara*, anger, and *onaas devarim*. Inappropriate conversation includes even appropriate words that takes place in the wrong time or location, such as idle talk in shul, especially during *davening*. These vapors rise up, form a cloud, and block our *tefillos* from getting through to Hashem. People speaking during *davening* are hindering the shul's *tefillos* from reaching Hashem.

This is the same *yesod* as that mentioned by the Chasam Sofer: *lashon hara*, *rechilus*, and *onaas devarim* all work to create a barrier to Hashem's acceptance of our *tefillos*.

How Does the Succah Protect Us From Lashon Hara?

David HaMelech states, תִּצְפְּנֵם בְּסֻכָּה מֵרִיב לְשֹׁנוֹת, *...protect them in a shelter from the strife of tongues (Tehillim 31:21)*. The *Nachalas David* (Rav Dovid Tevel)[9] writes that this *pasuk* implies that the mitzvah of *succah* protects us from *lashon hara*.

How does the mitzvah of *succah* offer us this spiritual protection? Rav Dovid Tevel writes that the word *succah* contains four letters: ס, ו, כ, ה. There are five parts of the mouth that contribute to speech; they are the teeth, tongue, palate, lips, and throat. The first letter of the word *succah* is ס, *samech*, which is a member of the letter group זסשרצ; they are formed with the teeth. The ו, *vav*, of *succah* is a member of the letter group בומפ; they are formed with the lips. The כ, *kaf*, of *succah* is a member of the letter group גיכק; they come from the palate. The ה, *hei*, of *succah* is in the letter group אהחע, which are guttural sounds formed in the throat. The tongue, however, has no representative letter in the word *succah*. The letters דטלנת, which are formed with the tongue, are not found in the word *succah*.

Rav Dovid Tevel explains that there is a very profound reason that the word *succah* does not contain any letters that require the use of the tongue. The tongue is protected by the four other parts of the mouth: teeth and lips in the front and palate and throat in the back. The purpose of the mitzvah of *succah*, he says, is to offer spiritual protection to a Jew to guard one's tongue and avoid speaking *lashon hara*. To symbolize this protection, there is no letter in the word *succah* that uses the tongue.

Guard Your Tongue – in the Succah!

Now we can understand why the *Mishnah Berurah* states that one should be very careful not to speak *lashon hara* in the *succah*: It is because doing so defeats the entire purpose of the *succah*!

The *Nachalas David* says that this also explains why the Yom Tov of Succos corresponds to the *Geulah Acharonah*, Final

Redemption. The *succah* protects us from speaking *lashon hara*, and we know that Mashiach will not come until we correct that sin. As the Gemara[10] states, the second Beis HaMikdash was destroyed because of *sinas chinam*, baseless hatred, and *lashon hara*. Until this is rectified, Mashiach cannot come.

☙ *Succos:*
The Best Time to Ask for the Beis HaMikdash

When we sit in the *succah*, it is the most opportune time to pray for the rebuilding of the Beis HaMikdash; therefore, we *daven,* הָרַחֲמָן, הוּא יָקִים לָנוּ אֶת סֻכַּת דָּוִד הַנּוֹפֶלֶת. Sitting in the *succah*, protected from *lashon hara* by the structure whose name does not contain any of the letters that require use of the tongue, we ask that the Beis HaMikdash be rebuilt. It is now that we are worthy of praying for the Beis HaMikdash, since we are rectifying our speech and guarding ourselves from speaking *lashon hara*.

☙ *Hashem Created the World With the Letter* ה

Hashem created the world with the word *Kah*, with the *yud* and the *hei*,[11] כִּי בְּיָ-ה ה' צוּר עוֹלָמִים. The *yud* stands for *Olam Haba*, and the *hei* for *Olam Hazeh*. Why did Hashem create this world with the letter *hei*? The Gemara[12] tells us that the open bottom of the *hei* is symbolic of this world, where it is easy for one to fall down and commit *aveiros*. But, one can always come back and do teshuvah through the opening on the *hei's* side, which symbolizes the Gate of Teshuvah that is never closed.

There is another explanation for why, of all the letters, Hashem chose to create the world with the letter ה. Of all the letter in the *aleph-beis*, the easiest letter to articulate is the letter *hei*. It requires nothing more than a breath of air: no tongue, palate, teeth, or lips are needed. Hashem created the world with the letter *hei* — whose name requires no effort to say — to symbolize that creating the world required no effort or action on Hashem's part. The entire Creation was extremely easy and simple for Hashem to accomplish.

The *mekubalim*[13] teach that a *succah* is symbolized by the letter ה, as a *succah* requires only two complete walls and a partial third wall to be kosher. This is exactly what we have in the letter ה: two complete sides and one partial wall.

The *yesod* of the *succah* is intended to bolster our *shemiras halashon* and to prevent us from speaking *lashon hara* and other wrongful modes of speech. How compelling it is, then, to have the *succah* represented by the one letter that does not require speech to articulate it.

‏‏✎ *Round Leaves Seem Ready to Speak*

Reb Chaim Karlenstein[14] quotes the *Mishnah*[15] stating that *tziftzafa* is *pasul*, invalid, for use as an *aravah* in the *Arba Minim*. A *tziftzafa* is an *aravah* with leaves that are round rather than long and narrow. The question then arises: Why do round leaves render an *aravah* invalid? Furthermore, why is this type of *aravah* referred to by the unique name, *tziftzafa*?

Reb Chaim Karlenstein explains as follows. The *Midrash* teaches[16] that the Four Species that we take on Succos represent four parts of the body: The *esrog* represents the heart, the *lulav* the spine, the *hadassim* the eyes, and the *aravos* represent one's lips, apparently in a closed position. The leaves of the *aravah* thus represent a closed mouth, indicating that we do not use our mouths to engage in inappropriate forms of speech. Round leaves do not have the appearance of a pair of closed lips. Rather, they look more like an open mouth, which is what we are seeking to avoid. This type of *aravah* is called *tziftzafa* because it looks like a mouth that is *mitzaftzef*, chirping. In the same vein, a *metzora* brings a *korban* of birds that are *mitzaftzefes*, chirping, to atone for his *aveirah* of having spoken *lashon hara*.

This is why an *aravah* with round leaves is *pasul*: We need the *aravah*, which symbolizes the closed mouth of the person who is careful not to speak *lashon hara*, to remind us, specifically on Succos, not to engage in prohibited speech.

∝ *Why the Kamatz Precedes the Patach*

Reb Chaim Karlenstein cites Rav Shamshon Raphael Hirsch, who writes that the *nekudah kamatz*, ָ, precedes the *nekudah patach*, ַ, in the order of the *nekudos*. The *kamatz* refers to a *peh kamutz*, closed mouth, while the *patach* refers to a *peh pasuach*, open mouth. *Kamatz* comes first to symbolize that a person's default position should be with a closed mouth, and one should open his mouth only when necessary.

∝ *Why Do We Strike the Aravos Against the Ground?*

This concept offers an incredible insight into the custom of *chibut aravah*, beating the bundle of *aravos* against the ground on Hoshana Rabbah. Rav Tzemach Gaon[17] explains, based on the above-mentioned *Midrash*, that by striking the *aravos*, which represent the lips, against the ground, we show Hashem that we understand that much of what we must do teshuvah for throughout the *Yemei HaDin* is for sins connected to speech. We show Hashem that we are going to rectify the sins of the mouth, and we are no longer going to engage in sinful forms of speech. The *pasuk* states, יִתֵּן בֶּעָפָר פִּיהוּ אוּלַי יֵשׁ תִּקְוָה, *Let him put his mouth to the dust — there may yet be hope* (*Eichah* 3:29). Sins of the mouth are among the worst — and among the most common. If one wants to achieve significant teshuvah, he must start with rectifying how he uses his mouth.

Chief among the sins of the mouth is *lashon hara*. On Succos, coming to a climax on Hoshana Rabbah, the final day of *kapparah*, we commit to never speaking *lashon hara* again and to stop using our power of speech for prohibited forms of speech. We demonstrate this commitment by striking the *aravos*, which look like lips, against the ground. We are symbolically placing our mouths in the dust, hoping that there will then be a chance for us to have a good year. Indeed, יִתֵּן בֶּעָפָר פִּיהוּ אוּלַי יֵשׁ תִּקְוָה.

Rav Tzemach Gaon offers another explanation. Until the last day of Succos, the accusers in *Shamayim* are active against the Jewish people, but on Hoshana Rabbah the *mikatregim*, prosecutors, are all silenced. Beating the "mouths" on the ground is indicative of the accusers being silenced.

∾ *Two Pshatim, One Yesod*

These two *pshatim* go hand in hand. Our committing to keep our mouths closed to inappropriate speech directly silences the accusers in *Shamayim*. The Chofetz Chaim[18] explains that when we speak ill of other people, when we pass negative judgment against our fellow man, we open the door for the same action to be directed toward us by the heavenly prosecutors who want our verdict to be a harsh judgment. But if we are careful to not point out deficiencies in other people, then in *Shamayim* they, too, will exhibit great restraint in pointing out our shortcomings.

The Yom Tov of Succos is focused on *zehirus*, caution, in one's *lashon*, speech. תִּצְפְּנֵם בַּסֻּכָּה מֵרִיב לְשׁוֹנוֹת, *the succah protects us from lashon hara.* We sit in the *succah* for eight days, guarding our mouths and showing Hashem how we will use our power of speech differently and appropriately. We then take the willow, the *aravah*, representative of one's lips, that can be used for inappropriate and sinful speech, and beat it against the ground. We have now arrived at a state where we can ask for rain.

As noted, rain is formed by the vapor of our mouth, by our speech. Having purified and sanctified our mouths and speech during Succos, thereby resetting the rain cycle, we are now fully equipped and worthy of asking Hashem for a blessed year of rain and hopeful of receiving a positive response. With our newly purified speech, the rain can truly be *gishmei berachah*, rains of blessing.

The Chofetz Chaim[19] writes that if we want to have the opportunity to see the Beis HaMikdash rebuilt, we must rectify that which led to its destruction. During the Second Beis HaMikdash era, the people learned Torah, they did mitzvos, but they did not have proper regard for one another, and they engaged in speaking *lashon hara*. Just as the sin of *lashon hara* was enough to cause the destruction of the Beis HaMikdash, it will most assuredly prevent the next Beis HaMikdash from being built! The Chofetz Chaim powerfully encourages us to rectify the sin of *lashon hara*.

On Succos we can achieve this. We repair our speech and can now ask Hashem to rebuild the Beis HaMikdash.

◁ *Why Is Succah a Segulah for Arichas Yamim?*

We can now understand a beautiful explanation as to why the mitzvah of *succah* is a *segulah* for longevity. The *pasuk* states, מִי הָאִישׁ הֶחָפֵץ חַיִּים אֹהֵב יָמִים לִרְאוֹת טוֹב, *Who is the man who desires life, who loves days of seeing good?* (*Tehillim* 34:13). Who is the man who desires *Olam Haba* and who would love to have a long life in this world? נְצֹר לְשׁוֹנְךָ מֵרָע וּשְׂפָתֶיךָ מִדַּבֵּר מִרְמָה, *Guard your tongue from [speaking] evil, and your lips from speaking deceit* (ibid., v. 14). The way to live a long life is to be careful not to speak *lashon hara*!

Thus, if one is careful to keep the mitzvah of *succah* and avoids speaking prohibited forms of speech, he will receive a long life and will be *zocheh* to sit in the *succah* for many years to come!

◁ *Succah: Both Succah Mamash and Ananei HaKavod*

The *pasuk* reads, לְמַעַן יֵדְעוּ דֹרֹתֵיכֶם כִּי בַסֻּכּוֹת הוֹשַׁבְתִּי אֶת בְּנֵי יִשְׂרָאֵל בְּהוֹצִיאִי אוֹתָם מֵאֶרֶץ מִצְרָיִם, *So that your generations will know that I caused Bnei Yisrael to dwell in succos when I took them out from the land of Egypt* (*Vayikra* 23:43). The Tannaim discuss whether this verse refers to material *succos* — Succos *mamash* — or to the *Ananei HaKavod*, Clouds of Glory.

Perhaps *both* opinions can be reconciled and synthesized. If one sits in his *succah*, in his hut, and speaks *divrei Torah*, words of purity and *kedushah*, then the vapor that issues from his speech forms a pure and holy cloud! Proper speech in the *succah mamash* will create *Ananei HaKavod*! On Succos, the *Ananei HaKavod* are created by the holy speech that one engages in while sitting in the *succah*, surrounded by the walls that protect him from speaking *lashon hara*.

May we be *zocheh* to utilize our mouths properly on the Yom Tov of Succos and to create sanctified air, purified vapor, and holy clouds — *Ananei HaKavod* — which are representative of *hashraas HaShechinah*, the resting place of the *Shechinah*. When we *daven*, הָרַחֲמָן, הוּא יָקִים לָנוּ אֶת סֻכַּת דָּוִד הַנּוֹפָלֶת, we pray that Hashem accept our *tefillos*, and we should be *zocheh* to see the rebuilding of the Beis HaMikdash speedily in our days.

ENDNOTES

1. סימן תרלט, ס״ק ב.

2. דרשות חתם סופר חלק ב הספד על ר׳ חיים הרש עמוד שעו.

3. תענית ו.

4. סנהדרין קיג, א.

5. תענית ב, א.

6. דרשות חתם סופר חלק ב הספד על ר׳ חיים הרש עמוד שעו.

7. ברכות לב, ב.

8. יערות דבש חלק א׳ עמוד פג.

9. הובא בליקוטי הגר״א על סוכות עמוד תכה-תכו.

10. יומא ט, ב.

11. מנחות כט, ב.

12. שם.

13. שם משמואל סוכות עמוד קע.

14. קונטרס בעניני חג הסוכות עמוד יח

15. סוכה פרק ג׳ משנה ג׳.

16. ויקרא רבה ל:יד.

17. תשובות הגאונים, שערי תשובה סימן שמ.

18. שמירת הלשון חלק א שער הזכירה פרק ב.

19. שמירת הלשון חלק ב פרק ז.

The Succah:
Breathe the Air — Live Long

❧ *Blessings and Benefits*

The mitzvah of *succah* certainly brings with it many blessings and benefits. One *berachah* that is particularly associated with the mitzvah of *succah* is *arichas yamim*, long life. The Torah says, חַג הַסֻּכֹּת תַּעֲשֶׂה לְךָ שִׁבְעַת יָמִים, *You shall make the Festival of Succos for a seven-day period* (*Devarim* 16:13). The Abarbanel and Ran have preserved a text from the *Pesikta* that is not extant in our versions of the *Pesikta*, stating that we derive from the word תַּעֲשֶׂה that if one sits in the *succah* this year, he will once again merit to sit in the *succah* next year: אִם עָשִׂיתָ כֵּן עַכְשָׁיו, יְהִי רָצוֹן שֶׁתַּעֲשֶׂה כֵּן לְשָׁנָה אַחֶרֶת, *If you do so now, may it be the will of Hashem that you will also be able to do so in the following year.* Hence, observing the mitzvah of *succah* offers the blessing of long life.* Although in the essay referenced below we have offered new insight into this special blessing, nevertheless, אֵין

---

* See "The Borders of Eretz Yisrael Encompassed in Your *Succah*," page 287, where we explain this explication of the *Pesikta* at length and bring down from Rav Naftali of Ropshitz and Rav Chaim Palagi *remazim* where the Torah alludes to the blessing of long life for those who scrupulously observe the mitzvah of *succah*.

בֵּית מִדְרָשׁ בְּלֹא חִידוּשׁ,* every time we delve into Torah matters we can find new insight and meaning, so let us endeavor to uncover new layers of understanding in this promise of the Torah.

✑ Succah = the Names of Hashem

The *Cheshek Shlomo*,[1] Rav Shlomo HaKohen M'Vilna, records an oft-quoted Kabbalistic idea. The word *succah* is typically spelled סוכה. The *gematria* of this spelling is ninety-one. The Four-Letter Name of Hashem — *Yud Kei Vav Kei* — is numerically equal to twenty-six, and the Name of *Adnus* — *Aleph Daled Nun Yud* — is sixty-five. Add these together and the sum is likewise ninety-one. Thus, *succah* reflects the combination and fusion of both of these Names of Hashem.

However, asks the *Cheshek Shlomo*, this is not the way the word *succah* is spelled in the Torah! Throughout the entire Torah, the word *succah* is always spelled *chaseir*, without the *vav*: סכה. Spelled this way, the *gematria* is only eighty-five.

✑ Succah = Shalom

The Chida[2] also quotes this idea, that the word *succah* is the combined *gematria* of these two Names of Hashem. He adds that if you write *Yud Kei Vav Kei* on one line, and then *Aleph Daled Nun Yud* below it, the letters that line up over each other are significant.

The first pairing is *yud* over *aleph*. *Yud* multiplied by *aleph* is still ten. *Hei* times *daled* is twenty. *Vav* multiplied by *nun* equals three hundred. Finally, *hei* times *yud* equals fifty. The sum of these is three-hundred eighty. This is the same *gematria* as the word *shalom*.** This explains why the *succah* is often referred to as *succas shalom*.

---

* Based on חגיגה ג.
** *Gematria im hakollel*; i.e., with the four letters.

～ The Dimensions of the Teivah

In *Parashas Noach*, the Torah records that the dimensions of the *Teivah* were 30 X 50 X 300 *amos* (*Bereishis* 6:15). Using this same pattern of multiplying the two Four-Letter Names of Hashem, the Malbim[3] offers a fascinating explanation to the significance of these dimensions. As we said above, *yud* times *aleph* equals 10, and *hei* times *daled* equals 20. Adding these together gives the first dimension of the *Teivah*: 30 *amos* wide. *Vav* times *nun* equals 300: a second dimension of the *Teivah*; i.e., its length. *Hei* times *yud* equals 50: the third dimension of the *Teivah*; i.e., its height. Thus, similar to the *succah*, the dimensions of the *Teivah* can be derived from these two Names of Hashem. The *Teivah*, too, was a *succas shaleim*, a *succah* of peace.

～ סֻכָּה *or* סוּכָּה?

But these calculations hold true only if the word *succah* is spelled with a *vav,* and it is never spelled with a *vav* in the Torah. *Succah* is always spelled *chaseir*, without the *vav*: סֻכָּה. One might note that in the verse, בַּסֻּכֹּת תֵּשְׁבוּ שִׁבְעַת יָמִים, *You shall dwell in booths for a seven-day period* (*Vayikra* 23:42), the word בַּסֻּכֹּת does have a *vav*, but that *vav* is not part of the word *succah*; rather, the *vav* after the *chaf* serves only to make the word plural. The word *succah* itself, in the singular, however, is never spelled with a *vav* in the Torah.

～ סֻכָּה *for Now;* סוּכָּה *When Mashiach comes*

The *Cheshek Shlomo* writes that there is one place in Tanach where *succah* **is** indeed spelled with a *vav*. The *pasuk* states, וַיְהִי בְשָׁלֵם סוּכּוֹ וּמְעוֹנָתוֹ בְצִיּוֹן, *Then His Tabernacle (succah) was in Jerusalem and His Dwelling in Tzion* (*Tehillim* 76:3). Here, the *vav* precedes the *chaf*.

Technically, the word *succah* should always be spelled with a *vav* between the *samach* and the *chaf*: סוּכָּה. However, there is an important reason it is never spelled this way in the Torah.

As noted, the word *succah* is numerically equivalent to two of the Names of Hashem. Until the Beis HaMikdash is rebuilt, *"ein HaSheim shalem,* Hashem's Name is not complete."[4] Therefore, until the Beis HaMikdash is rebuilt and Hashem returns to Tzion, the word *succah* is not spelled in its entirety. However, when Hashem will return to Tzion, then *succah* will be spelled *malei*, in its entirety.

The *pasuk* in *Tehillim* quoted above is telling us, וַיְהִי בְשָׁלֵם סוּכּוֹ, *when will the succah be complete,* spelled with the *vav,* וּמְעוֹנָתוֹ בְצִיּוֹן, *when the Shechinah will have returned to Tzion!* Only then can the *succah* be complete, because only then will the Name of Hashem be complete.

Even though now the word *succah* is spelled *chaseir,* without the *vav,* we must still recognize and appreciate the fact that when we enter the *succah* we are going into a structure that comprises a combination of two of the Names of Hashem. This is why it is *shalom,* since these two Names of Hashem, through the system of multiplication mentioned above, comprise the word *shalom.*

The *Mishnah*[5] teaches, לֹא מָצָא הַקָּדוֹשׁ בָּרוּךְ הוּא כְּלִי מַחֲזִיק בְּרָכָה לְיִשְׂרָאֵל אֶלָּא הַשָּׁלוֹם, *Hashem did not find a vessel that holds berachah, except for shalom, peace. Shalom* — which can be interpreted as a reference to the *succah* — is the greatest vehicle of *berachah!*

◈ *Two Unique Mitzvos*

The Vilna Gaon[6] writes that there are only two mitzvos in the Torah that one fulfills with his entire body, with all 248 limbs: *yeshivas Eretz Yisrael* and sitting in the *succah,* where one's entire body enters into the *cheftzah* of the mitzvah. This, too, is hinted at in the *pasuk* from *Tehillim* quoted above. When can one do a mitzvah *b'shleimus,* with the entirety of his being? וַיְהִי בְשָׁלֵם סוּכּוֹ וּמְעוֹנָתוֹ בְצִיּוֹן: in the *succah* and in *Tzion,* Eretz Yisrael. Furthermore, a person is not considered *shaleim,* complete, until he has fulfilled these two mitzvos.

❧ Halachic Ramification of the Gra

Rav Shlomo Zalman Auerbach writes[7] that this concept may have halachic ramifications. The Gemara[8] states that if one sleeps under a bed in the *succah*, he does not fulfill the mitzvah of *succah*. As Rashi explains, this is because there is an *ohel* between the person and the *succah*. *Ohel* is defined as a structure that is ten *tefachim* in height. According to the Gemara, the bed that is a *hefsek* between a person and the *succah* is one that is at least ten *tefachim* high. Following this reasoning, one who is sitting at a table in the *succah* may not be fulfilling the mitzvah *b'shleimus*! If the table is ten *tefachim* high, then it serves as an *ohel* over his legs. Hence, the lower part of his body is not in the *succah*. Since, according to the Gra, the full fulfillment of the mitzvah is accomplished only when one is in the *succah* with his whole body, the mitzvah would not be ideally fulfilled under these circumstances. Standing or sitting at a table lower than ten *tefachim* would allow one to fulfill the mitzvah *b'sheleimus* according to the Gra.

❧ Succah: Hashem's Embrace

Succah, which is numerically equivalent to two of the Names of Hashem, affords one the opportunity to be completely enveloped by the Ribbono shel Olam Himself. By entering the *succah*, a person's body is completely surrounded by and immersed in the *Shechinah*.

At the end of *Ne'ilah* on Yom Kippur, we say, "וַחֲבִיאֵנוּ בְּצֵל יָדוֹ, *protect me in the shade of Your hand.*" What does this petition refer to? Rav Shlomo Zalman Auerbach[9] explains this *tefillah* by noting that when one wraps his arm around another person in a hug, his arm surrounds the other person on three sides. The upper arm, forearm, and hand are actually symbolic of the precise dimensions of a halachic *succah*: two full walls and a *tefach*. This *tefillah* is thus referring to the mitzvah of *succah*; we are asking Hashem to embrace us in the *succah*, with which we are surrounded on three sides. Sitting in the *succah*, representative of two of His Names, is tantamount to receiving a hug from Hashem.

◠ *A Breath of Fresh Air*

Picture a patient who seeks a consultation with a physician. The doctor informs him that his symptoms represent a significant abnormality for which he will require heart surgery. After the surgery is performed, the patient is told that all went well and that the surgery was a success. His heart function has been restored to normal. However, the patient returns to the doctor after a few weeks, stating that while he definitely feels better than he had prior to the surgery, he does not feel that he has returned to how he felt prior to getting sick. The doctor reassures him that all the tests came back with excellent results, and tells him that he is simply weak from the surgery, and that he needs to convalesce. The doctor advises the patient to travel to a location where he can relax, rest, and be rejuvenated by the clear, fresh mountain air.

Says Rav Yosef Nechemiah Kornitzer,[10] during the Yamim Noraim we underwent surgical repair of our *neshamos*, but we are still in a weakened spiritual state. The Ribbono shel Olam then tells us not to worry; our *neshamos* have been cleaned by experiencing Rosh Hashanah and Yom Kippur. Now we merely need to convalesce and breathe in the spiritual air of the *succah*.

We go into the *succah*, breathe in the *Yud Kei Vav Kei* and the Name of *Adnus*, inhale the *Shalom*, and receive the hug from Hashem — and this helps to restore us to our maximal strength — spiritually and physically.

The above parable helps further our understanding as to how the *succah* helps us achieve *arichas yamim*: Going out of the house and immersing our entire being in the *Succah* — in the Ribbono shel Olam — where we can inhale the *kedushah* and be embraced by Hashem gives us the *zechus* for *arichas yamim*.

~ Lot and the Malachim: A Lesson in Bitachon

In *Parashas Vayeira* the Torah relates the incident of the *malachim* who came to save Lot and his family. The men of the city surround Lot's house, demanding that he hand over his guests. Lot offers the mob his daughters instead, beseeching them to leave his guests alone. After all, he says, these men came to my home trusting me to protect them. הִנֵּה נָא לִי שְׁתֵּי בָנוֹת אֲשֶׁר לֹא יָדְעוּ אִישׁ אוֹצִיאָה נָּא אֶתְהֶן אֲלֵיכֶם וַעֲשׂוּ לָהֶן כַּטּוֹב בְּעֵינֵיכֶם רַק לָאֲנָשִׁים הָאֵל אַל **תַּעֲשׂוּ דָבָר כִּי עַל כֵּן בָּאוּ בְּצֵל קֹרָתִי**, *"See, now, I have two daughters who have never known a man. I shall bring them out to you and do to them as you please; but to these men do nothing, **inasmuch as they have come under the shade of my roof**"* (Bereishis 19:8). Lot told the rabble, "Since they placed their trust in me, please do not harm them at all."

The Chofetz Chaim advances an incredible idea.[11] Let's analyze what Lot is telling the people of Sodom. He offers them his two unmarried daughters, but denies them access to his two guests. His stated reason for protecting the visitors was not because of the immoral and degenerate act that the residents of Sodom wanted to perform with them. He tells the people of Sodom that his visitors should be safeguarded for the simple reason that they had put themselves under his protection, and there is a moral obligation to protect someone who comes to you and trusts in you to provide protection. I must protect them, says Lot, כִּי עַל כֵּן בָּאוּ בְּצֵל קֹרָתִי, *for that is why they came under the shade of my home.*

Says the Chofetz Chaim, this gives us an incredible insight into the mechanism of *bitachon*. We are able to say to the Ribbono shel Olam, "Whether we deserve it or not, we are coming under Your protection. We are coming under Your *Tzeil*, Your Shade." Lot understood that if someone puts himself under your protection, you are then obligated to honor that trust. How much more so if we turn to Hashem and place our trust in Him, that He will surely come through for us. If we truly have *bitachon* in Hashem, then Hashem must honor our trust and provide what we are trusting Him to provide for us, simply because we are trusting Him to do so.

When Lot went to live in Sodom, he was looking to distance himself from Hashem, as the *pasuk* says, וַיִּסַּע לוֹט מִקֶּדֶם, *and Lot traveled from Kedem* (ibid., 13:11). His *emunah* had dramatically deteriorated. Yet he still understood that if someone places their complete trust in another, then that person is obligated to provide for him.

❧ A Revolutionary Insight Into the Succah

Rav Nosson Meir Wachtfogel, the Lakewood Mashgiach, suggests a revolutionary dimension of the mitzvah of *succah*.[12] When we come under the shade of the *succah*, we are conveying an unspoken message to HaKadosh Baruch Hu. We acknowledge that we do not know the outcome of the Yamim Noraim. When we enter into the *succah*, we are saying to Hashem that since we are placing our trust in Him, we should be provided for, whether or not we deserve it. By entering the *succah*, we show that we are coming under His protection. After all, the *succah* is the *Tzeil*, the Shade, of the Ribbono shel Olam.

Lot said that he must provide for the *malachim* כִּי עַל כֵּן בָּאוּ בְּצֵל קֹרָתִי, because they came under the shade of his roof for refuge. How could he turn them down? We, too, come under the protection of Hashem when we enter the *succah*, and for that reason alone, we warrant to be protected and answered. He is now obligated to provide for us, even if we did not merit a favorable outcome on Yom Kippur.

❧ Rebbe's Yissurim Reinforces This Lesson of Bitachon

The Gemara[13] discusses the *yissurim* that Rebbe suffered at the end of his life. Rav Yehudah HaNasi endured great suffering because of an event that occurred involving a calf that was being taken to be slaughtered. The calf came to Rebbe, burying its face under his cloak and crying. Rebbe told the calf to go to be slaughtered, since that is why it was created. The Gemara tells us that since Rebbe did not show mercy toward the calf, he was subjected to *yissurim*.

Asks Rav Nosson Meir Wachtfogel: What did Rebbe do that he deserved to be punished?[14] What he said was true; animals are indeed created for people to consume. As the Gemara[15] states, "סוֹף בְּהֵמָה לִשְׁחִיטָה, *an animal is destined to be slaughtered.*" Will each and every *shochet*, then, be subjected to *yissurim*?

With the *yesod* we have introduced, Rav Wachtfogel answers that indeed it is a mitzvah to *shecht* an animal; there is nothing improper in slaughtering an animal in order to eat it. However, if an animal seeks refuge under a person's cloak, crying and pleading for its life, then one must have *rachmanus*, mercy, on the animal. It does not matter that the animal was created to be *shechted*. Because it sought your protection, trusting in you, the animal creates a moral obligation for you to provide that salvation. Therefore, Rebbe should have offered the calf protection and prevented it from being slaughtered.

◈ *Lot's Shade ... an Actual Succah*

This principle that Lot asserted to the people of Sodom has uncovered a new dimension in the mitzvah of *succah*. We put ourselves under the protection of the *succah*, under the protection of Hashem, and therefore, regardless of whether we are worthy, we should receive salvation. Regardless of what we deserve, our *bitachon* in Hashem dictates that we should receive protection.

Incredibly, Rav Chaim Kanievsky[16] writes, based on *Tosafos*,[17] that the day that Avraham invited the *malachim* to sit under the tree was Succos. In that case, the next day, when the *malachim* came to Lot in Sodom, it was also the Yom Tov of Succos. How beautiful it is that Lot was not merely articulating the principle we have applied to the mitzvah of *succah*, but when he uttered the words, כִּי עַל כֵּן בָּאוּ בְּצֵל קֹרָתִי, he was referring to an actual *succah*, articulating this principle, that the refuge of the *succah* is the refuge of those who place their trust in HaKadosh Baruch Hu.

The phrase Lot had used to declare this principle is כִּי עַל כֵּן בָּאוּ בְּצֵל קֹרָתִי, *because this is why they came under the shade of my roof.* This clearly describes the trust and faith we are placing in Hashem by sitting in the *succah*, coming under the shade of His roof. In the *succah* we enter under the *tzeil d'mihemenusa*, the Shade of Hashem.

≈ Hashem Rewards Avraham With the Mitzvah of Succah

The *Midrash*[18] teaches us that we are *zocheh* to the mitzvah of *succah* in the merit of Avraham. When the *malachim* came to visit Avraham Avinu after his *bris milah*, Avraham told them, וְהִשָּׁעֲנוּ תַּחַת הָעֵץ, *recline beneath the tree* (*Bereishis* 18:4). Hashem told Avraham, "You told them to rest under the tree; I swear that I will repay you. In the *Midbar* I will envelop the Bnei Yisrael in the *Ananei HaKavod*, and in Eretz Yisrael I will give them the mitzvah of *succah*: בַּסֻּכֹּת תֵּשְׁבוּ שִׁבְעַת יָמִים, *You shall dwell in succos for a seven-day period* (*Vayikra* 23:42). When Mashiach comes, I will continue to repay you. וְסֻכָּה תִּהְיֶה לְצֵל יוֹמָם, *And there will be a succah (tabernacle) as a shade from heat in the daytime ...* (*Yeshayahu* 4:6).

Thus, the mitzvah is a reward for Avraham having told the *malachim* to rest and sit under the tree. But what is the connection? Why would Avraham's act of offering them to sit under a tree be rewarded with the mitzvah of *succah*? Why is one a reward for the other?

As we mentioned above from Rav Chaim Kanievsky, the very day that the *malachim* came to visit Avraham was on Succos itself. However, asks Rav Chaim, if it was Succos, why was Avraham sitting at the *pesach ha'ohel*, at the opening of the tent, and not in the *succah*? Rav Chaim answers that it was *k'chom hayom*; the day was exceptionally hot, and as a *mitzta'er*, one who is in pain, Avraham was exempt from *succah*! Rav Chaim offers another explanation: Avraham had moved closer to the open door because it was cooler there.

We know that Avraham Avinu kept the entire Torah. Therefore, explains Rav Chaim, when he invited the *malachim* to rest under the tree, he must have been referring to a tree that had been detached from the ground, and was therefore kosher as *schach*.

The above lends an explanation as to why Hashem rewarded Avraham's hospitality with the mitzvah of *succah*. Avraham Avinu invited the *malachim* to sit and rest under the shade of his *succah*, which he referred to as an *eitz*, a tree. Since he invited them to sit in his *succah*, Hashem repaid him in kind by giving his descendants the mitzvah of *succah*.

❧ *The Reward for Gemillas Chessed*

The *Yalkut Shimoni*[19] writes that the *koach*, the strength, of those who are *gomlei chessed* is very great. The reward for one who engages in *gemillas chassadim* is that he will earn the ultimate place of refuge when he passes away. His final resting place will not be in the shade of the orb of the Earth, it will not be in the shade of the sun, and it will not be in the shade of the angels or the animals. His final resting place will be in the shade of HaKadosh Baruch Hu.

The reward for doing *chessed* is protection under the shade of the Ribbono shel Olam Himself!

Rav Boruch Simon[20] beautifully applies this idea of the *midrash* to explain why the reward for Avraham Avinu was that his descendants received the mitzvah of *succah*. Avraham Avinu was performing *chessed* for the *malachim*, and, in fact, he was the ultimate *gomel chessed*. Therefore, his reward was that his descendants would receive the protection of the Shade of Hashem, in the form of the *succah*. This is the perfect reward, as the *Yalkut Shimoni* taught us that the reward for *chessed* is basking in the shade of Hashem.

As mentioned, when Lot said, כִּי עַל כֵּן בָּאוּ בְּצֵל קֹרָתִי, he was referring to his *succah*; that is why he argued that his guests warranted to be protected. Thus, a profound dimension of *succah* is that we beseech Hashem: We don't yet know what the outcome of our *din* on Rosh Hashanah and Yom Kippur will be. But it should not matter. Lot told the people of Sodom that the *malachim* came into his home for protection, and he is therefore morally obligated to protect them. So, too, do we come under the *Tzeil*, the Shade, of Hashem, expecting and believing that He will protect us, and He has the same moral obligation to do so. Hashem, we place our trust in You, and therefore, as we are surrounded in the *succah* by two of the Names of Hashem, may we be *zocheh* to the blessing of a long life, sitting in the *succah* for many years to come.

ENDNOTES

1. חשק שלמה סוף מסכת סוכה.
2. דבש לפי - מערכת ס׳ אות כז.
3. מלבי״ם נח:ו:טו.
4. רש״י בשלח יז, טז.
5. עוקצין ג, יב.
6. המאור הגדול - תהלים עמוד תס״ד.
7. כמוצא שלל רב סוכות עמוד קא.
8. סוכה ב, א.
9. הובא במבקשי תורה כרך ג׳ עמוד תמב.
10. דרשות רבינו יוסף נחמיה עמוד צז.
11. חפץ חיים על התורה פרשת וירא

פרק יט פסוק ח, זכור למרים פרק ה׳.
12. לקט רשימות (לייקווד תשסג) עמוד קמא.
13. בבא מציעא פה, א.
14. לקט רשימות (לייקווד תשסג) עמוד קמא.
15. ברכות יז, א.
16. טעמא דקרא וירא.
17. ראש השנה יא, א.
18. בראשית רבה מח:י.
19. ילקוט שמעוני רות אות תכב.
20. אמרי ברוך, וירא עמוד עט.

The Great Gift of Yom Tov: Beholding the Countenance of Hashem

≈ The Torah Reading of Shabbos Chol HaMoed

The Torah reading for Shabbos Chol HaMoed is taken from the end of *Parashas Ki Sisa*. This selection is most appropriate for Yom Tov, as this *leining* concludes with a brief discussion of the *Shalosh Regalim*. It culminates with the verse that captures the majestic experience of the three Festivals: שָׁלֹשׁ פְּעָמִים בַּשָּׁנָה יֵרָאֶה כָּל זְכוּרְךָ אֶת פְּנֵי הָאָדֹן ה' אֱלֹקֵי יִשְׂרָאֵל, *Three times a year all your males shall appear before the Lord Hashem, the God of Yisrael* (*Shemos* 34:23).

≈ Did the Reading Start Too Early?

What is curious, though, is the starting point of this Torah reading. The *leining* begins all the way back at *shlishi* in *Parashas Ki Sisa*, in *Shemos* 33:12.

There we read about a stirring exchange between Moshe Rabbeinu and HaKadosh Baruch Hu. Moshe fervently requests to experience and behold the Glory of Hashem. Hashem does not concede to his request, on the grounds that no mortal can see

His face and live. While this is certainly an important exchange, it seems completely unrelated to Yom Tov.

Although halachah dictates that on Shabbos we read a minimum of twenty-one *pesukim*, this could easily be fulfilled by beginning the reading from *chamishi*. We could start at *Shemos* 34:1, which reads, וַיֹּאמֶר ה' אֶל מֹשֶׁה פְּסָל לְךָ שְׁנֵי לֻחֹת אֲבָנִים, *Hashem said to Moshe, "Carve for yourself two stone tablets,"* and continue until the conclusion of the *parashah*. We would then have read twenty-six verses, generously fulfilling the halachic quota.

Why begin with *pesukim* that do not seem relevant to the theme of the *Shalosh Regalim*?

❧ The Soul of Yom Tov

וַה' הֵאִיר עֵינִי, *And Hashem illuminated my eyes*; thus I saw that herein lies the soul of the *Shalosh Regalim*. Moshe Rabbeinu was given a *besurah tovah*, a good tiding that gladdened his soul in the most profound way.

Earlier, Hashem had told Moshe that due to the sin of the Golden Calf, Hashem would no longer guide the Jewish people personally and intimately. Rather, He would send an angel to lead Klal Yisrael. Hashem now informed Moshe that He had reconsidered, as it were. He relented and would not be sending an angel to lead the Jewish people. Instead, Hashem said, פָּנַי יֵלֵכוּ וַהֲנִחֹתִי לָךְ, *My Presence will go and provide you rest* (ibid., 33:14). Moshe confirms this, saying, אִם אֵין פָּנֶיךָ הֹלְכִים אַל תַּעֲלֵנוּ מִזֶּה, *If Your Presence does not go along, do not bring us forward from here* (ibid. v. 15).

Moshe is now bolstered by Hashem's renewed commitment to personally remain close to and guide Bnei Yisrael. He then asks Hashem from the depths of his being, הַרְאֵנִי נָא אֶת כְּבֹדֶךָ, *"Show me now Your glory"* (ibid., v. 18). Hashem refuses: וַיֹּאמֶר לֹא תוּכַל לִרְאֹת אֶת פָּנָי כִּי לֹא יִרְאַנִי הָאָדָם וָחָי, *He said, "You will not be able to see My face, for no human can see Me and live"* (ibid., v. 20). Moshe wanted to experience and behold the *Pnei HaShechinah*, and Hashem said that this was not possible.

But then a concession was made. Hashem said to Moshe, וְרָאִיתָ אֶת אֲחֹרָי וּפָנַי לֹא יֵרָאוּ, *"...and you will see My back, but My face cannot be seen"* (ibid., v. 23).

What follows is my own interpretation. I am led to believe that this was not the only concession that Hashem made to Moshe. Moshe had saved the lives of the Jewish people through his prayer when Hashem had wanted to destroy us after the *Chet HaEigel*. Moshe had successfully beseeched Hashem to lead us personally instead of sending a *malach* in His stead. Moshe had earned the right to see the back of Hashem, which, *Chazal* reveal to us, refers to the knot of the back of Hashem's *tefillin shel rosh*.

I cannot help but think that this request of Moshe, הַרְאֵנִי נָא אֶת כְּבֹדֶךָ, which appears at the beginning of the reading of Shabbos Chol HaMoed, earned him one more concession from Hashem.

❧ Yom Tov Itself Is the Concession

Hashem tells Moshe that if he really wants to experience *Pnei Hashem*, the face of Hashem, if he really has such a strong desire to experience the full Glory of beholding the Divine, if he has such a longing to see His face, so to speak, then there is a way.

Says Hashem, as noted above, שָׁלֹשׁ פְּעָמִים בַּשָּׁנָה יֵרָאֶה כָּל זְכוּרְךָ אֶת פְּנֵי הָאָדֹן ה׳ אֱלֹקֵי יִשְׂרָאֵל, *Three times a year, all your males shall appear before the Lord Hashem, the God of Yisrael* (ibid., 34:23).

The gift of Yom Tov was Hashem acceding to Moshe Rabbeinu's request, "Show me Your Glory." While no person can see the face of Hashem, the experience of Yom Tov is, in some semblance, an experience of a Divine encounter, and is the closest we can come to beholding the *Pnei HaShechinah*.

Thus, the beginning of the Torah reading is critical to the theme of the *Shalosh Regalim*, as we begin by reading the heart-rending pleas of Moshe to experience the *Pnei HaShechinah*, and we conclude with the acquiescence of Hashem, in the form of the gift of Yom Tov.

HOSHANA RABBAH

Mysterious Shadows — Contemporary Responsibility

◦ *The Uniqueness of #21*

The *Mateh Moshe*,[1] a *talmud muvhak* of the Maharshal, quotes a *midrash* that relates that Hashem told Avraham Avinu, "I am unique, and you are unique. I will therefore give your children a day that is unique in its ability to provide atonement for their sins. This day is Hoshana Rabbah.

"I am unique," said Hashem, "as My Name *Aleph Hei Yud Hei* is numerically equal to 21. You, Avraham Avinu, are unique, as you are the twenty-first generation from the Creation of the world.* I am 21, and you are generation 21. I will give your children the 21st day of the year as a special day of atonement. It will be a unique day on the calendar."

This *midrash* implies a special connection between Avraham Avinu and Hoshana Rabbah. Let us explore this connection.

---

* There were ten generations from Adam to Noach, and another ten generations from Noach until Avraham. Avraham was therefore the twenty-first generation.

≈ Three Days of Atonement Correspond to the Three Avos

Another illustration of the connection between Hoshana Rabbah and Avraham is offered by the *Megaleh Amukos,* who presents an incredible idea,[2] stating that Rosh Hashanah, Yom Kippur, and Hoshana Rabbah, the three *Yemei Hadin,* Days of Judgment, correspond to the three *Avos.* Yitzchak Avinu represents *middas hadin,* and therefore corresponds to Rosh Hashanah. Yom Kippur is *Yom HaNora,* the awesome day, corresponding to Yaakov Avinu, who said, "מַה נּוֹרָא הַמָּקוֹם הַזֶּה, *How awesome is this place!*" (*Bereishis* 28:17)." Hoshana Rabbah corresponds to Avraham Avinu, since he is the twenty-first generation from the Creation of the world, and Hoshana Rabbah is the twenty-first day of the year.

Again, we see that Hoshana Rabbah is the day designated for Avraham. Let us try to uncover the depth of this association.

≈ The Arba Minim: Symbolic of the Four Types of Jews

The *Midrash*[3] says that the *Arbah Minim* that we use on Succos correspond to four different types of Jews. Some Jews learn Torah and do mitzvos. They are like the *esrog,* which has a pleasant scent and also tastes good. These Jews have Torah and *maasim tovim,* good deeds, to their credit, and they therefore "smell and taste" good. Some Jews do participate in learning Torah, but they do not do other mitzvos to accompany their Torah learning. Like the *lulav,* these Jews taste good but do not emit a fragrant aroma. Other Jews have mitzvos and *maasim tovim,* but they do not engage in learning Torah. These people are sweet-smelling but do not taste good, like the *hadassim.* Finally, there are those who have neither Torah nor *maasim tovim.* Like the *aravah,* these people have neither a fragrant aroma nor a delectable taste. On Succos we bring all four *minim* together; by bringing them together, the three species that have taste and/or aroma will help achieve atonement for the *aravah* that has neither.

∞ *Why Use the Aravah for Hoshanos?*

Based on this *midrash*, if we would have to choose one of the *Arba Minim* to use on its own as we *daven* to Hashem on Hoshana Rabbah, it would seem logical to take the *esrog*, which has both fragrance and taste. Perhaps there would be a *Yom Esrog*, holding an *esrog* aloft, showing Hashem a symbol of a Jew who has Torah and *maasim tovim*. Or, at the very least, we might choose one of the species that symbolizes a Jew who has either Torah or *maasim tovim*.

Of all the items to hold individually on Hoshana Rabbah, why do we choose the *aravah*, which has no aroma or taste and is symbolic of the Jew who has neither mitzvos nor Torah learning?[4] Why do we have a Yom HaAravah, the term the *Rishonim* used to refer to Hoshana Rabbah?

∞ *The Angels Came to Avraham on Succos*

To answer this difficult question, let us turn to the Gemara in *Meseches Rosh Hashanah*[5] that discusses the episode of the *malachim* who came to visit Avraham Avinu after his *bris milah*. *Tosafos*, according to the *Pnei Yehoshua*, explain that according to the Gemara these *malachim* visited Avraham on Succos. In fact, Rav Chaim Kanievsky[6] writes that the *eitz*, tree, mentioned in the *pasuk* וְהִשָּׁעֲנוּ תַּחַת הָעֵץ, *and recline beneath the tree* (*Bereishis* 18:4), was a tree that had been cut down and was being used as *schach* for the *succah*. [Avraham Avinu was sitting at the entrance, rather than inside the *succah*, because it was very hot, and a *mitzta'er*, one who is in pain, is exempt from the mitzvah of *succah*.]

∞ *Avraham Was Rewarded With the Mitzvah of Succos*

Avraham Avinu brought the guests into his home. The *Midrash*[7] tells us that Hashem told him that as a reward for his hospitality he would receive three rewards. The first reward would be the *Ananei HaKavod*, the Clouds of Glory, that would protect the Bnei Yisrael in the *Midbar*; the second reward, the mitzvah of *succah*; and the third reward, the great *succah* of *L'asid Lavo*, when Mashiach will come.

There must be some form of *middah kneged middah*, measure for measure, between Avraham hosting the *malachim* and the rewards he received. What is the connection between Avraham Avinu hosting his guests and the mitzvah of *succah*?

℘ *It's All in the Shadow*

The Gemara[8] teaches that there is a mystical means whereby a person can ascertain if he is going to survive the year. He should go into a dark house, and, if he can see the shadow of his shadow there, then he will live out the year. However, if the shadow does not have a shadow, then he will not survive the year. The Gemara does not advise doing this, since someone who does so may be frightened, which can be detrimental to one's *mazel*.

The *Rishonim* explain that this Gemara is referring to a specific night of the year.

At the incident of the *Meraglim*, Spies, the Torah states, 'אַךְ בַּה אַל תִּמְרֹדוּ וְאַתֶּם אַל תִּירְאוּ אֶת עַם הָאָרֶץ כִּי לַחְמֵנוּ הֵם סָר מֵעֲלֵיהֶם וַה' אִתָּנוּ אַל תִּירָאֻם, *But do not rebel against Hashem! You should not fear the people of the Land, for they are our bread. Their shadow [protection] has departed from them; Hashem is with us. Do not fear them!* (*Bamidbar* 14:9). Moshe Rabbeinu told the *Meraglim* not to be afraid but also not to rebel against Hashem. He tells them not to worry about the Canaanites because צִלָּם, *their [the Canaanites] shadow*, is gone, and Hashem is with us.

They don't have a shadow, and therefore there is no reason to fear them. The Ramban[9] explains that this *pasuk* refers to the night of Hoshana Rabbah, and this verse alludes to the tradition that one who is outside on that night and does not see the shadow of his shadow in the street will not survive the year.

Rabbeinu Bachya,[10] a *talmid* of the Ramban, writes that he heard from his rebbi, the Ramban, that on Hoshana Rabbah a person must see a shadow of his shadow in order to be included among those who will survive the year. He offers an explanation as to why this is so:

There are many celestial beings, with the sun being the most powerful. The sun even tries to show that it is dominant over human beings. When the sun beats down on us and we can block its rays, preventing them from reaching the ground, we demonstrate that we too are dominant entities. Therefore, the presence of a shadow is testament to our being a dominant force in the world. It shows that we have a significant presence, as we can prevent the sun's rays from reaching where they would otherwise go. However, if one's shadow is absent and the sun can shine unhindered, then this is a sign that the person does not exist. He is not an entity capable of blocking the rays of the sun.

The night of Hoshana Rabbah is when Hashem determines the outcomes for the coming year. If at that critical time a person is able to exhibit a shadow and block the light of the sun or the moon, he demonstrates that he is an entity, and he will survive the year. However, if a person does not have a shadow at this crucial juncture, then it is an omen that he does not have significance and that he is not a physical entity capable of blocking the light. This is indicative of a person unable to survive the year.

The *Avudraham*[11] relates an ancient custom that existed on the night of Hoshana Rabbah. People would dress in linen garments, go out into the field, undress, and extend their arms and hands. The digits of their right hand represented their sons, and the digits of their left hand represented their daughters. They would then analyze the shadows cast by the moonlight. The quality of the shadows of each appendage was then interpreted as to how the year would progress for the person represented by each shadow.

The *Rama*[12] also discusses this concept. He writes that in the shadows of the moon on the night of Hoshana Rabbah there are signs as to what will happen during the upcoming year for a person and his loved ones. However, some commentators say that one should not be particular about this, since it will lead to anxiety. Better to not pay attention to the shadows. תָּמִים תִּהְיֶה עִם ה' אֱלֹקֶיךָ, *You shall be wholehearted with Hashem, your God* (*Devarim* 18:13), and don't worry about the future, trusting that Hashem will take care of you.

Let us try to discover the deeper symbolism of "analyzing the shadows" and why seeing one's shadow on Hoshana Rabbah is of any significance.

≈ *Succah: A Reward for Avraham Avinu*

When Avraham Avinu brought his guests into his home, Hashem told him that as a reward he would receive the mitzvah of *succah*. Why is the mitzvah of *succah* a reward for *hachnasas orchim*, hospitality?

When the *malachim* arrived in the guise of nomads, Avraham thought that they were in fact Arabs who were idol worshipers. He would host his guests "*tachas kanfei HaShechinah*, under the wings of the *Shechinah*." Hashem said to him, "You are bringing the guests under the wings of the *Shechinah*; I will repay you with a gift: the *succah*." The *succah* is the shade of HaKadosh Baruch Hu, it is the shade of *emunah: tzila d'mhemenusa*.* For an entire week the Jewish people will have the tremendous *zechus* to sit in the *succah*, under the wings of the *Shechinah*. Thus, the mitzvah of *succah* is *middah kneged middah*, measure for measure. Avraham brought the unaffiliated under the wings of the *Shechinah*, and therefore he received the mitzvah of *succah*, during which we, his descendants, have the *zechus* of sitting under the protective wings of the *Shechinah*.

≈ *A Fundamental Principle*

Let us contrast how the Torah introduces Avraham Avinu with how the Torah introduces Noach.

Hashem told Noach to go into the *Teivah*, since He was

_____

* See "The *Succah*: Breathe the Air — Live Long," page 333, for an extensive discussion of this concept.

planning to bring the *Mabul*, the Flood. But before Hashem even spoke to Noach, the Torah gives us extensive background information as to who Noach was. The Torah states, וְנֹחַ מָצָא חֵן בְּעֵינֵי ה', *And Noach found grace in the eyes of Hashem* (*Bereishis* 6:8). The Torah continues, נֹחַ אִישׁ צַדִּיק תָּמִים הָיָה בְּדֹרֹתָיו אֶת הָאֱלֹקִים הִתְהַלֶּךְ נֹחַ., *Noach was a righteous man, perfect in his generations; Noach walked with Hashem* (*Bereishis* 6:9).

However, the Torah introduces Avraham without any accolades or anything complimentary at all. Seemingly out of nowhere, the first thing Hashem tells Avraham Avinu is "*Lech lecha,*" go to Eretz Yisrael (see *Bereishis* Ch. 12). Who is Avraham Avinu? His name is mentioned at the end of *Parashas Noach*, included in a listing with many others. However, the Torah does not relate any biographical or complimentary information about Avraham prior to Hashem speaking with him.

Avraham had no shortage of positive character traits. Avraham was the greatest *mekarev rechokim*, spreading the Name of Hashem to the masses. He was the consummate *baal chessed*. Yet the Torah is silent, telling us nothing about Avraham Avinu. A simple, "וַיֹּאמֶר ה' אֶל אַבְרָם, and Hashem said to Avraham," is how he is introduced to us.

This is a sharp contrast to how the Torah introduces Noach. Why?[13]

❧ *Unconditional Love*

The Maharal teaches one of the most fundamental principles of the entire Torah.[14]. In *Pirkei Avos*[15] we are taught, כָּל אַהֲבָה שֶׁהִיא תְלוּיָה בְדָבָר, בָּטֵל דָּבָר, בְּטֵלָה אַהֲבָה, Any love that is dependent on an external factor will dissipate when that factor is no longer present. For example, if one loves another person because of his appearance, wealth, or actions, then if these were no longer to be present, the love would cease to exist. This type of love is dependent on something that may only be temporary, and when that factor is no longer in play, the love falls away. However, וְשֶׁאֵינָהּ תְּלוּיָה בְדָבָר, אֵינָהּ בְּטֵלָה לְעוֹלָם, a love that is unconditional and independent of any external item will endure.

There is a fundamental difference between Noach and Avraham. Noach was an individual and when Hashem selected him, He selected only him. When Hashem spoke to Noach, He spoke to him and to him alone. Therefore, the Torah tells us why Hashem chose to speak to him: It is because Noach was a *tzaddik* and was worthy of having Hashem speak to him.

When Hashem spoke to Avraham, however, He was not merely choosing one man. He was choosing the entirety of Klal Yisrael. Hashem was choosing and including all of Avraham's descendants until the end of time.

Had the Torah written that Hashem spoke to Avraham because he jumped into the fire at Ur Kasdim or because he was *mekarev* people to serve Hashem or because he was a terrific host, we would have thought that the reason Hashem loves Avraham Avinu — and by extension why Hashem loves Avraham's descendants — is because of that attribute. This would render Hashem's love for Klal Yisrael conditional. It would be an אַהֲבָה שֶׁהִיא תְּלוּיָה בְדָבָר! What would then happen when we, as a nation, did not live up to the examples set for us by Avraham? If we ever ceased to maintain Avraham's attributes, then Hashem's love for us would cease!

Therefore, at this critical juncture in Jewish history, the Torah tells us that Hashem simply spoke to Avraham. Why? Just because. No special reason. The love Hashem has for us cannot be attributed to an external factor that could potentially cease to exist.

The inherent love that Hashem has for us is unparalleled, for no special reason. We are His children, and that is reason enough. A parent does not need a reason to love his child. He doesn't love him because he is cute or helpful around the house, but rather simply because he is his child. This is the kind of love Hashem has for us. Because we are His children, He loves us.

Where do we see that Hashem selected us to be His children, whom He loves unconditionally? It was when He instructed Avraham Avinu, *"Lech lecha."* He instructed Avraham to go, not because he was a *tzaddik*, not because he did *chessed*, and not because he was *mekarev* people. Avraham was all these and more, but that was not why Hashem loved him! This is not why Hashem spoke to him. Hashem's love for Avraham was not dependent on anything. Hashem loved him for no specific reason other than the fact that he was a child of HaKadosh Baruch Hu.

The Maharal says that this provides immutable hope in our generation. No Jew should ever think that he has sinned and conducted himself in a manner so that he is no longer eligible for Hashem's love. No one should ever think that Hashem would love him only if he learns and *davens* well, or if he engages in *maasim tovim*. Hashem's love for each and every Jew is independent of any external reason. There is therefore nothing that a Jew can do that would cause him to forfeit his eligibility for Hashem's love.

∾ Understanding Why We Take the Aravah

This is why we use the *aravah*, which is lacking in taste and smell, as it represents the person who does not have *maasim tovim* or Torah on his side. Says the *Shem MiShmuel*,[16] we wave the *aravah* and even place it on top of the *Aron Kodesh* to demonstrate to one and all that Hashem's love for us does not falter with our actions, as it is independent of what we do or what we don't do. We show that Hashem does not love us because we learn Torah or do *maasim tovim*. Rather, Hashem loves us merely because we are His children. By using the *aravah* we publicize the intrinsic value of being a Jew, regardless of action or conduct.

∾ Hoshana Rabbah vs. Yom Kippur

Yom HaAravah has a dimension that is greater even than Yom Kippur. On Yom Kippur, if we are worthy, then we can have a good outcome. If not, we won't. It depends on our actions. If we are an *esrog*, with Torah and *maasim tovim*, then we can have a *kapparah*. Even the *hadas* and the *lulav* have one redeeming attribute (either Torah or *maasim tovim*). But the *aravah* (i.e., the person who is bereft of Torah and of *maasim tovim*) has nothing going for it. It has no chance of *kapparah* on Yom Kippur. Yom Kippur is *middas hadin*, the attribute of strict justice, and the *aravah* does not stand a chance.

Hoshana Rabbah is different. The Gemara[17] gives us some insight as to what a person can achieve and the levels one can attain on Hoshana Rabbah. The mitzvah of the *Arba Minim* is הוּדְחָה, *set aside*, on Shabbos on the first day of Succos, yet the *aravah* on Hoshana Rabbah is taken even on Shabbos. The Sadducees did not accept that *aravah* is דּוֹחָה Shabbos. One year, Hoshana Rabbah fell out on Shabbos. People brought their *aravos* to the Beis HaMikdash and placed them in the *Azarah*, Courtyard. The Sadducees took the *aravos* and hid them under stones. The *amei haaretz*, unlearned people, found the *aravos* and gave them to the Kohanim, who took the *aravos*, stood them against the *Mizbei'ach*, and publicized that Yom Aravah is דּוֹחֶה Shabbos.

Who was it who saved the day on Hoshana Rabbah? Says the *Shem MiShmuel*, it was the *amei haaretz*, the unlearned people. It was not the *tzaddikim*, not the *talmidei chachamim*. Rather, it was the unlearned who rescued the *avodah* of the *aravah* on Hoshana Rabbah. The people in Klal Yisrael who are most similar to the *aravah* — lacking Torah and *maasim tovim* — were the ones who rescued the mitzvah of *aravah*.

On Hoshana Rabbah, the emphasis is not on *limud haTorah*. It is not on *maasim tovim*. An *esrog*, *hadas*, or *lulav* are not required. While we definitely strive to achieve these, they are not critical elements in earning Hashem's love. What we do need is the appreciation of the intrinsic value of being a child of HaKadosh Baruch Hu. We wave the *aravah*, as if to tell the Ribbono shel Olam that we know that all we need to do is wave the identity card that declares us to be Jews. Even if we are lacking Torah and *maasim tovim*, this is enough to allow us to benefit from and bask in Hashem's unconditional love. Even without Torah and *maasim tovim*, we are still eligible for Hashem's unconditional love. This is the power of Hoshana Rabbah. This is the message of the *aravah*.

☙ *The Otzar Chinam*

A *midrash*[18] relates that Hashem showed Moshe Rabbeinu Gan Eden and all the various storehouses in *Shamayim*. Hashem showed Moshe where the *s'char*, reward, for *tzaddikim* is stored until they pass away. As Moshe was taken from place to place, he asked Hashem about the purpose of each storehouse. Hashem explained: This one was for rewarding those who do mitzvos. That one is reserved to reward those who take care of orphans.

Eventually they came to a particularly large *otzar*, treasure house. Moshe asked whose reward was contained in this exceptionally large facility. Hashem told him that if one does mitzvos, then he will receive his *s'char* from a particular *otzar*. But people who do not do mitzvos do not have any *s'char* owed to them. Instead, they receive a share of the contents of this big *otzar*. This is known as the *otzar* of *matnas chinam*, unwarranted gifts, rather than rewards. The largest *otzar* in Heaven provides free gifts to people who did not earn their own reward.

What does someone have to do in order to be able to receive a free gift from this storehouse? How does one qualify? We all try to do mitzvos, learn Torah, do *maasim tovim*, and be able to one day receive our just reward. Who is *zocheh* to receive *matnas chinam* from the Ribbono shel Olam?

The *Shem MiShmuel*[19] explains that the free gifts contained in this large *otzar* are presented to people who appreciate the intrinsic value of being a Jew. If someone feels that he is a child of HaKadosh Baruch Hu, and that Hashem loves him unconditionally — just because he is a Jew — then that person is *zocheh* to a gift from the *otzar matnas chinam*.

This is the power of Hoshana Rabbah — the Yom HaAravah! We are loved by Hashem merely because we are His children. The *aravah* has no scent and no taste. Yet, some people have the custom to take the used *aravah*, on Hoshana Rabbah, and place it on top of the Aron Kodesh. This sends a very clear message. A person might have no Torah, no mitzvos, no *maasim tovim*, and be completely ineligible for any true reward. However, if he believes that he is deserving simply because he is Hashem's child, and he does not have to do anything to earn Hashem's love, then he will be eligible to earn a gift from the *otzar matnas chinam*. He is elevated higher than the Aron Kodesh. This is the highest level — the point at which we realize the intrinsic value that is inherent in every Jew, who are all considered *banim laMakom*.

In this sense, Hoshana Rabbah is even greater than Yom Kippur.[20] To receive a favorable *din* on Yom Kippur, one must be an *esrog*. Not so with Hoshana Rabbah. On Hoshana Rabbah even the *aravah* can be forgiven. On Hoshana Rabbah, it is enough for one to feel and appreciate the intrinsic value of being a Yehudi.

✑ *The Message of the Shadows*

We learned earlier that on the night of Hoshana Rabbah the way to determine how a person's year is going to progress is to analyze his shadow. Does this mean that we must have a shadow to be ensured a good *din* and a good year?

On Hoshana Rabbah, Hashem looks at each of us to see if He can give us gifts from the *otzar matnas chinam*. Hashem wants to see how much we appreciate the intrinsic value of being a Jew. Is that important to us? Do we regard that highly? Do we understand that the greatest success and source of happiness in the world is being a child of HaKadosh Baruch Hu?

What is the barometer that measures our level of appreciation of our intrinsic value as Jews? The barometer is "Do you have a shadow?" Every Jew has his own personal obligations. We have halachos we must follow, a *Shulchan Aruch* to instruct us in what we must do on a daily basis. We must perform all the mitzvos, and we all must be punctilious in halachah *k'chut hasaarah*, to a hairsbreadth. But to what degree do we value a Jew who does not do any of these things? How much intrinsic value do we give a Jew? After all, this is how Hashem bases the *din* of Hoshana Rabbah.

We look at what degree our sphere of influence has on other Jews. Do we have a shadow — do we exhibit influence on other Jews? Are we interested in the spiritual welfare of another Jew? That person may be very far from Hashem, and he may not have any Torah or *maasim tovim*. He may not have any obvious redeeming qualities as a Jew, but if we are still interested in him, then Hashem sees that we are *machshiv* a Jew simply because he is a Jew. Then we demonstrate an appreciation for the intrinsic value of a Jew. We understand and value what it means to be *banim laMakom*, children of Hashem, even without Torah and mitzvos. This is what the shadow represents: our influence that extends beyond ourselves, spreading to those who have no more going for them other than their identity as a Jew.

The *Yom HaAravah*, the Day of the Willow, is the day of *"ein bo Torah, v'ein bo maasim tovim."* On this day, the determining factor is how much one reaches out to other Jews. How much interest does one show in the spiritual growth of another Jew? Going to a *shiur*? Great — but do you invite along someone who may not have otherwise gone on his own to come along? Do you invite people for Shabbos or Yom Tov? Do you *daven* in a way that will inspire others to also *daven* well? If the answer is yes, then Hashem sees that you not only appreciate Torah and *maasim tovim*, but that you also value each Jew for the intrinsic value he has as one of the *banim laMakom*.

On the night of Hoshana Rabbah, Hashem looks to see if we have a *tzeil*, a shadow. Do we exert influence on those around us to serve Hashem better?

❧ *Hoshana Rabbah: Kneged Avraham Avinu*

This can help us understand the *Mateh Moshe's* teaching that Hoshana Rabbah is *kneged* Avraham Avinu. The *Mateh Moshe* cites the *midrash* that Hashem said to Avraham, "I am unique, you are unique; I will give you the most unique day of the year."

Avraham Avinu was the greatest *mekarev rechokim* of all time because he recognized that each Jew is intrinsically valuable as a child of Hashem, and his actions (or lack thereof) do not affect the inherent love Hashem as a Father has for him.

Avraham recognized this all-important concept: He truly felt that the value of each Jew is intrinsic, regardless of his actions. He truly believed that Hashem has an unconditional and inherent love for every Jew and that there was no Jew so far removed from the Ribbono shel Olam that he could not be taught Torah. Each Jew could be influenced to move from being an *aravah*, growing into a *hadas* or a *lulav*, and eventually into an *esrog*. This is exactly why Hashem chose Avraham; he did not need to ascribe any praise or accolade for Avraham's achievements, as alluded to by the manner in which Hashem spoke to Avraham. There is no introduction to Avraham, no biographical information is provided. וַיֹּאמֶר ה׳ אֶל אַבְרָם; simply calling him by name was enough, as God's love for him was inherent and intrinsic.

The Gemara[21] states that there are seven heavens: *vilon, rakiya, shechakim*, etc. The highest heaven is called *Aravos*. This highest level in *Shamayim* is the home to the storehouse of *matnas chinam*. The way to access this *otzar* is to truly feel the intrinsic value in every Jew, simply because they are *banim laMakom*.

This was the *koach* of Avraham Avinu. Because Avraham ascribed value to all Jews inherently, not because of their actions, he was infused with the inspiration to bring so many people *tachas kanfei haShechinah*, under the wings of Hashem's Divine Presence. Therefore, Hashem responded in kind and selected Avraham without needing a stated reason. That is why Hoshana Rabbah, the day of appreciating the intrinsic and inherent value of a Jew, is the day especially connected to Avraham Avinu.

On Hoshana Rabbah, we are able to appreciate that while we may have utilized the *Yemei Din* to obtain a good year based on the merit of our actions, on this night we are all eligible for a wonderful, sweet year just because Hashem loves us. Even if we are not deserving, we can still have a successful year full of *berachah* and *hatzlachah* by truly appreciating the intrinsic and inherent value of each and every Jew. We say to Hashem, "Look at this beautiful *aravah*, loved by You simply because he is a Jew. There is no better fortune than to be *banim laMakom*."

Going into Hoshana Rabbah knowing that "Hashem loves us *just because*" is the biggest *zechus* that we can marshal to be eligible to the treasures of the *otzar matnas chinam*. The litmus test of our conviction of this truth is based on whether we have a "shadow." Do we have a sphere of influence that encompasses other Jews? Taking interest in other Jews, even "*aravos*," Jews missing taste or aroma, without Torah or *maasim tovim*, demonstrates our appreciation of the fundamental value of the Jew. By elevating the status of the *aravah*, we can access the special *otzar matnas chinam* to which all Jews are eligible just because they are *banim laMakom*.

Going into Hoshana Rabbah with this *hashkafah* will allow each of us to merit a blessed, successful new year. Hashem truly loves each one of His children. The more we internalize this concept with conviction, the more He will allow us to share in the contents of His special reservoir of blessing to be *zocheh* to a year full of *berachah and hatzlachah*.

ENDNOTES

13. רמב"ן על התורה, לך לך יב, ב.

14. דרך חיים, מהר"ל על פרקי אבות פרק ה' פסוק י"ט.

15. פרקי אבות שם.

16. שם משמואל. הושענא רבא עמוד ר.

17. סוכה מג, ב.

18. שמות רבה מה:ו.

19. שם משמואל עמוד רא.

20. ע' קהלת יעקב דרוש ה' לרב שלמה קלוגר.

21. חגיגה יב:

1. מטה משה אות תתקנז.

2. מגלה עמוקות- ואתחנן אופן קג.

3. ויקרא רבה פרשה ל אות יב.

4. שם משמואל - הושענא רבה עמוד ר.

5. ראש השנה יא, א.

6. טעמא דקרא וירא.

7. בראשית רבה מח:י.

8. הוריות יב, א.

9. רמבן במדבר יד, ט.

10. רבינו בחיי שם.

11. אבודרהם - הושענא רבה.

12. רמ"א או"ח סימן תרס"ד סעיף א.

Nightlife and the Years of David HaMelech, According to the Zohar

❧ *Connection Between David HaMelech and Hoshana Rabbah*

As the final night of Succos,* Leil Hoshana Rabbah is the last night on which we invite the *Ushpizin*. The special guest of the night is David HaMelech. We recite, בְּמָטֵי מִינָךְ דָּוִד אוּשְׁפִּיזִי עִילָאִי דְּיַתְבֵי עִמִּי וְעִמָּךְ כָּל אוּשְׁפִּיזֵי עִילָאִי אַבְרָהָם יִצְחָק יַעֲקֹב מֹשֶׁה אַהֲרֹן וְיוֹסֵף.
If it pleases you, David, our supreme guest, I wish to sit together with you and all the heavenly guests, Avraham, Yitzchak, Yaakov, Moshe, Aharon, and Yosef.

What is the connection between Hoshana Rabbah and David HaMelech? Why is he our heavenly guest on the last day of Succos?

❧ *Why Do We Need a Second Day of Atonement?*

Rav Shlomo Kluger[1] asks: After experiencing the *Aseres Yemei Teshuvah*, culminating with Yom Kippur, why do we need

---

* The following day, Shemini Atzeres, is a רֶגֶל בִּפְנֵי עַצְמוֹ, *a separate Yom Tov.*

yet another day of *kapparah*, Hoshana Rabbah? As we know, Hoshana Rabbah is a great day of atonement, as it is referred to as the *Yom HaChosam HaGadol*, the Day of the Great Seal.[2]

Rav Kluger explains that the two days of *kapparah*, Yom Kippur and Hoshana Rabbah, parallel the two *korbanos temidim* that were brought daily in the Beis HaMikdash. The *midrash*[3] teaches that one *tamid* was brought in the morning; it was *mechapper* for *aveiros* committed during the preceding night. The second *tamid* was brought in the evening, to atone for the *aveiros* committed during that day. On Yom Kippur, we receive atonement during the day for the sins we committed over the course of the year during the daytime. If someone passes away on the night of Yom Kippur, then that Yom Kippur did not provide him with *kapparah*, because only the *day* of Yom Kippur atones.** Hoshana Rabbah, on the other hand, atones during the night, and it atones for sins committed during the night. This is why many have the custom to stay up late on the night of Hoshana Rabbah to learn Torah, many even staying up the entire night, which is not done on Yom Kippur.

This teaching can help us understand the recent momentum and attention Hoshana Rabbah has garnered in our very own times. In Biblical times, most sins were committed during the day, as darkness deterred people from many activities; thus, explains Rav Shlomo Kluger, the Torah describes Yom Kippur as the primary day to atone for one's sins. However, Hoshana Rabbah is not mentioned in the Torah as a day of atonement, since the sins it atones for, those committed during the night, were fewer in number.

Nowadays we can no longer say that most *aveiros* are committed during the daytime. Perhaps this is one factor in why there has been a renewed *chashivus* in maximizing Leil Hoshana Rabbah.

** See "The Divine Purity of the Name of Hashem That Manifests as Yom Kippur," page 235, for a detailed explanation of this concept.

⊷ Adam's Gifts (Plural) to David HaMelech

The *Yalkut Shimoni* states[4] that Hashem caused all the future generations to pass before Adam HaRishon. Adam saw that David HaMelech was fated to live for only three hours. Adam expressed shock at this short life span and asked Hashem how long he himself was supposed to live; Hashem told him that he would live one thousand years. Adam then asked Hashem if one is able to give gifts in *Shamayim*. When Hashem answered in the affirmative, Adam, with Hashem and the *malach* Mattatron, signed a contract stating that Adam was gifting seventy of his years to David HaMelech. In addition, Adam also gave David *malchus*,* royalty, and *zemiros*, the ability to sing *shirah* to Hashem.

Zayis Raanan is a commentary on the *Yalkut Shimoni* that was written by Rabbi Avraham Gambiner, the author of the *Magen Avraham*. He writes[5] that the gift of *shirah* that Adam bestowed on David was very significant. David is the only person in history who has permission to sing true *shirah* to Hashem. When we *daven*, our *tefillos* are based on those of David HaMelech and we *daven* to Hashem, *Habocher b'shirei David*, Who chooses the songs of David.

The *Zohar*[6] teaches that David was very grateful for the seventy years he received from Adam, stating כִּי שִׂמַּחְתַּנִי ה' בְּפָעֳלֶךָ בְּמַעֲשֵׂי יָדֶיךָ אֲרַנֵּן, *For You have gladdened me, Hashem, with Your deeds; at the works of Your hands I sing glad song* (Tehillim 92:5). Only one person in history was the personal handiwork of Hashem: Adam HaRishon, who was the *yetzir kapav*, fashioned by the hands, of HaKadosh Baruch Hu. David expresses the fact that Hashem made him rejoice via His handiwork, Adam, who gifted him seventy years of life.

---

* The *Zohar* says that Adam HaRishon was supposed to be king, but the monarchy was taken from him and given to David HaMelech (see זוהר ויחי דפו"י רמח).

❧ Why 1000 Years?

The *Midrash* states[7] that the silver basins in the *korbanos* of the *Nesiim* each were valued at seventy sacred *shekalim* — שִׁבְעִים שֶׁקֶל בְּשֶׁקֶל הַקֹּדֶשׁ — corresponding to the seventy years of life that Adam gifted to David. The original intent was for Adam to live forever; however, he was warned that he would die on "the day" he ate from the *Eitz HaDaas*; as the *pasuk* says, כִּי בְּיוֹם אֲכָלְךָ מִמֶּנּוּ מוֹת תָּמוּת, *for on the day you eat of it [the Eitz HaDaas], you shall surely die* (*Bereishis* 2:17). Hashem reckoned that day as what *He* considered a day in Heaven, which is one thousand human years, as the *pasuk* states, כִּי אֶלֶף שָׁנִים בְּעֵינֶיךָ כְּיוֹם אֶתְמוֹל כִּי יַעֲבֹר וְאַשְׁמוּרָה בַלָּיְלָה, *For even a thousand years in Your eyes are but a bygone yesterday, and like a watch in the night* (*Tehillim* 90:4). Interestingly, the *Midrash*[8] tells us that Hashem debated as to whether to keep this promise in human years or in Heavenly years, where one day is equivalent to 1000 years. He ultimately opted for 1000 years, and therefore Adam was able to live 930 years after giving 70 of them to David.

❧ David's Fate Altered

In the *Sefer HaLikkutim*, the *Arizal* teaches[9] that David HaMelech was destined to be a *nefel*, an unsustainable fetus, who was not expected to survive more than a few hours. Why? Why should he have been doomed to so short a life span?

The *Arizal* explains that David HaMelech was the *gilgul*, reincarnation, of Adam HaRishon. Although Hashem had told Adam that he would die on the day he would eat from the *Eitz HaDaas*, this decree was not carried out as originally stated. Instead, Hashem planned to fulfill this promise through David, who was supposed to die on the day he was born to fulfill the verse, כִּי בְּיוֹם אֲכָלְךָ מִמֶּנּוּ מוֹת תָּמוּת. Hashem then altered the decree by allowing Adam to give David seventy of his years. Subsequently, David spent the rest of his life trying to correct Adam HaRishon's sin of the *Eitz HaDaas*, which brought *misah*, death, into the world. To balance Adam's *aveirah*, David's role, as Adam's *gilgul*, was חַי וְקַיָּם, *to live and endure*. He would not sleep even *shishim nishmin*, sixty horse-breaths, since sleep is one-sixtieth of death. Various opinions interpret this statement to mean either three minutes, thirty minutes, or three hours.[10] Furthermore, David's descendant, Mashiach, will further rectify Adam's having brought *misah* to the world by accomplishing the opposite: by performing *Techiyas HaMeisim*, Revivification of the Dead.

The name אדם, *Adam*, hints at this: אדם forms the *roshei teivos* of **A**dam, **D**avid, and **M**ashiach.

The Gemara[11] states that David HaMelech knew he was destined to pass away on Shabbos. In an effort to thwart the *Malach HaMaves*, Angel of Death, David spent every Shabbos learning Torah throughout the day. He knew that the Angel could not approach him while he was learning. The *Malach HaMaves* was able to circumvent David's plan only by shaking the branches of a tree in the garden outside his window. The sound distracted David from his learning, providing the *Malach HaMaves* the opportunity to take his *neshamah*.

The *Shevilei Pinchas* points out[12] that the shaking of the leaves of the **tree** alludes to the fact that David HaMelech, a *gilgul* of Adam HaRishon, was dying at the age of seventy years because of Adam HaRishon's sin of eating from the *Eitz HaDaas*, the **tree** in Hashem's Garden.

✎ Why Seventy Years?

Why did Adam give David specifically seventy years? The *Chida*, in his commentary to the *Zohar*, *Nitzutzei Oros*, explains.[13] In *Parashas Lech Lecha*, the *Zohar*[14] writes cryptically that "David HaMelech only had seventy years, given to him by Adam HaRishon; it is entirely the secret of wisdom; everything down here is all in the secret Above."

The *Chida* explains that there are seven *sefiros*, mystical manifestations of Divine attributes: *Chessed, Gevurah, Tiferes,*

Netzach, *Hod*, *Yesod*, and *Malchus*. Avraham Avinu represents *Chessed*; Yitzchak Avinu, *Gevurah*; Yaakov Avinu, *Tiferes*; Moshe Rabbeinu, *Netzach*; Aharon HaKohen, *Hod*; Yosef, *Yesod*; and David HaMelech, *Malchus*. (Interestingly, Yosef is number 6, and the *gematria* of Yosef, 156, is six times the *gematria* of the Name of Hashem, *Yud Kei Vav Kei*.)

David HaMelech represents *Malchus*, the seventh *middah*. This final *middah* encompasses all the other *middos*. Each of the *middos* contains ten *middos* within it; thus, *Malchus* contains seventy *middos* in all. This, the *Chida* explains, is why Adam HaRishon gave David seventy years of his life.

✎ *The Gift of Years: Not Only From Adam*

In *Parashas Vayishlach*, however, the *Zohar* writes[15] that David's seventy years came from an entirely different source. The *Avos HaKedoshim* gave a number of their years to David HaMelech. Avraham Avinu, Yaakov Avinu, and Yosef all gave some of their years to David HaMelech.* Yitzchak is the exception; he did not give any of his years to David HaMelech because Yitzchak and David both come from the same kabbalistic root.

The *Zohar* explains that Avraham Avinu gave David HaMelech five years. Avraham had been destined to live for 180 years, and he gave 5 years to David, reducing his own life span to 175. Yaakov was meant to live as long as Avraham, but he passed away after 147 years. He donated 28 years to David HaMelech; thus, a total of 33 years were given to David by Avraham and Yaakov.

---

* Yosef is considered an *av* and also one of the sons. As the *pasuk* says, בְּנֵי-יַעֲקֹב וְיוֹסֵף סֶלָה, *the sons of Yaakov and Yosef, Selah* (*Tehillim* 77:16). This is also why Yosef is mentioned at the end of *Parashas Vayechi*: וַיָּמָת יוֹסֵף, *And Yosef died* (*Bereishis* 50:26), and again in *Shemos* 1:6: וַיָּמָת יוֹסֵף וְכָל אֶחָיו וְכֹל הַדּוֹר הַהוּא, *Yosef died, and all his brothers and that entire generation.* Yosef is in *Sefer Bereishis*, the *Sefer HaAvos*, and also in *Sefer Shemos*, the *Sefer HaBanim*, since he was classified as both. See פחד יצחק פסח מאמר מט.

Yosef HaTzaddik lived for 110 years, instead of the 147 that he would have expected as that is the number of years that his father lived. This is because Yosef donated 37 years to David. This brings the total number of years donated by Avraham, Yaakov, and Yosef to seventy. This is why David lived for seventy years. Therefore, says the *Zohar*, although David was not supposed to live at all, he lived only because of the years he received from Avraham, Yaakov, and Yosef.

The *Zohar* then explains why Yosef was the most generous donor to David. Yosef is unique because the *Navi* Amos refers to him as a *tzaddik. The pasuk says,* עַל מִכְרָם בַּכֶּסֶף צַדִּיק, *for their selling a righteous man [Yosef] for money (Amos 2:6). As a *tzaddik,* Yosef donated many more years than even Avraham and Yaakov combined.

∾ Why Didn't David Live for 140 Years?

With this second teaching of the *Zohar*, we are faced with two obvious problems. First, since Adam HaRishon had already given David seventy years, why did Avraham, Yaakov, and Yosef have to give him years as well? Second, now that David was the recipient of this second set of 70 years, why did he not live for 140 years, the sum total of these years?[16]

The *Ohr HaChamah*[17] offers the following explanation: When the sin of the *Eitz HaDaas* took place, Adam's donation of 70 years became corrupted; it was sullied and defiled by the *aveirah* he had committed. Adam then returned as a *gilgul*, in the form of each of the *Avos*, when he donated a total of 70 years to replace the first gift of time. Thus, the two gifts came from the same source — from Adam — but the second gift replaced the first, corrupted donation.

The *Ben Ish Chai*[18] offers another explanation: Although Adam gave David 70 years of his life, he later retracted his offer. David then required a different source of years, which he received from the *Avos*. This is why David asks, הוֹדִיעֵנִי ה׳ קִצִּי, *Let me know my end, O Hashem (Tehillim 39:5), to learn if the years given to him by Adam were lost completely and only the 70 years given by the *Avos* remained. If Adam's years were not lost, David would therefore live longer than the 70 years donated by the *Avos*. After all, Adam lived only 930 years, so David hoped that perhaps he would still receive those years as well.

In his commentary on the Siddur, *Shaar HaShamayim*, the *Shelah HaKadosh* explicates the source of the contention that Adam HaRishon retracted his gift of years. The *Shelah* comments on the *pesukim,* אַל תִּבְטְחוּ בִנְדִיבִים בְּבֶן אָדָם שֶׁאֵין לוֹ תְשׁוּעָה: תֵּצֵא רוּחוֹ יָשֻׁב לְאַדְמָתוֹ בַּיּוֹם הַהוּא אָבְדוּ עֶשְׁתֹּנֹתָיו: אַשְׁרֵי שֶׁקֵל יַעֲקֹב בְּעֶזְרוֹ שִׂבְרוֹ עַל ה׳ אֱלֹקָיו, *Do not rely on nobles, nor on a human being, for he holds no salvation. When his spirit departs, he returns to his earth, on that day his plans all perish. Praiseworthy is one whose hope is Yaakov's God, whose hope is in Hashem, his God (Tehillim* 146: 3-5). The *Shelah* asks,[19] Who are these nobles whom we cannot trust? And further, why is Hashem referred to here as "Yaakov's God"? He explains that when Adam was one day old, he asked Hashem how long he would live. Hashem told him he would live for one thousand years; however, as the *Shaarei Teshuvah* writes, even if someone were to live two thousand years, when his final year comes, he will wonder where all the time went. He will not believe that his years are coming to a conclusion.

Thus, when Adam HaRishon reached year 930, which was to be his final year, he regretted his decision and wanted to live longer. Hashem told him that he should learn from his descendant Yaakov that one should always keep his promises and never go back on his word; as we see in *Parashas Vayeitzei,* וַיִּדַּר יַעֲקֹב נֶדֶר לֵאמֹר, *Then Yaakov took a vow (Bereishis* 28:20) — and he kept it.

The *Shelah* explains the *pesukim* quoted above. אַל תִּבְטְחוּ בִנְדִיבִים, *Don't trust noble, generous people*; i.e., Adam HaRishon — בְּבֶן אָדָם שֶׁאֵין לוֹ תְשׁוּעָה, *in Adam, who holds no salvation;* תֵּצֵא רוּחוֹ יָשֻׁב לְאַדְמָתוֹ, בַּיּוֹם הַהוּא אָבְדוּ עֶשְׁתֹּנֹתָיו, *on the day he is supposed to return to the earth, all hope will be lost for you;* אַשְׁרֵי שֶׁקֵל יַעֲקֹב בְּעֶזְרוֹ, *fortunate is the one who is helped by the God of Yaakov,* because Hashem showed Adam how Yaakov kept his promise.

From this *Shelah* we see that David alludes to Adam's regretting his gift of time. Ultimately, the *Ben Ish Chai* then teaches us that an alternate source of years was needed, and Yaakov received 70 years from the *Avos*.

℘ *The Sacred Nights of David HaMelech*

In *Midbar Kadeimos*,[20] the *Chida* offers a third explanation of why David HaMelech, having received two separate gifts of 70 years, did not live for 140 years. David never slept — and he never tasted the taste of death, since sleep is one-sixtieth of death. Therefore, he lived 70 years during the day, and another 70 years at night. Adam gave David the days, and the *Avos* gave him the nights. David did in fact live the equivalent of 140 years, since he never slept.

The *Shevili Pinchas*[21] offers a beautiful *remez*. David HaMelech writes, מָה אָהַבְתִּי תוֹרָתֶךָ כָּל הַיוֹם הִיא שִׂיחָתִי, *O how I love Your Torah! All day long it is my conversation* (Tehillim 119:97). The Gemara[22] teaches, "יְמֵי חַיֶיךָ הַיָמִים, כֹּל יְמֵי חַיֶיךָ הַלֵּילוֹת, *The 'days of your life' refer to the days. 'All' — the word* כֹּל — *includes the nights.*" Thus, when David HaMelech writes that he loves the Torah so much that כָּל הַיוֹם, *all day long*, it is what he discusses, he is saying that he learned Torah all night as well. The word כָּל indicates that he learned and spoke about the Torah of Hashem all night long, just as he did during the day. Had he slept at night, he would have lived for 140 years, but he loved the Torah so much that he chose to cut his life span in half by utilizing the nights in as productive a manner as he did the days.

Furthermore, David HaMelech states, גַּל עֵינַי וְאַבִּיטָה נִפְלָאוֹת מִתּוֹרָתֶךָ, *Unveil my eyes that I may perceive wonders from Your Torah* (ibid., 119:18). עֵינַי, *my two* ע*'s;* i.e., seventy days and seventy nights. David HaMelech represents the concept of not relegating *limud HaTorah* only to the daytime, but also using our nights for Torah study.

⚭ David Must Be the Ushpizin
for Leil Hoshana Rabbah

Earlier, we quoted Rav Shlomo Kluger's reason as to why, since we already have Yom Kippur, we need Hoshana Rabbah. As noted, Yom Kippur is *mechapper* on *aveiros* committed during the day, while Hoshana Rabbah atones for *aveiros* committed at night.

Perhaps this is why the *Ushpizin* for Hoshana Rabbah is none other than David HaMelech. He theoretically could have lived for 140 years, but he utilized half of those years for productive nights. He epitomizes the concept of *limud HaTorah* by night in addition to day. Certainly, of all *aveiros* that can be done at night, the one we are most liable and culpable for is *bitul Torah*.

The Rambam[23] writes that even though it is a mitzvah to learn Torah by both day and night, a person will acquire most of his wisdom by learning at night. Therefore, someone who wants to merit the crown of Torah should be careful to utilize each and every night for learning Torah. One should not waste even a single evening with excessive or unnecessary sleeping, eating, drinking, idle conversation, or the like.

⚭ Hoshana Rabbah
Is Not Mentioned in Torah Shebichsav

Interestingly, there is no explicit mention of Hoshana Rabbah in the *Torah Shebichsav*. However, there are many *remazim* that bring out the unique spiritual qualities of Hoshana Rabbah that would fall into the category of *Torah Sheb'al Peh*. For example, Rabbi Bachya writes[24] that the world was created on the twenty-fifth of Elul. The *gematria* of Hashem's Name, *Yud Kei Vav Kei*, is 26. Twenty-six days from the twenty-fifth of Elul is Hoshana Rabbah: it is the twenty-sixth day of Creation. The *Mateh Moshe*[25] uncovers a remarkable *remez* by examining the *gematrios* of the letters of *Yud Kei Vav Kei*: 10 = י, representing the ten days from Rosh Hashanah to Yom Kippur. 5 = ה; add five more days to reach Succos. 6 = ו; add six more days to arrive at Hoshana Rabbah. As the letter *hei* has already been expounded, it need not be explicated again.

Why isn't Hoshana Rabbah mentioned in *Torah Shebichsav*? The *Midrash* teaches us that Moshe Rabbeinu went up on Har Sinai to receive the Torah, he was taught *Torah Shebichsav* during the day, and *Torah Sheb'al Peh* at night. In this way, he was able to differentiate between day and night. From here the *Mishnah Berurah* derives that although the *mekubalim* advise against learning *Torah Shebichsav* at night, it is not halachically forbidden. Rather, *l'chatchilah*, it is preferable to arrange one's learning of *Torah Shebichsav* for the day and *Torah Sheb'al Peh* for the night, to pattern after the way Hashem taught Moshe Rabbeinu.

As stated, the *kapparah* of Hoshana Rabbah is for the *aveiros* of the night. Prime among the *aveiros* of the night is the sin of *bitul Torah*. Not coincidentally, nighttime is also the preferable time to learn *Torah Sheb'al Peh*. Small wonder, then, that the references and allusions to Hoshana Rabbah are found only in the *Torah Sheb'al Peh*. Yom Kippur, on the other hand, is *mechapper* on the days and on the *bitul Torah* of the day — when one should be focusing on *Torah Shebichsav*. Therefore, Yom Kippur is explicitly mentioned in *Torah Shebichsav*.

As we emerge from the *Yamim Noraim* foremost on our minds should be how we spend our evenings. Our evenings should consistently be dedicated to learning Torah. As the Rambam taught, most of one's wisdom is acquired at night. On Leil Hoshana Rabbah, the night of the Heavenly guest David HaMelech, let us emulate the ways of *Adoneinu* David, who utilized all his nights for Torah and may we thus be *zocheh* to Mashiach ben David, who will usher in the Final Redemption.

ENDNOTES

1. חכמת התורה - ר׳ שלמה קלוגער - הובא באוצרות התורה סוכות עמוד רמד-רמה.
2. רבינו בחיי כד הקמח-ערבה.
3. במדבר רבה פרשה כא, אות כא.
4. ילקוט שמעוני בראשית אות מא.
5. זית רענן בראשית אות מג.
6. זוהר בראשית דף נה עמוד א.
7. במדבר רבה יד:י״א.
8. בראשית רבה י״ט:כ.
9. ספר הליקוטים פרשת האזינו.
10. ביאור הלכה סימן ד׳ סעיף טז׳ ,קיצור שולחן ערוך סימן ב׳ ס״ק ח.
11. שבת ל, ב.
12. שבילי פנחס בראשית מאמר לב, עמוד קעה-קעו.
13. ניצוצי אורות להחיד״א [הובא בשבילי פנחס שם עמוד קעו].
14. זוהר הקדוש פרשת לך-לך דפו״י דף צא:, אות שמה.
15. זוהר פרשת וישלח דפו״י דף קסח עמוד א-קסח עמוד ב.
16. שבילי פנחס שם עמוד קעט.
17. אור החמה על הזוהר [הובא בשבילי פנחס שם עמוד קעט-קפ].
18. בן יהוידע שבת ל.
19. סידור שער השמים, פסוקי דזמרה.
20. מדבר קדמות מערכת ד אות ו.
21. שבילי פנחס שם.
22. ברכות יב, ב.
23. רמב״ם הלכות תלמוד תורה פרק ג הלכה יג.
24. רבינו בחיי - כד הקמח - ערבה.
25. מטה משה אות תתקנז.

David Restores the Missing Daleds and Seals Death Forever in the Final Mem

✆ David: The Seventh Guest

Let us continue to explore the connection between David HaMelech and the holy night of Hoshana Rabbah.

✆ Why Seven Hakafos?

The *Rokeach*, Reb Eliezer M'Germeiza, uncovers an incredible *remez* from the Torah reading for Hoshana Rabbah. The *pesukim* listing the *nesachim*, libations, of Succos seem to be similar for each day of Yom Tov. However, there are a number of discrepancies in the *pesukim* for each day. For example, the Gemara[1] *Meseches Taanis* (2b) points out that there is an extra *mem* in the *pesukim* of the second day in the word וְנִסְכֵּיהֶם.[2] There is an extra *yud* on day six in the word וּנְסָכֶיהָ,[3] and there is another extra *mem* on the seventh day, where it says כְּמִשְׁפָּטָם.[4] This is a *remez* to *nisuch hamayim*, as the extra letters spell the word מַיִם.

On Hoshana Rabbah, the *pasuk* reads, וּבַיּוֹם הַשְּׁבִיעִי פָרִים שִׁבְעָה אֵילִם שְׁנַיִם כְּבָשִׂים בְּנֵי שָׁנָה אַרְבָּעָה עָשָׂר תְּמִימִם: וּמִנְחָתָם וְנִסְכֵּהֶם לַפָּרִים

לָאֵילָם וְלַכְּבָשִׂים בְּמִסְפָּרָם כְּמִשְׁפָּטָם, *And on the seventh day: seven bulls, two rams, fourteen lambs within their first year, unblemished. And their meal-offering and their libations for the bulls, the rams, and the lambs, in their proper numbers in their requirements* (Bamidbar 29:32-33). The Rokeach writes[5] that these verses allude to the practice that we perform on Hoshana Rabbah: We circle the *bimah* seven times as we carry the *Arba Minim* and recite the *Hoshanos*. Everything has a source in the Torah. The *remez* to this custom is found in the *pasuk* quoted above, which refers to the *minchas nesachim* that accompanied the *korban mussaf* on the seventh day, Hoshana Rabbah. Each of the seven words in this *pasuk* ends with the letter *mem*. All the other days contain only six final *mems* (*mem sofis*) in the verse describing their *nesachim*. The extra *mem* on the seventh day, making seven *mem sofis* in a row, serves as a clue that on this day we make seven complete circles around the *bimah* on Hoshana Rabbah.

What is the significance of the letter *mem*? Of all the letters, why is the letter *mem* (and specifically the *mem sofis*) used as a *remez* that we encircle the *bimah* (or, in the times of the Mikdash, the *Mizbei'ach*) seven times on Hoshana Rabbah?

☙ Four Days of Judgment

The Mishnah[6] tells us that the world is judged four times during the year. On Pesach the world is judged for the grain (i.e., *parnassah*). On Shavuos the world is judged for the fruit of the coming year. Rosh Hashanah is the *Yom HaDin* for mankind, the day on which humans are judged. On Succos Hashem judges the world for water.

The judgment for water that takes place on Succos seems to be given more attention than the judgments that take place on Pesach and Shavuos. After all, Hoshana Rabbah is given quasi-High Holiday status, for it is the *chasimah*, the seal, for the judgment on water. We don't have a comparable day of sealing during Pesach or Shavuos for their respective judgments. Why?

The Tur explains[7] that the seriousness of the judgment of

Succos is because water is the one thing without which we cannot live. In the words of the Tur, "כָּל חַיֵּי אָדָם תְּלוּיִין בְּמַיִם, Man's life depends on water." We can live without grain and without fruit, but not without water. Therefore, since *hakol holech achar hachitum*, everything goes after the conclusion, the all-important culmination of the judgment for water is on Hoshana Rabbah.

Let us try to uncover another dimension to the significance of the awesome day of Hoshana Rabbah.

⌔ *How Can the Yetzer Hara Be Slaughtered?*

Meseches Succah[8] states that in the future, at the End of Days, Hashem will slaughter the *yetzer hara*. However, the *yetzer hara* is not a physical entity and does not have a physical body. How, then, will Hashem slaughter him?

The Baal Shem Tov explains [9] that the name of the *Malach HaMaves*, Angel of Death, whom we refer to as the *yetzer hara*, is סמא"ל. This name resembles one of the seventy-two Names of Hashem: סא"ל. Adding a *mem* to the Name of Hashem produces the name of the *yetzer hara*.

Rashi writes[10] that we find three *pesukim* in *Shemos* 14:19-21 that have seventy-two letters each. When we set the words of these *pesukim* one over the other — in the format *yoshar, hofach, yosher* (straight, reversed, straight) — each vertical column of three letters (starting with the first letter of the first *pasuk*, the last letter of the middle *pasuk*, and the first letter of the third *pasuk*) spells out another three-letter Name of Hashem. As noted, one of these seventy-two Names of Hashem is סא"ל, which has the *gematria* of 91. If this were to be the name of the *Malach HaMaves*, he would be a *malach kadosh*, a holy angel, as his name would be the same as one of the Names of Hashem. Adding an extra letter to the *Shem Hashem* is toxic and causes this *malach* to bring death to the world. The fatal letter that changes Hashem's Name into the name of the *Malach HaMaves* is the letter *mem*.

The Baal Shem Tov explains why the letter *mem* was chosen

from all the letters of the *aleph-beis* to transform the holy Name of Hashem into the name of the *Malach HaMaves*. It is because the letter *mem* stands for *misah*, death. Therefore, once the *mem* is added to the Name, it transitions into the *Malach HaMaves*, into the *yetzer hara*.

When the Gemara says that in the End of Days, Hashem will slaughter the *Malach HaMaves*, it is not meant to be taken literally. Rather, at the time of *Techiyas HaMeisim*, when *misah* is no more, Hashem will merely remove the letter *mem* from the name of the *Malach HaMaves*,[11] causing the name to actually morph into a *shem kadosh*, a holy name, which happens to have the same *gematria* as *succah*. The *Malach HaMaves* will become a *malach hachaim*, angel of life; Hashem will have effectively brought about the "death" of the *Malach HaMaves*.

ᔌ *Why Does the Letter Mem Stand for Misah, Death?*

The origin of the concept that the letter *mem* stands for *misah* is the *Zohar*.[12] The Torah tells us, during the incident of the *Eitz HaDaas*, וַתֵּרֶא הָאִשָּׁה כִּי טוֹב הָעֵץ לְמַאֲכָל וְכִי תַאֲוָה הוּא לָעֵינַיִם וְנֶחְמָד הָעֵץ לְהַשְׂכִּיל וַתִּקַּח מִפִּרְיוֹ וַתֹּאכַל וַתִּתֵּן גַּם לְאִישָׁהּ עִמָּהּ וַיֹּאכַל. *And the woman perceived that the tree was good for eating, and that it was a delight to the eyes, and that the tree was desirable as a means to wisdom, and she took of its fruit and she ate; and she gave also to her husband with her, and he ate* (Bereishis 3:6). The *pasuk* states that Chavah took "מִפִּרְיוֹ," *of its fruit*. It could have merely said that she took פֵּרְיוֹ, *its fruit*. Why does the Torah add the extra *mem*? Says the *Zohar*, whenever *misah*, death, is about to come to the world, there will be a "floating *mem*." When Chavah was about to eat from the *Eitz HaDaas*, she took the fruit and along with it, the letter *mem*, and that *mem* was then searching for a partner.

Every letter in the *aleph-beis* seeks a partner. The *aleph* is partnered with the *tes*, the *beis* with the *ches*, *gimmel* with *zayin*, *daled* with *vav*, etc. Only the letters *hei* and *nun* do not have partners. This offers new meaning to the *pasuk*, הֵן עָם לְבָדָד יִשְׁכֹּן,

Behold, Klal Yisrael dwells alone (Bamidbar 23:9), meaning without anyone to be partnered with, like the letters in the word הֵן, the *hei* and the *nun*, that don't have partners.

When Chavah went to eat from the *Eitz HaDaas* and the *mem* was floating, it was searching for a partner. It partnered with the *vav* and the *taf*. This *pasuk* has four words that begin the *vav-taf* letter combination: *va'teire, va'tikach, va'tochal, va'titein*: וַתֵּרֶא הָאִשָּׁה כִּי טוֹב הָעֵץ לְמַאֲכָל וְכִי תַאֲוָה הוּא לָעֵינַיִם וְנֶחְמָד הָעֵץ לְהַשְׂכִּיל וַתִּקַּח מִפִּרְיוֹ **וַתֹּאכַל** **וַתִּתֵּן** גַּם לְאִישָׁהּ עִמָּהּ וַיֹּאכַל.

When the *mem*, which was floating alone, chose the *vav* and *taf* combination as its partner, it produced מָוֶת, *maves*: death. The *Zohar* says that this is how *misah* came to the world. Chavah did not take "*piryo, its fruit*," but rather "**mi**'*piryo, of its fruit*." She took the letter *mem* and she connected it to the *vav-taf*, thereby bringing *misah* to the world.

♋ *Pinchas Used the Mem Against Zimri*

The *Zohar* continues: When Pinchas saw the obscene behavior of Zimri, he acted to defend the honor of Hashem. The *gematria* of the name Pinchas (פִּינְחָס) is 208. Having seen the *aveirah* being performed, he was garbed with the *Middas HaDin*, the Attribute of Justice, similar to Yitzchak Avinu, who we are taught represents *Din*. The *gematria* of Yitzchak (יִצְחָק) is likewise 208.

When Pinchas saw Zimri committing this heinous act with Kazbi, he knew that this would be an act that would bring *misah*, death, into the world. Therefore, he also saw the floating letter *mem*. He knew he had to act to grab the *mem* before the *Satan* did.

The Torah tells us, וַיַּרְא פִּינְחָס בֶּן אֶלְעָזָר בֶּן אַהֲרֹן הַכֹּהֵן וַיָּקָם מִתּוֹךְ הָעֵדָה וַיִּקַּח רֹמַח בְּיָדוֹ, *Pinchas son of Elazar son of Aharon HaKohen saw, and he stood up from amid the assembly and took a spear in his hand (Bamidbar 25:7)*. Pinchas took his own 208 and combined them with the *mem*, which he had rescued from the *Malach HaMaves*, making a total of 248: רֹמַח. He took a *romach*, spear, which is numerically equal to 248. The *romach* of Pinchas, his spear, was the 208 of his name combined with the floating *mem* that he was able to capture. The *mem* is the *mem* from the *Eitz HaDaas*, from the word *mi'piryo*. By attaching it to his 208, he produced a *romach*, a spear, with which to put an end to the perverse acts of Zimri and Kazbi and defeat the plague.

❧ *The Sin of the Eitz HaDaas Brought Maves Into the World*

When Adam and Chavah ate from the *Eitz HaDaas*, it was the letter *mem* that brought *misah* into the world.

The *Arizal*, brought in the writings of Maran Ovadia Yosef, discusses the episode of the sin of the *Eitz HaDaas*.[13] The *pasuk* there states, וַיֹּאמֶר ה׳ אֱלֹקִים לָאִשָּׁה מַה זֹּאת עָשִׂית וַתֹּאמֶר הָאִשָּׁה הַנָּחָשׁ הִשִּׁיאַנִי וָאֹכֵל, *And Hashem God said to the woman, "What is this that you have done!" The woman said, "The nachash, serpent, deceived (seduced) me and I ate"* (*Bereishis* 3:13). The word Chavah uses, הִשִּׁיאַנִי, is not found anywhere else in Tanach. There are many other, more commonly used phrases that Chavah could have used to indicate that she had been seduced and persuaded by the *nachash* to consume the forbidden fruit. Why did she use this unique terminology?

❧ *The Nachash Stole the Daleds*

The *Arizal* teaches a secret about two of Hashem's Names. We know that the Name of *Adnus* is spelled *aleph, daled, nun, yud*, and the Name *Shakkai* is spelled *shin, daled, yud*. The *Arizal* teaches that the serpent is a thief who stealthily stole the *daled* from each of these Names, leaving the letters *shin* and *yud* from *Shakkai*, שי, and the letters *aleph, nun,* and *yud* from the name of *Adnus*, אני. Together, these remaining letters spell שִׁיאַנִי! The deceit of the *nachash* represents the two Names of Hashem, minus the two *daleds*.

Chavah, then, is saying that the *nachash*, "Hishiani." He stole the two *daleds*, one from *Adnus* and one from *Shakkai*. Our *avodah*, then, is to restore these two stolen *daleds*. The only way to rectify the *cheit* of Adam HaRishon is to put the two *daleds* back where they belong! How can we accomplish this? Who has two extra *daleds* that can be used to restore these Names of Hashem?

◎ *Learning Torah Restores the Daleds*

The *Arizal* writes that there is only one way to get the two *daleds* back. Shlomo HaMelech declares in *Mishlei*, אַשְׁרֵי אָדָם שֹׁמֵעַ לִי לִשְׁקֹד עַל דַּלְתֹתַי יוֹם יוֹם לִשְׁמֹר מְזוּזֹת פְּתָחָי, *Praiseworthy is the person who listens to me, to hasten to my doors every day, to guard the doorposts of my entranceways* (*Mishlei* 8:34). Shlomo HaMelech is saying, fortunate is the one who is diligent by my doors, or, literally, *daleds*.

The letter *daled* is spelled the same as the word door: דלת, *deles*. Thus, Shlomo is teaching us that by being diligent at the doors of Torah, we can restore these two missing *daleds*. Learning Torah brings life into the world. This can counteract the *misah* brought into the world by the serpent. Crossing the threshold of the *beis midrash* in the morning, going to learn Torah, represents the first *deles*, restoration of the first *daled*. Going to learn again in the evening is the second *deles*, the restoration of the second *daled*. Doing this restores the two *daleds* and it completes the two Names of Hashem. The name of *Adnus* and the name *Shakkai* are now whole again. Praiseworthy is the one who can restore the two *daleds* to the *Shem Hashem* by learning Torah in the morning and in the evening.

◎ *Krias Shema Restores the Daleds*

The *Yalkut Reuveni*[14] presents a slightly different way to understands how to restore the two *daleds*. In *Shema*, we say, שְׁמַע יִשְׂרָאֵל, ה' אֱלֹקֵינוּ, ה' אֶחָד. בָּרוּךְ שֵׁם כְּבוֹד מַלְכוּתוֹ לְעוֹלָם וָעֶד, *Hear, O Yisrael: Hashem is our God, Hashem, the One and Only. Blessed is the Name of His glorious kingdom for all eternity.* The *daled* at the end of each of these two *pesukim* restores the *daleds* of the Names of Hashem that were removed by the *nachash*.

The Gemara[15] states that we are obligated to learn Torah by day and by night. The minimal means whereby one can fulfill this obligation is to recite *Shema* in the morning and evening. Therefore, we can suggest, these two ways of restoring the *daleds* to the Names of Hashem are really one approach. Preferably one should attempt to restore the two *daleds* with actual *limud HaTorah*, but at the very least, the two *daleds* should be restored by reciting *Shema* twice a day.

In *Selichos*, which we recite before Rosh Hashanah and during the *Aseres Yemei Teshuvah*, we declare the following: דְּפַקְנוּ דְלָתֶיךָ, דְּלָתֶיךָ דָּפַקְנוּ ... נָא אַל תְּשִׁיבֵנוּ רֵיקָם מִלְּפָנֶיךָ, We bang at Your doors, at Your doors we bang; please do not turn us away empty-handed from before You. We mention two doors. Rav Shaul Brach teaches[16] that these two doors refer to the doors that we need to utilize to restore the two *daleds* to the Names of Hashem. דָּפַקְנוּ דְלָתֶיךָ, the *beis midrash* in the morning, and דְּלָתֶיךָ דָּפַקְנוּ, the *beis midrash* in the evening. By learning in the *beis midrash* morning and evening, we restore the *daleds* to the Name of *Adnus* and to the Name of *Shakkai*.

❧ *Stolen Daleds or Floating Mem?*

Although we may have read the incident of Adam and Chavah as a simple narrative, we learn that behind the scenes the serpent was actually tampering with the letters that are the very building blocks of existence. The following problem arises: With which letters did the *nachash* tamper? On the one hand, the *Zohar* teaches that he grabbed the floating *mem* and attached it to the letters *vav* and *taf*. On the other hand, the *Arizal* teaches that he stole two *daleds* from the Names of Hashem. Which one was it? Did he grab the floating *mem* or did he steal the *daleds*?

❧ *Mem vs. Mem Sofis*

The standard letter *mem*, known as the open *mem*, can appear at the beginning or middle of a word, while a *mem sofis*, the closed *mem*, appears only at the end of a word. We find two exceptions in Tanach, one in which there is a regular *mem* at the end of a word, and one in which there is a *mem sofis* at the beginning of a word.

The first exception is seen when the *Navi* Yeshayahu proclaimed, לְמַרְבֵּה [לְמַרְבֵּה] הַמִּשְׂרָה וּלְשָׁלוֹם אֵין קֵץ עַל כִּסֵּא דָוִד וְעַל מַמְלַכְתּוֹ לְהָכִין אֹתָהּ וּלְסַעֲדָהּ בְּמִשְׁפָּט וּבִצְדָקָה מֵעַתָּה וְעַד עוֹלָם קִנְאַת ה' צְבָקוֹת תַּעֲשֶׂה זֹּאת, *Upon the one with the greatness in dominion and the boundless peace that will prevail on the throne of David and on his kingdom, to establish it and sustain it through justice and righteousness, from now to eternity. The zealousness of Hashem, Master of Legions, will accomplish this!* (*Yeshayahu* 9:6): In the time of Mashiach there will be abundant authority and rulership. There will be endless peace when the throne of David is firmly established. The word used to describe the abundance of authority during the *Yemos HaMashiach*, *marbeh*, is spelled with a *mem sofis* at the beginning of the word.

The second exception is seen as Nechemiah spoke about the walls of Yerushalayim that were breached and were in need of repair. The *pasuk* says, וָאֵצְאָה בְשַׁעַר הַגַּיְא לַיְלָה וְאֶל פְּנֵי עֵין הַתַּנִּין וְאֶל שַׁעַר הָאַשְׁפֹּת וָאֱהִי שֹׂבֵר בְּחוֹמֹת יְרוּשָׁלַם אֲשֶׁר הַמְפֹרָצִים [הֵם פְּרוּצִים] וּשְׁעָרֶיהָ אֻכְּלוּ בָאֵשׁ, *And I went out at night through the Gate of the Valley, toward the direction of the Serpent's Spring to the Dung Gate; I contemplated the walls of Yerushalayim which had been breached, and its gates consumed by fire* (*Nechemiah* 2:13): The word הֵם is spelled with an open *mem* at the end of the word, הֱמ, instead of a *mem sofis*.

Why is there a *mem sofis* in the middle of the words *marbeh* and an open *mem* at the end of the word *heim*, where we would expect there to be a *mem sofis*?

Rabbeinu Bechaya explains[17] that one *mem* is an *arev*, guarantor, for the other. In *Nechemiah* we are learning about the walls of Yerushalayim that were breached. This is represented by the open *mem*, in place of a closed *mem sofis*. Like the *mem*, the city should be closed, but instead its gates were destroyed and its wall were open. What will guarantee that one day Hashem will fill in and seal up the breaches in the wall of Yerushalayim? The *pasuk* in *Yeshayahu* tells us, לְמַרְבֵּה הַמִּשְׂרָה וּלְשָׁלוֹם אֵין קֵץ, where there is a *mem sofis*, a final *mem*, at the beginning of a word. This word is a guarantor, an *arev*, that the day will come that Hashem will take the breached and broken wall and will repair it. He will seal the holes in the wall closed, like the *mem sofis*. This will transpire when the throne of David will be established with abundant authority.

The open *mem* represents *churban*, destruction. It represents *misah* and tragedy. The closed *mem*, on the other hand, is representative of the *Acharis HaYamim*, the End of Days. The open *mem* is *maves*, and when בִּלַּע הַמָּוֶת לָנֶצַח, *He will eliminate death forever* (*Yeshayahu* 25:8), then Hashem will seal up the *mem*, and the closed *mem* will signify the end of death and destruction.

❧ Shas: From Open Mem to Closed Mem

In *Shushan Eidus*, Rabbi Binyamin Zev Berkowitz's commentary on *Ediyos*,[18] he makes the great observation that the *Mishnayos* begins with an open *mem*, מֵאֵימָתַי, and it ends with a closed *mem*, a *mem sofis*, the word שָׁלוֹם. What is the significance of this? He explains, based on the idea we learned above from Rabbeinu Bachya, that the open *mem* represents *galus*, exile, and tragedy and destruction; the closed *mem* signifies redemption and the end of death, when Hashem will swallow up death forever. The *avodah* of learning *Shas* is to transition the world from the open *mem* of מֵאֵימָתַי קוֹרִין אֶת שְׁמַע בְּעַרְבִית, of the first *Mishnah* in *Shas*, and develop it into the era of the End of Days by reaching the closed *mem* of the final letter of *Shas*, ה׳ עֹז לְעַמּוֹ יִתֵּן, ה׳ יְבָרֵךְ אֶת עַמּוֹ בַשָּׁלוֹם! Our goal is to seal shut the *mem* and thereby death forever.

The *Midrash*[19] teaches us that the *geulah sheleimah*, the final redemption, will only come about as the result of the *zechus* we acquire from learning *mishnayos*! Why is learning *mishnayos* the key to redemption? The *Shushan Eidus* explains that by journeying through *Shas*, which begins with an open *mem* we are able to seal off and close the *mem* of *misah*, and turn the *mem* of מֵאֵימָתַי into the ultimate שָׁלוֹם of *Acharis HaYamim*.

Chazal tell us, אֵין מַיִם אֶלָּא תּוֹרָה, there is no *mayim*, water, other than Torah. We can suggest that this is so because, like the word *mayim*, Torah begins with the open *mem* and ends with the closed *mem*. By learning Torah properly, one can seal the *mem* closed, thereby protecting himself from *churban*, *tzarah*, and difficulties, like the word *mayim*, which begins with the open *mem* and ends with a closed *mem sofis*.

◎ Mem Sofis = Daled + Daled

The *Shushan Eidus* then adds an interesting insight. He reveals that the *mem sofis* really consists of two letters that interlock with each other: it is made up of two interlocking *daleds* at a 90-degree angle. The two *daleds* combine and form a final *mem*. The *Satan*, however, has chiseled away at the final *mem*, prying it open to form an open *mem*, unlocking the two *daleds* that had held it together. What is the process and procedure by which the *Satan* can open up the final *mem*?

◎ How the Satan Opens the Mem

B'siyata d'Shmaya, we can suggest an exhilarating approach. When a person is *davuk baTorah*, attached to learning Torah, and fulfills אַשְׁרֵי אָדָם שֹׁמֵעַ לִי לִשְׁקֹד עַל דַּלְתֹתַי יוֹם יוֹם (*Mishlei* 8:34), he will merit the two doors/*daleds* connecting and interlocking to form a sealed and completely closed *mem sofis*. When the *mem* is closed as a result of a person being *davuk* to Torah, it is חַיִּים הִיא לַמַּחֲזִיקִים בָּהּ, *life for all who grasp it*, and בִּלַּע הַמָּוֶת לָנֶצַח, *there is no maves* — no *tzaar*, no pain, no tragedy — just *chaim l'olmei ad*, eternal life.

The problem arises when a person weakens in his commitment to Torah and his attendance in the *beis midrash* slackens off. Then the final *mem* opens and the *daleds* separate. Now there is an opening for the *Satan* to enter.

Thus, the *Satan's* actions in introducing the open *mem* and stealing the two *daleds* are all part of one plan. When a person does not go to the *beis midrash* twice daily, the two *daleds* of the closed *mem* are no longer sealed, and now they are available for the *Satan* to take them. It is a two-step process. The *mem sofis* is a closed letter because it is comprised of two *daleds* fused and sealed together. Step One is the *Satan* opening up the two *daleds* that were fused together. In Step Two, once the *mem* is open, the *Satan* can move in and take them.

L'asid Lavo, when Mashiach comes, Hashem will remove the *mem* from the *Satan*. Until that time, however, the *Satan* has successfully pried open the *mem*, exposing and releasing the two *daleds*, which he then stole.

∾ *How to Seal the Mem Forever*

Who can successfully seal shut the two *daleds* and construct the final *mem*?

Adam HaRishon was responsible for the *cheit* of the *Eitz HaDaas*. Hashem had intended Adam to live for a thousand years, but he lived only 930 years. The *midrash* says that he gave seventy of his years to David HaMelech.

The *Arizal* takes this further. David was not merely given the seventy years from Adam, he was in fact the reincarnation of Adam HaRishon! Through the sin of the *Eitz HaDaas*, Adam brought *misah* into the world. Now, when he returned as David HaMelech, he brought life. דָּוִד מֶלֶךְ יִשְׂרָאֵל חַי וְקַיָּם, David, the king of Israel, lives and endures. Adam brought death into the world; when he returned as David, he would not even sleep שִׁיתִין נְשָׁמִין, sixty horse-breaths, since sleep is one-sixtieth of death. The *Arizal* adds that the name Adam — אָדָם — forms the *roshei teivos*, initial letters, of Adam, David, Mashiach.

Adam HaRishon caused the final mem to be pried open. David HaMelech, then, is responsible to seal the *mem* shut. He is well equipped to do so, as his name contains the two *daleds* necessary! In his name, the *daleds* are separated by a *vav*: a *vav hachibur*, which is a letter that joins words, and in this case letters, symbolizing that David will fuse the two *daleds* and seal the *mem* closed.[20]

When describing Chavah's action at the *Eitz HaDaas*, the Torah says, *vatikach mi'piryo*. That was when the *Satan* acquired the *mem*, which he cracked open to extract the two *daleds*. *Hishiani*: he grabbed the two *daleds*, leaving the Names of Hashem incomplete. David HaMelech comes along and says, מָה אָהַבְתִּי תוֹרָתֶךָ כָּל הַיּוֹם הִיא שִׂיחָתִי, *O how I love Your Torah! All day long it is my conversation* (*Tehillim* 119:97). He does not say, "*Kol Yom*," as would be expected. He added the *hei*: *kol hayom*. The extra letter *hei* teaches us that David HaMelech learned Torah at night as well as during the day. He did not sleep at night; rather, he fulfilled the *pasuk* from *Mishlei* quoted above, אַשְׁרֵי אָדָם שֹׁמֵעַ לִי לִשְׁקֹד עַל דַּלְתֹתַי יוֹם יוֹם. By going to the *beis midrash* in the morning — the first *daled* — and going to the *beis midrash* in the evening — the second *daled* — he is able to restore the *daleds* to their rightful place. Through the *vav hachibur* of his name, David is able to fuse the *daleds* and seal the *mem* closed again. It is no longer *hishiani* — now the Names of *Adnus* and *Shakkai* are restored and complete. *Aleph, daled, nun, yud*, and *shin, daled, yud*. In this manner, the *Satan* is overcome, while דָּוִד מֶלֶךְ יִשְׂרָאֵל חַי וְקַיָּם.[21]

As noted, the *pasuk* in *Yeshayahu* states (9:6): לְמַרְבֵּה [לְמַרְבֵּה] הַמִּשְׂרָה וּלְשָׁלוֹם אֵין קֵץ עַל כִּסֵּא דָוִד וְעַל מַמְלַכְתּוֹ לְהָכִין אֹתָהּ וּלְסַעֲדָהּ בְּמִשְׁפָּט וּבִצְדָקָה מֵעַתָּה וְעַד עוֹלָם קִנְאַת ה' צְבָ-אוֹת תַּעֲשֶׂה זֹּאת. *When will there be endless peace on the throne of David?* לְמַרְבֵּה הַמִּשְׂרָה: when the regular *mem* is sealed off and transformed into a closed *mem sofis*.

Rav Eliyahu Gutmacher[22] explains that, as we said above, the name אדם stands for Adam, David, and Mashiach. In this case, the name of Mashiach, which starts with an open *mem*, is alluded to in the name אדם with a *mem sofis*, a closed *mem*. This is because Mashiach will thrive in the era when he successfully seals the *mem* shut and transforms the open *mem* into *bila maves lanetzach*.

❧ David Must Be the Ushpizin for Day Seven

Upon analyzing the *pesukim* in the incident when Chavah ate from the *Eitz HaDaas*, we know that the *mem* of וַתִּקַּח מִפִּרְיוֹ is symbolic of *misah* that was introduced into the world. As noted above, the *Zohar* points out that in these *pesukim* we find four words that contain the *vav-taf* letter combination, to which the *mem* is now connected.

However, upon a careful examination of the entire passage, we find, remarkably, seven *vav-taf* letter combinations

וַתֹּאמֶר הָאִשָּׁה אֶל הַנָּחָשׁ מִפְּרִי עֵץ הַגָּן נֹאכֵל. וּמִפְּרִי הָעֵץ אֲשֶׁר בְּתוֹךְ הַגָּן אָמַר אֱלֹקִים לֹא תֹאכְלוּ מִמֶּנּוּ וְלֹא תִגְּעוּ בּוֹ פֶּן תְּמֻתוּן. וַיֹּאמֶר הַנָּחָשׁ אֶל הָאִשָּׁה לֹא מוֹת תְּמֻתוּן. כִּי יֹדֵעַ אֱלֹקִים כִּי בְּיוֹם אֲכָלְכֶם מִמֶּנּוּ וְנִפְקְחוּ עֵינֵיכֶם וִהְיִיתֶם כֵּאלֹקִים יֹדְעֵי טוֹב וָרָע. **וַתֵּרֶא** הָאִשָּׁה כִּי טוֹב הָעֵץ לְמַאֲכָל וְכִי תַאֲוָה הוּא לָעֵינַיִם וְנֶחְמָד הָעֵץ לְהַשְׂכִּיל **וַתִּקַּח** מִפִּרְיוֹ **וַתֹּאכַל וַתִּתֵּן** גַּם לְאִישָׁהּ עִמָּהּ וַיֹּאכַל. **וַתִּפָּקַחְנָה** עֵינֵי שְׁנֵיהֶם וַיֵּדְעוּ כִּי עֵירֻמִּם הֵם וַיִּתְפְּרוּ עֲלֵה תְאֵנָה וַיַּעֲשׂוּ לָהֶם חֲגֹרֹת. וַיִּשְׁמְעוּ אֶת קוֹל ה' אֱלֹקִים מִתְהַלֵּךְ בַּגָּן לְרוּחַ הַיּוֹם וַיִּתְחַבֵּא הָאָדָם וְאִשְׁתּוֹ מִפְּנֵי ה' אֱלֹקִים בְּתוֹךְ עֵץ הַגָּן. וַיִּקְרָא ה' אֱלֹקִים אֶל הָאָדָם וַיֹּאמֶר לוֹ אַיֶּכָּה. וַיֹּאמֶר אֶת קֹלְךָ שָׁמַעְתִּי בַּגָּן וָאִירָא כִּי עֵירֹם אָנֹכִי וָאֵחָבֵא. וַיֹּאמֶר מִי הִגִּיד לְךָ כִּי עֵירֹם אָתָּה הֲמִן הָעֵץ אֲשֶׁר צִוִּיתִיךָ לְבִלְתִּי אֲכָל מִמֶּנּוּ אָכָלְתָּ. וַיֹּאמֶר הָאָדָם הָאִשָּׁה אֲשֶׁר נָתַתָּה עִמָּדִי הִוא נָתְנָה לִי מִן הָעֵץ וָאֹכֵל. וַיֹּאמֶר ה' אֱלֹקִים לָאִשָּׁה מַה זֹּאת עָשִׂית **וַתֹּאמֶר** הָאִשָּׁה הַנָּחָשׁ הִשִּׁיאַנִי וָאֹכֵל (*Bereishis* 3:2-13):

This group of seven *vav-tav* combinations implies that the letter *mem* was *mechaber*, connected to, these seven pairs. Who can seal shut all seven of these open *mems* that were connected to these seven letter combinations? Who can close them all and seal them into closed *mems sofis*? David, the seventh *Ushpizin*, whose turn to visit our *succah* is Leil Hoshana Rabbah, the night of Hoshana Rabbah.

The *Rokeach*[23] points out that in the *pesukim* of the *korbanos* of Hoshana Rabbah there are seven *mems sofis*, seven closed mems.

וּבַיּוֹם הַשְּׁבִיעִי פָּרִים שִׁבְעָה אֵילִם שְׁנָיִם כְּבָשִׂים בְּנֵי שָׁנָה אַרְבָּעָה עָשָׂר תְּמִימִם. וּמִנְחָתָם וְנִסְכֵּיהֶם לַפָּרִים לָאֵילִם וְלַכְּבָשִׂים בְּמִסְפָּרָם כְּמִשְׁפָּטָם , *And on the seventh day: seven bulls, two rams, fourteen lambs within their first year, unblemished. And their meal-offering and their libations for the bulls, the rams, and the lambs, in their proper numbers, in their requirements* (Devarim 29:32-33).

It is the responsibility of David HaMelech, who is the *Ushpizin* of the seventh day, to seal shut the open *mem* that appeared with the seven *vav-tav* letter combinations at the time of the sin of the *Eitz HaDaas*.

Through his *limud HaTorah* of day and night, being diligent at the doors of the Beis Hamedrash, David will acquire the two *daleds*. Through his *vav hachibur*, he will fuse the *daleds*, effectively sealing off all seven *mems*, thereby eradicating the *Satan* and *misah* from the world. He will usher in the era of *bila hamaves lanetzach*, the days of *Techiyas Hameisim*, the Revivification of the Dead.

דָּוִד מֶלֶךְ יִשְׂרָאֵל חַי וְקַיָּם is *merumaz*, alluded to, in the *pasuk* that is specific to Hoshana Rabbah: וּמִנְחָתָם וְנִסְכֵּיהֶם לַפָּרִים לָאֵילִם וְלַכְּבָשִׂים בְּמִסְפָּרָם כְּמִשְׁפָּטָם. The seven final *mems* of Hoshana Rabbah, the day of David, will swallow death forever.

Hoshana Rabbah is the last day we are Biblically commanded to sit in the *succah*. The *gematria* of the word *succah* is 91, corresponding to the *gematria* of the future name of the *Satan* without his *mem* (סאיל), without the *maves*. May the *kedushah* and positive influences, the *hashpa'os*, of the *succah*, remain with us the entire year, and may we be *zocheh* to a *shenas chaim veshalom, ad biyas goel tzedek, bimheirah veyameinu.*

ENDNOTES

1. תענית ב, ב.
2. במדבר כט, יז.
3. שם פסוק לא.
4. שם פסוק לג.
5. פירוש רוקח, במדבר פרק כ'ט פסוק לב-לג.
6. ראש השנה טז, א.
7. טור או"ח סימן תרסד.
8. סוכה נב, א.
9. תולדות יעקב יוסף, הובא בבעל שם טוב, בראשית אות קמט.
10. סוכה מה, א ד"ה אני והו.
11. קהלת יעקב (ערך סמאל) הובא בליקוטי מאמרים שבילי פנחס בראשית מאמר ל.
12. זוהר הקדוש פינחס אות תסד-תסו דפו"י דף רלז:
13. ענף עץ עבות ב:יט.
14. ילקוט ראובני בראשית, עמוד 80
15. נדרים ח, א.
16. דבר המלוכה, סליחות, עמוד א.
17. רבינו בחיי ויחי, מז:כח.
18. שושן עדות, סוף מסכת עדיות.
19. ויקרא רבה ז:ג.
20. שבילי פנחס בראשית מאמר כח, עמוד קנה.
21. ספר הליקוטים פרשת האזינו.
22. חידושי רבי אליהו גוטמאכר, חגיגה יא., עמוד רטז.
23. פירוש רוקח פנחס, כט:לב-לג.

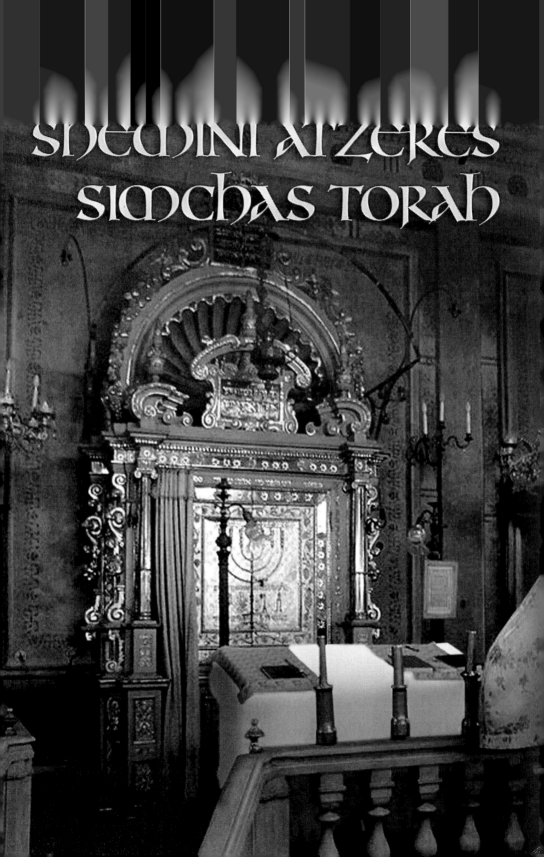

SHEMINI ATZERES
SIMCHAS TORAH

Shemini Atzeres: Pure Ecstasy, So Ask Hashem for Your Heart's Desire

≈ The Happiest Day of Zman Simchaseinu

The Vilna Gaon was known to have been very joyous throughout the Yom Tov of Succos.[1] On Shemini Atzeres, the Gra was exceptionally exuberant. His level of *simchah* on this day exceeded that of all the days of Succos. Succos is זְמַן שִׂמְחָתֵנוּ; however, it is Shemini Atzeres that possesses the highest level of *simchah*.

What is it about Shemini Atzeres that engenders more *simchah* than the other days of Succos?

≈ Why Is Shemini Atzeres Missing?

Rav Shlomo Kluger writes[2] that there are three *parshiyos* in the Torah that discuss the Yamim Tovim: *Parashas Emor, Parashas Pinchas,* and *Parashas Re'eh.* In *Emor,* when the Torah discusses Succos, it mentions Shemini Atzeres as well. Likewise, when the Torah discusses the Yamim Tovim and their *korbanos* in *Pinchas,* Succos and Shemini Atzeres are both mentioned. However, in

Re'eh the discussion of the *chagim* includes Succos (as a seven-day Yom Tov), while Shemini Atzeres is glaringly absent! Why doesn't the Torah include Shemini Atzeres in its discussion of the Yom Tov of Succos in *Parashas Re'eh*?

ᘯ *Isn't It a Chag?*

The *Shulchan Aruch*[3] discusses the insertions that we add into the *davening* on the various Yamim Tovim. On Shemini Atzeres we incorporate the words, "שְׁמִינִי חַג הָעֲצֶרֶת הַזֶּה,"* into our *tefillos*. The *Rema* comments that since we never find the title *chag* ascribed to Shemini Atzeres anywhere in the Torah, one should omit the word *chag* and say only, "יוֹם שְׁמִינִי עֲצֶרֶת הַזֶּה."

Why shouldn't Shemini Atzeres be called a *chag*? When the Torah refers to a Yom Tov as a *chag*, what quality is being referred to, and why doesn't it apply to Shemini Atzeres?

ᘯ *The Greatest Eis Ratzon*

In his *sefer, Moed L'chol Chai*,[4] R' Chaim Palagi shares an incredible idea about Shemini Atzeres. He writes that one should be exceptionally careful with the *tefillos* of Shemini Atzeres, as they should be recited with intense *kavannah*. The *tikkun*, rectification, achieved in the days from Rosh Hashanah to Shemini Atzeres is completed on the day of Shemini Atzeres, and all that was achieved depends on Shemini Atzeres. In addition, during the entire period of the Yamim Noraim, no other day is as much of an *eis ratzon* as Shemini Atzeres. It is the day that is most conducive to Hashem being attentive to a person's *tefillos* and granting all that is requested. Since the unique power of Shemini Atzeres is an opportunity to be capitalized upon, it is fitting to spend the day engaged in introspection, learning Torah, and asking Hashem to fulfill one's needs.

What is so special about Shemini Atzeres that it is the ultimate

---

* These are the words in Nusach Ashkenaz. Those who *daven* Nusach Sefard say, "*Shemini Atzeres HaChag hazeh*."

day for having a person's *tefillos* answered? Why is it the greatest day of the year to *daven*?

❧ Why Are There Fewer Korbanos on Shemini Atzeres?

Throughout Succos, the Kohanim offered fourteen sheep daily. Over the course of seven days, this totals ninety-eight sheep; they are *kneged*, in counterpoint to, the ninety-eight *kelalos*, curses, that were uttered on Har Eval (see *Devarim* Chs. 27-28). There were also seventy oxen offered over the Yom Tov of Succos, *kneged* the seventy nations of the world. On Shemini Atzeres, however, only a single ox and a single ram were brought as *korbanos*.

The *Midrash Tanchuma*[5] offers an explanation for the *korbanos* of Shemini Atzeres, which are much fewer in number than the offerings brought on the preceding days of Succos. Hashem is telling the Bnei Yisrael that over the course of the preceding seven days, they sacrificed seventy oxen on behalf of all the nations of the world. Now, says Hashem, it is time to bring a *korban* for yourselves, on behalf of Klal Yisrael. This is comparable to a king who threw a week-long party. He invited all of his subjects to his party, and there were many, many participants. Once the week passed, he turned to his beloved and says, "We have fulfilled our obligation to all of our subjects, and we partied with them. But now, I want to have a private party just with you." For this private, intimate party, simple party fare was sufficient. A small piece of meat, some vegetables — nothing extravagant or fancy.

Similarly, Hashem tells the Bnei Yisrael, "All the offerings you brought on Succos were brought on behalf of the other nations of the world. Now, on the eighth day, let's have a special day just for us, and we will be content with whatever you offer — a single ox and a single ram."

The Bnei Yissaschar[6] comments that if Hashem wants to spend the final day with His beloved Klal Yisrael, it would seem to make more sense for there to have been even more *korbanos* brought, as one might think that the king would want to have an even bigger party with his beloved than he did with all the commoners in his country. Hashem would presumably want to have a bigger and better party with His children, whom He loves and cares for. Why is the celebration Hashem has with the nations of the world so much more elaborate than the party He throws for His children?

The reason is that on Shemini Atzeres Hashem chooses to celebrate and spend time with us: quality personal time, one on one. A *chassan* and *kallah*, alone for the first time in the *yichud* room, are not going to spend the time focusing on eating a meal. Food is not important; it is a distraction. What is important is being together. In this situation, a big meal would be an unwanted distraction that would not enhance the shared quality time. The seventy nations are needed, but they are not beloved to Hashem. They are not loved intrinsically. If Hashem wants to celebrate with them, it requires a lavish party with many delicacies.

But Hashem does love the Bnei Yisrael intrinsically, and He wants to spend quality time just being with us. A small *seudah* allows for a more intimate setting in which Hashem and Klal Yisrael can spend time together. A simple meal, with less focus on the external trappings, allows us to have a more meaningful visit with Hashem. It allows Hashem to enjoy the essence of Bnei Yisrael on their own, without the trappings of an elaborate celebration. The *hanaah*, pleasure, that Hashem wants is derived by spending time with His beloved nation, whose pure essence Hashem wants to enjoy without distraction. Therefore, Hashem instructed us to bring a relatively simple offering, consisting of only a single ox and a single ram.

ᴔ *The Most Intimate Day With Hashem*

With this new understanding behind the reason for the limited *korbanos* of Shemini Atzeres, we can appreciate that Shemini Atzeres is the day on which we enjoy the most intimate relationship with Hashem; we are closest to Him on this day. It is the day on which Hashem celebrates the very essence of Klal Yisrael, appreciating our intrinsic value, in a manner He does not do on any other day of the year.

≈ Three Stages of Marriage

On Shavuos, we celebrated the first part of our marriage to Hashem. Hashem gave us the Torah on Shavuos. In our *tefillos* we say, "תּוֹרָה צִוָּה לָנוּ מֹשֶׁה מוֹרָשָׁה קְהִלַּת יַעֲקֹב, *The Torah that was commanded to us by Moshe is the heritage of the Congregation of Yaakov"* (*Devarim* 33:4). The word *morashah* is interpreted as *me'orasah*, betrothed, as in the first step of the marriage ceremony, which is referred to as *kiddushin* or *eirusin*, as Hashem gave us the Torah as a *kinyan*, act of acquisition, just as the groom gives the bride a ring. The second stage of our marriage to Hashem, the *chuppah*, the *nesuin*, takes place in the *succah*. The *succah* represents the *Mishkan*, and it serves as the wedding canopy in the marriage of Hashem and Klal Yisrael.

Yichud, even more intimate than *nesuin*, takes place when we are alone with Hashem. It is the next step in establishing our marriage to the Ribbono shel Olam, and it is this that we achieve on Shemini Atzeres.[7]

The *Midrash*[8] states that once the seven days of Succos end, Hashem says to us, "Now you and I can rejoice together, *yachad* (*lashon* of *yichud*), and I will not trouble you to bring many *korbanos*. One ox and one ram will suffice."

≈ Two Types of Simchah

Rav Moshe Shmuel Shapiro[9] points out a fundamental difference between the *simchah* of Succos and the *simchah* of Shemini Atzeres. The *pasuk* in *Parashas Emor* states, וּלְקַחְתֶּם לָכֶם בַּיּוֹם הָרִאשׁוֹן פְּרִי עֵץ הָדָר כַּפֹּת תְּמָרִים וַעֲנַף עֵץ עָבֹת וְעַרְבֵי נָחַל **וּשְׂמַחְתֶּם לִפְנֵי ה׳** אֱלֹקֵיכֶם שִׁבְעַת יָמִים, *You shall take for yourselves on the first day the fruit of a citron tree, the branches of date palms, twigs of a plaited tree, and brook willow, and **you shall rejoice before Hashem**, your*

God, *for a seven-day period* (*Vayikra* 23:40). We are to rejoice before Hashem: *lifnei Hashem*. Hashem is in *Shamayim*, and we rejoice before Him. On Shemini Atzeres, however, *Chazal* say, "אֲנִי וְאַתֶּם נִשְׂמַח בְּיַחַד, *you and I rejoice together.*" The joy, the *simchah*, on Succos is that of Klal Yisrael *before* Hashem; they are as two separate entities. The *simchah* of Shemini Atzeres is different; it is that of Hashem and Klal Yisrael rejoicing together, as one. Hashem rejoices with us, and we rejoice with Him.

✑ Why Isn't Shemini Atzeres Called a Chag?

The Chasam Sofer,[10] in the name of the *Rama Mifano*, explains why the title *chag* is bestowed upon all the Yamim Tovim except for Shemini Atzeres. The word חַג, *chag*, refers to a חוּג, *chug*, a circle. A Yom Tov is referred to as a circle because it revolves around something. The focal point of the circle of each Yom Tov is the mitzvah of that Yom Tov. Rosh Hashanah revolves around *shofar,* the focal point of its circle. Yom Kippur revolves around the mitzvah of *inui*, the five prohibitions of the day. Succos revolves around the *Daled Minim*. Pesach's focal point is the mitzvah of *matzah*. Shavuos revolves around the *Shtei HaLechem*, the two loaves of bread that were brought as a *korban*.

There is only one Yom Tov that does not revolve around a single mitzvah. Shemini Atzeres has no mitzvah around which to revolve. There is no object that is specifically used on Shemini Atzeres for a mitzvah unique to the holiday.

Why is this? Why doesn't Shemini Atzeres have a mitzvah to be performed on it, a focal point around which it revolves?

The answer is that the focal point of Shemini Atzeres is Hashem. Shemini Atzeres revolves around Hashem. It is as if Hashem is telling us to not become distracted by performing the mitzvos of the day, because that would take attention from the true focal point of the day: Hashem.

We can also view all the Yamim Tovim as collectively forming a single circle. All the festivals reside on the outer edge of the circle, along the perimeter. They surround the hub of the circle, the very center, which is where Shemini Atzeres is located. With this understanding, all the Yamim Tovim constitute a *chug*, a circle, around the center, around Shemini Atzeres.

The mitzvah of Shemini Atzeres is rejoicing with Hashem personally, without any distractions. Few *korbanos*, no special mitzvos. Just us and the Ribbono shel Olam *b'yichud* — together as one.

✑ *The Greatest Joy Explained*

Now we can understand why the Vilna Gaon had the greatest joy on Shemini Atzeres. This is the one day on which we rejoice just with Hashem, just with the *Shechinah*, and not even with the need for any item that is to be used for a mitzvah of the day.

✑ *Only Joy: Ach Samei'ach*

The Vilna Gaon quotes[11] the *pasuk* regarding the Yom Tov of Succos that states, "וְהָיִיתָ אַךְ שָׂמֵחַ, *and you will be completely joyous*" (*Devarim* 16:15). The Gemara[12] interprets this verse to mean that even the night of Shemini Atzeres is to be included in the mitzvah of rejoicing. The word *ach* comes to include the night of Shemini Atzeres.

The Gra asks, Since the word *ach* is an exclusionary term that is generally used to stress "only this and NOT that," how can it be used here to include an additional time period in the mitzvah of simchah? *Ach* excludes; it does not include!

The Gra answers, the word *ach* is indeed excluding here. The *pasuk* is telling us that until this point in the Yom Tov of Succos, there were many mitzvos to be performed: *succah, lulav, esrog, hadas, aravah,* and *Simchas Beis HaSho'eivah*. However, now, on Shemini Atzeres, none of these mitzvos apply any longer. *Only* the mitzvah of *simchah* remains: *ach samei'ach.*

The main mitzvah of Shemini Atzeres is *simchah*, rejoicing with the Ribbono shel Olam Himself.

❧ Shemini Atzeres — The Greatest Day to Have Your Prayers Answered

The *Zohar*[13] explains why Shemini Atzeres is the greatest day of the year on which to *daven* for anything one needs. The seventy nations of the world received *berachah*, blessing, throughout the week of Succos as the Kohanim offered seventy oxen, one for each nation. Hoshana Rabbah marks the end of their period of *berachah*. After Hoshana Rabbah, the nations enter into a time of judgment.

The Bnei Yisrael, however, are exactly the opposite. Our judgment began on Rosh Hashanah, and it concludes on Hoshana Rabbah. We then enter into a period of *berachah*. The very next day, on Shemini Atzeres, we are invited to delight with the King and receive *berachos* for the entire year. And, writes the *Zohar*, no one is included in these joyous festivities with the Ribbono shel Olam other than Bnei Yisrael. Having a private audience with the King affords us the unique opportunity to request whatever is on our minds. This is a special day reserved for us and Hashem to enjoy each other's company, and this intimate moment is further enhanced by the King granting the requests of the subjects with whom He is celebrating. It is for this reason that the *pasuk* states, אֲהַבְתִּי אֶתְכֶם אָמַר ה׳, *I loved you, says Hashem* (*Malachi* 1:2).

This is why there is no greater day for *tefillah* and *bakashos*, requests, than Shemini Atzeres.

❧ The Unique Setting of Sefer Devarim

Rav Shlomo Kluger[14] quotes a *Yalkut Reuveni*. The Torah states, אֵלֶּה הַדְּבָרִים אֲשֶׁר דִּבֶּר מֹשֶׁה אֶל כָּל יִשְׂרָאֵל, *These are the words that Moshe spoke to all Yisrael* (*Devarim* 1:1). Moshe Rabbeinu spoke these words to Klal Yisrael, in front of Hashem. Hashem was present, listening and enjoying every word of Torah! Throughout the Torah, Hashem would teach Moshe something, and he would then turn around and teach it to the Bnei Yisrael, but not necessarily in the Presence of Hashem. *Devarim*, on the other hand, was different. Hashem was present when Moshe taught *Devarim* to Bnei Yisrael.

∾ Why Shemini Atzeres Is Not Mentioned

This, explains Rabbi Shlomo Kluger, is why Shemini Atzeres is not mentioned in *Parashas Re'eh*. Shemini Atzeres is testimony to the exceptional, indescribable love Hashem has for us, His children. Mentioning Shemini Atzeres is tantamount to proclaiming effusive praise for Hashem. However, since Hashem is listening to everything Moshe is saying in *Sefer Devarim*, He would hear this high praise as well.

Chazal have taught us that one can only mention part of a person's praiseworthy attributes while in his presence: מִקְצָת שִׁבְחוֹ שֶׁל אָדָם אוֹמְרִים בְּפָנָיו.[15] We don't mention a person's full praise, all their qualities, when he is there. As the *midrash* teaches us, we are only permitted to say part of Hashem's praise in His direct Presence, while we can say the full list of His praises when He is not being directly addressed. The *pasuk* says, אִמְרוּ לֵאלֹקִים מַה נּוֹרָא מַעֲשֶׂיךָ, *Say unto God, "How awesome are Your works!"* (*Tehillim* 66:3): Directing praise to Hashem, we only mention "*mah nora.*" But when we are not directly addressing Hashem, then we proclaim, הוֹדוּ לַה׳ כִּי טוֹב כִּי לְעוֹלָם חַסְדּוֹ, *Give thanks to Hashem for He is good, for His kindness endures forever* (*Tehillim* 136:1).

Mentioning Shemini Atzeres would be akin to mentioning the ultimate praise of Hashem, since it is such an incredibly special day. Hashem gifting Shemini Atzeres to us is the greatest praise we can say! Therefore, it cannot be mentioned in Hashem's Presence, and it is therefore omitted from the discussion of Yom Tov in *Parashas Re'eh*.

ENDNOTES

1. מעשה רב אות רלג.

2. קהלת יעקב דרוש סג, הובא באוצרות
   התורה עמוד רסב.

3. שולחן ערוך אורח חיים סימן תרסח
   סעיף א.

4. מועד לכל חי, רבי חיים פלאג'י, סימן
   כ'ה סעיף א'. הובא בזמן שמחתינו
   עמוד תנג.

5. מדרש תנחומא פרשת פנחס.

6. בני יששכר תשרי מאמר י"ג. וגם בינה
   לעתים, דרוש יז, דרוש לשמיני חג
   העצרת.

7. זמן שמחתינו מאמר מז עמוד תמו-
   תמז.

8. ילקוט שמעוני פינחס רמ'ז תשפב.

9. זהב משבא מרב משה שמואל שפירא,
   הובא בזמן שמחתינו עמוד תמו.

10. דרשות חתם סופר סוכות עמוד מז.

11. קול אליהו פרשת ראה אות קיד.

12. סוכה מח, א.

13. זוהר הקדוש חלק ג' לב:א, הובא בזמן
    שמחתינו עמוד תנ.

14. קהלת יעקב דרוש סג.

15. בראשית רבה פרשה לב , ג.

Simchas Torah: What to Think While You're Dancing — The Seven Habits of Highly Effective Dancers

∾ Deepening Our Understanding of Our Avodas Hashem on Simchas Torah

The *Chovos HaLevavos* writes[1] that we must constantly strive to upgrade and deepen our understanding of Torah, the *tefillos* that we say, and all aspects of our *avodas Hashem*. We must work on deepening our appreciation of mitzvos. As we grow older, we need to understand and appreciate the practices we engage in on a deeper and more sophisticated level. If we don't, we are in danger of observing the Torah and mitzvos on the same elementary, simplistic, and basic level as when we were younger.

These words of the *Chovos HaLevavos* can most appropriately be applied to the celebration of Simchas Torah. To many, Simchas Torah is a day that is observed in the same way it was observed in their youth. It is a day for the children who parade to the shul with their flags, candies, and toy *Sifrei Torah*. Let us endeavor to enhance and develop a more sophisticated understanding of the sanctity of the day. Let us try to deepen our appreciation for Simchas Torah so we can have an awareness for the great spiritual achievements and accomplishments that are available on the very last day of this season of elevation.

✑ *The Way It Was*

Here is a glimpse of how Simchas Torah was celebrated in days gone by. Rav Avigdor Miller wrote an article describing how Simchas Torah was celebrated as he witnessed it in Slabodka:*

> When it was time for a *simchah*, the yeshivah was unequaled. Simchas Torah was a tremendous event in the yeshivah; we had a list of eighty-five *niggunim* that we had to sing that day. We worked all day long dancing around and around. First we came for *davening* (Shacharis and Mussaf), and then we went home to eat, returned for Minchah, and then made the *hakafos* until nighttime. There were some Lithuanian police standing around because some of the bums in town tried to shoot needles at the yeshivah boys through the windows. The town had deteriorated very much, and the behavior of some of the youth was inappropriate. In general, the town was antagonistic to the yeshivah. The yeshivah was packed, and all day long the boys danced around, repeating the same song over and over again. You see, the words of the song themselves were *mussar*, so when you repeated it over so many times with such an intensity of happiness it becomes very deeply rooted in your mind. The *simchah* had a tremendous effect on the people.

We learn that one of the objectives of Simchas Torah in the days of old was accomplished by internalizing the words that

---

* *The World That Was: Lithuania,* page 47. Peninim Publications, 1997.

are sung over and over again. Many great ideals are articulated in the songs of Simchas Torah. We chant the words תּוֹרַת ה' תְּמִימָה אֲנָא עַבְדָּא דְקֻדְשָׁא, and מְשִׁיבַת נָפֶשׁ, כִּי מִצִּיּוֹן תֵּצֵא תוֹרָה וּדְבַר ה' מִירוּשָׁלָם בְּרִיךְ הוּא numerous times as we sing them over and over again. By listening attentively and internalizing the words we repeat again and again, like a *mussar seder*, we can integrate, ingrain, and engrave these concepts in our consciousness.

∽ *The Seven Habits of Highly Successful Dancers*

Although all *minhagai Yisrael* are laden with so many levels of meaning and there are endless benefits that accrue to those who observe them properly, let us present seven goals and *kavannos* to have while dancing that can significantly transform our Simchas Torah into a most elevated experience.

The *Mishnah Berurah* states[2] that on Simchas Torah the custom in many communities was for even many elders to dance as they recited praises for the Torah. Therefore, one should strengthen himself to dance and sing for *kavod HaTorah*, as we find that David HaMelech expended tremendous energy dancing fervidly in front of the *Aron* of Hashem with all his strength (*II Shmuel* 15:16). David publicly displayed his overwhelming *simchah shel mitzvah*, joy in doing a mitzvah.

The *Mishnah Berurah* then cites the *Arizal*[3] as having stated that the highest summit of *kedushah* that he was able to achieve was a product of his having rejoiced in the *simchah shel mitzvah* with all his strength. Likewise, the Vilna Gaon was known to dance with all his might before the *Sefer Torah*.

We know that the *Arizal* attained incredible levels of *ruchniyus*. He was privy to unique revelations to which others were not *zocheh*. The *Chida* writes that the *Arizal* even had access to the ashes of the *parah adumah*, the Red Heifer. The *Arizal* said about himself that he experienced an extraordinary torrent of Torah that sought to emanate from his mouth. And, had he opened his mouth a little wider, the Torah would have poured forth in an uncontrollable jet. The greatness of the *Arizal* is incalculable and yet the *Mishnah Berurah* cites that the highest level he reached was when he rejoiced over doing a mitzvah.

These examples are brought in the context of Simchas Torah to teach us that possibly the highest *madreigah* a person can reach, the loftiest height that a person can achieve, is not on Rosh Hashanah, Yom Kippur, or Hoshana Rabbah; rather, it is on Simchas Torah by rejoicing over the Torah.

◈ The First Objective: Display True Simchah shel Torah and Achieve the Highest Madreigah

The first objective we should bear in mind on Simchas Torah is to be aware that as we dance, through the proper *simchah shel Torah* we will be elevating ourselves to the highest possible *madreigah*. The loftiest spiritual level we could ever hope to achieve will become accessible to us through exhibiting and truly feeling proper *simchas haTorah*. Simchas Torah therefore is an opportunity to reach the greatest *madreigos*.

◈ Repair the Pegam in One's Neshamah

R' Chaim Palagi also cites[4] the custom brought in the *Mishnah Berurah* that even many *zekeinim*, elders, dance vibrantly on Simchas Torah. Furthermore, even though we normally do not dance on Shabbos or Yom Tov, on Simchas Torah it is permitted due to the *kavod haTorah* that results. He then brings from the *Chemdas Yamim* that one who engages in exhibiting and extolling true *simchas haTorah* is fortunate, because this will repair any *pegam*, defect, that his *neshamah* may have incurred because he had not given the proper honor and respect to the Torah in the past. One can be redeemed from these deficiencies and past grievances by displaying true *simchas haTorah* on Simchas Torah. This is another great achievement that can be accomplished on Simchas Torah.

❧ *The Second Objective: Assure That the Torah Will Endure in Your Family*

R' Chaim Palagi declares that one who is *zahir*, careful, and makes sure to rejoice with the Torah on Simchas Torah is assured that Torah will never cease from his descendants. If one wants to ensure that the Torah will remain with his family forever, he should rejoice with great excitement over the Torah!

R' Chaim Palagi then states in the name of the *Chemdas Yamim* that he saw a great Rav who danced with ecstatic joy on Simchas Torah. It was testified about this rav that for the next three generations he merited a wondrous line of descendants who were *talmidei chachamim* and *marbitzei Torah*. All who knew him realized that this was due to the outstanding level of *simchah* that he displayed on Simchas Torah.

HaRav Ovadia Yosef's father was nicknamed Gali. This nickname has its source in the great joy, *gilah*, that he would display on Simchas Torah. His fathering such an incredible son was attributed to the merit of his great *simchas haTorah*. He would dance with all his strength and would inspire others to dance as well. He would sing, "שִׂמְחוּ בַה' וְגִילוּ צַדִּיקִים," with enthusiastic fervor and intensity. He would also visit many different shuls and wish their *chassanei Torah* a warm *Mazel Tov*.

A proper display of *simchah* on Simchas Torah not only elevates us, but it also assures that Torah will remain with our descendants. It will assure the continuity and perpetuity of Torah in each person's family. The success of our children in their learning and in their dedication to HaKadosh Baruch Hu can be deeply influenced by the level of *simchah* we display on Simchas Torah.

❧ *The Third Objective: Internalize and Solidify Kabbalos*

We celebrate Shemini Atzeres as a day added to Succos because Hashem declares, *"Kashah Alai preidaschem"*; i.e., Hashem does not want us to take leave of His Presence.[5] Rav Hutner[6] wonders how an extra day will resolve such an issue. Whatever difficulty was experienced when considering Klal Yisrael departing after Hoshana Rabbah still remains! It just delayed the inevitable for one day. How does that ease the difficulty of us leaving? There must be something about the additional day that alleviates the longing and prevents the sadness that would otherwise occur at the conclusion of the *chag*.

Rav Hutner cites the Targum, who translates *atzeres* in this context as "כנש," which Rav Hutner teaches us means "incubation." He writes that the purpose of Shemini Atzeres is to be "קולט," to deepen and further ingrain within us all the lofty *madreigos* we have achieved during Elul and the Yamim Noraim. Throughout Elul, Rosh Hashanah, and Yom Kippur, we grew and made *kabbalos*, accepting upon ourselves practices to increase our *zechusim*. We committed to *daven* better, to learn more, to remove distractions that stand between us and our *avodas Hashem*. We undertook to be more careful in how we speak to our children and spouses.

In honor of all the *kabbalos* we have made, we dance on Simchas Torah, on the day added by Hashem. This is not merely an extra, added day; rather, it serves to incubate all the growth we've achieved, and it helps us integrate those *kabbalos* into our lives to make them permanent. We review all those commitments and incorporate them into our minds and hearts. As we dance around the Torah, the physical dancing serves to engrain our commitments into our beings, making them part of us and firmly embedding them into our newly improved selves. The dancing helps us internalize our commitment to be more dedicated servants of Hashem, more loyal subjects, and more carefully adherents of the mitzvos.

This deepened commitment is what the "extra" day of Shemini Atzeres serves to accomplish, and it is another component of the *avodah* of the dancing on Simchas Torah. As we dance around the *bimah* with great *simchah*, each time we stamp our feet, let us deeply stamp and engrain these commitments into our hearts.

◌ *The Fourth Objective: We Never Take Leave of the Torah*

Elsewhere, Rav Hutner[7] discusses the extra day that Hashem added to the Yom Tov of Succos because He feels a loss, so to speak, as we take our leave of Him: *Kashah Alai preidaschem.* How does adding on a day make it easier for Hashem as we take our leave of Him?

In this extra day, in Shemini Atzeres, says Rav Hutner, lies the heart of the Jewish people, the pulse of Klal Yisrael.

If we are really taking leave of Hashem, then delaying a day has no impact and does not change the situation. What does change the status quo is that now we are not alone as we take our leave of Hashem; we are accompanied by the Torah. Our ties to the Torah are never severed; we never take leave of the Torah. The Torah shields and saves us even when we are not actively involved in learning it.

Rav Hutner teaches us yet another *yesod*. Rejoicing with the Torah is the way in which we are now able to part from Hashem. Were it not for Simchas Torah, we would not be able to part from Him. Were we to part from Hashem immediately after Rosh Hashanah, we would have attained new heights with the *Yom HaDin*, but we still could not take the *shofar* with us. Neither the fast of Yom Kippur nor the *Arba Minim* and the *succah* can be taken with us after the respective Yom Tov has passed.

But there is one thing that *can* come along with us as we part from the Ribbono shel Olam: The Torah. Even when we are not actually engrossed in the Torah, even when we are not actually learning Torah, the Torah is still with us, protecting us. As we recite in the *hadran*, "לָא נִתְנְשֵׁי מִנָּךְ מַסֶּכֶת ... וְלָא תִתְנְשֵׁי מִנָּן, we will not forget [the Torah], and [the Torah] will not forget us."

We deliberately dance with the Torah, as a way to show that although all the other *tashmishei kodesh* cannot be taken with us, we can hold onto the Torah, and it will serve to protect us throughout the coming year, even when we are not actively engaged in it.

Thus, the fourth objective is to contemplate that we dance and celebrate with the Torah for Torah is our very lifeblood from which we never have to separate.

∝ The Fifth Objective: Simchah for All the Torah We Plan to Learn — No Limits!

Rav Hutner relates[8] an incident concerning the *Chiddushei HaRim*. Two students of the *Chiddushei HaRim*, two *talmidei chachamim*, were dancing on Simchas Torah. The *Chiddushei HaRim* commented that one of them would tire before the other. As they continued to dance, his prediction proved accurate, and one tired well before the other. His *talmidim* asked him how he had known.

He answered that the dancer who tired first is in fact a much more learned *talmid chacham*. He was dancing as a celebration of all the Torah he had learned this past year. Every *masechta* he had completed gave him tremendous joy, and he danced to celebrate these achievements. But what he already learned is finite, and therefore the dancing will ultimately come to an end.

The second dancer, however, is dancing to celebrate his new aspiration and longing to learn more in the coming year. He is dancing for the Torah he plans to learn in the coming year. Torah that is yet to be learned knows no boundaries — it is infinite — and therefore the dancing, too, has no boundaries or limits.

The Gemara[9] states if one really wants to do a mitzvah and some external force or circumstance prevents him from doing it, Hashem considers it as if he has in fact performed the mitzvah in question.

Rav Yonasan Eibeshutz explains[10] that when Hashem calculates the value of this type of mitzvah — a mitzvah that the person really wanted to do but couldn't actually perform — He gives the would-be doer the reward of one who performs a perfect mitzvah. He is rewarded as if he had done the mitzvah to its utmost, with total perfection, which is a stage that people who actually do the mitzvah can almost never attain.

When we do a mitzvah, it is performed with all our human imperfections, limitations, and flaws. We might do a mitzvah in haste, thus belying the importance of the mitzvah, or our attention may be divided and our thoughts not entirely focused on the mitzvah at hand. However it manifests itself, human shortcoming creeps into all we do, and these mortal attributes serve to detract from the perfection of a mitzvah being performed in a truly ideal fashion.

Not so with someone who receives reward from Hashem for an intense desire to perform a mitzvah that is out of his reach for a reason beyond his control. In this case, the reward he receives is the reward he would merit if he were to truly perform the mitzvah in the purest, holiest, most pristine manner. His reward will be much greater than that of one who actually did the mitzvah.

The second dancer, who is dancing for all the Torah he wants to learn, fits into this category. The Torah he aspires to learn has no limit; it is infinite, it is not bound by human limitations in energy and time. This gives him superabundant *simchah*, and he dances with boundless energy. He will not tire as easily when he dances.

On Simchas Torah, we are *mesamei'ach*, joyous, about the oceans of Torah we want to learn, the Torah that we anticipate mastering in the coming year. *Chumash, Neviim, Kesuvim, Mishnayos*, Gemara, *Midrash, poskim* — there is so much to learn. It is *rechavah min hayam*, wider than the ocean. Thinking of this will infuse our dancing with extra strength. As we dance on Simchas Torah, we should contemplate the fact that we are showing tremendous *simchah* for the Torah we plan to learn in the coming year.

৶ The Sixth Objective: Topple the Wall Between Us and Hashem

The *Chida*[11] records the *tefillah* that should be recited before each *hakafah*. It reads, יְהִי רָצוֹן מִלְפָנֶיךָ ה' אֱלֹקֵינוּ וֵאלֹקֵי אֲבֹתֵינוּ, שֶׁבְּכֹחַ הַקָּפוֹת אֵלּוּ תַּפִּיל חוֹמַת הַבַּרְזֶל הַמַּפְסֶקֶת בֵּינֵינוּ לְבֵינֶךָ, וְנִהְיֶה מוּקָפִים מִתּוֹרָה וּמִצְווֹת מִבַּיִת וּמִבַּחוּץ, וְנִדְבַּק בְּךָ וּבְתוֹרָתֶךָ תָּמִיד, אָנוּ וְזַרְעֵינוּ וְזֶרַע זַרְעֵינוּ,
May it be Your will, Hashem, that with the strength of these

hakafos the iron wall that separates You from us should fall, and we should be surrounded and encircled by Torah and mitzvos, both inside and out; We should always cling to You and Your Torah — we and our descendants.

The *Chida* is teaching us that when we embrace the Torah and dance around the *bimah*, we can break through whatever impediments are preventing us from serving Hashem properly. Whatever prevents us from getting close to HaKadosh Baruch Hu can be removed and overpowered with the *hakafos* that we perform on Simchas Torah. The wall that exists between us and Hashem, the wall that does not allow us to truly feel Hashem's Presence when we *daven*, the wall that prevents us from connecting to Hashem when we learn, is toppled by the power of our *hakafos*, with the strength of our *simchas haTorah*.

As we dance on Simchas Torah, our objective is to break down and eradicate any barriers that exist in our lives that are impediments to our true service of Hashem. By showing that we have *kavod HaTorah*, we break through the spiritual wall and thereby allow a much closer relationship to develop between ourselves and the Ribbono shel Olam.

❧ The Seventh Objective: Daven! The Hakafos Are an Auspicious Time for Tefillah

Rav Yerucham Olshin[12] recollects what he heard as a child from his grandmother. Her father would say that in his city of origin (Dinov, the city of the *Bnei Yissaschar*) it was a well-known and accepted fact that during the dancing on Simchas Torah one could accomplish more with his *tefillos* than he could with all the *tefillos* of the rest of the year.

When the *chazzan* proclaims, "אָנָּא ה׳ הוֹשִׁיעָה נָא, *Please, Hashem, save us now*," it is the most powerful *ana Hashem* of the entire year! Reciting this *tefillah* properly can achieve more than the same *tefillah* can accomplish at any other time of the year. "אָנָּא ה׳ הַצְלִיחָה נָא" represents the best chance a person has to *daven* for *hatzlachah*. "אָנָּא ה׳ עֲנֵנוּ בְיוֹם קָרְאֵנוּ." This was known and accepted: *Daven* with exceptional *kavannah* during the *haka-fos*! These special *tefillos* can effect much more than *tefillah* on any other day of the year!

Rav Olshin cites the *teshuvos* of the Klausenberger Rebbe,[13] who mentions that even though his grandfather, the *Divrei Chaim*, did not recite the aforementioned *yehi ratzon*, his other *zeide*, the Bnei Yissaschar, did. Furthermore, the Klausenberger Rebbe related that he heard from the *ziknei chassidim* that during the dancing of one single *hakafah* on Simchas Torah in Dinov, there was more crying and more tears shed than on all the other days of the Yamim Noraim combined! These were *bechiyos*, tears, of *simchah*.

◈ *Crying Out to Hashem*

The final objective of the dancing is *tefillah m'toch rikud*," crying out to Hashem through dance to express our joy and happiness in the Torah. *Tefillos* during this auspicious time are the most powerful *tefillos* of the year.

As noted above, when one is *b'simchah*, he can reach the highest possible *madreigah*. More than that, it is also a time of powerful *tefillah*. We are going to cry out, "אָנָּא ה' הוֹשִׁיעָה נָּא. אָנָּא ה' הַצְלִיחָה נָּא. אָנָּא ה' עֲנֵנוּ בְיוֹם קָרְאֵנוּ." We will recite *tefillos* beginning with every letter of the *aleph-beis*.

We must realize that dancing on Simchas Torah is an opportunity, and perhaps the greatest *eis ratzon* of the entire year,* since Simchas Torah is considered part of Shemini Atzeres and we are still in a personal audience with Hashem.

Therefore, the time of dancing is a time to *daven* for one's own achievements in *ruchniyus*. It is also a time to *daven* for one's children; it is a time to safeguard the perpetuity of Torah in one's family.

These are the habits of highly effective dancers.

May all of our *tefillos*, may all of our *avodah*, may all of our

---

* See "Pure Ecstasy, So Ask Hashem for Your Heart's Desire," page 395, for more on this topic.

she'ifos and aspirations come to fruition through the merit of Simchas Torah. We hope all of our *tefillos* will be accepted and we will merit to reach great heights. May we be *zocheh* that the continuity of Torah remains in our families and may we merit בָּנִים וּבְנֵי בָנִים עוֹסְקִים בַּתּוֹרָה וּבְמִצְוֹת, עַל יִשְׂרָאֵל שָׁלוֹם.

ENDNOTES

1. חובות הלבבות שער חשבון הנפש פרק ג חשבון כד.

2. משנה ברורה סימן תרס״ט סעיף קטן יא.

3. שער הכוונות ריש דרושי חג הסוכות.

4. מועד לכל חי סימן כ״ה ס״ק מא.

5. רש״י אמור כג:לו.

6. מאמרי פחד יצחק סוכות מאמר ע״ב, אות ו״ז.

7. מאמרי פחד יצחק סוכות מאמר נ״ח.

8. מאמרי פחד יצחק סוכות מאמר נז.

9. ברכות ו, א.

10. יערות דבש חלק ב׳ דרוש ב׳ עמוד כד-כה.

11. ספר עבודת הקודש, חלק ציפורן שמיר, אות יב.

12. ירח למועדים סוכות, מאמר פה, דף תקפט, footnote רנד.

13. שו״ת דברי יציב חלק א סימן ע״ה.